ENGAGING CHILDREN
IN SCIENCE

ANN C. HOWE
University of Maryland at College Park

LINDA JONES
California State University, Northridge

Merrill, an imprint of
MACMILLAN PUBLISHING COMPANY
New York

MAXWELL MACMILLAN CANADA
Toronto

MAXWELL MACMILLAN INTERNATIONAL
New York   Oxford   Singapore   Sydney

Cover Art: Susan Sturgill
Editor: Linda James Scharp
Developmental Editor: Molly Kyle
Production Editor: Julie Anderson Tober
Art Coordinator: Lorraine Woost
Photo Editor: Anne Vega
Text Designer: Susan E. Frankenberry
Cover Designer: Thomas Mack
Production Buyer: Pamela D. Bennett
Illustrations: Precision Graphics

This book was set in Janson by V & M Graphics, Inc., and was printed and bound by Book Press, Inc., a Quebecor America Book Group Company. The cover was printed by Phoenix Color Corp.

Macmillan Publishing Company
113 Sylvan Avenue, Englewood Cliffs, NJ 07632

Library of Congress Cataloging-in-Publication Data
Howe, Ann C.
      Engaging children in science/Ann C. Howe, Linda Jones.
        p.   cm.
      Includes bibliographical references and index.
      ISBN 0-675-21186-7
      1. Science—Study and teaching (elementary)—United States.
   2.   Education, Elementary—United States—Activity programs.
   I.   Jones., Linda, 1932–   .   II. Title.
   LB1585.3.H69   1993
   372.3'5044'0973—dc20
                                                                        92-11635
                                                                            CIP

Printing: 3   4   5   6   7   8   9   Year: 4   5   6   7

Photo Credits: All in-text photos supplied by Linda Jones (author), except those on p. 24, UPI/Bettmann Newsphotos, and p. 39, Harvard University News Office. Photos at opening of chapters are credited to the following individuals: Andy Brunk, p. 2, 78, 200; Jim Cronk, 292; Kevin Fitzsimons, p. 20; Linda Jones, 128, 238; Mark Madden/KS Studios, p. 98, 262, 316; Tom McGuire, p. 170; Anne Vega, p. 54; and Ernie York, p. 346.

PREFACE

Engaging Children in Science is a guide to an activity-based course in science teaching methods for both preservice and inservice elementary teachers. The science program described in this book is based on the belief that children build their own knowledge from their own experiences. This *constructivist* approach to teaching is based on the view that knowledge cannot be acquired simply by absorption through the senses, but by active thinking and doing. Learners take what they hear or see or perceive and construct their own personal understanding. When learning is viewed this way, it becomes clear that the teacher has a responsibility to provide the special type of learning environment and experiences that allow children to construct their own knowledge.

It is the goal of this book to model what it teaches—to provide you, the reader, with an environment that enhances your ability to construct your own understanding about how children learn science and how you can implement strategies to capitalize on how children learn best. With that goal in mind, an important feature of the book is an extended case study that follows the interaction between an experienced teacher and a teacher in training: Ms. Oldhand and Mr. Newman. Strategically placed descriptions of "Ms. O.'s" methods of teaching science will help you visualize how the strategies described in the book are used in actual classroom situations. As the reader, you are invited to "listen in" on conversations between Ms. O. and Mr. Newman as they discuss the challenges of implementing strategies in real classrooms.

But science involves more than learning strategies to teach facts, concepts, and processes. It also involves the assumptions, attitudes, and beliefs of the children you will teach. A child's years in elementary school span a period of dramatic physical, mental, and emotional growth. The teacher's primary role is often seen as increasing students' knowledge, but the most effective teachers also play an important role in fostering growth in other aspects of their students' lives. We believe effective teachers play a significant role in promoting the growth of their students' independent, responsible thinking and actions, or, to put it another way, their students' growth toward autonomy.

To be autonomous means to be responsible for one's own actions—to govern oneself in accordance with rules and within the bounds of appropriate expectations. It also means to think independently and arrive at one's own conclusions. Children need to know that they can think for themselves and that their own thoughts are worthwhile and valuable to themselves, their classmates, and their teacher. We take the point of view that teachers can promote autonomous thought and action by the way they teach and interact with their pupils, and that helping children become autonomous should be an important goal for science teaching.

In the 1960s a great effort was made to reform elementary science education. Scientists, teachers, and other educators believed strongly that few of the goals of science education could be achieved through the traditional methods of lecture, memorization, and recitation. The reform programs were excellent in every way, yet today the programs are used in few classrooms and educators are still struggling with the same issues. Why? We believe that one important reason for the under-utilization of those reform programs lay in the faulty assumption that a set of good curriculum materials was all that was needed. The teacher's role was underestimated. Teaching is complex and demanding, but the existence of so many good teachers attests to the fact that teaching is not too complex to learn. *Engaging Children in Science* is intended to help you meet the challenges of the profession you've chosen.

NOTES ON THE TEXT STRUCTURE

After an opening chapter on the modern view of science, the book lays the theoretical foundation for constructivism by describing the positions of Piaget, Bruner, Vygotsky, Kohlberg, and Papert. The next two chapters show how current research can be applied to science teaching, including classroom management, teacher expectations, and goals of science teaching.

The central section allows students to construct their own knowledge of science processes and learn how to use them as the basis for teaching science concepts to children. Starting with Direct Instruction and moving through Guided Discovery to Group and Individual Investigations, the text guides students step-by-step toward becoming competent and confident to teach science. Science processes are taught through activities designed for the students themselves. As they move through the book and carry out the activities, students learn to use science processes as a means of reaching the cognitive, affective, psychomotor, and social goals of science teaching and to help their pupils become autonomous learners.

Integrating science with other subjects is treated in a separate chapter before the closing section on evaluation of instruction and reflective teaching. Provided throughout are lesson plans, unit plans, and references to resources for teaching.

Included in each chapter are questions for discussion in class, activities for the students to complete outside of class, and a list of research references.

ACKNOWLEDGMENTS

We would like to thank the following individuals for their thoughtful reviews of our manuscript: Joel Bass, Sam Houston State University; Glenn D. Berkheimer, Michigan State University; Roger T. Cunningham, The Ohio State University; Larry E. DeBuhr, University of Missouri—Kansas City; Richard W. Griffiths, California State University, San Bernardino; Stanley J. Henson, Arkansas Tech University; Karen K. Lind, University of Louisville; E. Robert Moore, University of Nevada, Las Vegas; Lawrence C. Scharmann, Kansas State Univeristy; John R. Staver, Kansas State University; Robert L. Steiner, University of Puget Sound; Marla Stone, Texas A & M University.

The authors extend their sincere thanks to the students of California State University, Northridge, for their valuable suggestions on early drafts of the manuscript and for tolerating picture-taking during their student-teaching lessons. Further appreciation for assistance with the photographs goes to the teachers and pupils of Vena Avenue School, Canterbury Street School, and Balboa Magnet School in the Los Angeles area, especially to Liz and Ken for posing as Ms. O. and Mr. Newman. We also extend our thanks to Linda Scharp for her continuous editorial guidance and support throughout the several years of writing and production, and to the other editorial staff, each of whom made special contributions to this effort.

—Ann C. Howe
Linda Jones

Contents

CHAPTER 3

EVERYDAY TEACHING SKILLS

55

C H A P T E R 4

EXPECTATIONS AND GOALS

79

C H A P T E R 5

DIRECT INSTRUCTION

99

CHAPTER 6

BASIC SCIENCE PROCESSES
129

CHAPTER 7

GUIDED DISCOVERY
171

CHAPTER 8

ADVANCED SCIENCE PROCESSES   201

CHAPTER 9

APPLICATIONS AND TECHNIQUES FOR GUIDED DISCOVERY
239

CHAPTER 10

GROUP INVESTIGATIONS
263

CHAPTER **11**

INDIVIDUAL AND CLASS PROJECTS

APPENDIX **A**

SCIENCE TOPICS FOR THE ELEMENTARY SCHOOL   375

APPENDIX **B**

PIAGET TASKS   385

INDEX   399

1

SCIENCE IN THE ELEMENTARY SCHOOL

▼ Joe Newman, teacher candidate, is discussing elementary science with his cooperating teacher, Ms. Oldhand.

Mr. Newman: I don't feel very confident about teaching science. I loved science in elementary school, but I'm nervous about teaching it myself.

Ms. Oldhand: I'm glad to hear that you liked science in elementary school. What courses did you have in high school and college?

Mr. Newman: I had all the required courses and they were OK, but science wasn't my main interest so I concentrated on other things.

Ms. Oldhand: Well, it was about the same with me. Some of my teachers gave interesting lectures, but the theories weren't connected with anything I felt I had experienced. Fortunately, I later had some opportunities to learn about hands-on science for children. Now, I'm really enthusiastic about it.

Mr. Newman: That's great. What makes you so enthusiastic?

Ms. Oldhand: The children enjoy hands-on science so much. I use that built-in motivation to bring in as many other subjects as possible—it makes sense to integrate science into the rest of the school day. The experiences with materials are so meaningful for the children that they actually want to write about those experiences, read background material, and even use the computer for something other than games.

Mr. Newman: I'm concerned about being able to find the time to get all the materials organized.

Ms. Oldhand: Teaching this way was time-consuming at first, but now the children do most of the setup and all of the clean-up.

Mr. Newman: OK, I'm convinced you've made it work. Now I just have to convince myself that I can do it, too.

Ms. Oldhand: That's the first step. And if you believe this kind of teaching is worthwhile, you'll be able to learn how to do it in a fairly short time. You know, you don't have to learn everything in one day. Watch me start the mealworms unit this afternoon. Then I'll help you plan one of the lessons for next week.

Mr. Newman: You make it sound so simple.

Science can be the most exciting subject in the elementary school for both children and teachers if science is an active, hands-on subject that children learn through doing, not listening or memorizing. Science provides both enormous scope for the teacher's imagination and many opportunities for integration with other subjects. This book about science learning and teaching has been written to help teachers and future teachers open children's minds to the natural world—the world of plants and animals, rocks, water, and the sky.

Young children learn best when they experience things themselves and then have time to think about those experiences as well as talk about what they have seen and

▼ Mr. Newman and Ms. Oldhand discuss the mealworm unit.

done. Observing, measuring, collecting, and classifying—some of the ways of learning that work best in science—come naturally to most children. When you help children learn about the world through their own activity and thought, you reinforce their natural interests and curiosity.

Perhaps your interest in science began as a child, and you are now anxious to pass on a love of the subject to your pupils. Maybe you had a teacher who kindled this interest, or maybe your parents shared with you their own interest in some area of science. To you, science is an exciting subject full of opportunities for exploring the world.

Others of you probably first took required science courses in high school and college—you may have no recollection of having had science in elementary school. Science has not always received a high priority in elementary schools, and sometimes it gets left out altogether. High school and college science courses can seem quite abstract and demanding for those who have had no opportunity to build a foundation in elementary school. Students who lack confidence in mathematics may feel disadvantaged in science courses as well. If you fit one of these descriptions, you are not alone. The authors of this book want to reassure you that we have kept you in mind and have not assumed that all readers have positive memories or feelings about science.

We believe, however, that everyone who wants to become a good teacher can learn to present science activities in ways that are natural, interesting, and fulfilling for pupils. You have only to believe in your own ability to learn new things and to open up your mind to the ideas in this book. You can be able to help your future pupils develop positive attitudes about science and strong self-images as problem solvers. In the process you can begin to understand some things that you never fully understood before. If you are one of those who already enjoy science and want to pass on your interest to others, this book will help you develop the skills needed to engender similar interest and enthusiasm in your pupils.

As you become a teacher, we hope you will learn to trust your own ability to learn and teach science. Richard Feynman, a Nobel laureate in physics, had this to say in a talk he gave to science teachers at a national meeting:

> You teachers . . . can maybe doubt the experts once in a while. Learn from science that you *must* doubt the experts. . . . When someone says, "Science teaches such and such," he is using the word incorrectly. Science doesn't teach anything; experience teaches it. If they say to you, "Science has shown such and such," you might ask, "How does science show it? How did the scientists find out? How? What? Where?" It should not be "science has shown," but "this experiment, this effect, has shown." And you have as much right as anyone else, upon hearing about the experiments (but be patient and listen to all the evidence) to judge whether a sensible conclusion has been arrived at. (Feynman, 1968)

One reason all of you can become good elementary science teachers is that children love hands-on learning. That is the natural way to learn; your main job is to provide the situation and teach them how to function within its boundaries. In such a context, science ideas will be concrete rather than abstract, and your role will be to guide a learning encounter rather than to tell about or explain concepts.

Another reason all of you could become good teachers is that this book—and your instructor—will help you acquire the skills you need to be successful. As you learn how to guide students through activities and discussions of the kind described here, you will gain confidence in your own ability to have a positive effect on student learning. Self-efficacy, the name given by psychologists to this sense that what you do can make a difference, is one of the few teacher characteristics shown to be related to student achievement (Woolfolk & Hoy, 1990). To be effective, you must believe that what you do will have an effect. You must also show children that what they do will have an effect. Goodwill is not enough. Particularly with girls and with minority children, you will need to develop teaching strategies that give each child a sense of self-efficacy—a belief in his or her own ability to learn science as well as the motivation to take responsibility for that learning.

WHAT SCIENCE IS

Scientists proceed on the belief that the world is understandable and that there are discoverable patterns throughout nature. Science is a way of finding out what those patterns are. Scientists use both their own senses and various instruments—sometimes very complicated ones—to observe the world; they use their minds and imaginations to create theories and hypotheses to explain what they have observed. We, too, can use our senses and our minds to see patterns all around us: the rising and setting of the sun, the cycle of the seasons, the migration of birds, the tide coming in and going out.

The desire to know more about the natural world has probably always been a part of the human experience, certainly since the beginning of recorded history. In more recent times an explosion of scientific knowledge has occurred with far-reaching consequences. Just since the beginning of this century, the application of scientific knowledge has changed almost every aspect of the way we live. Some of the most important changes are the exploration of space, the changes in the diagnosis and treatment of disease, the discovery and use of atomic energy, the use of computers, and new methods for the production of food. Changes in the way we think have been perhaps less dramatic though just as important. At one time people attributed natural phenomena and events to evil or benign forces in the universe; now we look for rational or logical explanations. We believe it is possible to predict and control many of the forces of nature, even though we have not yet been successful in controlling everything we would like to. Many ideas that once seemed farfetched and even ridiculous are now part of our general knowledge. For example, it would be hard to find an educated person today who does not believe that bacteria and viruses cause disease, but this germ theory of disease was hotly debated and denied by intelligent people a little over a century ago.

Science is both knowledge and ways of finding out—that is, both content and process. To be scientifically literate a person needs to have knowledge of the concepts and theories of science and, in addition, to have some understanding of how this knowledge has been obtained in the past and is still being learned today. Science will never be a finished body of knowledge because new ideas and theories are always being proposed and new discoveries are being made. Things taken for granted can turn out to be different from what they were thought to be.

Consider how Albert Einstein, the famous twentieth-century physicist, defined science:

> Science is not just a collection of laws, a catalogue of unrelated facts. It is a creation of the human mind, with its freely invented ideas and concepts. Physical theories try to form a picture of reality and to establish its connection with the wide world of sense impressions. (Einstein & Enfield, 1938)

Some scientific concepts come from direct experience or observation; these are often called concrete concepts. For example, a child can directly observe the life cycle of a butterfly. No sequence of logic or leap of insight is required to understand that interesting changes take place along the way from egg to adult. A child can also notice that beetles go through similar changes in their life cycle. At this point the child might overgeneralize that all insects have larval and pupal stages. This misconception could easily be refined by providing some additional insect cultures to observe, such as crickets or mantises. Notice that the refinement is also based on concrete experience.

Other scientific concepts appropriate for direct experience have aspects requiring abstract thought. An example is sinking/floating. Anyone can observe that some objects float and some sink when placed in water. Observing the sinking/floating behavior of objects is a concrete experience. Certain conclusions about sinking and floating also can be drawn at a concrete level. For example, metal things sink, wooden things float. But as more and more exceptions to these conclusions become apparent, the firmness of the early understanding begins to slip. For example, some kinds of wood sink, and waterlogged wood also sinks; but metal cups float. The Queen Mary floats! An adequate concept of sinking/floating—one that will explain and predict any floating/sinking system—requires abstract thinking that coordinates the density (weight per unit volume) of the object to the density of the liquid. Not all elementary pupils will be able to understand sinking/floating in this way.

Some science ideas are quite abstract and are not easily presented in any concrete way. The growth of knowledge about the spherical shape of the earth is an interesting example of the use of explanatory concepts in science. Before anyone actually sailed around it, many thinkers had postulated that the earth was round, though everyday experience told them, as it tells us, that the earth is flat. Thinking of the earth as a sphere was at first a scientific theory that explained many puzzling things not explained by the flat-earth idea and that supported a variety of predictions. For example, Columbus predicted that he could get to the Orient by sailing west and that he would not fall off the edge, because a sphere has no edge. His voyages supported the second prediction, but the first prediction was not borne out until Magellan's crew sailed around the globe.

All of the thinking that originally went into formulating the idea of the round earth was based on indirect evidence. And even though the idea had proved to be correct, it was not until the last half of the twentieth century, some 500 years later, that the entire earth was actually seen in one glance. The famous photograph taken by the Apollo astronauts on their way to the moon was literally an eye-opener. Many people, including news commentators, remarked that they always knew that the earth was round, but they never really believed it until they saw that picture.

BUILDING ONE'S OWN KNOWLEDGE

The kind of science program described in this book is one in which children build their own knowledge from their own experiences, from both doing and thinking. "Hands-on" must be accompanied by "minds-on." Having interesting things for the children to do is not enough; thinking and talking about what they have done must be part of the science program, too. In this way children build their own knowledge from their own experiences.

The idea that people must build their own knowledge from their own experiences and thought is called *constructivism*. Constructivists believe that real understanding occurs only when children participate fully in the development of their own knowledge. They describe the learning process as self-regulated transformation of old knowledge to new knowledge, a process that requires both action and reflection on the part of the learner. Contrast this idea of learning with the opposite idea, that children learn by absorbing what they are told or that their minds are like blank pages on which teachers can write. The research of cognitive psychologists and science educators over the past decade has shown that what children learn greatly depends on what they already know. Knowledge and understanding grow slowly, with each new bit of information having to be fitted into what was already there.

You may be thinking at this point that there are certain things a pupil simply must be told and then asked to remember, and you wonder how the memorization of facts fits into this idea of learning. Undoubtedly, some things have to be committed to memory without explanation, such as your telephone number, the name of the street you live on, the names of trees and birds and flowers, and so on. We all need a mechanism for remembering and retrieving these kinds of numbers and words, and there will be things of this kind that you will want your pupils to know. But learning of this kind is a lower-level mental function; although some may be necessary, it should not be the main emphasis or even an important emphasis of your teaching. Science teaching should lead to a deeper understanding of relationships and interrelationships, of causes and effects, of how we know what we know and how we can find out more. These concepts require higher-level thinking and should not be treated as facts to be memorized. This is the kind of knowledge that must be constructed by each person in his or her own way.

KINDS OF KNOWLEDGE

The knowledge that children bring with them to school is not all acquired in the same way. For instance, we might say that a certain child knows the alphabet, knows that ice is cold, and also knows why shadows are longer in late day than at noon. We could also say that the child knows how to play with other children. The way the child has arrived at knowing is different in each of these cases. A child learns the alphabet by memorization, learns that ice is cold through experience, learns about relationships in the natural world through thinking about experiences, and learns about getting along with others through social interaction.

These four kinds of knowledge are described in more detail below. The terms used—as well as the basic idea of kinds of knowledge—are derived from Jean Piaget's work, though the terms are not exactly the same as he used. An interesting and useful discussion of kinds of knowledge can be found in Kamii and DeVries (1978).

Social-arbitrary knowledge is arbitrary in the sense that someone, at some time, decided that this is the way it would be. Included in this category are names, symbols, conventions, rules, and procedures. These have been defined by other people—or the society as a whole—and are learned from other people, either directly (by being told) or indirectly (by reading or from watching television). An easy way to understand this concept is to think about languages; what English speakers call a *house* is called *maison* in French, *casa* in Spanish, and *ie* in Japanese. All these words refer to the same thing. In some countries cars keep to the right, whereas in others they keep to the left. This is an arbitrary rule or convention.

Physical knowledge arises from direct experience and observation of objects and events. A person really knows that ice is cold only if ice has been experienced. Examples of physical knowledge include the knowledge that rocks sink in water and wood floats, that water runs downhill, and that caterpillars turn into moths or butterflies. This kind of knowledge can be discovered by oneself and universally rings true. Learning experiences that lead to physical knowledge are the heart of science in the primary grades.

Logical knowledge encompasses concepts, conclusions, and higher-order ideas derived from thinking about observations or experiences. This kind of knowledge must be constructed by the learner. It cannot be acquired by observation alone and it cannot be learned from being told; it has to be constructed in the mind of the learner. Young children think that a ball of clay broken into pieces will weigh more than it weighed before it was broken up. Weighing the clay before and after will not convince them; they think the scales are wrong! Eventually, however, they come to understand that, logically, the amount of clay cannot change when it is broken up and that the clay has to weigh the same.

Social-interactive knowledge is gained through interaction with other people, including how to get along with others, how to understand the feelings of others, and how to work cooperatively. Children have to grow into the knowledge of others that allows them to see something from another's point of view. This is not the knowledge of rules of behavior but a deeper understanding of the ways of compromise and cooperation.

These four kinds of knowledge, or ways of knowing, will be described and illustrated more fully in later chapters of this book, but an example here may be helpful. Consider an elementary science lesson about a balance beam. The names of the parts (arm, fulcrum, etc.) are social-arbitrary knowledge; the way the balance behaves when objects are hung on the arms is physical knowledge; the mathematical relationship between the masses of the objects and the distance from the fulcrum on a beam that is balanced is logical knowledge; knowing how to work in harmony with a partner is social-interactive knowledge.

MISCONCEPTIONS OR ALTERNATIVE CONCEPTUAL FRAMEWORKS

The kinds of knowledge with which we are most concerned in this book are physical knowledge and logical knowledge. Before you can help your pupils use their observations and experiences to construct their own logical knowledge, you will have to understand the ideas, concepts, and generalizations they bring to class. Since children develop ideas and beliefs about the natural world long before they are formally taught, what is already in their minds may be quite different from what teachers want them to learn.

In recent years there has been much interest in the ideas of the natural world and the laws of nature that children have developed spontaneously or have misinterpreted from what they have been taught in school. Among the terms used to describe these ideas are "naive ideas," "misconceptions," "alternative conceptions," and "alternative conceptual frameworks." Many of them have been described and studied. An early description of Swiss children's ideas about living and nonliving things (Piaget, 1951) was followed by a similar but more detailed study of Canadian children's ideas about the same subject (Laurendeau & Pinard, 1962). Studies of American children show that they, like their counterparts in other countries, develop many ideas about living things (including the human body) that would surprise many of their teachers. Examples include what happens to food once eaten, where various organs are located, and what is the nature of blood. Misconceptions about physical phenomena are as widespread as those about living things (Carey, 1985).

CHILDREN'S IDEAS ABOUT THE EARTH

Studies of children's notions about the earth and gravity illustrate how they try to reconcile their own experience of the world with what they have been taught or have heard. The first of several studies was carried out at Cornell University (Nussbaum & Novak, 1976). Subsequent studies included one conducted in Israel (Nussbaum, 1979), one in Nepal (Mali & Howe, 1979), and one in California (Sneider & Pulos, 1983). All of these studies, conducted in such widely separated places, yielded similar results.

In the original research, children from two second grade classes were individually asked a series of questions designed to elicit the notions about the earth that they actually believed. When first asked about the shape of earth, all children said that, of course, the earth was round like a ball. On further questioning it became clear that almost two-thirds of the children believed that the earth is flat. They had been taught in school that the earth is round "like a ball," but their experience told them that the earth is flat. Since what they were taught was contradicted by their own experience, they had to work out a way to reconcile the two opposing ideas. Figure 1.1 illustrates what some of the children were thinking when they said the earth is round while actually believing that the earth is flat. These notions correspond with the numbered drawings in Figure 1.1:

1. The hills and mountains are round; that's why we say the earth is round.
2. The round earth is in the sky somewhere; we are on a different earth.
3. The earth is a flat disk, shaped like a pancake.
4. The earth has a flat plane through the center with the sky above and rocks, water, and dirt underneath.

Audio-tutorial lessons were given to the children with the objective of changing their ideas, but at the end of the series of lessons the number who still believed in the flat earth was almost as large as before instruction. They had constructed their own

▾ FIGURE 1.1
Children's notions
of the earth

Source: Adapted from figure in "Development of Earth and Gravity Concepts Among Nepali Children" by G. Mali and A. Howe, 1979, *Science Foundation 63*, (5), p. 687. Copyright © 1979 by John Wiley & Sons, Inc. Adapted by permission.

alternative frameworks for thinking about the earth, and they did not give up their own beliefs as the result of having a few lessons. Not only in this case, but in many others as well, researchers have shown that children hold onto their beliefs tenaciously, changing them only reluctantly and over a period of time.

Thus, telling children what you want them to learn will have little effect when the ideas they already have are strongly held. Adding a new fact to what they already know is not enough to bring about a conceptual change. In order to understand a new concept they have to restructure their thinking.

Most children grow up with some cultural beliefs that they cling to even when those beliefs become untenable. Did you believe in Santa Claus when you were a child? If you did, it did not trouble you that Santa was supposed to go all over the world in one night and squeeze in and out of chimneys. When you noticed that not all children lived in houses with chimneys, you accepted your parents' explanation that Santa could just as easily enter houses through doors. Finally, you began to wonder how anyone could get around the world in one night, and you noticed some other very strange things as well. At this point you had what psychologists call cognitive dissonance. There were quite a few things that did not fit together, and you heard rumors from other children that Santa was not real. But you were not ready to give up the idea because it was an important part of your whole belief system. Eventually, you abandoned the idea of a Santa Claus. For most people, this is associated with some mental distress.

The conceptual change that takes place when children give up firmly held beliefs about the world as they experience it is somewhat analogous to giving up the idea of Santa Claus or the Tooth Fairy. Admittedly, giving up the idea of the flat earth may not be traumatic, but there are similarities in that it takes a long time and a lot of evidence to convince yourself that what you thought was true is not really the way things are.

The Santa Claus example illustrates another important point about learning. Learning about the world does not take place in a social vacuum; interactions with other people, in conjunction with experiences and mental activity, constitute a source of knowledge. Knowledge construction is only rarely a solitary process and is, rather, one that occurs in the context of social interactions (Driver, 1989).

TEACHING TO PROMOTE UNDERSTANDING

One important finding from research on children's misconceptions is that children may actually understand very little of what the teacher has told them about science. Over and over again researchers have found that teaching by telling does not necessarily lead to understanding or a conceptual change when children already have their own ideas about the subject.

Teachers and researchers working with Rosalind Driver have identified features that are present when science is taught from a constructivist perspective. Things a teacher would do include:

- Identify and build on the knowledge that learners bring to lessons.
- Allow the learners to develop and restructure this knowledge through experiences, discussions, and the teacher's help.
- Enable pupils to construct for themselves and to use appropriate science concepts.
- Encourage pupils to take responsibility for their own learning.
- Help pupils develop understanding of the nature of scientific knowledge, including how the claims of science are validated and how these may change over time. (Driver, 1989, p. 86)

Science in the elementary school offers a number of special opportunities and unique vantage points shared neither by other subjects nor by science instruction at other levels. Elementary school studies are usually recognized as preliminary to any specialization, and all students at a school study the same things. Elementary school normally provides general background for living as a responsible and participating citizen in a democratic society.

By the time an adolescent gets to secondary school, specialization of interests and abilities has often occurred, resulting in the selection of some courses of study and the avoidance of others. If students have had negative science experiences before they get to high school, they usually take only the required minimum number of courses, thus cutting themselves off from many science-related careers and from the scientific understanding needed by every citizen. In the elementary school, on the other hand, all students take science regardless of what they will study in the future. Therefore, a good science program makes sense at every grade level. In today's climate of utilitarianism, students sometimes shun studies not directly related to career preparation, but the quality of people's lives depends on more than just economic factors. Science is about developing reasoning skills, mental outlooks, and an openness to new information. All citizens need these skills to lead a rich and fulfilling mental life, as well as to enable them to make independent decisions about important societal issues.

BASIC KNOWLEDGE OF SCIENCE

The view that all citizens should have a common understanding of what science is, as well as some knowledge of the most basic ideas of modern science, prompted the American Association for the Advancement of Science to bring together in 1988 a group of prominent scientists and educators to make recommendations for the improvement of science education at all levels, from kindergarten through grade 12. Their report, *Science for All Americans* (National Council for Science and Technology Education, 1989), begins with the premise that all Americans should have the knowledge, skills, and attitudes that will make them scientifically literate. The report defines scientific literacy as (1) the awareness that science is a human enterprise with strengths and limitations, (2) understanding of the key concepts and principles of science, (3) a familiarity with the natural world and recognition of its diversity and unity, and (4) the ability to use this knowledge for individual and social purposes. The report recommended that schools teach less and teach it better and teach for broader understanding rather than just to cover material. The authors of the report asserted that elementary school science should "enhance childhood"; that is, science should be taught not only for some future benefit but also to make life richer and more rewarding for children as they experience it.

The group identified broad areas of knowledge considered as basic in physical science, life science, and the human body. These broad areas can be taught at many levels and in many ways. Details and facts are not important in themselves and are only useful to the extent that they lead to understanding of the principles involved.

The focus is on depth of understanding and on using knowledge of science in the choices everyone makes in daily life.

The recommendations in *Science for All Americans* are much broader than any list of topics could indicate, but some of the basic areas of knowledge are listed below along with our interpretation of how each might be translated into the elementary science curriculum.

Physical Science

- *The universe.* Children should become aware of the sun, the stars, and the planets and know that we are part of a very large universe.
- *The earth.* The shape of the earth, its motion around the sun, its climates, winds, oceans, and fresh water, and its changes through time are phenomena that children should gradually come to understand as they move through the elementary grades.
- *Forces that shape the earth.* Children should understand the effects of wind, water, animals, plants.
- *The structure of matter.* Elementary science should include the study of observable states of matter—solid, liquid, and gas—and the changes brought about by heat and other forces but should leave atoms, electrons, and other invisible particles for study in later years.
- *Energy transformations.* Observable phenomena associated with heat, light, sound, electricity, and mechanical energy can form an experiential basis for later study.
- *Motion and forces.* Changes in speed, the action of magnets, and the pull of gravity should be observed by elementary children.

Life Science

- *Diversity of life.* The observation and study of the wonderful variety of living things should be an important part of elementary science at all levels.
- *Heredity.* Observation and discussion of easily observed inherited characteristics should be addressed in elementary science.
- *Cells.* Upper elementary children should begin microscopic and other exploratory activities associated with cells.
- *Interdependence of life.* Food webs, parasitic relationships, and ecosystems can be the basis for many interesting activities.
- *Flow of matter and energy.* Elementary science should include study of the effect of sunshine on plants and basic natural cycles.
- *Evolution of life.* This concept requires a level of abstract thinking that is beyond the reach of all but a few elementary children.

The Human Organism

- *Human identity.* The similarities that make us human should be discussed.
- *Life cycle.* Birth, growth, and death of human beings should be discussed.
- *Basic functions.* Elementary school students should study the derivation of energy from food, protection from injury, internal coordination, reproduction.

▼ Experience with magnets leads to later understanding of forces and motion.

As you study this book you will see many examples of lessons and activities that teach simple concepts related to these basic scientific ideas. These are not ideas that children, or anyone else, can learn by memorization or by listening to the teacher. People have to build knowledge and understanding gradually from their own experiences and from their own thinking.

TEACHING METHODS

The report *Science for All Americans* also makes these main recommendations about how science should be taught:

- Reduce the amount of material covered so that more time can be devoted to developing thinking skills.

- Emphasize the connections among science, mathematics, technology, and other areas of the curriculum.
- Start teaching with questions rather than with answers. Students should be actively engaged in "the use of hypotheses, the collection and use of evidence, and the design of investigations and processes."
- Encourage students' creativity and curiosity.
- Focus on the needs of *all* children.

GOALS FOR SCIENCE IN THE ELEMENTARY SCHOOL

There is remarkable agreement among scientists and educators about what an elementary science program should be and about the kinds of activities that children should engage in. From these sources, as well as from our own experience, we believe that the important goals for children in elementary science are to:

- Develop and maintain a curiosity about the world around them.
- Observe and explore their environment and organize those experiences.
- Develop the technical and intellectual skills needed to make further study of science possible.
- Build an experiential basis for understanding important concepts in science.
- Relate what they learn in school to their own lives.

Other goals are for children to enjoy science and to develop positive attitudes about school. Children who enjoy school and see their needs met there are more likely to become active learners and successful students.

The purpose of this book is to help you learn teaching methods and attitudes that will allow you to carry out the recommendations and reach the goals listed above. The teaching methods you will learn emphasize the importance of asking questions, promoting independent thinking, building on children's ideas, encouraging children's engagement in activities, and emphasizing science processes rather than memorization of facts. As you work your way through this book, you will find plans for lessons and units that demonstrate how to put these ideas into practice.

▼ SUMMARY

Science means different things to different people. It does not mean the same thing to the person who "doesn't like science" that it means to the research scientist or to someone who has developed an interest in some branch of science.

Scientific literacy for all Americans is a goal that has not been reached but one that we can all work toward. A distinguished group of scientists and educators have developed a list of the ideas they believe are most important in science and have suggested ways that science should be taught to enhance the development of these ideas.

There are different ways of studying science; what is appropriate at one level may not be appropriate at another level. For children from the age of five to eight or nine, finding out about the environment through their active involvement in observation, classification, and other simple means is what is most important. As children move into the upper elementary grades they may be ready to plan and carry out simple experiments, that answer questions that are of interest to themselves. Children of this age, as well as those who are younger, learn best through active physical involvement followed by thoughtful discussion.

Teachers should not ignore the explanations and ideas about life and the environment that children bring with them to class, since most of these ideas are firmly held and not easily given up. Common sense and courtesy, in addition to current research, will tell you that it is important to let children express their ideas freely and without ridicule. This will allow you to identify their misconceptions and help them move toward acceptance of more logical explanations.

The purpose of this book is to help you become an enthusiastic and effective science teacher. In the next chapter you will find some ideas that will help you understand how children's minds develop and how they learn. The succeeding chapters explain practical ways to work with your pupils to help them become active, responsible learners.

▾ DISCUSSION QUESTIONS

The following questions are for you to think about and then discuss with the whole class or a small group. You may wish to write out an answer before you come to class.

1. How would you define science to someone from a totally different culture?
2. Think back to your own childhood and recall a misconception that you once had about something in your environment. (For example, many children think there are little people inside the TV set.) What caused you to change your mind?
3. If you plan to explore the environment with children, then you necessarily will be studying animals. Is there anything you are squeamish about? If so, how will you get over your squeamishness so as not to pass it on to your pupils?
4. What is your reaction to Feynman's message to teachers?
5. What potential do you see for using science to help children become more responsible? In what ways, if any, is this potential different in science than it is in other school subjects?
6. What experiences might cause a child to dislike science? How might dislike of science influence the child's future?
7. Discuss the relationship of gender to science achievement and attitude. What can an elementary teacher do about it?

▼ REFERENCES

Carey, S. (1985). *Conceptual change in childhood.* Cambridge, MA: MIT Press.

Driver, R. (1989). The construction of scientific knowledge. In R. Millar (Ed.) *Doing science: Images of science in science education* (pp. 83–106). London: Falmer Press.

Einstein, A. & Enfield, L. (1938). *The evolution of physics.* Cambridge, England: Cambridge University Press.

Feynman, R.P. (1968). What is science? *The Physics Teacher, 7*(6), 313–320.

Kamii, C., & DeVries, R. (1978). *Physical knowledge in preschool education: Implications of Piaget's theory.* Englewood Cliffs, NJ: Prentice Hall.

Laurendeau, M., & Pinard, A. (1962). *Causal thinking in the child.* New York: International Universities Press.

Mali, G., & Howe, A. (1979). Development of earth and gravity concepts among Nepali children. *Science Education, 63*(5), 685–691.

Nussbaum, J. (1979). Israeli children's conceptions of the Earth. *Science Education, 63*(1), 83–93.

Nussbaum, J., & Novak, J. (1976). An assessment of children's concepts of the Earth using structured interviews. *Science Education, 60*(4), 535–550.

Piaget, J. (1951). *The child's conception of the world.* London: Routledge and Kegan Paul.

Sneider, C., & Pulos, S. (1983). Children's cosmologies: Understanding the Earth's shape and gravity. *Science Education, 67*(2), 205–221.

Woolfolk, A., & Hoy, W. (1990). Prospective teachers' sense of efficacy and beliefs about control. *Journal of Educational Psychology, 60,* 327–337.

CHILDREN'S THINKING AND LEARNING

▾
_____

The study of children's thinking has occupied some of the most original minds of the twentieth century and continues to be a subject of intense interest to psychologists, cognitive scientists, and teachers. We have chosen five of these who have had great influence and who share the constructivist view of how knowledge is acquired.

In the previous chapter we explained that the idea that knowledge must be constructed by each person is called constructivism. Constructivism stands in direct opposition to the view that children have empty heads waiting to be filled with what the teacher tells them and what they read in textbooks. Although there are facts or pieces of information that children learn through memorization, this kind of learning is only of lasting value if used as a building block for a larger body of knowledge that has meaning for the learner. To understand this concept, you have only to recall the vocabulary of a foreign language you once learned but never used or the dates you once memorized for a history test.

The main ideas outlined in this chapter should provide a background for your thinking about what science to teach, when to teach it, and how to teach it. You may elsewhere have studied the ideas of some or all of the thinkers described here, but this chapter is designed to help you understand how their ideas may be useful to you in teaching science. At the end of the chapter you will find a short section on recent research that will highlight several issues of current interest to researchers in science education. First, however, the following classroom demonstration will help you understand how knowledge of children's thinking can improve your teaching of science.

▾ A CLASSROOM SCENE

Mr. Newman discovered that his first graders became upset if they thought that he was not absolutely fair about everything. They became particularly upset if they thought that one person got more juice than another at juice time. After Mr. Newman had seen this happen several times he planned a lesson to convince his pupils that he was always fair, even though it might appear that one child had more than another. He found six small glass jars of different sizes and shapes in his apartment and took them to school. The next day he set the jars in a row on a table and had the children sit on the rug, where all could get a clear view of the demonstration. He carefully measured 100 ml of colored water and poured it into the first jar. Then he asked one of the children to help him measure exactly 100 ml of water and pour it into the second jar. Figure 2.1 shows what the children saw after 100 ml of water had been poured in each jar.

Mr. Newman explained that each jar had exactly the same amount because he had measured very carefully. Even though the amounts did not look the same, they were the same.

The children did not appear interested in what Mr. Newman was trying to explain. And since they did not ask questions about the amounts in the jars, Mr. Newman thought it was clear and obvious to everyone that all the jars had the same amount of liquid. Actually, the children seemed to be more interested in

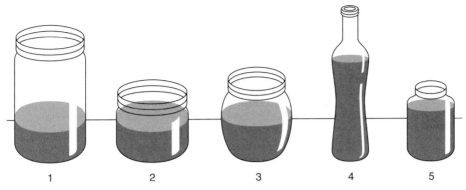

▼ FIGURE 2.1
Mr. Newman's jars

the jars than in the amounts of liquid in them, asking questions about where the jars had come from and what they had originally contained.

Juice time came soon after this lesson, and Mr. Newman was prepared with two different kinds of plastic drinking cups and a measuring cup to portion out the juice. He could not believe his ears when a big argument broke out between two children with different-sized plastic cups. Most puzzling to him was that these were two of the brightest children in the class; both were reading well above grade level. The boy with the larger cup started to cry because he thought he had less juice.

Mr. Newman, at wit's end over this episode, could hardly wait until school ended to talk with Ms. Oldhand about what had happened. He could not understand why the children did not believe their own eyes especially when he thought he had made it all so clear and logical. He could not understand why his lesson did not work. [*Can you think of reasons why Mr. Newman's lesson didn't work?*]

When Mr. Newman found Ms. Oldhand and told her what had happened, she explained that he had presented the children with a task similar to one devised by Jean Piaget to study children's thinking. She suggested that Mr. Newman would understand why his lesson had not had the expected outcome if he learned more about Piaget.

JEAN PIAGET

Although many people's ideas have enhanced our understanding of children's thinking, the person whose ideas have had the greatest impact over the past half century is Jean Piaget (1896–1980). Piaget, a Swiss developmentalist who spent most of his life in Geneva, was interested in finding out what goes on in children's minds as they try to make sense of the world around them. Piaget's work has been of particular interest to science teachers because an important goal of science teaching is for children to understand the world around them. Many teachers have turned to Piaget for insight and help in reaching this goal.

His research method was simply to sit down with a child and ask a series of questions. At times his questions concerned something the child had often observed, such as clouds or the sun. More often, the questions focused on simple objects or an apparatus, such as balls of clay or a pendulum.

The questions of most interest to science teachers were designed to find out how a child thinks about things encountered in daily life. Piaget showed that young children do not think logically by adult standards and that it takes many years for

▼ Jean Piaget

children to mature into thinking about things in a logical way. Of course, Piaget and his co-workers interviewed many, many children in the course of their studies. Their conclusions were based on patterns of thinking that they repeatedly found in the responses of children.

You should get a better idea of Piaget's work and how it relates to science teaching from some examples of children's responses to the questions he asked. In Chapter 1 you learned about four kinds of knowledge that children may acquire—social-arbitrary, physical, logical, and social-interactive. Example 1 focuses on logical knowledge.

EXAMPLE 1: CONSERVATION OF QUANTITY

The first example, taken from *The Child's Conception of Number* (Piaget, 1965), presents responses from children who were asked questions related to conservation of quantity (a concept that Mr. Newman assumed his children understood). The word *conservation*, used here as usually used in science, refers to the principle that a substance, an object, or a set of objects remains the same, regardless of changes in form or appearance, if nothing is added or taken away. For example, if 100 grams of water is frozen, the substance changes in appearance but has the same weight as before. This would be an illustration of the principle of conservation of weight. Conservation (and the idea of identity) is a principle basic to all science; many of Piaget's experiments deal with conservation. As you study this series of children's responses, think about Mr. Newman's classroom demonstration.

The child is shown two glasses of equal dimensions, each containing the same amount of liquid. The contents of one of the glasses is then poured into two smaller glasses, and the child is asked whether the combined amount in the two smaller glasses is the same as the amount in the original glass. The liquid may then be poured from one of the smaller glasses into two even smaller glasses. Each time, the questioner asks the child whether the total amount in the smaller glasses is equal or not equal to the amount in the original glass, which had been left undisturbed.

As you read the following interviews with Laura, Jed, and Art, keep in mind each child's age.

LAURA, AGE 4

Questioner: I am going to give you a glass of orangeade and give your friend, Mary, a glass of lemonade. I think both of you have the same amount to drink. What do you think?

Laura: I think we both have the same amount.

Questioner: Are you sure?

Laura: Yes.

Questioner: Now Mary pours hers into two different glasses. [*Pours Mary's lemonade into two small glasses.*] Does she still have the same amount as you?

Laura: No, I have more.

▼ FIGURE 2.2
Mary's and
Laura's glasses

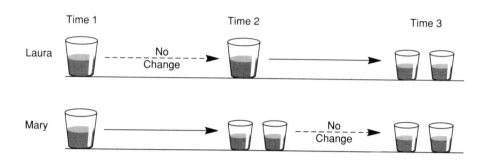

Questioner: Why?
Laura: Because you put less in.
Questioner: Now I'm going to pour your orangeade into two glasses that are the same size as the ones Mary has. [*Pours liquid into two glasses.*] Now, does one of you have more than the other?
Laura: No, the same.

The liquid is poured back and forth. Each time Laura affirms that the amounts are the same if the glasses are the same size and different if the glasses are of different sizes. As the liquid is poured back and forth, the child continues to say that the amounts are equal or unequal with no apparent awareness of any contradiction.

JED, AGE 5

Glasses and liquids are presented as in the previous example and the same questions are asked.

Questioner: Here are two glasses, one of lemonade and one of orangeade. Do both glasses have the same amount?
Jed: Yes.
Questioner: Are you sure?
Jed: Yes.
Questioner: When I pour the lemonade into two smaller glasses is there the same amount of lemonade in these two glasses together as there is in this glass of orangeade?
Jed: Yes, it's the same. [*Jed examines all three glasses carefully.*]
Questioner: Now, when I pour the lemonade in this glass into three small glasses is there the same amount in the three together as there is in this glass of orangeade? [*The glass of orangeade remains unchanged since the beginning.*]
Jed: There's more in the three glasses.
Questioner: And if I pour it back into the two?
Jed: Then there will be the same here [*pointing to the two smaller glasses*] as there [*pointing to the original glass of orangeade*].

ART, AGE 7

The child is presented with a glass of lemonade and several smaller glasses.

Questioner: If I pour your drink into these two [smaller] glasses, will you still have the same amount to drink?

Art: Yes, it's the same.

Questioner: I'm pouring Roger's drink into two smaller glasses and then pouring part of the lemonade from one of the glasses into another glass. Will he still have the same amount as before?

Art: Yes. [*Art says this with conviction.*]

Questioner: And if I pour yours into four glasses?

Art: It'll still be the same.

Questioner: How do you know?

Art: I just know. Once you know you always know.

CLASSIFYING CHILDREN'S RESPONSES

The responses of the children can be classified into three categories, based on their use of logical thinking. The first child gave prelogical responses. She did not understand that the amount of liquid remained the same regardless of the size or shape or number of the containers that it was poured into. The second child was beginning to understand the concept, but he contradicted himself without, apparently, being aware of the contradictions. The third child had mastered the concept and was absolutely sure of the correctness of his answers. In Piagetian language we would say that Art had attained the concept of conservation of quantity. (Piaget used the term "conservation of continuous quantity," though this task is sometimes referred to as "conservation of liquid" or "conservation of liquid amount.")

One of Piaget's important discoveries is that children have their own reasons for thinking the way they do about the things they see happening around them; convincing them to change their minds is difficult. Children construct their own realities, and there is a certain logic in the frameworks they construct. For young children, appearance is what matters. If something *looks* smaller, in the child's mind it *is* smaller.

Piaget believed that a child's ability for logical thinking develops gradually just as many other abilities do. No one expects first graders to have the hand-eye coordination that will allow them to produce the kind of handwriting that is expected of sixth graders. Similarly, no one should expect first graders to have the same degree of mental coordination that will allow them to "put two and two together" in order to arrive at a logical conclusion about the relative amounts of liquid in two glasses.

Piaget used the idea of stages to describe the way children's logical thinking progresses from infancy through adolescence. When Piaget's work first became widely known to science educators, they thought it was important to test children to pinpoint the "Piagetian stage" of each child. Today the emphasis has shifted. Most educators and psychologists now believe that development tends to be a continuous process rather than one of stops and starts, though experience tells us that growth is more rapid at some times than at others. Also clear is that what a person can learn in any area depends on how much he or she already knows in that area. Piaget's system of stages is now generally considered to be a useful shorthand for describing the capabilities that may be expected of children within a given age range rather than a rigid system with no exceptions or gray areas.

Piaget defined and described four stages in the growth of logical thinking, from infancy through adolescence, each stage characterized (1) by the typical behavior that a child exhibits in response to a specific task and (2) by what Piaget inferred was going on in the child's head. Although there has been much disagreement over Piaget's interpretation of children's behavior, there has been remarkable concensus that the actions and responses he discovered and described are found among children everywhere. The tasks Piaget used have been given to children in almost all parts of the world with remarkably similar results.

STAGES OF MENTAL DEVELOPMENT

A short description of each stage follows, with approximate ages at which they occur (Flavell, 1963). As you read about the stages, remember that the ages are approximate and that the descriptions are general, barely scratching the surface of Piaget's discoveries about children's thinking. Table 2.1 should also help you form an overall picture of a child's cognitive development.

1. SENSORIMOTOR INTELLIGENCE (0–2 YEARS)

Starting with only the reflexes of the infant, the child gradually learns to adapt to the environment by coordinating perception and action. Through trial and error the child learns to manipulate objects for the purpose of achieving concrete goals of action, though the child does not use language or other symbols to represent action until near the end of this period.

2. PREOPERATIONAL (2–7 YEARS)

The child begins to think about and represent action rather than simply to act; the child is able to engage in inner, symbolic manipulations of reality. The child also develops the ability to recall the past, represent the present, and anticipate the future, but the child still cannot use logic to solve problems. In this period parents and teachers are often surprised to find that a child who can already read well and do simple arithmetic will give illogical answers to questions about such things as the movement of the moon or conservation of matter.

3. CONCRETE OPERATIONAL (7–11 YEARS)

The child is now acquiring a system with which to organize and manipulate the immediate environment without the contradictions and perplexity that were present at the earlier stage. The child can think logically about real objects and gradually acquires the ability to perform the operations of adding, subtracting, multiplying, dividing, measuring, classifying, ordering, and comparing. The child can focus on transformations rather than final states and now understands the principle of conservation in some areas and eventually in most areas. In many cases the child is helped by having concrete objects to manipulate as an aid to thinking, though the child can think about some things without having objects present if these have been part of his or her experience.

4. FORMAL OPERATIONAL (12 AND OVER)

The adolescent becomes able to think logically and abstractly, to deal effectively with possibilities as well as realities. Now the adolescent can use propositional and hypothetical-deductive thinking; that is, he or she can think about "what if?" and "suppose" and does not have to refer to actual objects or parts of the real world as a basis for thinking. The adolescent's thinking can go beyond actual experience to include possibilities as well as realities. As in the other stages, these abilities do not come all at once; there is a gradual transition from one period to the next.

Most children in elementary school will be in the second or third stage of this development sequence. They need a science program that gives them many experiences with real objects in a setting that challenges them to think about and to represent what they see and do. Experience with objects is necessary but experience alone is not enough; both thinking about the experience and explaining it in words and pictures are also important.

Piaget's description of developmental stages is the most widely known aspect of his work, and many books have focused on ways to determine what stage a child might be in or what percentage of children of a given age are in each stage. Piaget

▼ TABLE 2.1
Piagetian stages of mental development

STAGE	DEVELOPMENT
Sensorimotor (0–2)	Learns to coordinate perception and action and to manipulate objects to attain goals; begins to use language
Preoperational (2–7)	Begins to think about his or her own actions, to plan, and to use language with clarity and precision; in problem solving, tends to focus on only one variable at a time; not aware of contradictions in logic
Concrete Operational (7–11)	Begins to think logically about things within own experience; can perform arithmetic operations; becomes aware of logical contradictions
Formal Operational (12 and over)	Becomes aware of the form as well as the content of problems; can think logically and abstractly about things and ideas outside own experience; can handle multiple variables and conflicting ideas

himself, however, put more emphasis on what a child's progression through the stages showed about the development of knowledge and understanding. Piaget's central concern was with the question, "How do we come to know what we know?" His answer was that we must construct our own knowledge and understanding; knowledge cannot be transmitted intact from one person to another. Children can memorize facts and be taught how to do many things, but they cannot really understand a phenomenon or a relationship—such as the relation of the sun to the earth—except by thinking about it and putting the pieces together in their own heads. This, the essence of Piaget's theory of mental development, is the basis for the constructivist view.

In example 1, you saw how one kind of knowledge, logical knowledge, develops. Example 2 involves both physical knowledge and logical knowledge.

EXAMPLE 2: THE MOON

In this example, taken from *The Child's Conception of the World* (Piaget, 1965, pp. 216–221) responses are given by children of different ages to the same questions. These interviews should give you insight into how children think about the things they observe in the world around them. Among the subjects Piaget asked children to talk about was their ideas and beliefs about the moon. He and his co-workers asked children from age 6 to 12 the question, "When you go for a walk at night what does the moon do?" The interviews that follow contain responses that are typical of children at three stages of development.

JIM, AGE 6

Questioner: When you go out for a walk at night what does the moon do?
Jim: It goes with us.
Questioner: Why?
Jim: Because the wind makes it go.
Questioner: Does the wind know where you are going?
Jim: Yes.
Questioner: And the moon too?
Jim: Yes.
Questioner: Does it move on purpose to go where you are going or because it has to?
Jim: It comes so as to give light.
Questioner: Where did you go for a walk?
Jim: In the park. The moon went too.
Questioner: Did it see you?
Jim: Yes.
Questioner: Does it know when you go for a walk in the park?
Jim: Yes.
Questioner: Does it care?
Jim: Yes, it does.
Questioner: Does it know your name?
Jim: No.

Questioner: Does it know there are houses?
Jim: Yes.

SUE, AGE 9

Questioner: When you go out for a walk at night what does the moon do?
Sue: It follows us.
Questioner: Why?
Sue: Because it's high up and everyone sees it.
Questioner: If you and I were walking in opposite directions, which of us would the moon follow?
Sue: It stays still because it can't follow two at the same time.
Questioner: When there are a lot of people in the town what does it do?
Sue: It follows someone.
Questioner: Which person?
Sue: Several people.
Questioner: How does it do that?
Sue: With its rays.
Questioner: Does it move?
Sue: Yes, it moves.
Questioner: How does it do that?
Sue: It stays still and its rays follow us.

PAM, AGE 10

Questioner: When you go out for a walk at night what does the moon do?
Pam: When you're walking you'd *say* that the moon was following you, because it's so big.
Questioner: Does it really follow you?
Pam: No. I used to believe it followed us and that it ran after us but I don't believe that any more.

These answers, typical of the answers of a large number of children, show the development of the idea that the moon is independent of us. The development of this idea requires both physical knowledge and logical thinking. Children who had never seen the moon and had no physical knowledge of it would hardly have been stimulated to think about it and acquire the logical knowledge as expressed by Pam. Because Piaget found similar answers among many children, he believed that these ideas arise spontaneously, based on direct observation and the child's own thinking. In this example, a progression is evident from the idea that the moon's role and function is to be helpful to us, to an unresolved contradiction (the moon "follows us" but "always stays in the same place") and, finally, to an understanding that the moon does not respond to us in any way.

This example of how children think about a natural phenomenon that all of us have experienced gives a science teacher a lot to think about. If children have these misconceptions (or alternative conceptual frameworks) about the moon, what do they think about the sun, about clouds, the wind and the rain? Is it possible to change their beliefs just by explaining things to them? Just explaining did not work in the case of the juice and the glasses. Is it any more likely to work in the case of objects as far away and as mysterious (to them) as the moon, the sun, and the wind?

From a Piagetian perspective, the task of the teacher is to provide the learning environment, the materials, and the tasks that will stimulate and encourage children to construct knowledge for themselves. Talking to children, or even demonstrating, will not teach them that the amount of water remains the same when poured from one container to another; they have to construct this knowledge for themselves through their own experience of acting on objects as well as through their own thinking. Seeing is not always believing for children; they have to experience things for themselves.

One way to construct for yourself a better understanding of how children think is for you to have experience in presenting Piagetian tasks to children and hearing their responses firsthand. Directions for administering a representative sample of such tasks are given in Appendix B.

JEROME BRUNER

Piaget's chief interest lay in discovering the origin and nature of knowledge as it develops in the mind of the child. He asked how we come to know what we know, and he developed a new vocabulary for describing the child's progress, through a series of stages of mental development, from prelogical thinking to a sophisticated use of logic in late adolescence. He did not discover, however, what outside forces or experiences (in addition to natural growth and maturation) propel a child from one stage to another. This problem he left to others, one of whom was American psychologist Jerome Bruner (b. 1915).

Bruner, who has acknowledged a debt to Piaget, used tasks devised by Piaget in studies on children's thinking. Bruner, however, went beyond a description of stages to consider not only how children think but also how children learn and how they can best be helped to learn. Some of his ideas about curriculum and instruction are directly related to what is proposed in this book (Bruner, 1966).

PROBLEM SOLVING

Probably the most important issue that Bruner addressed was how to stimulate and encourage children's thinking in the classroom. Problem solving constitutes one obvious way to encourage thinking, but Bruner noted that children encounter two kinds of problems in school. The most dominant problem for most children is the problem of finding out what it is that the teacher wants. When a child is confronted with a problem in arithmetic, for example, the first thing that pops in the child's mind is not, "What is the best way to tackle this problem?" Instead, the child thinks, "What did the teacher say about this kind of problem? How does the teacher want me to work this problem?" In other words, the child tries to please the teacher rather than focus on the problem. Teaching that leads to this kind of thinking discourages independent thinking as well as mastery of a subject.

Children encounter the other kind of problem all too seldom in school: problems that give children the experience of real problem solving, that is, the experience of solving problems that are of interest to them and for which they have to invent or create a solution. These problems can be solved in more than one way or have more than one acceptable solution. Problems of this kind cannot be solved by remembering an algorithm such as "multiply by two and take the square root" or "first measure the weight and volume and then make a graph."

Figure 2.3 shows a very simple problem of the second type. Suppose this is a drawing that shows the blocks and streets in a town. John lives at X and his friend lives at Z. What is the shortest way to go from Z to X? How many different ways can you go from Z to X?

Children who have never had experience in school with problems that require independent thinking are at first nervous and uncertain about how to proceed. The teacher has to reassure them both that their suggestions will not be dismissed and that there are more ways than one to solve the problem. The teacher is not going to show them the "correct solution" at the end. An example of an activity from a curriculum project that was much influenced by Bruner's ideas may clarify what is meant by creating a solution.

Clay Boats is a unit designed for elementary and junior high children, though high school and college students also find it interesting. The teacher rolls into balls equal amounts of clay for each group of two to four children. Each group has available a supply of washers, small tiles, or some other small objects of approximately equal weight. Each group also has a pan or some other container for water. Pupils are told to see whether they can make the clay float. Sooner or later everyone finds out that a boat or saucer shape is necessary to make the clay float. A subsequent problem is to determine how much "cargo" their boats can support without sinking. After each group has determined this, reported it, and compared results with other groups, the children are given the next problem: to find the boat shape that will hold the most tiles. Again the groups work together to solve the problem, and results are reported, compared and discussed (Educational Development Center, 1969).

▼ FIGURE 2.3
Blocks and streets

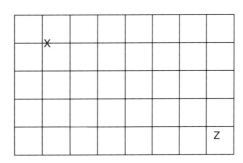

In this series of tasks, children have to act on their own ideas, and no special knowledge learned in school is useful in solving this problem. They are essentially left on their own, with only casual suggestions by the teacher for those who cannot get started. Bruner pointed out that in order to include this kind of problem solving the teacher has to want it, encourage it, and provide materials that make it possible. For Bruner, though, such problem solving is the heart of good teaching.

MODES OF REPRESENTING KNOWLEDGE

Bruner observed that one of the characteristics of intellectual growth is the child's increasing ability to communicate what he or she has done or plans to do. That is, the child becomes increasingly adept at representing experience or knowledge. Bruner identified three different forms of representing experience and used the words *enactive, iconic* and *symbolic* to describe these three modes of representation. The child begins with the enactive mode, then develops the iconic mode, and finally develops the symbolic, although at all stages of life people can and do use all three modes.

Enactive representation is experience translated into action. Anyone who has tried to teach a child to ride a bicycle or to play tennis, as Bruner points out, has become aware of the inadequacy of words. In those cases we represent what we know through action, not words. There are many instances where the old axiom "action speaks louder than words" can be applied in teaching—some things cannot be taught except by showing children what is supposed to be learned. How to use equipment, such as a balance or a microscope, is a good example, though there are many things best taught by action rather than words. Everyone accepts this principle in sports, music, and art education, but it applies as well in many aspects of science teaching.

Iconic representation depends upon visual or other sensory means of organizing information. Just as there are many things best taught by showing how, there are others best taught by using a drawing, a picture, or a diagram. In science teaching it is important to have children learn to use this method of representing their own experience. For example, children who have set up an electric circuit are more likely to remember what they have done and to understand it if they represent the system by making a diagram or drawing of it.

Symbolic representation depends on the use of words or mathematical symbols to express experiences, ideas, the past, the present and the hypothetical future. This is the most powerful as well as the most advanced form of representation. Without language and symbols, science could not exist. Facility with language and mathematics is surely one of the chief goals of science teaching. This is an ability that must be developed in children, because if this form is developed then the other forms of representation will be more effective for most of the science taught in elementary school.

Understanding and being able to use these three modes of representation will allow you to adapt your teaching to different learning objectives and to the needs of different children. You will recognize that some things are taught best by using enactive methods whereas others require visual means of presentation as well as symbols and words.

THE SPIRAL CURRICULUM

In Bruner's view, the curriculum should involve the mastery of skills that will in turn lead to the mastery of more powerful skills. This process is in itself motivating and rewarding. He believes that there is an appropriate version of any skill or knowledge that can be taught at whatever age one wishes to begin and that the curriculum should be built as a spiral; that is, the teacher and the learner come back again and again to the same topic, each time increasing and deepening understanding.

Consider, for example, the idea of acceleration, an important concept in physics. How do young children get the "feel" of acceleration? Riding a sled, roller skating down a hill, running down a steep bank, or watching a ball rolling down a hill, are a few ways that a child can experience acceleration through the senses. This is learning in the enactive mode. As a teacher, you can ask the children to recall their experiences and talk about how it feels to go faster and faster. If there is a hill nearby, you can take the class outside to watch objects accelerate as they roll down the hill.

A few years later, the children will be given the materials for performing an experiment with cylinders rolling down an inclined plane. They will learn to measure how fast the cylinder rolls and be taught a way to represent that action on a chart, which is a means of iconic representation and a way to advance their understanding. They will then be given a term—*acceleration*—to describe what happens. At that point, they will have used enactive, iconic, and symbolic means to represent the same concept.

Now, fast forward to physics class in high school, where one of the topics is acceleration. Because of the spiral curriculum adopted by the school, the physics teacher is confident that pupils in the class have had experiences and performed simple experiments involving acceleration. Now they are ready to carry out more complex, detailed experiments and, finally, to learn a formula expressed in mathematical symbols. The teacher will work problems on the board and assign problems for the pupils to solve. In theory, they will have constructed an understanding of acceleration through Bruner's three modes—the enactive, the iconic and the symbolic. But if, as often happens, acceleration is an idea that has never previously been discussed or represented in school, for most pupils the formula will have little relation to the world of their experience. They will learn to work the problems by memorizing the formula.

On the other hand, for those fortunate pupils whose experience has included talking, thinking about, and representing acceleration from time to time throughout their school years, the formula will represent a concept that can now be understood in a deeper and more meaningful way. The new learning builds on what they have already learned. Some of them will turn and say to each other, "Do you remember when Ms. Oldhand took us out to the hill behind the elementary school and showed us how a basketball went faster and faster as it rolled down the hill? I've always remembered that." Some other examples of how a spiral curriculum might be developed are given in Table 2.2.

In order to carry out Bruner's ideas, the teacher has to be an active problem solver with an attitude of openness to pupils' ideas and the expectation that pupils will be active and enthusiastic learners. There is no formula or set of rules for inquiry teach-

▼ TABLE 2.2
The Spiral Curriculum

ELEMENTARY	MIDDLE SCHOOL/JUNIOR HIGH	SENIOR HIGH
Experiences with objects that float or sink	Measuring mass and volume; calculation of M/V	Calculation of specific gravity; Archimedes Principle
Observing changes in colors of acids and bases using indicators	Neutralization of acids and bases by mixing measured volumes	Titrations; using volumes, moles, etc.

ing than can capture the essence of Bruner. For him the important thing is the process, not the product. The teacher as well as the children must become involved in the process.

LEV VYGOTSKY

Vygotsky (1896–1934), a Soviet psychologist, was born in the same year as Piaget but died at an earlier age, leaving work that was little known in the United States for decades. Now that it has become available, we can see that he had some very interesting and stimulating ideas about the socialization and education of children that are relevant to science teaching. He, like Piaget and Bruner, emphasized the importance of seeking meaning that goes beyond perception. "I do not see the world simply in color and shape," he wrote, "but also as a world with sense and meaning" (Vygotsky, 1976, p. 546).

Vygotsky was familiar with Piaget's early work and wrote one of his early books in response to some of Piaget's ideas about the role of children's language in mental development (Vygotsky, 1926). He, like Piaget, believed that the learner constructs knowledge; that is, what children know is not a copy of what they find in the environment but is, instead, the result of their own thought and action, mediated through language.

Although both of these thinkers focused on the growth of children's knowledge and understanding of the world around them, Piaget placed more emphasis on the child's internal mental processes and Vygotsky placed more emphasis on the role of teaching and social interaction in the development of science concepts and other knowledge. Vygotsky also believed that language plays a central role in mental development; in this way, perhaps, he had more in common with Bruner. Bruner has, in fact, written that Vygotsky influenced his own thinking (Bruner, 1985).

DEVELOPMENT OF MENTAL FUNCTION

Vygotsky believed that development depends both on biological (natural) forces and on social (cultural) forces. Biological forces produce the elementary functions of memory, attention, perception, and stimulus-response learning; social forces are necessary for the development of the higher mental functions of concept development, logical reasoning, and judgment. A main difference between lower (elementary) and higher mental functions is a shift from outside control to inner control. Through social interaction the child gradually assumes more responsibility and becomes more self-directed and autonomous.

In practical terms this means that what children can do and learn in school depends, at every age, on their attention span, their ability to remember, and various other biologically determined factors. But this is only part of the story. What they can do and learn also depends on the interactions that take place among the children and between children and adults, especially parents and teachers. Through social interaction, including interaction with teachers, children become conscious of their basic mental functions and become able to use those functions in their growth toward self-control, self-direction, and independent thinking and action. As discussed in a later section, a good science program helps children develop the characteristics of self-control, self-direction, and independent thinking along with the development of science concepts and processes.

INTERACTION AS A FORCE IN DEVELOPMENT

Vygotsky's ideas were developed through observation of children in the context of their daily lives, including school and family. His writings emphasize the importance of interactions between children and adults or older peers as the main force in cognitive, or mental, development. In his view, children learn best by having tasks set for them that are just beyond their present capability and then having guidance from an adult or older peer.

Think of how this happens in a family between parents and children or between older and younger children. When the toddler is learning to speak, the parents exaggerate the shape of their mouths in forming words for the child to repeat. They are modeling the behavior for the child. Parents who say "please" and "thank you" to their children are also modeling a behavior they want the children to acquire, and this technique works much better than telling children to be polite in a home where the adults are not polite to one another or to the children. Children learn to swim or hit a baseball by a combination of being taught and watching other people who are more skillful.

How can you use these ideas in teaching science? By applying the same general principles at school that good parents apply at home, a teacher can set tasks that are just beyond what pupils can do on their own but that are attainable with the teacher's help. This is like building scaffolds for the learner to climb to higher levels. At first, the individual learner must depend on the teacher to be shown what to do, but gradually the learner masters the task and gains control over a new function or concept. Everyone has had the experience of "going through the motions" in working a science problem or learning a new laboratory skill. Then, at some point that could not have been predicted, an understanding is gained, as well as a higher level of mastery and control.

As teachers, our aim is to provide the environment and the circumstances that make it possible—even probable—for our pupils, day by day, to master new skills and learn new things. Some of the ways that this can be done are:

- *Modeling.* The teacher models the behavior or skill to be taught or encouraged until the pupils can internalize the behavior. For example, if you, as the teacher, use the metric system consistently and reflexively, the children will accept that system as the way things are measured in science class.
- *Peer tutoring.* The expectation that individual children will help each other is incorporated into the teaching strategies used in the classroom. You will have to teach your pupils how to be good tutors and how to accept tutoring, and you will have to plan to assign pupils to be tutors or be tutored.
- *Cooperative learning.* Planned grouping of children is used as a regular part of instruction. Cooperative learning methods (which will be described later in this book) take advantage of pupil interaction as a means of promoting both academic and social learning.

A Vygotskian perspective suggests a classroom where active exchanges between children themselves and between children and teacher are an ongoing part of daily life. From these exchanges and interactions, children construct meaning and knowledge. The teacher sets tasks that are just beyond the learners' current levels of competence and provides the help that learners need to reach higher levels. That help may take various forms, but an important aspect will be opportunities for children to work together, to give and receive verbal instructions, respond to peer questions and challenges, and to engage in collaborative problem solving. If you establish a classroom where this is the normal way for pupils to behave, you will have little trouble using hands-on methods for science lessons. Children will know how to share equipment, to work in groups, and to ask questions about things they do not understand or know how to do.

LAWRENCE KOHLBERG

Lawrence Kohlberg (1927–1987), another constructivist who built on the foundation laid by Piaget, concentrated his study on the development of moral reasoning rather than logical reasoning. He, like Piaget and others, based his theory on studies of the responses of children and adolescents to questions asked during individual interviews. He presented situations in which a choice has to be made between conflicting ethical or moral values, situations in which a person wants to do what is right but can find no way to avoid undesirable consequences. A simple example of such a situation that children confront is whether to tell if they see a good friend cheating on a test. From responses to situations of this kind, Kohlberg arrived at a developmental theory of moral reasoning.

Kohlberg's inclusion in the short list of thinkers discussed in this chapter supports the belief that science at the elementary level cannot be taught in a moral vacuum. The years in elementary school are a time of growth in all dimensions, including the

▼ Lawrence Kohlberg

moral dimension. The children you teach live in a world of moral dilemmas, many of which are brought on by the uses and misuses of science. They are better able to make hard choices if their moral development has kept pace with their increasing knowledge and understanding of science.

STAGES OF MORAL DEVELOPMENT

Kohlberg sought to show that children's development of a sense of right and wrong, as well as the ability to make moral choices and to act on them, is a slow process that occurs over many years. He, like Piaget, defined stages of development, each of which has characteristics that differentiate it from the other stages. These stages are outlined briefly below.

Level I   Pre-conventional

- *Stage 1* is characterized by the unquestioning acceptance of the right of authority figures to exercise power and to demand obedience to rules; the motivation is to avoid punishment. The child says, "I will do what the teacher wants me to do because I have to obey the teacher or I will be punished."
- *Stage 2* is characterized by obedience to rules when it is in one's own self-interest as well as a concern with fairness in all exchanges. The child says, "I am afraid I'll get caught if I don't play by the rules." Children spend a lot of time making sure that all rules are adhered to.

Level II   Conventional

- *Stage 3* is characterized by children's wanting to do what they think is the right thing; the children want to live up to expectations of others. They try to have good motives, and they believe in trust, loyalty, and gratitude. They have a desire to maintain rules and a social order that supports good behavior.
- *Stage 4* is characterized by a belief in institutions and laws, except where there is a conflict with one's duty to be loyal, truthful, and honest and to uphold other social values. A person considers individual relations in terms of their place in the social system. For instance, there are situations in which the individual is torn between wanting to obey the law and wanting to be loyal to a friend.

Level III   Post-conventional or Principled

- *Stage 5* is characterized by development of an awareness of the variety of opinions and values held by people, as well as a recognition that most values and rules are relative to a group or culture. One recognizes that some values, such as life and liberty, are above or beyond the reach of relative values and must be valued in all societies.
- *Stage 6* is characterized by a belief in the validity of universal moral principles and a sense of personal commitment to them. The highest principle is justice: the equality of human rights and respect for the dignity of individuals.

EDUCATIONAL IMPLICATIONS

Just as Piaget believed that children must construct their own logical knowledge, Kohlberg believed that children must construct their own moral knowledge. Kohlberg's view was that a child cannot become a moral person by memorizing rules of behavior any more than that child can become a logical thinker by memorizing ways to work problems. Trying to teach children to be "good" by admonishing them to obey a set of rules is equated by Kohlberg to giving them a bag of tricks to pull out at appropriate moments, a method that has had notably poor results. Kohlberg's ideas can be put to practical use in two main ways.

First, keep in mind that children are at a lower stage of moral development than you are. They must pass through the earlier stages before they can reach the higher ones. In class discussions that center on what is the right thing to do in situations that arise in the classroom, you must take account of the stage of the children—they do not have an adult point of view. You can help them to see things from other children's perspectives and to construct for themselves the rules by which they will live.

Second, establish a classroom atmosphere in which each child is respected and in which you as a teacher are scrupulously fair to all pupils. Fairness is extremely important for children in elementary school, most of whom are not beyond Kohlberg's stage 3. Children at that stage become uncertain and anxious in any situation in which they cannot depend on the adult in charge for fair treatment. Remember Mr. Newman's class at the beginning of this chapter? The teacher was motivated to have a lesson on conservation because the children thought he was not being fair in giving out juice. When children are concerned and upset about lack of fairness, their attention is diverted from the lesson. Take care to be fair in assigning duties, in allocating equipment to groups, and in the amount of time you spend with individual children or groups. A more extensive discussion of this point can be found in Siegal (1982).

Kohlberg's ideas are important in the context of science teaching because of the guidance they can provide in establishing a classroom where the interactions between teacher and pupils—both as individuals and as a group—are guided by moral and ethical considerations. One consideration is fairness: being fair and letting children know that you will be fair in all your dealings with them. Another consideration is respect: letting children know that you respect them and expect them to respect each other. Science cannot be well taught when children's social and emotional development are not taken into account. At a higher level, Kohlberg reminds everyone that the advance of science can lead to difficult moral issues.

SEYMOUR PAPERT

Seymour Papert belongs with the constructivists because he believes that children construct their own meaning from their experiences, and he, perhaps more than the others, has worked to give children a mechanism for doing this. Papert, a professor of education and mathematics at the Massachusetts Institute of Technology, began his academic career as a mathematician and later developed an interest in artificial intelligence (AI) and computational theory. AI is an attempt to create in machines what is called intelligence in people. To figure out how to make such a machine, it becomes necessary to study what human intelligence is. This led him eventually to Geneva from 1958 to 1963 where he, like Bruner, studied with Piaget.

LOGO OR TURTLE GEOMETRY

Papert is most often associated with the computer programming language Logo, and this is the area of greatest educational impact so far in his career. The great contribution of Logo is that it allows children to use the computer as a tool to improve their ability for logical thinking.

Logo was developed for children to learn and use with ease and enjoyment. With only a few minutes of instruction, a user can do fascinating and significant things. But Logo is not simply a "baby language"; it is a full-fledged computer language capable of highly sophisticated products. Just as English is learned in a simple form by youngsters but is capable of use in the highest forms of literature, Logo can be said to have neither floor nor ceiling. The form of Logo most used in schools is Turtle Geometry.

A triangular object called the Turtle appears in the center of the computer screen, and it can be moved forward and back and turned left and right by commands typed on the keyboard. When the Turtle moves from one position to another, it leaves a trace on the screen. In addition to the command, however, the user must also enter a number. For example, FORWARD 100 draws a line that is twice as long as one

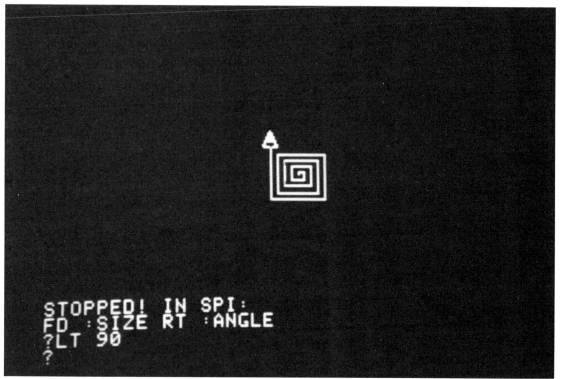

STOPPED! IN SPI:
FD :SIZE RT :ANGLE
?LT 90
?

▼ This photo shows the original Apple Logo turtle. The turtle in more recent versions of Logo has a different shape. Permission granted by Logo Computer Systems, Inc. (LCSI), Montreal, Ontario, Canada.

produced by FORWARD 50, and LEFT 90 makes the Turtle turn left by 90 degrees. By giving appropriate commands to the Turtle, the child can draw things on the screen and can print out whatever has been drawn. Later, the child learns how to "teach" the Turtle to remember; in other words, the child learns how to write programs. The child can then invoke the program he or she has written by typing the name given to that program, causing the drawing to be redone by the Turtle as many times as the program name is entered.

One can easily see how using Logo to draw interesting things could result in the child's understanding of concepts such as angles and variables. This learning is significant because it is connected to other meanings in the child's mind and can therefore be used for further learning. Learning about angles and variables in this way is very different from memorizing definitions from a textbook.

Another feature of Logo is its modular nature. Simple programs can be put together to produce a superprogram. This building-block approach to programming has much in common with the constructivist view that knowledge is put together by the knower. Putting together two simple programs (or figures drawn by the Turtle) to form a connected, larger program (or figure) can be considered a model of the way a learner puts together disconnected pieces of knowledge (small concepts) in order to form a larger concept.

MAKING SENSE

A more powerful type of learning also results from using Logo—developing a strategy for learning. That strategy could be described in this way: In order to learn something, first make sense of it. Papert criticizes the traditional science curriculum as placing too little value on making sense. Logo helps children become aware that, in order to learn something, one must first make sense of it by thinking about it. This concept leads into thinking about how to think, an ability that has often been considered too abstract for children. Papert asserts that the microcomputer has opened the door for earlier and more advanced mental growth than was possible before. By providing learners with the Turtle as an "object to think with," ideas previously known only through abstraction are given concrete embodiment, and are therefore much more accessible to children. Logo allows the learner to externalize his or her expectations or intuitive notions into the concrete form of a program, where those notions are accessible to reflection.

Take, for example, the production of the figure of a square on the computer screen. This is a figure that every primary child can be expected to be familiar with, but now the child is confronted with the problem of telling the Turtle how to make a square. This problem requires some thought about something the child has probably not thought much about before. Starting from a point somewhere on the screen, the learner must think exactly what has to be done to make a square. The feedback is immediate and informative. If the program does not function as expected, it can be studied and "debugged." Errors or programming bugs, says Papert, "are not seen as mistakes to avoid like the plague, but as an intrinsic part of the learning process" (Papert, 1980a, p. 153). The learner is thus placed in better command of the learning process and can construct her or his own knowledge.

Learning more about Logo, and becoming a participant in learning with your pupils, will help you understand the potential Papert's ideas have for children and learning. This passage written by him may give you the flavor of his thought: "I believe with Dewey, Montessori, and Piaget that children learn by doing and by thinking about what they do. And so the fundamental ingredients of educational innovation must be better things to do and better ways to think about oneself doing these things" (Papert, 1980b, p. 161). Piaget said that children learn by acting on objects and thinking about the consequences or results of their actions. For example, when children put a weight on a balance (an act), they can see whether the balance beam goes up or down (the result). In that way, they learn about the balance. Papert took this idea one step further by inventing something new for children to act on that would give them immediate and clear feedback about the result. In addition, Logo contains the potential for going from the simple to the very complex. Thus, the learner can continue to build on what has been learned, incorporating what is already known into a more and more complex construction, and having to think about her or his own thinking in order to move ahead.

RECENT RESEARCH

Most science educators today could be called constructivists. A consensus has formed that knowledge of science must be structured and restructured by the learner, that learning is more than memorization, that understanding is what matters, and that each learner must "put it all together" in his or her own head. But big questions remain. How does this happen? What brings it about? What are the mechanisms of conceptual change?

Recent research in science education has approached these questions from several perspectives and proposed alternative hypotheses. In most cases the researcher starts from the premise that, beginning long before the start of formal schooling, the learner already has well established ideas, beliefs, and concepts. The researcher then asks how this knowledge is restructured to become more consistent and coherent, as well as closer to the accepted scientific explanation for the process or phenomenon in question. The research areas described below all address these questions; there is some overlap among them, and many unresolved problems that are being studied from more than one perspective.

PIAGETIAN AND NEO-PIAGETIAN RESEARCH

Piagetian theory has been used as the framework for much research in science education. Many researchers have tried to show (1) that specific science concepts can only be understood after a child has reached a certain stage of development and (2) that, conversely, when a child has reached a stage, such as concrete operational, then the teacher can be assured that the child can learn concepts that could not previously have been learned. These views have had to be changed in the light of the results of research.

Piaget's work is no longer considered an infallible guide to teaching science, though it has inspired an almost overwhelming amount of research by others. Perhaps the most important outcome of research based on Piaget's work was described by Confrey (1990) as "the belief that teaching is most effectively improved when the teacher learns to listen to students' thoughts and to interpret students' actions and thoughts from their perspectives as children" (p. 11). The current understanding of the importance of listening to children and to seeking their explanations for what they say and do is probably Piaget's most enduring legacy.

Learning has been shown to be more domain-specific than it was formerly thought to be by Piagetians. In other words, learning depends on prior knowledge in a particular field as well as on the level of reasoning. What you can learn at a given moment about chemistry, for example, depends on what you already know about chemistry as well as on your ability to reason at a certain level. In one subject you may operate at the concrete operational level; in another subject, at the formal operational level (see, for example, Linn, 1983, or Lawson & Wollman, 1976). Other variables, such as spatial ability and psychosocial factors, also appear to influence reasoning, and many Piagetians have now incorporated Vygotsky's ideas into their own thinking about the factors that influence learning. One aspect of Piaget's theory that has been universally retained, though, is constructivism.

One group of researchers, sometimes called Neo-Piagetians, believe that an important factor in children's reasoning ability is the amount of information they can hold at one time in working memory, and that this capacity increases with age. In this view, children cannot understand density, for example, because they cannot simultaneously consider the two variables of volume and mass. As the amount of memory space in the brain increases, more information can be processed at one time (Pascual-Leone, Goodman, Ammon, & Subelman, 1978). That is, young children can think about only one thing at a time, but as they get older they become able to keep two things in mind at once. Some researchers explain children's lack of understanding of the conservation principle as the inability to consider two dimensions (for example, height and width of glasses of liquid) at the same time. Although teachers cannot influence the amount of memory capacity available, they can frame problems and tasks in ways that reduce the demand for working memory. One way to do this is to break problems down into steps; another is to avoid giving younger pupils problems or tasks that require them to consider two variables at once.

INFORMATION PROCESSING

Another framework for studying the problem of how learners construct knowledge is that of information processing. Several important lines of research are based on the idea that the human brain functions as an information processor, somewhat analogous to a computer. Using computer programs to model human thinking has been one of the features of this line of research. This perspective has led to studies in general problem solving and, more recently, to studies of problem solving in science. Much of this work has been carried out with adolescents or college students, though some work has focused on younger children.

One important and interesting finding is that when a person has learned something well, that person tends to organize what has been learned into "chunks" of information and then, in effect, think with those chunks (Simon, 1974). For example, when you first moved to where you now live, you had to learn how to get to campus. If you were driving, you paid careful attention to where to turn right or left; if you were on a bus or train, you watched carefully for the place to get off. Soon, however, you could do all this without paying attention to it; the pattern had become a routine filed somewhere in your brain under "getting to campus." The same principle works in other areas. If you are a bridge player, you can look at many hands and know right away what you will be able to bid because you have learned to recognize a certain combination of cards. Studies of chess players have shown that this is how expert players think and that this way of thinking is their great advantage over nonexperts (Chase and Simon, 1973). Learning to recognize a pattern and to "chunk" that information is an important part of constructing knowledge. As a science teacher you can help pupils learn to do this.

Research on problem solving in science has shown that the way students deal with information influences how they solve problems. Some pupils look at all the separate bits of information and try to attack the problem without really processing the information; others read the problem, think about it and try to bring to mind anything they already know that might help them solve the problem. Of course, those in the latter group have more success (Flavell, 1976). As a consequence, teachers can improve their pupils' problem-solving abilities by teaching them the steps or procedures that are used by good problem solvers.

Although little research has been done on problem solving by children, research on computer programming conducted with adolescents may be applicable to problem solving in learning science. Linn and co-workers (Linn and Dalbey, 1986; Linn, Sloane, & Clancey, 1987) have found that teachers who emphasize or teach specific procedures are more effective, especially with middle-ability pupils. (The brighter pupils figure these procedures out on their own.) The results of this research provide further evidence of the need to help pupils understand what they are taught in a way that will allow them to recognize patterns, organize information, and integrate knowledge in order to construct meaning for themselves. One outcome of this work has been the clarification of the difference between *procedural knowledge* and *declarative knowledge*. Procedural knowledge refers to the procedures used to solve problems or complete tasks; it tells a person how to do something. Declarative knowledge refers to what a person knows about a subject. Both kinds of knowledge are used in solving a problem.

CHILDREN'S MISCONCEPTIONS

The children's misconceptions about the moon described earlier constitute only one among many areas about which children have misconceptions or "unscientific" ideas. Eylon and Linn (1988) have produced a list of commonly held misconceptions about 16 important concepts from the physical and life sciences. The extent of the misconceptions and the difficulty of changing them has received a good deal of attention among science educators, though no one should have been surprised to learn that children form their own ideas about things they see around them (Schoenfeld, 1983). Nor should it have been surprising to learn that children's beliefs influence their receptiveness to new information. After all, the essence of science is to wonder about the things observed in the natural world.

Several instructional approaches have been tried to persuade children to give up their naive notions about natural phenomena and accept established scientific concepts or explanations. Some evidence shows that allowing children with different views to discuss their ideas and argue among themselves is more conducive to change than instruction by a teacher, even when this instruction takes place on an individual basis (Johnson and Howe, 1975).

▼ FIGURE 2.4
A fifth grader's
concept map for
water

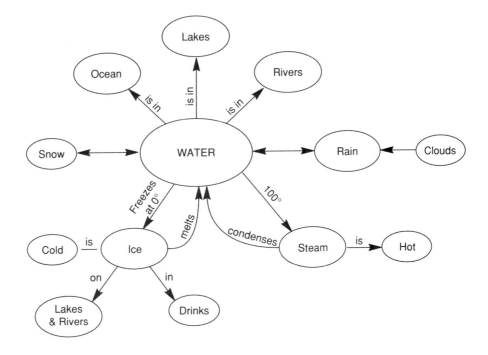

Another approach to changing children's concepts is a strategy called *concept map-ping*, which focuses on the relationships between concepts. Each concept is part of a network of other concepts. For example, the concept of blood circulation in the body is related to concepts of the heart, veins, arteries and pumping. One way to use con-cept mapping is to ask each pupil to draw a "map" that connects related concepts; the maps help the teacher understand the children's thinking and provide some guidance for instruction. Figure 2.4 shows a concept map for water. Novak (1985), one of the foremost researchers in science education, developed concept mapping as one way to help students "learn how to learn." There is no agreement about what teachers can do to change children's misconceptions, but there is agreement that the process takes time, that children come to school with their own ideas, and that adults should listen to children to find out what they are thinking and take into account their "miscon-ceptions" about natural phenomena.

Although these results of recent research may or may not pass the test of time, they offer some suggestions for science teachers. Research indicates that what chil-dren can learn depends as much on what they already know in an area as on their level of logical thinking. Another useful idea is that information is processed and remembered in "chunks"; thus, once a procedure, for example, is well learned it becomes automatic and does not have to be thought about in order to be used. Finally, much evidence shows that teachers need to take into account the preconcep-tions or misconceptions that children already have when they intend to teach an im-portant concept.

▼ SUMMARY

The common thread that ties everything together in this chapter is constructivism, the belief that meaningful knowledge must be built up, or constructed, by the learner. This belief is considered from different points of view by the thinkers whose ideas were discussed.

Piaget described how a child's ability for logical thinking develops partly through natural maturation and partly through interactions with the objects and people in the child's surroundings. Understanding Piaget's stages of mental development will help you decide what activities are appropriate for the children you are teaching so that you can match instruction to the children's level of development. Remembering Piaget's view that the learner must construct knowledge for him or herself will help you be patient with your pupils as they try to absorb and internalize new ideas. Piaget, a giant in his field, had a profound influence on the others discussed in this chapter.

Bruner examined ways in which instruction can promote the mental development that Piaget described. In his view, instructional materials should be structured and sequenced so that mental development is reinforced by a curriculum that returns to important concepts again and again throughout the school years, each time with a more sophisticated and inclusive interpretation.

Another important aspect of Bruner's work is his emphasis on the ways a person represents what that person knows. He describes three modes of representation—the enactive, the iconic, and the symbolic—and points out their uses both as means of instruction and as ways for children to represent knowledge. Instruction, for Bruner as well as for Piaget, should be a process in which the pupil is actively engaged with materials of all kinds and learns to represent the new knowledge through action, drawings, or words.

Vygotsky's main contribution to the understanding of children's learning is in the importance he attached to the role of interaction between child and adult or child and older peer. For Vygotsky, this was the main force in learning of all kinds. He believed that children learn by being helped to do things that they are not yet competent to do alone but in which they can become competent with the assistance of another person.

Kohlberg's ideas on children's moral development help teachers remember that the planned curriculum is not all that is learned in the classroom. As a teacher you should also be concerned about the moral climate of your classroom and about the moral as well as the cognitive development of your pupils. Learning will be enhanced in a classroom where the teacher shows respect for each individual and creates an atmosphere of fairness and trust.

Papert is known for his development of the computer language Logo, which was designed specifically for learning. As with the other learning theorists presented here, he was strongly influenced by Piaget. The unique area of Papert's contribution is in suggesting that the stages of development described by Piaget are not as limiting as was once thought. He proposes a model of learning in which complex ideas and autonomy in learning are accessible to young learners when they are provided with a good "object to think with," the good object in this case being the Logo Turtle.

Recent research has built on the work of these thinkers and has brought new insights and ideas to the study of children's thinking, including extensive work on the discovery of children's ideas about a great number of natural phenomena. There is now more emphasis on studying how children think in specific situations than on general cognitive development or thinking in general. Cognitive scientists have added a new dimension to the study of thinking by examining how people process, store, and retrieve the information they receive as well as how beginners and experts differ in using information to solve problems.

Table 2.3 should help you put together the main ideas presented in this chapter.

▼ DISCUSSION QUESTIONS

1. In his book, *Toward a Theory of Instruction*, Bruner wrote, "There is an appropriate version of any skill or knowledge that may be imparted at whatever age one wishes to begin . . ." (p. 35). What do you think he meant by that statement? Try to defend or refute the statement with examples. Select one important process or concept in science and discuss appropriate versions for primary children and for upper elementary children.
2. What does it mean to *create* an answer to a problem? Give an example of a problem that has more than one answer.
3. The following moral dilemma is similar to one posed by Kohlberg.

   A young woman is very ill. Her husband has been told by her physician that she probably does not have long to live but that there might be some hope if he could obtain a new and experimental medicine being used in cases similar to hers. The husband finds out that there is a pharmacist in the city who has a small supply of this medicine but that it is prohibitively expensive. He goes to the pharmacist and begs for a supply of the substance, but the pharmacist tells him that he himself has paid an enormous amount for the medicine and cannot afford to give it away. That night the husband breaks into the pharmacist's store and steals some of the medicine. Was it wrong for him to steal the medicine? Would it have been right for him to let his wife die rather than steal?

   Write your answer to this dilemma and bring it to a class, ready to discuss it with the class or a small group. In discussing this question, think about what your highest values are. Is it more important to follow the rules that a society has decided are important for the well being of everyone or to save one person's life?
4. Can you remember a time when you felt that a teacher or other adult did not treat you fairly? Looking back on it, can you understand the adult's point of view or do you still think the treatment was unfair?
5. If you had to add a summary of one other person's ideas to this chapter, whose ideas would you add? Discuss other thinkers who might influence your teaching.

▶ TABLE 2.3
Constructivism in Science Teaching

SCHOLAR	MAJOR IDEAS OR THEMES	IMPLICATIONS FOR SCIENCE TEACHING
Piaget	Children acquire knowledge by acting and thinking. Knowledge is classified as physical, logico-mathe-matical, or social. Development of logical thinking is a maturational process. Understanding of natural phenomena depends on logical thinking ability.	Provide environment to encourage independent action and thought. Distinguish between kinds of knowledge in planning instruction. Be aware of children's level of logical thinking.
Bruner	Children learn by discovering their own solutions to open-ended problems. Knowledge is represented in enactive, iconic, and symbolic modes. Appropriate ways can be found to introduce children to any topic at any age. The process of learning is more important than the product.	Use open-ended problems in science regularly and often. Use all three modes of teaching and testing for understanding. Emphasize processes of science. Teach concepts and processes that will lead to further learning.
Vygotsky	Children learn through interaction with peers and adults. Knowledge is built as a result of both biological and social forces. Language is a crucial factor in thinking and learning. Children need tasks just above their current level of competence.	Encourage pupils to work together and to learn from each other. Encourage children to explain what they are doing and thinking in science. Set tasks that challenge children to go beyond present accomplishment.
Kohlberg	Children learn moral and ethical behavior by example rather than by teaching. Moral development is a slow, maturational process. Moral dilemmas that have no easy solution are part of life.	Set example of fairness and honesty in your own behavior. Guide discussion of problems as they arise and allow children to suggest solutions. Include science-related societal problems in class discussion.
Papert	Children learn when they can make sense of what they are learning. The computer can be a tool for explaining children's ability to think. Children can learn to think about their own thinking.	Make sure that children understand the meaning of their class activities. Make the computer a tool for new learning, not a substitute for a book. Encourage and model thinking about thinking.
Recent Research	Learning is domain-specific. Misconceptions about natural phenomena interfere with new learning. Both procedural and declarative knowledge are important.	Expect greater competence in familiar topics than in unfamiliar ones. Probe to find out what misconceptions children bring to science class. Distinguish between kinds of knowledge in planning science instruction.

▼ ACTIVITIES FOR THE READER

1. A few representative Piaget Tasks are given in Appendix B. If you have never had the opportunity to present these tasks to children and to reflect on their responses, you should do it now. This will give you very valuable insight into children's thinking.
2. a. Write a plan for a series of classroom activities that you would use to help children develop the concept of conservation of liquid amount, that is, the knowledge that the amount of water does not change when it is poured from one container to another.
   b. Would you expect all the children in your class to attain the objectives of the activities planned in part a? Explain your answer.
3. Select an important concept in science and write short lesson plans to show how you would teach it at three different levels so that each level is built on the previous one, as in the acceleration example.
4. Give an example of each of the following:
   a. something that you might teach in the enactive mode
   b. something that you might teach in the iconic mode
   c. something that you might teach in the symbolic mode
5. Make up a dilemma that you could use in your class. Invent a situation that could actually happen in the lives of children and that might arise in your class or among your pupils. Explain what questions you will ask and how you will classify the answers.

▼ REFERENCES

Bruner, J. (1966). *Toward a theory of instruction.* Cambridge, MA: Harvard University Press.

Bruner, J. (1985). Vygotsky: A historical and conceptual perspective. In J. Wertsch (Ed.), *Culture, communication and cognition: Vygotskian perspectives.* Cambridge, England: Cambridge University Press.

Chase, N., & Simon, H. (1973). Perception in chess. *Cognitive psychology*, 4, 55–81.

Confrey, J. (1990). A review of research on student conceptions in mathematics, science and programming. In Cazden, C. (Ed.), *Review of Research in Education.* Washington, DC: American Educational Research Association.

Eylon, B.-S., & Linn, M. (1988). Learning and instruction: An examination of four research perspectives in science education. *Review of Educational Research*, *58*(3), 251–301.

Educational Development Center (1969). *Teachers guide for clay boats.* New York: McGraw-Hill.

Flavell, J. (1963). *The developmental psychology of Jean Piaget.* Princeton, NJ: Van Nostrand.

Flavell, J. (1976). Metacognitive analysis of problem solving. In L. Resnick (Ed.), *The nature of intelligence*. Hillsdale, NJ: Erlbaum.

Johnson, J., & Howe, A. (1978). The use of cognitive conflict to promote conservation acquisition. *Journal of Research in Science Teaching*, 15, 234–237.

Lawson, A., & Wollman, W. (1976). Encouraging the transition from concrete to formal operational functioning: An experiment. *Journal of Research in Science Teaching*, *13*(5), 413–430.

Linn, M. (1983). Content, context and process in adolescent reasoning. *Journal of Early Adolescent Reasoning*, 3, 63–82.

Linn, M., & Dalby, J. (1986). Cognitive consequences of programming instruction: Instruction, access and ability. *Educational Psychologist*, *20*(4), 191–206.

Linn, M., Sloan, K., & Clancy, M. (1987). Ideal and actual outcomes from precollege Pascal instruction. *Journal of Research in Science Teaching* 24(5), 467–490.

Novak, J. (1985). Metalearning and metaknowledge strategies to help students learn how to learn. In L. West and A. Pines (Eds.), *Cognitive structure and conceptual change* (pp. 189–207). New York: Academic Press.

Papert, S. (1980a). *Mindstorms*. New York: Basic Books.

Papert, S. (1980b). Teaching children thinking. In Taylor, R. P. (Ed.), *The computer in the classroom: Tutor, tool, tutee*. New York: Teachers College Press.

Pascual-Leone, J., Goodman, D., Ammon, P., & Subelman, I. (1978). Piagetian theory and neo-Piagetian analysis as psychological guides in education. In J. M. Gallagher & J. A. Easley (Eds.), *Knowledge and development* (Vol. 2, pp. 243–289). New York: Plenum.

Piaget, J. (1965). *The child's conception of the world*. Totowa, NJ: Littlefield, Adams & Co.

Piaget, J. (1965). *The child's conception of number*. New York: Norton.

Schoenfeld, A. (1983). Beyond the purely cognitive: Belief systems, social cognitions, and metacognitions as driving forces in intellectual performance. Cognitive *Science*, 7(40), 329–363.

Siegal, M. (1982). *Fairness in children*. New York: Academic Press.

Simon, H. (1974). How big is a chunk? *Science*, 183, 482–488.

Vygotsky, L. (1976). Play and its role in the mental development of the child. In J. S. Bruner, A. Jolly, & K. Sylva (Eds.), *Play*. New York: Penguin.

Vygotsky, L. (1926). *Thought and language*. Cambridge, MA: The M.I.T. Press.

EVERYDAY TEACHING SKILLS

CHAPTER OUTLINE

▼
_____

Most of us have grown up hearing from our elders many popular sayings of folk wisdom. Because these sayings have been familiar since before we were old enough to reason, we tend to accept them as true without much thought. In some cases, these sayings have paired and opposite meanings, as in "Look before you leap" and "He who hesitates is lost." So much for popular wisdom! A couple that are worth thinking about are:

- The best way to learn to swim is to jump off the deep end.
- There are two ways to do anything: the right way and the wrong way.

Each saying has an appealing simplicity, and each has at least a grain of truth. Although it is true that you cannot learn to swim without getting your feet wet, the consequences of jumping off the deep end as a first lesson can be pretty dire. Even those who somehow avoid drowning will probably have a bad attitude, or at best, poor technique. Learning to avoid drowning is not the same as learning to be a skilled and happy swimmer. The grain of truth in the second saying is that there is almost always a wrong way to do anything—there are, in fact, usually a great many wrong ways. There are also a great many right ways to do most things. The more complex the "thing" being done, the more right and wrong ways there are to do it.

Teaching is extremely complex. One aspect of teaching is to learn the connections between particular teacher behaviors and particular pupil outcomes. Your beliefs about children and how they learn will influence your behavior, and your behavior will, in turn, influence pupil behavior. The notion of "right" and "wrong" can be limiting to a teacher's professional growth. More useful is to think of teacher behaviors as effective and ineffective for a particular goal. What is effective in one situation or for one goal may be ineffective for other situations or goals. This book takes the viewpoint that teachers can become aware of their own assumptions and behaviors, recognize the probable effects of these behaviors, reflect on their effectiveness, and make a conscious effort to act in ways that are likely to achieve particular teaching goals. There is no one "right" way to be a teacher. The best anyone can do is to develop a repertoire of behaviors, a sensitivity to pupils' needs, and a growing sense of when to do what to produce desired effects. Albert Einstein had a saying that is not folk wisdom yet but should be: Everything should be as simple as possible, but no simpler.

Oh, no! I'll never learn how to teach—it sounds too complicated! Don't despair. You will learn. You will not drown because you will not be thrown into the deep end. First, you will learn some techniques. Then you will get a chance to try them out. It will be something like learning to swim under the supervision and direction of instructors who love to swim and love to teach.

This chapter introduces some ideas and considerations for teaching in any subject area. Some readers will already be familiar with these ideas and may not need to study this chapter. For others, it will set the stage for later chapters by providing the background of basic skills on which to build competence as a science teacher.

TEACHER CONCERNS

If university courses are thought of as answers to questions, it could be said that some education courses are answers to questions that have not been asked, at least not by students. In these courses, students often feel a lack of relevance to their needs and interests. Sometimes methods courses share this negative rating. Teachers with a bit more experience tend to rate the same courses much more positively. One way to look at this problem of perceived relevance was described by Fuller (1969); her idea was that beginning teachers are concerned with their own survival in the system. Only after these early concerns are resolved can teachers turn their attention to higher levels of concern, such as whether pupils are learning and what should be taught. For student teachers, behavior management seems to consume the day. Although this concern cannot be resolved simply by reading or discussing, some attention will be given to it here.

CLASSROOM MANAGEMENT

Universally, the major concern of beginning teachers is keeping order and avoiding any embarrassing discipline problems. Virtually all beginning teachers worry about classroom control. If you are a beginning teacher who still has this early concern, take comfort in the notion that your feelings are quite normal and will begin to abate with experience. Once the early concern is accepted as normal, you can begin to gather potentially useful information. The following sections should serve as starting points in learning to manage a classroom in a way so that it becomes a learning environment.

WHY WE NEED CLASSROOM MANAGEMENT

Until the early teacher concerns are resolved, a beginning teacher might be stuck on the idea that the purpose of classroom management is to preserve the teacher's dignity and avoid embarrassment. Once the teacher has passed that concern, the actual purpose becomes more apparent: many normal, acceptable home behaviors are disruptive when multiplied by thirty and packed into the confines of a small classroom. Thus, restrictions of freedom become necessary in order to provide an appropriate environment for learning. Each pupil has to give up some freedom of movement in order to gain freedom from disorder and disruption of learning. Although the obvious goal of managing behavior is to provide an environment conducive to learning, a subtle goal is for children to practice controlling impulses and to develop consideration for the needs of others.

Children become uncomfortable and nervous when they feel that no one is in control. Even well-behaved children will test the limits and sometimes break the rules, but they want to know that they will not be allowed to go too far. Most children seem to know instinctively that they need adult guidance and protection.

ABOUT GENERALIZATIONS

There are no absolute rules that always work in every situation, but there are some guidelines that will help very much most of the time. In open discussions about behavior management, beginning teachers often respond to broad statements with the "yes but" syndrome. A student-teaching seminar or methods-class discussion, in which several beginning teachers dispute a generalization on the basis of experiences in their own classrooms, has a dampening effect on more than just the mood of the instructor. There is certainly an emotional justification in questioning the usefulness of an idea that does not always work, and there are many cases today in which children bring severe problems to the classroom. Such problems often require special solutions (some of which will be discussed in later chapters). But even if you are a new teacher in a troubled classroom, it is important for you to understand normal systems and normal children. Otherwise, no progress toward ideals can be made. Likewise, it is important to understand general guidelines for behavior management, even when one's own situation requires many exceptions to those guidelines. Otherwise, every solution to every problem would be unique and have no relevance for other applications. "Playing by ear" in every case is an extreme and unworkable solution. The teacher would spend all of his or her time controlling each problem individually, and the pupils would be deprived of any opportunity to learn to take responsibility for their own behavior.

ESSENTIAL TEACHER BEHAVIORS

Kounin (1970) reported on a pioneering series of research studies done by him and his associates to examine how teacher behavior affects classroom management. A surprising finding was that when successful and unsuccessful managers were compared, no particular differences were found in the way they responded to pupil misbehavior. Later studies have verified and extended these results (Anderson et al., 1980; Emmer et al., 1980; Brophy & Good, 1986; Doyle, 1986).

Researchers were determined to find out what made the difference between successful and unsuccessful classroom managers. If it was not the action taken by the teacher when a child misbehaved, what was it? The secret turned out to be prevention of inappropriate behavior. Teacher behaviors that prevent discipline problems have been summarized from the research and reported by Good and Brophy (1987). They found four teacher behaviors that provide the most prevention.

With-it-ness, sometimes described as having eyes in the back of one's head, is mainly an awareness of what is happening in the whole classroom at all times. It involves use of ears as well as eyes to monitor noise level and take action when a "crescendo" is beginning to build. A teacher with this kind of awareness, and with a consistent history of intervention in potentially disruptive pupil behavior, conveys to pupils a sense of with-it-ness that prevents most problems from happening in the first place.

An ability to do more than one thing at a time allows a teacher to keep an eye on learning groups while holding a direct lesson with others. This ability also lets a teacher respond to outside questions and manage routine jobs without seriously interrupting the main activity.

Maintaining lesson momentum means being well-prepared and organized enough to avoid stopping to look at notes or backtracking after false beginnings. It means making judgments to ignore minor daydreaming but to intervene in situations that could escalate into disruptions. It also means minimizing the disruption to the lesson that such a teacher intervention itself causes.

Providing variety and challenge in independent work means assigning tasks that hold the pupils' interest. If the content is too hard or if the procedure is unclear, pupils will give up. If the task is too easy or overly repetitious, pupils will be bored. Either situation means wasted learning time and potential management problems.

In summary, appropriate pupil behavior is achieved by teachers who are flexible, businesslike, aware of potential trouble building up, and sensitive to pupils' needs and abilities. These traits cannot be developed simply by reading a methods book but require the experience of being in charge of a real classroom. Experience alone is not enough, however; also essential is to understand the needs and abilities of pupils. In order to find a workable middle ground between "don't-move-a-muscle" rigidity and "anything goes" anarchy, consider these generalizations about children:

- Children are still immature, prone to impulsiveness, and often lacking in judgment. A child may be bright, but is rarely wise. Responsibility must be learned by practice, even though this means that there will be some mistakes. Without the freedom to make mistakes, children cannot learn to be responsible.

- Children are not born difficult; they learn that behavior if adults around them do not sufficiently respect their potential for growth and their current limitations. Children who have been taught to be difficult can usually be untaught. Exceptions to this generalization include children with certain learning disorders or retardation. Until a problem child is so diagnosed by a specialist, however, the regular classroom teacher should not hold lower expectations for him or her than for any other pupil in the class.

- Children are naturally curious and interested in objects and relationships. They want to learn about things that interest them. School learning does not have to be drudgery. A resourceful teacher seeks ways to bring curriculum into the sphere of children's natural interests.

- Children naturally overdo things when confronted with a novel task. Those who do not overdo at first may actually be timid or repressed. When planning an activity that involves new materials or new freedoms, the teacher who takes this natural tendency into account will have fewer problems. With guidance, the children will learn to exercise restraint and to appreciate the feeling of accomplishment produced by consciously varying the amount of energy used to produce different effects. The first encounter with the situation, however, is almost always characterized by excess. A corollary of this rule is that children cannot handle too much novelty at once. In planning a science lesson that involves something new, the teacher should introduce only one element of novelty at a time. When there is more than one thing being overdone at the same

▼ Introduce novelty a little at a time to avoid overwhelming children.

time, it is almost impossible even for normally well-behaved children to avoid falling apart.

- Children know they are less effective in the world than adults. They yearn alternately to be more powerful and to be more secure. It is normal for children to test limits. If they find no limits, or if the latitude of freedom exceeds their ability to manage on their own, they are likely to get into trouble. This generalization is closely related to the idea of overdoing in novel situations. Even while they are being disruptive or engaging in dangerous behavior, children are usually unconsciously asking for the security of adult control. They sense that they are not always able to control their behavior and that someone else needs to do so.

PREVENTING INAPPROPRIATE BEHAVIOR

In addition to developing the essential teacher behaviors, a teacher must establish standards and consequences for guiding pupil behavior and to help the pupils understand why the standards are necessary. This step is important: you cannot expect much cooperation unless pupils understand why the rules are necessary.

Standards means a set of general rules of conduct; *consequences* means what happens when a standard is violated. In your reading, you may see the terms *sanctions* or *penalties* used in much the same way as *consequences*. To begin, decide on a few absolute requirements that are not open to debate. Then, depending on the age and maturity of your pupils, you may decide to involve them in formulating additional standards and, possibly, more consequences. The number of each should be kept to a few, however. Children's imaginations are rather limited when it comes to thinking of appropriate examples. A better way to involve them in the process is to discuss actual or potential disruptions and give them some alternative solutions to discuss and choose from. In any case, the pupils should be directly taught the standards and consequences. Instruction of this sort requires several lessons at the beginning of the year, with frequent, regular review thereafter.

DEALING WITH MINOR MISBEHAVIORS

When inappropriate behavior is not serious and stops on its own, the teacher is advised to ignore it. Two examples are momentary pencil tapping and brief talking. If these or similar potential distractions continue for a longer time, an emotionally neutral intervention is called for, such as establishing eye contact, making a gesture, or standing near the pupil. With young children, a gentle touch often works, though this may be less effective with older pupils. Remember that the main idea is to continue the lesson or activity with a minimum of disruption. Calling on a pupil to gain renewed participation also fits here. None of these problems is serious and thus should not be the cause of embarrassment. Embarrassment of the pupil in question is noticed by the others and can itself constitute a disruption of the lesson. A simple redirection of attention is all that is usually necessary.

APPLYING CONSEQUENCES IN MORE SERIOUS CASES

When inappropriate behavior goes beyond the minor type, the teacher must intervene in a consistent, expected manner. If penalties are applied inconsistently, they will cease to be regarded as consequences and discipline will collapse. Because it is hard to foresee every situation, some teachers are apprehensive about using a system in which negative consequences are invoked in a seemingly automatic way. Shouldn't there be occasions when exceptions are made? First, a clarification is needed: not all negative consequences are punishments. In fact, punishment should be used only as a last resort; although punishment can control behavior, it has little or no effect in changing attitudes or in teaching acceptable behavior (Bandura, 1969). A series of consequences of increasing impact on the pupil can be used. The first offense could call simply for a reminder. For many pupils, a reminder is enough. A second offense by the same pupil could entail a short conference with the teacher, during which the pupil is required to describe the unacceptable behavior and identify the class standard that has been violated. The penalty for a third offense could be to have the pupil devise a plan for correcting the problem. Glasser (1977) has described a 10-step plan for difficult behavior problems that moves through a series of consequences of increasing impact.

LEARNING TO PREVENT BEHAVIOR PROBLEMS

Some teachers use a comprehensive management system, such as Assertive Discipline (Canter & Canter, 1979), Teacher Effectiveness Training (Gordon, 1976), Logical Consequences (Dreikurs & Cassel, 1972), or Reality Therapy (Glasser, 1969, 1986).

Such systems (and there are others) require time and effort to learn. Some teachers learn a system through in-service training provided by the school or district administration. Other teachers take the initiative to learn a system through reading or university courses. Each of these systems has its particular strengths and weaknesses; one may be more effective than another in a certain situation. If you would like to know more about such systems, you may wish to read *Teacher's Guide to Classroom Management* (Duke & Meckel, 1984), in which nine approaches are described and compared in specific situational examples.

All of these systems are based on the principles of behaviorism. Since we have made a strong case for constructivism earlier in the book, you may ask why we have included techniques drawn from behaviorism. The reason is a practical one: these methods have been shown to be effective in helping many teachers establish a classroom environment in which learning is possible. As helpful as these approaches may be, it should be noted that many teachers have become excellent classroom managers without using any of these systems. Whether you decide to use one of these approaches or develop your own, there are certain factors common to all effective classroom management, sometimes referred to as the three Cs: clarity, communication, and consistency.

Clarity in your own expectations is essential. If you are not sure what kinds of behavior to expect and what kinds you will not tolerate, then you will have to settle each problem on a case-by-case basis. That method will not work for long. Advance planning is needed to think about the needs for general class rules of behavior—standards—and the consequences for deviating from them. In any case, you must decide ahead of time how to present the standards and consequences to the class. All of these decisions must be made, and your thinking on the matter must be clear.

Communication is essential to transfer your expectations to the pupils. Remember that children are not just little adults. They have very limited capacity to make judgments. It is unrealistic to expect children to regulate their own behavior by judging its appropriateness. Although a goal of teaching is to help children become more responsible, do not forget that they have quite a way to go. During the elementary school years, following clearly communicated standards is enough to expect.

Consistency in applying consequences is essential to the success of any management system. The secret to getting children to take responsibility lies entirely in their learning a highly predictable sequence of cause and effect. They are quick to learn when they see that every single infraction meets with the same undesirable consequence. When there are exceptions to enforcement, infractions continue and even increase in number. When a child is not sure whether he or she can get away with something, the child is tempted to test the limits of the system. The quickest and most humane way to teach responsibility while maintaining order is to enforce the classroom standards by using prearranged consequences uniformly, immediately, and without exception.

Once you have gained confidence in your ability to prevent or handle problems, you may want to develop your own methods. But one way or another you must have a classroom in which children can go about their work without continual or major disturbances. Principles of behavior management have been emphasized because that subject is a concern of beginning teachers. But an important factor in children's behavior is the level of their involvement in learning activities, the subject of the next section.

PUPIL INVOLVEMENT

The amount of time children spend in school in the United States has often been contrasted with the amount of time in school in other countries. It seems obvious to many people that if a pupil spends more time working on a skill or thinking about an idea, then that pupil will learn more than if less time had been spent. There are several ways to think about this time factor, however. One way is as *time-to-learn*. A 20-minute lesson offers twice as much time-to-learn as a 10-minute lesson. Another way to look at time is as *time-on-task*. This quantity is measured by a trained observer who keeps track of how much time is spent "off-task." For example, time spent sharpening pencils, gazing out the window, or visiting socially would be subtracted from a pupil's time-on-task score. Another way to think about amount of exposure to a task, however, that has to do with the quality of the engagement as well as the amount of time, is called *pupil involvement*. When measured as pupil self-reports of attention, pupil involvement has been shown to have more to do with achievement than either time-to-learn or time-on-task (Wittrock, 1986).

When involvement happens, it can easily be observed by the teacher. Highly involved pupils are oblivious to things that normally distract them, because they are very busy and locked onto the task. Left to work on their own without teacher encouragement, they persist at the task much longer than at normal academic tasks.

The research on attention has been focused on all academic tasks, including listening to the teacher and routine seat work. If the definition of academic tasks is broadened to include hands-on and interactive activities such as labs and computers, the picture of pupil attention span and pupil involvement changes radically. Labs and computers are much closer to children's natural interests than is passive schoolwork. The term *labs* implies hands-on activities with concrete materials in which the pupil has some freedom, even if a small amount. Children who would not choose to spend their spare time at academic tasks may spend hours playing with construction sets, or watching bugs, or interacting with pets. Such activities are not just pleasant pastimes but important learning experiences of real and highly significant value to the child's

▼ Highly involved students keep on task and do not get into trouble.

mental and emotional development. Why would a child voluntarily choose to educate him- or herself in this way? Because it is natural for children to be curious and to seek learning.

Learning is only unnatural when removed from individual interests and curiosity. Although society needs to start early with a child's schooling, individual teachers can make schooling more humane by trying to match the methods and activities more closely to children's natural interests and needs.

The learning activity types listed in Figure 3.1 are in the approximate order of difficulty children have in maintaining attention over time. There are some qualifications and exceptions to the sequence, but in general, the lower on the list, the harder it is for children to maintain lengthy attention. The activities higher on the list are more concrete in nature. There is another factor working as well and that factor is interaction. In the bottom two activities, the pupil is essentially a passive receiver of information. Even in reading, there is some control of pace and sequence by the child. In the top three activities, real interaction occurs; something happens in response to what the pupil does, and vice versa.

These two factors, concreteness and interaction, are the main determinants of pupil involvement. Keep this chart in mind when you plan your science lessons, and

▼ FIGURE 3.1
Comparing
activity types by
involvement

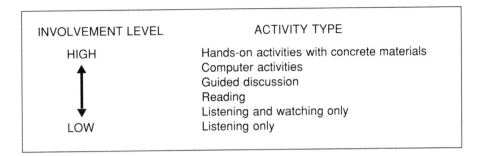

INVOLVEMENT LEVEL	ACTIVITY TYPE
HIGH	Hands-on activities with concrete materials
	Computer activities
↕	Guided discussion
	Reading
	Listening and watching only
LOW	Listening only

always try to think of a way to meet the objectives by planning to use methods as high on the list as possible.

The mind has an appetite for learning in the same way that the stomach has an appetite for food. The mind craves knowledge and understanding of its surroundings. The kind of learning sought by the child's mind is firsthand experience. A beginning teacher once asked, "Do you mean there are things that you can't learn from reading?" Yes, from reading you can't learn how a banana smells, or what color the sky is, or how it feels to pet a kitten. You might learn the word *blue* from reading or from hearing spoken language, but unless you have previously had some firsthand experience with things that are blue, the word conveys no meaning. Words, after all, are a wonderful way to communicate when they cause the reader or listener to recall a firsthand experience. If no experience lends meaning to the words, no real learning can occur.

Teachers must constantly remind themselves how limited the experience base of a child is. A kindergartner was born only 60 months ago. There just has not been time for a five-year-old to have had many experiences. Even older elementary-age children have amazing gaps in their experience that adults may not think to consider. For example, many children, even from affluent families, have never eaten or examined a fresh orange. This is true even in orange-growing regions, because many parents give their children frozen or ready-prepared orange juice. When teachers keep this limited experience base in mind, they are less likely to expect children to maintain attention for long periods of time during low-involvement activities such as listening. Without an extensive experience base, too many words and sentences seem meaningless. Extended listening is hard work even for adults; for children, even a very few minutes may be too hard.

Several ways are useful in minimizing the amount of time spent in low-involvement activities. One is to modify activities to increase the involvement level. Instead of long lectures, break up the information with questions to check for understanding. Children can also be invited to ask questions or give comments. These changes move the involvement to a higher level. Any spoken information input should be carefully planned to avoid unnecessary details, as well as to keep things brief. Some beginning teachers tend to ramble on and on, repeating themselves and using unnecessary and uncommunicative expressions such as "you know." This kind of problem can be helped by careful planning.

A second way to increase pupil-involvement is to spend more time in high-involvement activities. Some teachers may avoid lab-type activities, computer lessons, and activity centers because they are too much trouble or because the teachers feel insecure about them. This book should help you learn to use these powerful high-involvement methods with confidence and effectiveness.

A third way to increase involvement is to increase your own teaching efficiency. Learning time that is wasted waiting in line for supplies—or waiting while the teacher finds a piece of chalk—not only breaks the momentum and lowers the pupil involvement level but also sets the stage for inappropriate pupil behavior.

VERBAL TECHNIQUES

The verbal behavior of the teacher sharply determines the level of pupil involvement. Teaching techniques that involve spoken language are crucially important and as a consequence will occupy a large segment of many chapters of this book. This section begins the discussion with a brief look at some simpler aspects of teacher talk.

GIVING INFORMATION

Giving information is what many people think teaching is all about. Most teachers would challenge the notion that it is the only or even the main function of the teacher, but every teacher still must know how and when to give information verbally. As mentioned in the section on pupil involvement, listening is hard work for children and generates a low level of involvement. Therefore, it is important to keep content information-giving as brief as possible.

Learning to listen is an important instructional goal in itself, and you may ask, "How about using a science lesson to help pupils improve their listening skills?" This sounds like a fine example of killing two birds with one stone, but in reality the strategy does not work. Children have a hard time managing more than one task at a time, thinking about too many different things at once, or handling excessive novelty in general. Think about the games "Simon Says" and "May I?" The challenge that makes them interesting is having to do two things at once. Even at the adult level, adding style requirements to a test makes the test harder. An example is the television quiz show "Jeopardy!" in which contestants must not only think of answers but also give them in the form of a question. A seemingly simple, but additional, demand of this type can greatly increase the difficulty of the mental task, sometimes called cognitive load. When you decide to have a lesson to teach listening skills, choose some neutral or "enrichment" information to use as a context rather than the developmental content upon which later understandings will depend.

Because listening is so hard and generates such a low involvement level, every means must be taken to simplify and shorten it. Failure to do so results in two potential problems: (1) the information is not heard or not understood and (2) behavior problems often ensue.

GIVING DIRECTIONS

Giving directions is one of the teacher's tasks that sometimes gets neglected in methods books and courses. You just tell them what to do, right? Well, not quite. The same difficulties described for giving information apply to listening to directions. In classrooms where the routine is rarely broken, pupils learn how to do regularized tasks sooner or later, through individualized instruction if necessary. Classroom business that is truly routine should be regularized in order to move smoothly and efficiently through the day's activities. If collecting milk money or lining up for recess is still a time-consuming hassle one month after school begins, something is wrong. On the other hand, instructional procedures and learning activities need a certain amount of variety to engage and hold the interest of pupils. Learning where to draw the line between stultifying sameness and overwhelming unpredictability is something that comes with experience and careful thought. An effective teacher varies instructional activities and therefore must be a good direction-giver, because she or he will be introducing new ways to do things now and then and cannot rely entirely on pupils' ingrained procedural actions.

The style of giving directions is similar to the style used in direct teaching of content information. In both, verbal information is being given by the teacher and active listening is required. The main difference is the nature of the information being given: substantive (content) information or procedural (what to do) information. To the learner, there is little or no difference.

There are many ways to teach science content, only one of which is giving information directly. One way may work better in a certain situation, another way in a different situation. Once two or more methods are mastered, the teacher can choose the one that promises to be most effective in a given set of circumstances. There is much less variation in effective ways to give directions. When working with elementary pupils, certain ways will almost always work when introducing a new procedure.

It is of primary concern to establish an atmosphere of openness and trust as early in the school year as possible. Pupils must be able to ask procedural questions without fear of embarrassment or put-downs. In classes where an open atmosphere is absent, pupils will prefer to risk doing things wrong rather than openly admit that they do not understand. In a lesson designed to teach how to listen to directions, encourage nondistracting hand raising—or some other prearranged signal—when clarification is needed. If days or weeks later, however, you accuse a pupil of not paying attention when she asks for clarification, your atmosphere of openness goes out the window. Pupils learn from such teacher behavior not to trust you and, possibly, not to trust teachers in general.

In the book *Teaching Science as Continuous Inquiry: A Basic* (Rowe, 1978, pp. 433–35) discusses giving directions for science activities, especially those involving concrete materials. The following list of suggestions is based in part on her work.

Guidelines for Directions

1. Be clear in your own mind exactly what you want the pupils to do. Do not change your mind after you start talking.

2. Be as brief and clear as possible. Plan carefully by writing down exactly what you plan to say. Then go back and cut out all unnecessary information. Ask another adult to critique your directions for clarity.

3. Maintain the sequence in your directions that you want carried out in the procedure. Try to avoid this type of behavior: "Oh, I forgot. Before you put beans in the pans, you should attach the pans to the balance beam."

4. Give directions before passing out materials. There is no earthly way that verbal directions can compete for pupils' attention with concrete materials to be touched and fiddled with.

5. Give directions in short segments. Stop after each segment to get feedback on understanding. If no hands are up, ask for questions. Check also for facial expressions suggesting puzzlement. Watch for inattentiveness or decrease in interest. Whispering may indicate lack of comprehension ("What does attach mean?"). A brief pause can give pupils an opportunity to consolidate the information. Often, teachers move on to give more directions while pupils are still thinking about the previous direction.

▼ Charted directions reinforce spoken directions and serve as a memory aid.

6. Develop sensitivity to any use of words that may be unfamiliar to pupils. Use new words in known contexts. New words and old words used in a new way should be explained or illustrated.

7. When possible, demonstrate with materials as you give directions.

8. With all but the very youngest children, use chart paper or a chalkboard to list the steps. Write only the key words or very short sentences. The chart serves as reinforcement for your spoken directions and as a memory aid later, not as the main information source.

9. Until you have complete confidence that the children feel safe in asking for clarification, ask for a volunteer to give back each step when you finish your directions.

So far you have looked at the two simplest kinds of teacher talk, giving content information and giving procedural directions. The more complex interactive verbal techniques will be introduced in later chapters.

PLANNING

Classrooms in which children are highly involved in interesting and meaningful learning activities—in which they give attention to the teacher when that is needed and in which there are few disruptions or behavior problems—do not just happen. Such classrooms are the result of careful planning with attention to both the overall goals and the details of the daily activities.

Although there are always decisions to be made on the spot while you are in the midst of teaching, there are other decisions that can and should be made much earlier, during the planning stage. The lesson objectives, the specific materials to be used, the pupils who are to be involved, the time of day to introduce the lesson, and many more such decisions should be settled during planning. In Chapter 4 you will find some guidelines for selecting teaching methods to achieve different goals.

Virtually everything that can be planned ahead of time should be. Does this mean that a decision is locked into place once planned? Of course not. Once a lesson is underway, many contingencies of the real world may demand that the plan be modified. Whatever the purpose of a particular lesson, the main principle of instruction that always applies is this: Teaching is not merely transmitting information; rather, teaching is bringing together curriculum and the learner in a way that is appropriate to the learners' needs, thus enhancing meaningful learning. This principle means that the teacher must constantly assess the pupil's understanding and fine tune the delivery of the lesson as it unfolds. Occasionally, a teacher will discover partway through a lesson that the pupils are simply not ready for it. In that case, the best decision is to "abandon ship," or terminate the lesson. When the goal is understanding rather than information, this type of decision becomes possible.

It is crucial, however, to think through the plan in detail even if many changes have to be made later. Leaving details to be worked out at the last minute is a formula for disaster. Two aspects of planning that should be a daily concern are (1) determining instructional objectives and (2) evaluating the lesson.

INSTRUCTIONAL OBJECTIVES

The first detail of lesson planning should be the decision about the objectives of the lesson. The objectives of any particular lesson will depend on broader goals, such as those outlined in Chapter 1 and elaborated in Chapter 4. Each unit will have goals drawn from the overall goals and related to them, but specific objectives should be determined and kept in mind for every lesson. Thus, you should never begin a lesson without having a clear idea of the objectives for the pupils. You should know what you expect them to learn. Without keeping objectives in mind, there is a tendency for the days to drift by without reaching the important instructional goals. Your actions will be designed to help the pupils reach the objectives of the lesson.

DETERMINING PERFORMANCE OBJECTIVES

Many teachers have found it helpful to think in terms of *performance objectives*, statements of what the pupil should be able to do by the end of the lesson that he or she was not able to do before. The purpose of focusing on performance (or behavior) is to make the new ability easier for the teacher to observe. You may have studied behavioral objectives before, but you likely will find that the way they are used in this book will be somewhat different. Some writers, emphasizing that lesson outcomes must be measurable, have placed a criterion of acceptable performance in the objective, for example, "The pupil will be able to name the bones in the human body with 75-percent accuracy." Such precision is unnecessary, even undesirable, for an individual lesson at the elementary level, partly because measuring each objective for each pupil at this level would take an inordinate amount of class time.

The two main functions of performance (or behavioral) objectives are to guide the teacher in lesson planning and in deciding whether a lesson is successful or not. The emphasis is on lesson evaluation rather than pupil evaluation. Identifying the observable behaviors that should result from the instruction allows the teacher to decide whether the lesson has "worked" or whether it needs to be revised and retaught. A secondary function of performance objectives does involve pupil evaluation, but every lesson need not always result in a grade or mark for every pupil. Some people have criticized the idea of using performance objectives because there are so many worthwhile aims of instruction that are difficult or impossible to describe in behavioral terms and because "behaviorization" tends to trivialize the objectives by emphasizing their less important aspects. These criticisms ring true, but performance objectives are still useful in certain applications. One of these applications is helping beginning teachers learn to think clearly and systematically about planning. To avoid misuse of behavioral objectives, the following limitations are stressed:

- The use of performance objectives should be limited to the lesson level and not extended to larger instructional entities, such as units or courses.
- Performance objectives should never be used as the only source of evaluative data from which grade reports or other permanently recorded pupil evaluations are made.
- Nothing more serious than whether to redo a lesson should be based entirely on performance objectives.

WRITING PERFORMANCE OBJECTIVES

A good way to start is to think of what you hope to accomplish by teaching the lesson. In other words, what is the lesson *goal*? This goal can be stated in ordinary, everyday language. Suppose you are doing a primary-grade lesson on magnets. You want the pupils to find out the action of magnets on different materials. Also, because you know that some of the pupils worked with horseshoe magnets last year, you want them to realize that magnets can come in other shapes as well. You have the beginnings of a lesson with these two general goals:

- Find out that magnets attract some metals and not other materials.
- Find out that magnets can have different shapes.

The next step is to figure out what you can observe during or after the lesson that will let you know that the pupils were able to find out these two ideas. You have stated the new things they will know; now ask yourself, How will I know that they know? What new things will they be able to do as a result of the new knowledge? You could say that knowing or finding out are things to do. True, but the problem is that it is very hard to observe children knowing or finding out. You want to have evidence that an objective has been met. So you will ask yourself, Is there some kind of observable behavior that could serve as an indicator? This indicator may or may not be spontaneous behavior. You may decide to ask pupils to do something that will let you know that they understand the goals. This task you ask them to do may be a regular part of the lesson, or it may be just for letting you know.

Here are some action verbs that are useful in writing behavioral objectives. All of them refer to a specific behavior or performance.

list	state	differentiate
name	identify	describe
construct	distinguish	perform alone
demonstrate	create	group
classify	design	measure
organize	select	order sequentially
predict	infer	compare

There is nothing magical about these words, and their use in a sentence does not guarantee that a useful behavioral objective will result. Usually, additional words or phrases are needed to spell out observable behavior more specifically. How can you tell whether an objective will be useful or not? Decide if it suggests to you a specific action you can see or hear. If you read an objective and the action seems a bit vague, the statement probably needs more work. The following are some examples of useful objectives that could be developed to serve as indicators for the two general lesson goals. Which or how many of them you would select would depend on your own ideas of how the lesson should proceed and what is important about this lesson. By the end of the lesson, the learner will be able to:

- Distinguish magnets from nonmagnets by their actions on other objects.
- Describe the action of a magnet on metals and nonmetals.
- Group a set of materials into two sets: (1) attracted by magnets and (2) not attracted by magnets.

- State a rule about the relationship of shape and magnetic activity, such as "not all magnets are horseshoe-shaped" or "not all horseshoe-shaped metal things are magnets" or "some magnets are round and some are bar-shaped."
- Predict which objects in an unknown set will be attracted by magnets based on whether they are metallic.

Writing the objective helps to clarify it in your own mind. After it is written you will need to decide whether the language of the objective is specific enough to allow you to observe the performance. If the language lacks specificity, you can add examples or modifiers. The main idea is to give yourself a way of judging whether or not the pupils are learning what was intended. An additional benefit of going through this mental exercise is that interesting and useful activities are often suggested by specific objectives that might not have otherwise come to mind. Can you create some more objectives to add to the list?

EVALUATION

One purpose of writing performance objectives is to have a way of evaluating a lesson. In later chapters you will read about ideas for evaluating individual pupils' performance and progress in science; this section suggests a way of thinking about evaluation that will be useful as you plan for instruction in any subject.

The idea of evaluation makes many beginning teachers uncomfortable, perhaps because of personal experience with test anxiety. This raises the question of just what the word *evaluation* suggests to these teachers, as well as what evaluation actually is. There are many misconceptions on this subject; perhaps by examining them, you can reduce your anxiety and let in a bit of light:

Misconception 1: Evaluation means formal paper-and-pencil tests.

Misconception 2: The purpose of evaluation is to determine grades.

Misconception 3: Evaluation lets the teacher find out who cannot or will not do the work.

Misconception 4: Evaluation is done during time that is set aside for that purpose only.

Misconception 5: Evaluation is something the teacher does to the pupil.

In most misconceptions there is an element of truth, but the problem is that they are simplistic, that is, overly simplified. To paraphrase Einstein, these ideas are simpler than possible.

Purposes of evaluation vary. The determination of grades for report cards is only one purpose—one that has very little usefulness to the teacher. Grades serve the purposes of principals and parents much more than those of teachers. In contrast, evaluation of instruction and of pupil progress are of great use to teachers. Although these two purposes can be discussed separately, they are highly interlinked. The teacher asks, "How are they doing?" and then, based on the answer, makes instructional decisions. If most or all of the pupils did poorly, the lesson or activity obviously needs to be modified and retaught. If only a few pupils had trouble, individualized remedies for the few are called for. Although the lesson probably will not be retaught, modifications may be made to improve the lesson for use with the next class.

In your reading, you may have encountered the terms *formative* and *summative* in relation to evaluation. Summative evaluation is simply a summing up of information for the purpose of grading. Formative evaluation, on the other hand, involves helping to form the instruction and the pupil's progress. Formative evaluation is the kind done to see if a lesson is working, or whether a pupil is having trouble. Instructional decisions such as lesson revision, setting up extra practice centers, or providing feedback to pupils are based on formative evaluation. Notice that formative evaluation is dynamic and ongoing, whereas summative evaluation is static and suggests an end point.

Ways of evaluating include paper-and-pencil tests but also a host of other methods. Paper-and-pencil tests provide a way of getting information about many pupils in a short time. But the usefulness of the information to the teacher is not usually as great as that derived from more informal means, such as pupil products and informal or structured observation during work.

With these thoughts in mind, take another look at the misconceptions.

Misconception 1: Evaluation means formal paper-and-pencil tests. There are many ways to evaluate pupil performance. Paper-and-pencil tests are sometimes important for administrative reasons, but other means are usually more useful to teachers.

Misconception 2: The purpose of evaluation is to determine grades. Grading is mostly an administrative function. Evaluation also serves important instructional purposes, as explained above.

Misconception 3: Evaluation lets the teacher find out who cannot or will not do the work. Other aspects of pupil evaluation assess progress in affective and social areas. Attitudes are important to investigate. Also, how is the pupil progressing in learning to be responsible? How to do these important assessments will be covered in later chapters. In addition to assessment of pupil progress in all areas, evaluation should also provide information on whether the lesson is adequate or needs revising.

Misconception 4: Evaluation is done during time that is set aside for that purpose only. While this may be true in formal tests, most of the time instruction and evaluation are going on at the same time. Not only do pupils learn from evaluation, but also teachers who have learned to value a diagnostic philosophy of instruction are observing and asking questions during a lesson to better understand the nature of any difficulty pupils may be experiencing. The diagnostic teacher watches for the effect of information on the pupils' behavior, and is alert to possible misunderstandings. Another excellent time to evaluate by informal observation is when pupils are working with concrete materials, because this is when they are "thinking with their hands" in an openly visible way. The teacher who does not do several things at the same time is a limited and probably ineffective teacher. Paper-and-pencil tests are the most noticeable evaluations to pupils. Other types of assessment are done all the time, but are invisible to those being assessed.

Misconception 5: Evaluation is something the teacher does to the pupil. There is more to it than this. The teacher is also evaluating the lesson, the unit, the learning center, or any other part of the instruction. This is the beginning of self-evaluation as a teacher. In addition, older children can be taught to begin evaluating themselves. A part of learning to take responsibility for one's behavior is learning to take responsibility for one's own learning.

CLASSROOM ENVIRONMENT

Physical factors in the classroom can play an important part in the emotional atmosphere and the efficiency of instruction, both of which relate directly to ease of management and orderliness. Certainly everyone would agree that a classroom should be a busy and happy place, perhaps even a neat and clean place. But there is still a great deal of variation in the way classrooms look.

Consider two classrooms, Room A and Room B. Room A has colorful bulletin boards, busy learning centers, a reading corner with soft seating, and neat storage of many kinds of materials. The double desks are arranged in pairs so that four pupils form a natural work group facing each other. The teacher's desk stands in the back of the room, and a carpet covers the floor near the front chalkboard for group lessons. Fish, animals in cages, and plants occupy various corners and nooks. Room B has individual desks in straight rows with all pupils facing forward toward the teacher's desk at the front. There are centers and bulletin boards, but all of the children are at their desks.

In which classroom would you rather be a pupil? In which would you rather be a teacher? What do the differences say about the teachers' philosophies? Are there some reasons for selecting more features from Room A and other situations when it would be better to have a room more like B? Deciding how to arrange and provide for a classroom environment that enhances instructional goals is more complex than the either/or choice described here, but several important aspects are touched on. These are some of the matters that will be discussed in specific instructional contexts.

DEALING WITH COMPLEXITY: AN ANALOGY

A beginning student teacher asked her university supervisor how to handle a particular situation. The supervisor replied that it depended on many factors and began to explain some of the various options. The student teacher, however, grew restless and finally interrupted, "Don't confuse me with all that! Just give me the one-two-three's." Certainly, the supervisor should have found a way to respond that would have been more directly relevant to the student teacher's needs. Nevertheless, there are very few "one-two-three's" in learning to teach. Every successful teacher makes literally thousands of decisions every day. You may well respond, "That sounds awful! How does anyone survive in that sort of pressure cooker?" Well, consider an analogy. Almost every adult in the United States drives a car. Driving is a complex and demanding skill. The penalty for too many mistakes can be death or a whole host of lesser evils. Yet, we are usually able to function as drivers without being paralyzed by fear and indecision. Try to think back to when you learned to drive. It did not all happen at once. First you learned and practiced the mechanical aspects of operating the controls of the car. Later you learned the rules of the road and practiced driving in street traffic. Only after you had developed these skills did you dare to enter the freeway and tackle tricky interchanges at rush hour. What was happening to the early skills as you progressed to the more advanced ones? Are you consciously thinking about how to steer, accelerate, and brake (and maybe even shift) while you maneuver through a freeway interchange? Probably not; probably you are able to manage these early skills in an almost automatic way, a sort of mental cruise control. A similar process allows you to move through all kinds of skill hierarchies. There is one difference, however: it is human nature to quickly forget what it was like not to know something just as soon as you learn it. You will be much more effective as a teacher if you can retain the memory of that pre-knowledge state, because retaining that memory makes you able to relate to the learning process in your own pupils.

Learning to be an effective teacher is complex but not too complex to learn. You just need to think about what you are doing and not let the mental cruise control become too automatic. Just as many driving decisions are made as you drive along, many teaching decisions cannot be made in advance but depend on unforeseeable circumstances. On the highway your decisions depend on what is happening all around you; on a busy highway you have to be alert at every moment. In the classroom your decisions will also depend on what is happening around you, and you also have to be alert at every moment. These "in-progress" decisions teachers must make include how to involve all the pupils, whether to interrupt the lesson to correct misbehavior, whether to use variations in language or to stress repeatedly the same words, whether to accept an incomplete pupil response or to take time to probe for more depth, whether to make a major excursion from the planned lesson in response to unexpected pupil reactions, and many, many more. As you see, most of these decisions involve knowing and reflecting on what you are doing, being aware of what is happening around you, and modifying your own thinking and actions accordingly.

▼ SUMMARY

The most common concern of beginning teachers is whether they will be able to establish and maintain a classroom in which children work productively and peacefully without rude or disruptive behavior. This is recognized as a legitimate concern because of the importance of providing an environment that is conducive to learning.

Certain teacher behaviors and attitudes have been found to be effective deterrents to inappropriate pupil behavior. Suggestions were made for handling minor problems and serious disruptive behavior, and a list of classroom management systems based on behaviorist principles was provided.

The level of pupil involvement is an important factor in pupils' classroom behavior; using activities that have a high level of involvement is the preferred way to promote learning and prevent undesirable behavior. A teacher's careful use of verbal techniques is also an important factor in obtaining pupil participation and involvement.

Planning that includes determining performance objectives and a means of evaluating the lesson will assist the teacher in keeping the goals of instruction in mind and in deciding whether a lesson is leading to pupil progress. Evaluation can be a tool that the teacher uses to determine whether her or his own objectives for the lesson have been met and how to modify instruction to enhance pupil progress.

▾ DISCUSSION QUESTIONS

1. What are your greatest concerns as a prospective or beginning teacher?
2. The research suggests that many teachers who know how to respond to pupil misbehavior in a satisfactory way are still poor managers. Explain.
3. If you have visited different elementary classrooms, you probably noticed a wide variety in the amount of pupil movement, the accepted noise level, and the general impression of order (or disorder). What are some factors that are involved? What do you think would work best for you? Why?
4. If you were planning to introduce science activities with concrete materials for the first time to your class, what are some considerations to keep in mind?
5. What are some ways you might introduce behavior standards with a new class?
6. What are the differences among penalties, negative consequences, and punishment? If any of these are required, which are most effective for controlling behavior? For teaching responsibility?
7. Can a warning be a consequence? Should there always be a certain number of warnings before penalties are applied? Is it kinder sometimes to overlook or forgive an infraction?
8. What can a teacher do to increase involvement? Make a list and compare with those of your classmates.
9. Are some kinds of learning unnatural? Give examples.
10. Which requires more planning, giving content information or giving procedural directions? Explain. What kinds of problems could arise with each, and how could you avoid them?

▾ ACTIVITIES FOR THE READER

1. For each of the following lesson ideas, write one or more lesson goal statements and some performance objectives to use with the goals.
   a. Collect and bring to class different insects. Compare and find out similarities and differences.
   b. Make a map of the classroom to the scale of 1m = 1cm.
   c. Collect, compare, and classify forms and patterns of leaves.

2. For each of the following faulty objectives, identify the problems and make a stab at fixing them:
   a. The pupil will learn the names of the major parts of a plant.
   b. The teacher will describe the major body parts of a mealworm.
   c. The student will pay attention while the teacher demonstrates how to use the microscope.
   d. The student will check the correct answers on the worksheet.
   e. The class will recall the types of conditions they have seen seeds grow in.
   f. The learner will help decide what things to look for when evaluating the experiment.
   g. Make comparisons regarding the contents of several jars.
   h. Write rules or formulas to help them with problem solving.
3. Choose one of the lesson activities from Activity 1 and write the directions you would give to pupils for doing it. As a group, critique your directions, using the suggestions in this chapter as criteria.

▼ REFERENCES

Anderson, L., Evertson, C., & Emmer, E. (1980). Dimensions in classroom management derived from recent research. *Journal of Curriculum Studies, 12,* 343–356.

Bandura, A. (1969). *Principles of behavior modification.* New York: Holt, Rinehart and Winston.

Brophy, J., & Good, T. (1986). Teacher behavior and student achievement. In M. Wittrock (Ed.), *Handbook of research on teaching* (3rd ed.). New York: Macmillan.

Canter, L., & Canter, M. (1976). *Assertiveness discipline: A take charge approach for today's educator.* Seal Beach, CA: Canter.

Doyle, W. (1986). Classroom organization and management. In M. Wittrock (Ed.), *Handbook of research on teaching* (3rd ed.). New York: Macmillan.

Dreikurs, R., & Cassel, P. (1972). *Discipline without tears.* New York: Hawthorn Books.

Duke, D., & Meckel, A. (1984). *Teacher's guide to classroom management.* New York: Random House.

Emmer, E., Evertson, C., & Anderson, L. (1980). Effective classroom management at the beginning of the school year. *Elementary School Journal, 80,* 219–231.

Fuller, F. (1969). Concerns of teachers: A developmental conceptualization. *American Educational Research Journal, 6,* 207–226.

Glasser, W. (1969). *Schools without failure.* New York: Harper & Row.

Glasser, W. (1986). *Control theory in the classroom.* New York: Harper & Row.

Good, T., & Brophy, J. (1987). *Looking in Classrooms* (4th ed.). New York: Harper & Row.

Gordon, T. (1974). *T. E. T.: Teacher effectiveness training.* New York: David McKay.

Kounin, J. (1970). *Discipline and group management in classrooms.* New York: Holt, Rinehart and Winston.

Rowe, M. (1978). *Teaching Science as Continuous Inquiry: A Basic* (2nd ed.). New York: McGraw-Hill.

4

EXPECTATIONS AND GOALS

▼ Ms. Sanchez, a beginning teacher, talks over a problem with her mentor, Ms. Oldhand.

Ms. Sanchez: Ms. Oldhand, I need some help with one of the low-achieving pupils in my class. Stephen's record shows that he has always been near the bottom of the class, beginning in first grade. He's a nice kid and has never been a behavior problem. But lately he doesn't even seem to be trying, and he is beginning to be a little bit of a show-off. I'm afraid that he'll start being a behavior problem as well as a low achiever unless I can do something to change his attitude.

Ms. Oldhand: Well, you have a good start on the problem because you assume that you can do something to turn the situation around. Would you like for me to sit in your class and see whether I can come up with some things for you to try?

Ms. Sanchez: Yes, I think that's a very good idea.

The next day Ms. Oldhand observed the class.

Ms. Sanchez: I'm glad you could observe my class this morning. You could see for yourself that Stephen is not interested in what's going on in class and that he tries to call attention to himself.

Ms. Oldhand: Yes, I did see that, and I agree with you that something needs to be done to help Stephen. There were several things that I noticed that I wonder whether you are aware of. I noticed that when you asked Stephen a question—which was a very easy one—you only gave him a second to answer. And when he hesitated, you turned to another pupil and asked her to give the answer. Why didn't you give Stephen more time?

Ms. Sanchez: It seemed pretty clear that he didn't know the answer, and I didn't want to embarrass him.

Ms. Oldhand: But when you asked a question of Mary—who I know is a very bright girl—and she hesitated, you gave her a clue and waited long enough for her to think of a reply. Why did you give her more time than you gave Stephen?

Ms. Sanchez: I gave her more time because I knew that she could come up with an answer if she just thought about it.

Ms. Oldhand: In other words, you *expected* Mary to be able to answer the question you asked her, but you *didn't expect* Stephen to be able to answer the question you asked him. Stephen may be a low achiever, but he's smart enough to figure out that your expectations for him are very low.

Ms. Sanchez: Are you suggesting that Stephen could do as well as Mary if I changed my expectations?

Ms. Oldhand:	No, I'm not suggesting that. Expectations aren't magic. I am saying that I believe Stephen knows that you don't expect him to be able to master the work in this class, and that makes him think, "What's the use? Even the teacher doesn't think I can do this work." If he thought you *believed* he could do the work and *expected* him to do the work, he might try harder to live up to your expectations. That way he could get positive feedback and wouldn't have to try to get attention by showing off.
Ms. Sanchez:	It's hard for me to believe that my expectations influence the way I interact with Stephen, but I think I'll tape record the next question-and-answer session and listen to the tape to see whether you're right about this.

TEACHER EXPECTATIONS

Have you ever felt that you had to do something in order to live up to someone's expectations for you? All of us have expectations about what will happen in certain circumstances, and we often have expectations for ourselves and for other people. This section presents some important ideas about teachers' expectations for themselves and their pupils as well as some possible outcomes of these expectations.

To serve as a focus for discussion, take a moment to write your reaction to the following statements. For each statement, choose from these possible reactions: Strongly Agree, Agree Somewhat, Disagree Somewhat, or Strongly Disagree.

1. It is unreasonable to expect all pupils to pass.
2. Schoolwork is necessary but usually boring.
3. In today's hectic classroom, dealing with pupils as individuals is not feasible.
4. Some children just do not want to learn.
5. Some children will disregard the rules no matter what the teacher does.
6. A teacher who does everything "by the book" can expect smooth sailing.

A book describing research on teacher expectations, *Pygmalion in the Classroom* (Rosenthal & Jacobson, 1968), became famous after it was published in 1968. The authors reported the results of a research project in which researchers told a group of teachers that certain children in their classes were "late bloomers" and would make a spurt in achievement during the year. Actually, the children had been chosen at random, and the researchers had no objective reason to believe that they were different from any of the other children in the classes. But the teachers believed that those children were different and thus raised their expectations for the children. As a result (according to the authors), the designated children actually did achieve at a higher level than they had before. A valid conclusion seemed to be that when the teachers expected them to do better, the children did do better. This book became controversial when the findings could not be duplicated by some other researchers. But the book was important, nevertheless, because it focused attention on the need for teachers to have high expectations for all of their pupils.

Research carried out since publication of that book has shown that a teacher's expectations for a pupil affect the teacher's behavior toward that pupil, and the teacher behavior has an effect on pupil achievement. Figure 4.1 shows how the process might work.

Suppose a certain science teacher does not expect girls to be as interested in science as boys are and, therefore, does not expect girls to do as well in science. How might this expectation unconsciously affect the teacher's behavior? One thing a teacher might do would be to give different assignments to boys and girls when groups are formed. Girls might be assigned—or "allowed"—to be recorders while the boys do the experiments. This would give boys an active role and girls a passive role. Since children learn by doing, not by watching, the result likely would be that the girls would not learn as much as the boys, and the teacher's expectations would be confirmed. This is what is called a self-fulfilling prophecy—the teacher's behavior brought about what he or she expected to happen.

Suppose the teacher, taking a different tack, had thought, "Why shouldn't girls do as well as boys in science? I'm going to be careful to see that girls and boys have the same opportunities to learn in this class, and I'll expect all of them to do well." The teacher would organize the class so that all pupils had an opportunity to do some of the experiments and all took a turn being recorder.

It may seem natural for teachers to have lower expectations for low-achieving pupils than for high-achieving pupils, but this attitude can be discouraging and even damaging to the low achievers, who know they are being treated differently in class. Differential treatment can further lower those students' achievement (Brophy & Good, 1970). The ways that teachers have been found to treat high and low achievers differently include:

- Calling on low achievers to answer questions in class less frequently (Adams & Cohen, 1974; Rubovits and Maehr, 1971).
- Waiting less time for low achievers to answer questions asked by the teacher. Since the teacher does not expect the pupil to know the answer, the teacher moves on quickly to someone else (Brophy & Good, 1970; Rowe, 1974a, 1974b).

▼ FIGURE 4.1
Pupil achievement affected by teacher expectations

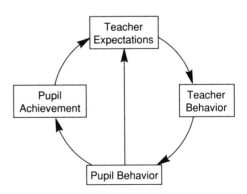

- Dismissing low achievers' ideas. The teacher does not expect the low achievers to have good or useful ideas, though creativity and school achievement are not necessarily related (Martinek & Johnson, 1979; Martinek & Karper, 1982).
- Giving briefer answers to questions of low achievers. Since the teacher does not expect the low achiever to understand anyway, less time is spent explaining (Cooper, 1979).

In all these cases the teacher's behavior communicates to the low-achieving pupil that the teacher does not expect him or her to know the answer or to have good ideas or to be able to understand the learning task. These cause the pupil to become discouraged and lose interest, and the teacher expectation becomes a self-fulfilling prophecy.

Some have suggested that teachers should neither look at pupils' previous records nor talk to other teachers about individual pupils in order to prevent forming negative expectations. Such denial seems unreasonable. What a teacher does with the information is the important thing. Information from the past can be useful in helping a teacher diagnose a pupil's problems and plan instruction that will meet the pupil's needs. Teachers should trust their own judgment and good intentions. The way to avoid harmful expectations is not to restrict information but to become more aware of negative, unconscious assumptions and expectations. All teachers have unconscious assumptions and expectations that are often based on false premises.

Consider the responses you made to the series of statements near the beginning of the chapter. Those statements were designed to help you increase your awareness of any unconscious assumptions that might influence your teaching behaviors. If you are a sophisticated professional well acquainted with the research and harboring no unexamined assumptions, you would have disagreed strongly with all the items. If you are just beginning in the profession, however, you may have had different reactions. The main idea here is simply to create a focus for discussion, so consider now what the best research-based thoughts on these topics are.

1. It is unreasonable to expect all pupils to pass. [*strongly disagree*]

Teachers should expect all pupils to meet at least the minimum specified objectives. Although all pupils cannot reasonably be expected to do equally well, a teacher can establish reasonable minimal objectives for each class. Most pupils will be able to exceed the minimal objectives, and the teacher should try to stimulate this development as far as possible.

2. Schoolwork is necessary but usually boring. [*strongly disagree*]

Teachers should expect children to enjoy learning. When teachers have a positive attitude toward schoolwork, they present the material in ways that make their pupils see it as enjoyable and interesting. Tasks and assignments, including practice exercises, are presented without apology, as activities valuable in their own right. The teacher with a negative attitude about learning behaves differently. A teacher might see learning as necessary but unpleasant. This teacher may be apologetic and defensive about assignments and will often resort to bribery, trying to generate enthusiasm artificially through overemphasis on contests, rewards, and other external incentives.

Or a teacher might be an authoritarian, presenting learning as a bitter pill to be swallowed—or else. In either case, the pupils will quickly acquire a distaste for school activities, thus reinforcing the teacher's expectations.

3. In today's hectic classroom, dealing with pupils as individuals is not feasible. [*strongly disagree*]

As a rule, teachers should think, talk, and act in terms of individual pupils. This does not mean that teachers should not practice grouping or that terms such as "low achievers" should not be used. Teachers do sometimes lose sight of the individual Juan Martinez or Jennifer Jones among the "bluebirds" or the "dinosaurs," however. There are certain teacher behaviors to watch for as warnings that a stereotype has begun to structure the teacher's perception of a pupil. Among these behaviors are continual references in speech to group names to the exclusion of individual names, and an overemphasis on differences between groups. These warning signs are especially important when the groups in question are the more permanent ones of economic status, ethnicity, or gender.

4. Some children just do not want to learn. [*strongly disagree*]

The teacher should assume that each child wants to learn, is able to learn, and is hoping to learn. The teacher's job is to create the situation in which each child can make progress. A teacher who does not realize this may act as if the pupils are expected to learn on their own with no help from the teacher. If a pupil does not catch on immediately after one demonstration—or does not do his work correctly after hearing the instructions one time—the teacher reacts with impatience and frustration. The real art of teaching is not just in giving information, but in listening to pupil responses and in observing pupil behaviors as sources of information, and then using the information to design further learning experiences.

5. Some children will disregard the rules no matter what the teacher does. [*strongly disagree*]

The teacher should expect all pupils to follow the rules. Some teachers have a hand in creating serious discipline problems. Usually the cause is failure to establish and enforce appropriate rules of behavior. Adherence to rules is usually obtained rather easily by teachers who establish fair and appropriate rules, who are consistent in what they say, who say only what they really mean, and who regularly follow up with appropriate action whenever necessary. Appropriate action produces credibility and respect; the pupils are clear about what the teacher expects of them and know that they are accountable for meeting these expectations.

6. A teacher who does everything "by the book" can expect smooth sailing. [*strongly disagree*]

Although positive expectations may go a long way toward solving and preventing problems, they will not prevent or solve all problems. Expectations are not automatically self-fulfilling, though positive expectations are necessary and important. To the extent that positive expectations initiate behavior that does lead to positive effects, they help prevent and solve problems. The benefits of positive expectations simply would not be gained if these expectations were not there in the first place. All teachers, however, have some difficulties from time to time; to expect perfection of yourself as a teacher or of your pupils at all times is unrealistic.

GOALS OF ELEMENTARY SCIENCE

Teacher expectations are directly related to accomplishing the goals of science education, not only the goal of scientific literacy for all students but various other goals as well. The teacher's expectation must be that all pupils will be able to make progress toward reaching the goals. The goals for science in the elementary school were stated in broad terms in Chapter 1. The teacher's job is to translate those general goals into day-to-day classroom activities that will eventually lead to their accomplishment. This section is about the kinds of goals that will guide your thinking as you plan for instruction day to day.

A goal is simply a destination or desired end for some endeavor. There are goals of education, goals of elementary science education, and goals of a science unit or lesson. The first decision you will make in planning lessons is to decide what the goals of the lesson are. The purpose of setting goals is to guide planning and implementation of a project so that the project does not go off in all directions or mistakenly change course along the way. The main way that *goals* will be used in this book is as a general statement of purpose. In a dictionary, you will find that the word *objective* has about the same meaning as *goal*. In this book, *objective* denotes a specific goal—namely, a performance objective as described in Chapter 3—and its use is confined to individual lessons.

TYPES OF GOALS

A general approach to articulating the goals of education (including, but not limited to, science education) was developed by Benjamin Bloom, who is widely regarded for his leadership in classifying educational goals into *domains* and (along with others) for developing taxonomies of the domains (Bloom, 1956; Krathwohl, Bloom, and Masia, 1964; Harrow, 1972). Bloom's three domains are:

1. *Cognitive domain* (knowledge of facts, concepts, and intellectual skills)
2. *Affective domain* (feelings, attitudes, and values)
3. *Psychomotor domain* (motor skills, such as small and large muscle control)

For the purpose of planning instruction in elementary science, an expansion of the list seems appropriate. The cognitive domain is divided into two subcategories, and a new domain, the social domain, is added:

1. Cognitive domain
   a. Content knowledge (facts, concepts, and higher-level ideas)
   b. Science process skills (inquiry skills such as observing, inferring, classifying, and measuring)
2. Affective domain (feelings, attitudes, and values)

3. Psychomotor domain (motor skills, such as small and large muscle control)
4. Social domain (skills of getting along with others)

Each of these domains contains a hierarchy of educational goals. The lowest level is memorization of facts and words—that is, objectives that do not require thinking, only memorization. At the next levels, children apply the knowledge they have gained to the task of solving problems. High-level goals include analyzing situations, synthesizing information, and applying critical thinking and evaluation skills to real-world problems.

It is interesting to compare these goals of education with the Piaget-derived kinds of knowledge (described in Chapter 1), since goals of education are tied to desired knowledge. Social-arbitrary knowledge and logical knowledge would fall into the cognitive domain, physical knowledge would probably fall into the cognitive and psychomotor domains, and social-interactive knowledge would fall into the social domain. This comparison is made as a reminder that there are many ways to classify anything of interest.

Consider how the goals from Bloom's taxonomy might be translated into goals for elementary science teaching. Some examples of goals from an intermediate grade unit on electricity are given below. Although you may not be familiar with the actual content of such a unit, reading over the goals should give you an idea of what type of activities are used, some of the methods used, and possibly the values of the teacher who planned the unit. First are goals from the cognitive domain:

Cognitive Content Goals
- Know the elements of a simple circuit and their arrangement.
- Diagram actual circuits using standard electrical symbols and construct actual circuits from provided diagrams.
- Know the effects of adding resistance to a circuit.

Cognitive Process Goals
- Predict and verify arrangements of elements that will cause a bulb to light.
- Test a prediction about whether a bulb will light.
- Infer pathways inside a mystery circuit board based on an observed result.
- Measure the brightness of a bulb with a simple meter.

In Chapter 2, you read about research that has clarified the difference between declarative and procedural knowledge: declarative knowledge refers to what a person knows about a subject, while procedural knowledge refers to the procedures used to solve problems or complete tasks. In the examples from the cognitive domain, the cognitive content goals can be considered as declarative-knowledge goals and the cognitive process goals as procedural-knowledge goals. The difference is sometimes explained as the difference between "knowing that" and "knowing how". In most of your science lessons you should try to have both kinds of goals. Notice that the statement of goals does not tell you what the children will do to learn about circuits. That will be up to you as you plan your lesson.

Goals from the affective domain are not accomplished in isolation but simultaneously with the other goals of instruction. Part of your responsibility as a teacher will be to model the behaviors exemplifying affective goals, and to reinforce them as you observe evidence of their use among your pupils. Goals from the affective domain are:

- Show curiosity and persistence in working with materials and related problems.
- Behave responsibly toward use and care of materials.

Since "hands-on" activities are the heart of a good elementary science program, children need to learn to use equipment and apparatus with care and skill. This will be easier for some children than others, but the same can be said for cognitive tasks. As a teacher, you can have the expectation that all children—except, possibly, the physically handicapped—will acquire increasing skill in the psychomotor domain while they are also achieving the cognitive goals of a lesson. Here is a goal from the psychomotor domain:

- Handle circuit elements and connectors with increasing skill.

It is essential to promote social goals when children are actively pursuing cognitive and psychomotor goals through active work, often in groups. If children are to learn from each other they must be able to work together in harmony (at least, most of the time). A goal from the social domain is:

- Show cooperation and courtesy in group work.

MATCHING INSTRUCTION TO GOALS

Once you have decided on the goals of the lesson, you will think about the best way to reach the goals considering your situation and the children you are teaching. If the principles of constructivism are used as a guide, you will plan the lesson or unit with as many opportunities as possible for the children to be engaged in activities that will stimulate their thinking and lead them to construct new knowledge for themselves. By the end of the lesson they should understand something in a different way or know something that they did not know before.

AUTONOMY LEVELS

The preface of this book introduced the idea that a goal of science teaching is to develop autonomous learners and thinkers. The word *autonomous* means "self governing." To be autonomous means to be responsible for one's own actions, to think independently and arrive at one's own conclusions. Autonomy is related to science and science teaching because science demands that everyone thinks for him- or herself. Science includes facts and theories, but its real essence is the ability to consider evidence and draw a conclusion, and that ability requires independent, or autonomous, thinking. Teachers will shortchange children unless those children are guided toward learning to think for themselves. Teachers want children to know that they can think for themselves and that their own thoughts are worthwhile and valuable.

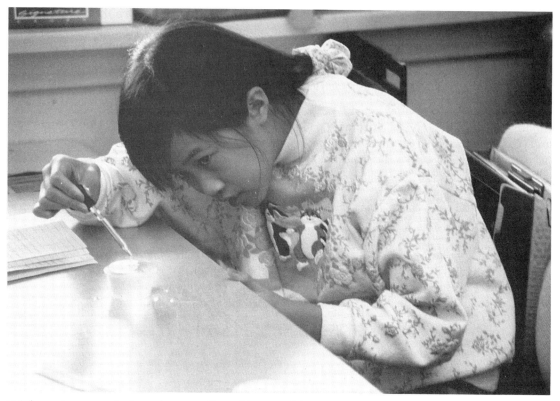

▼ The real essence of science is to consider evidence and draw one's own conclusions.

This book takes the point of view that teachers can promote autonomous thought and action by the way they teach and interact with their pupils. Table 4.1 classifies three well-known teaching methods according to goals of instruction and the level of pupil autonomy. The chapters that follow describe how you can teach science at the three autonomy levels represented by Direct Instruction (Level 1), Guided Discovery (Level 2), and Group Investigations and Independent Projects (Level 3). These ideas will become clearer as you study the table.

AUTONOMY LEVEL I

When the goals of a lesson are to learn a series of procedures or to memorize information to be recalled later, then Direct Instruction, at Autonomy Level I, may be a suitable method. Autonomy Level I, the lowest level in the classification, is essentially teacher-centered in that the teacher has responsibility for all the instructional decisions. The teacher controls the source and flow of information as well as pupil movement and behavior. The pupils have little or no voice in determining the content, methods, procedures, or pacing of the lesson. Most

▼ TABLE 4.1
Autonomy Levels

	LEVEL I	LEVEL II	LEVEL III
Goals for Pupils	Learn and practice procedures Receive and remember information Learn behavior standards	Make procedures automatic Learn from direct experience Internalize behavior standards	Devise procedures Design, carry out learning experiences Plan and work cooperatively in group
Type of Instruction	Direct Instruction	Guided Discovery	Group Investigation Independent Projects
Role of Teacher	Provide information, guide practice Determine pacing and timing Set & enforce behavior standards	Provide and guide learning experiences Ask questions, keep on task Allow for more student responsibility	Motivate pupils Monitor progress Assist with practical problems Monitor cooperative group behavior
Role of Pupil	Follow directions Answer teacher's questions Maintain expected behavior	Participate in learning activities Ask questions, listen to others Take responsibility for own behavior	Plan and participate in learning activities Devise questions to answer by investigation Take responsibility for group behavior Carry through

beginning teachers find learning to teach at Autonomy Level I easier than learning to teach at the higher levels, because there are fewer variables to keep in mind and fewer decisions to make once the lesson is in progress. Level I lends itself more consistently to an algorithmic formulation or a concisely prescriptive model and is therefore both easier to plan and critique and easier to present. Because pupils have fewer choices, they are less likely to get lost on sequence or procedure. This translates to fewer behavior problems for the beginning teacher to manage. These advantages make Autonomy Level I a natural place for beginning teachers to start in the development of their teaching repertoire. There are, however, a number of limitations to teaching at this level, one of which is that such teaching does not promote the goal of increasing independence as much as teaching at the higher levels.

In Chapter 5 you will see an example of a Direct Instruction lesson designed to teach pupils how to use a piece of apparatus. This method of instruction may be appropriate for a short lesson at the beginning of a unit, such as a lesson on identifying rocks and minerals or on learning to use instruments that will be needed later. Some units cannot be started until pupils have mastered certain essential procedures or learned some essential information. At this level of autonomy the role of the teacher and the role of the pupils are well-defined and should be made clear at the beginning of the lesson. The teacher sets the pace and the pupils follow the teacher's directions.

AUTONOMY LEVEL II

Guided discovery is a general term for teaching methods that introduce more flexibility into the lessons, and these methods have been classified as Autonomy Level II. When the goals of the lesson are for the pupils to use the procedures in further learning, to learn from their own actions and experience, and to learn to work with others, Guided Discovery is an appropriate means to accomplish the goals. Now the pupils are given more responsibility and independence; they work in groups, talk to each other, ask questions, and decide how to divide up the work, how to tackle the problems they are given, and—to some extent—how to pace their own work. Their freedom is limited, of course, but the teacher acts as a guide rather than as a taskmaster.

As you gain experience and confidence from success with teaching at Level I you will be able to consider the more complex aspects of decision making required by a higher level. To the inexperienced observer, Level II lessons look deceptively easy. The pupils seem interested and businesslike; the teacher seems to take a back seat in running the lesson. But that inexperienced observer is like someone who has entered a theater in the middle of a movie. The beginning of the movie would show how the teacher developed this amazing increase in responsibility by means of deliberate instruction done in carefully thought-out stages. Children can learn to behave responsibly, to manage materials effectively, and to become independent learners—if they are taught those skills.

AUTONOMY LEVEL III

A third level of pupil responsibility and independence comprises teaching based on individual and group projects, in which pupils have more choice in the content and method of learning than at Level II. The exact division between any two levels is arbitrary, but it is possible to illustrate each of the levels with descriptions of appropriate activities. How to prepare children to handle this additional freedom, as well as some specifics of project management, are the subjects of Chapter 10.

Autonomy Level III is the realization of the constructivist perspective in science teaching. At this level children are well on the way to becoming autonomous learners who have confidence in their own ability to solve problems and to construct meaning for themselves. This level of autonomy is the goal toward which you will have been aiming as you worked patiently to help your pupils develop the attitudes, habits, and skills that are needed to learn independently, to be curious and creative, and to have confidence and initiative (Kamii & Joseph, 1988). Instruction at this level does not exclude other kinds of instruction; it includes them, but it also goes beyond them. Children will still be naming and classifying, recording observations, measuring, and estimating, but now these processes and procedures will be used in the context of a larger goal. The processes that were once themselves the goals of instruction have become the tools for reaching other, more inclusive goals.

COMPARING AND CONTRASTING LEVELS

As you examine Table 4.1 and move across from Level I to Level II, notice how the role of the teacher changes from the role of one who provides information and guides practice to one who motivates, stimulates, and encourages pupils to do their own thinking and acting. The teacher's role also changes from setting and enforcing standards of behavior for individual pupils to assisting pupils in monitoring their own behavior and to setting standards for group behavior.

Notice, also, how the role of the individual pupil changes from answering the teacher's questions to asking questions and listening to other pupils' questions, and finally to thinking of questions to be answered through an investigation. The pupil's responsibility for her or his own behavior increases from simply doing what is expected and defined by the teacher to taking responsibility for that behavior and, finally, to taking some responsibility for the group's behavior by reminding classmates when they are getting too noisy or disturbing others.

There are important similarities among the teaching methods at the various autonomy levels, as well as points of contrast. First, concrete experience is always important. Real materials and firsthand experiences, as opposed to vicarious experience, should form the basis of every possible initial learning. Second, various extended practice activities are appropriate at all levels, among them the learning center. Center activities can be designed to function at different autonomy levels; specific designs will be described in later chapters.

▼ Learning centers can function at different autonomy levels. This mealworm center provides extended experience at the guided-discovery level.

There is another similarity among the three autonomy levels. Each level is useful for certain types of learning or lesson goals. Methods involving Levels II and III require a greater number of judgments and other complex teaching skills—much more than just "turning the children loose with materials" is involved. Until the teacher is confident enough to teach at the higher autonomy levels, direct instruction at Level I may be the best method, but this book is intended to help you develop a repertoire of teaching skills and methods so that you can choose the method that will accomplish the goals of the lesson.

MOVING FROM LEVEL I TO LEVEL III

Notice in Table 4.1 that in each section there is a progression toward self reliance and responsibility for one's own learning. If you follow the goals across from Level I to Level III, you will see that the goal in Level I is to learn and practice procedures, the corresponding goal in Level II is to make the procedures automatic, and the goal in Level III is to devise (or design) one's own procedures.

An example that concerns teaching children to measure area may help you understand how this progression would work in practice. The first goal would be to "learn and practice procedures," at Level I. You could plan a series of lessons in which children first measure area by covering a surface with paper squares. The number of squares could then be counted and area of the surface reported as so many "area units." Later in the series of lessons, pupils could be taught to find the area of irregular tagboard cutouts by tracing them on square-centimeter grid paper and using a system for deciding which squares to count. If you look down Table 4.1 to the Role of Teacher, you will see that the teacher should provide information, guide practice, determine the pacing and timing, and set standards of behavior. These will be Direct Instruction lessons, so the Role of Pupil would be to follow directions, answer questions, and follow the rules set by the teacher. Children would stay in their seats, but they would have lots of materials and time to handle them. The teacher would guide their practice of the measuring skills being taught. Over the following weeks the pupils would have many opportunities to practice measuring area. These lessons would all be directed towards the goal of "learn and practice procedures."

If you look at the middle column of the table, Level II, you will see the goal "make procedures automatic." Now the Role of the Teacher is to guide learning experiences rather than just guiding practice. Now the goal is for the pupils to use the skill to measure a variety of objects and in so doing to make the skill automatic. By practicing the measurement of area in many different contexts, pupils would learn to make judgments more easily about which squares to count. They would also come to understand which type of measuring device to choose for particular situations. For example, tracing a footprint on grid paper is convenient, but to measure area of a long and thin object, placing individual square unit models on the object may work better. Making the skill automatic takes time and practice. (Think back to how complicated it all seemed when you were learning to ride a bike or drive an automobile and you will appreciate this point. What is now automatic once took a great deal of concentration.) As measuring area becomes an automatic procedure, accuracy and estimation become part of the process, so that care in measuring becomes automatic and estimation ensures that a large mistake is noticed immediately. Since measuring is an integral part of many of the experiments and investigations that children will be doing later, this phase of learning is very important.

If you look at the right column of the table, Level III, you will see the goal "devise procedures." When measuring can be accomplished with little thought given to the procedures, pupils can then make decisions about what and how to measure as they plan their projects and experiments. By this time they will have moved up to a higher grade and will be able to assume more responsibility in many ways. That is, they can devise procedures for measuring because they have learned the basic processes and can put their attention on the investigation rather than on the procedures themselves. For example, a group of pupils working together on a project may decide that they need to measure the area covered by the shade of a tree. To do this they will have to devise procedures, since this is a new problem that requires the use of the skills they have learned but is not a problem they have been taught to solve. Now the Role of the Teacher is to motivate, monitor progress and assist where necessary. The pupils are assuming the main responsibility for their own work.

As you study the Autonomy Level table again, follow each section across from Level I to Level III. You will see that each section shows a progression similar to the example of measuring area. Look at Pupil's Role. The first line shows the place of questions in science instruction. At the beginning the pupil answers the teacher's questions; then the pupil is allowed and expected to ask questions and listen to other pupils' questions; finally, the pupil participates in the group as questions are devised to be answered by investigation. Questions and questioning is a powerful means of teaching and learning science at all three levels but the responsibilities of pupils and teacher are different at different levels. If you understand these differences and learn to teach science at all levels, you will have a repertoire for science teaching that will allow you to motivate and engage pupils in discovering the excitement of learning about the natural world.

▼ SUMMARY

High expectations are crucial in creating an atmosphere for learning. It is hard for children who are not expected to do well to have the motivation and incentive to succeed. This concept is particularly important for teachers to remember when they are relating to children who have traditionally been thought to be "different"—children with disabilities, minority children, poor children, or any others who may have been labeled as "problems." Sometimes girls are not expected to do as well as boys in science because science has not been a traditional subject for women. While teachers increase their awareness of the role of expectations in pupil achievement, they also have to be realistic and not expect all children to have the same abilities and interests. The first section of this chapter sought to help you develop the skill of setting reasonable expectations and working with children so that they can learn science.

Expectations have a strong influence on instructional goals. Goals of instruction set by Bloom were described and applied to a science activity. The relation of instructional goals to instructional methods was made explicit in a table of Autonomy Levels, showing a progression of goals, activities, teacher roles, and pupil roles, all tending toward an increase in pupil responsibility and autonomy.

▼ DISCUSSION QUESTIONS

1. How can you expect all the pupils to do passing work when you read in the paper that 10 percent of children in your school district fail?
2. How much about the past records of pupils in a class is useful for the teacher to know at the beginning of the school year?
3. How do teacher expectations interact with affective, psychomotor, and social goals?

4. Do you agree or disagree that pupil autonomy, defined as independence and responsibility, should be a goal of science teaching? Explain your answer.
5. What factors limit the amount of pupil autonomy that may be possible in a classroom?

▼ ACTIVITIES FOR THE READER

1. Write out a plan for actions that Ms. Sanchez can take to deal with the problem outlined in her conversation with Ms. Oldhand.
2. An example of a cognitive content goal was given as follows: Know the elements of a simple circuit and their arrangement. Outline three plans for teaching a lesson to achieve this goal, using three levels of pupil involvement as shown in Chapter 3.
3. Make a list of behaviors you would look for as evidence that (a) psychomotor, (b) affective, and (c) social goals were being reached.
4. Select another example from the elementary science curriculum and write descriptions of how it could be taught at Autonomy Levels I, II, and III.

▼ REFERENCES

Adams, G., & Cohen, A. (1974). Children's physical and interpersonal characteristics that affect student-teacher interactions. *Journal of Experimental Education, 43,* 1–5.

Bloom, B. (Ed.). (1956). *Taxonomy of Educational Objectives: Handbook I, Cognitive Domain.* New York: McKay.

Brophy, J., and Good, T. (1970). Teachers' communication of differential expectations for children's classroom performance: Some behavioral data. *Journal of Educational Psychology, 61,* 365–374.

Cooper, H. (1979). Pygmalion grows up: A model for teacher expectation communication and performance influence. *Review of Educational Research, 49,* 389–410.

Harrow, A. (1972). *A Taxonomy of Educational Objectives: Handbook III, Psychomotor Domain.* New York: McKay.

Kamii, C., & Joseph, L. (1988) *Young children continue to reinvent arithmetic: 2nd Grade.* New York: Teachers College Press.

Krathwohl, D., Bloom, B., & Masia, B. (1964). *Taxonomy of Educational Objectives: Handbook II, Affective Domain.* New York: McKay.

Martinek, T., & Johnson, S. (1979). Teacher expectations. Effects on dyadic interaction and self-concept in elementary-age children. *Research Quarterly, 50,* 60–70.

Martinek, T., & Karper, W. (1982). Canonical relationships among motor ability, expression of effort, teacher expectations, and dyadic interactions in elementary-age children. *Journal of Teaching and Physical Education, 1,* 26–39.

Rosenthal, R., & Jacobson, L. (1968). *Pygmalion in the classroom: Teacher expectation and pupils' intellectual development.* New York: Holt, Rinehart & Winston.

Rowe, M. (1974a). Pausing phenomena: Influence on quality of instruction. *Journal of Psycholinguistic Research, 3*, 203–224.

Rowe, M. (1974b). Wait-time and rewards as instructional variables, their influence on language, logic, and fate control: Part I, Wait-time. *Journal of Research in Science Teaching, 11*, 81–94.

Rubovits, P., & Maehr, M. (1971). Pygmalion analyzed: Toward an explanation of the Rosenthal-Jacobson findings. *Journal of Personality and Social Psychology, 19*, 197–203.

CHAPTER $\blacktriangledown$ 5

DIRECT
INSTRUCTION

CHAPTER OUTLINE

▼
_____

This chapter describes a method of planning and presenting lessons called *direct instruction*, also known as direct teaching and teacher-centered instruction. A direct-instruction lesson comprises specific types of activity that are carried out in a specific sequence. Using this structure ensures inclusion of many important elements of lesson presentation. Because decisions about structure are made during the planning stage, the number of instructional decisions the teacher must make during the progress of the lesson is greatly reduced. Direct instruction works well for many lesson topics and is much favored by administrators for two reasons: it is relatively easy to learn, and it can be used effectively by beginning teachers.

Direct instruction is the use of the traditional methods of lecture, demonstration, seat work, recitation, and feedback. The method is sometimes referred to as teacher-centered instruction because virtually all the instructional decisions are made by the teacher. The level of pupil autonomy is low. Pupils are generally not free to pace their own learning, to move about the room, to discuss their work with other pupils or to follow up interesting ideas they come across in the course of the lesson. When this kind of lesson is operating as planned, the pupils' attention is focused on the lesson objective as determined by the teacher. Thus, direct instruction constitutes a series of actions taken by the teacher to bring about a predetermined learning outcome. This method is not to be confused with simply talking to pupils or "discussing" a topic when all the discussion is actually teacher talk.

Researchers have attempted to discover relationships between what teachers do and how well students learn. Many studies have used achievement (gains made by students on tests of content) as the indicator of learning; these studies are called teacher-effectiveness research. From this work, there has emerged a consensus about the most effective behaviors for teachers to employ in teaching basic skills in the early grades. In a comprehensive review of more than 200 such studies, Brophy and Good (1987) summarized the findings as follows:

> At least two common themes cut across the findings. One is that academic learning is influenced by the amount of time students spend in appropriate academic tasks. The second is that the students learn more effectively when their teachers first structure new information for them and help them relate it to what they already know, and then monitor their performance and provide corrective feedback during recitation, drill, practice or application activities. (p. 366)

The second theme implies these steps in a direct-instruction lesson: review of previous related material, presentation of new skill or content, guided practice, independent practice, and closure. The specific sequence of these steps (described more fully later in this chapter) is called the direct-instruction model. There is general agreement among researchers that using this model is more effective than using individualized or discovery methods for teaching basic skills in fourth grade and below (Rosenshine and Stevens, 1987). In reading and mathematics, the subjects in which most of the teacher-effectiveness research has been carried out, basic skills are easy to identify. In mathematics, basic skills would include multiplication facts (such as 5 times 5) and use of a multiplication algorithm for computation involving numbers larger than 10. Some mathematics skills that are beyond the basics include estimating and problem solving. In reading, basic skills would include word attack, as compared to comprehension, which is a higher-level skill. In science, identifying basic skills proves more difficult, because science is less hierarchical and sequential than either reading or mathematics. Many science educators would agree, however, on two areas of science instruction that could be called basic skills, and thus these two are taught effectively by the direct-instruction model: (1) learning to use tools and equipment for later application in science activities and (2) learning to use basic scientific processes such as observing, communicating, classifying, and measuring.

It would seem reasonable that many elements of the direct-instruction model could be extended to include older pupils and higher-level objectives. Indeed, research on the model is continuing and may someday clearly indicate whether there are limits and, if so, where they are. Regardless of future findings, this direct, explicit teaching is clearly appropriate where the objective is a straightforward skill and the pupil is young. A straightforward skill is one that can be taught in a step-by-step manner and reinforced by practice and application.

The usefulness of direct instruction for science is limited. This would be the method of choice primarily for teaching specific, stepwise procedures—how to use equipment, for example. Learning to use certain basic science processes can also be procedural—learning to construct and use graphs, for example. But procedural learning of this type constitutes only a small percentage of instruction in any science program. Additionally, there may be some science procedures that are less clear-cut, and that could be presented either directly or indirectly. The great majority of science instruction should take the form of guided discovery or projects—methods that more closely parallel the way science is done by scientists. A major reason for the inclusion in this book of direct instruction as a legitimate teaching method is to provide for the developmental needs of the beginning teacher. The direct-instruction model is an excellent device for teaching beginning teachers how to plan a well-structured lesson. And an understanding of the direct-instruction model and the interrelation of its elements should provide the beginning teacher with a reasonable basis from which to understand the more complex guided-discovery model (described in Chapter 7).

PLANNING AND PRESENTING A DIRECT-INSTRUCTION LESSON

Several main parts make up a direct-instruction lesson plan. Each will be briefly described. Then a structured lesson plan for the balance lesson will be described. Finally, the idea of each component will be explained in more detail. First, though, read a general description of one of Ms. Oldhand's lessons.

MS. OLDHAND'S BALANCE LESSON

▼ In this lesson, Ms. Oldhand's second-grade pupils learn to use an equal-arm pan balance. Although the balance is an interesting example of a lever, today Ms. O. mainly wants her pupils to learn to use the balance as a tool. Later, the pupils will need to use the balance to compare and measure weights of objects.

To save space, the balances are stored disassembled in boxes. In this lesson, Ms. O. wants each pupil to learn to put a balance together, learn the names of the parts, and get the general idea of how the balance works when objects are placed in the pans. First, she shows the class how to put a balance together, explaining each step and naming the parts as she does so. Next, she shows them what happens when objects are placed in the pans. Then she asks individual pupils to come to the front of the class to try doing these things themselves. They come one at a time, and their work is watched by the others and closely monitored by Ms. O. When a problem arises, the pupil is helped in some way so that each mistake is gently corrected before the next step is taken. Then all the children get a chance to practice the new skills at their desks. Today, Ms. O. decides to have them work in pairs. As they work, she circulates to help as needed—to encourage, to acknowledge accomplishments, and to provide special advanced tasks for those that finish early.

LESSON PLAN PARTS

A direct-instruction lesson plan has eight main parts. As you read the description of each part think about Ms. Oldhand's balance lesson. Can you decide what would be written for each of these parts?

1. *Performance objective(s)*. Statement of what the pupils will be able to do after the lesson that they could not do before.
2. *Materials*. List of materials that must be prepared or assembled for the lesson.
3. *Motivation*. What the teacher does to create interest or focus attention at the beginning of the lesson.
4. *Presentation*. What the teacher does to give information on how to meet the lesson objectives. Presentation is usually accomplished by showing, telling, or both.
5. *Guided Practice*. What the teacher does to provide closely supervised practice on the lesson objectives with immediate feedback on correctness. Guided practice is normally done one pupil at a time, with the others observing both the practice and the teacher feedback.
6. *Independent practice*. What the teacher does to provide independent practice for all the pupils at once. Teacher supervision is individualized.
7. *Closure*. What the teacher does to close the lesson. For closure, a teacher may decide to review, summarize, relate to previous lessons, or otherwise pull the lesson together.
8. *Appraisal*. What the teacher does to evaluate whether the lesson was a success.

In addition to these eight main parts for the direct instruction lesson plan, additional parts may be added for clarity. In Lesson Plan 5.1 given here as an example, the grade level, a descriptive topic title, and a materials preparation statement are examples of optional lesson-plan parts.

▼ LESSON PLAN 5.1 (Autonomy Level I)

GRADE LEVEL: 2

TOPIC: Getting Acquainted with the Equal-Arm Balance

PERFORMANCE OBJECTIVES

By the end of these activities, the pupil should be able to:

1. Assemble a pan balance from provided components.
2. Name and Identify the parts of the balance: base, support, fulcrum, beam, and pans.
3. Describe the general behavior of the pan balance when objects are put into and taken out of the pans, such as "When one pan goes up, the other goes down" or "You can make the beam even by adding to the high pan or taking away from the low pan."

MATERIALS

For the teacher:

- parts for one pan balance
- several one-inch cube blocks

For each pair of pupils:

- parts for one balance
- 10 one-inch blocks
- 2 balance worksheets (see Figure 5.1)

MATERIALS PREPARATION

Place materials at each double desk during lunch or recess. When pupils return, have them sit on the front rug.

MOTIVATION

Ask "Have you ever played on a seesaw? Sometimes it is called a teeter-totter." Ask what happened if a heavy child and a light child tried to seesaw together. "If you didn't know who was heavier, how could you find out with a seesaw? Today you will learn about a pan balance, a science tool something like a seesaw. We can use it to find out which things are lighter and which are heavier."

PRESENTATION

1. Teacher demonstration: "Watch very closely while I show you how to put your pan balance together." Name the parts as you put the balance together (base, support, fulcrum, beam, pans).

▾ FIGURE 5.1
A balance
worksheet

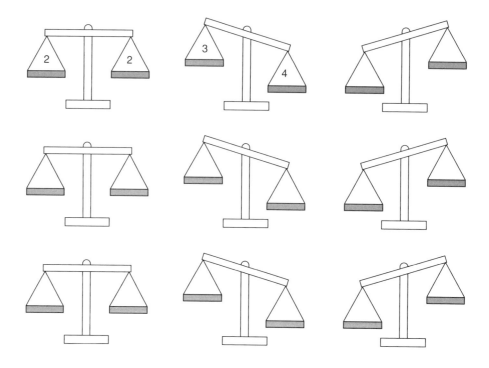

2. When assembly is complete, hold a block over one pan. Ask, "What do you think will happen to the beam?" Take a few responses without comment, and then place the block in the pan. Continue adding blocks to alternate pans. Ask, "Who wants to predict what will happen when I put this on the pan?" Then, without comment, do it.

3. Write the names of the balance parts on the board and go over them with the class.

GUIDED PRACTICE

1. Take the demonstration balance apart. Hold up the parts one at a time and ask for their names. Ask a pupil to come up and do a step of the assembly job and to describe what he or she does using the correct names of parts. Continue by asking "Who can show us the next step?" If someone has trouble, ask another pupil to help. As a last resort, do the assembly yourself, using the names of parts in clear, direct sentences.

2. Ask questions about the behavior of the balance, such as, "Who can tell how to make the balance go down on this side?" (Up on this side, down on the other side, etc.) Regardless of answer, have that child come up and do what he or she suggested. The balance will provide feedback. "Who can make the balance beam even? Is there another way to make the beam even?" Ask pupils to use the names of the balance parts as they demonstrate. Correct any incorrect naming of parts.

3. During part 2 of Guided Practice, begin drawing sketches of balances on the board to show the actions demonstrated.

INDEPENDENT PRACTICE

1. Prepare the pupils to return to their desks by giving directions for the seat work. Hand out a worksheet to each pupil and explain how it corresponds to the diagrams drawn on the board. The worksheet consists of diagrams of balances in left-pan-up, right-pan-up, and even beam positions (several of each). Explain that each will work with a partner to put the balance together and then to make the balance look like the pictures by adding or removing blocks. They should record their work by writing a number in the pan of each diagram to show how many blocks were required to make the balance look that way.

2. Give a prearranged signal for the pupils to return to their seats. As they work, circulate to help as needed.

CLOSURE

Give the signal for attention. Announce that time is up for the lesson and that more balance work will continue later in the week. Ask the pupils to take the balances apart and put the parts in the box. When this is done, the table monitors should collect the boxes.

▼ Hands-on activities can be used in direct instruction.

APPRAISAL

Informal observation during the Independent Practice and responses on the worksheets will provide information for deciding whether the objectives have been met.

EXPLANATION OF LESSON PLAN

In this section, the parts of the lesson plan are explained in some detail, each part supported by research and expert opinion. The lesson-plan parts fall into two different categories: sequencers and organizers. *Sequencers* include motivation, presentation, guided practice, independent practice, and closure, all of which are bound together in a time sequence and occur one after another. Sequencers can also be called *learning activities*. By contrast, the *organizers*—performance objectives, materials, and appraisal—are not together as a sequence; rather, they help the teacher organize thoughts about the total lesson. The performance-objective and materials parts generally are not things the teacher "does." The appraisal is something the teacher does, but the time in which appraisal happens is not fixed. It may occur simultaneously with other lesson parts, afterward, or both. All the parts have a strong and necessary relationship to one another.

1. PERFORMANCE OBJECTIVE(S)

The point of stating the objectives as pupil performance or behavior is to make them observable and therefore easier to appraise. Not all the behaviors that pupils do during a lesson, though, need to be significant new abilities. Many desirable pupil behaviors are simply procedural; that is, the behaviors do not indicate new abilities but are simply "housekeeping" actions necessary to the progress of the lesson. Examples of procedural (or nonsubstantive) behaviors in the balance lesson are:

- Sitting on the front rug
- Discussing the activity with a partner
- Taking the balance apart
- Passing the boxes to the end of the table

All of these behaviors are important to the lesson's progress but are not in themselves new abilities acquired as a result of the lesson activities.

2. MATERIALS

What materials would be most effective for your objectives? What quantities would be optimal? The ideal should be considered first. Then, if there are constraints, adjustments can be made with the conscious recognition of the compromise being made. In the balance lesson, Ms. O. decided to have her pupils work in pairs because she wanted to encourage pupil-to-pupil interactions, not because there was a shortage of balances. Suppose she had decided that it was important for every pupil to work alone with a balance, but she had only 10 balances. She could have chosen to do the lesson with successive groups of 10 while the other pupils did something else. After you have decided what and how many materials you will use, list them in a way that helps you organize for teaching. You will find that designating the number of each material needed is a helpful way to plan. Notice how this was done in the balance plan.

The one-inch blocks used in the balance lesson were selected because they were simple, uniform, and available. Many primary classrooms have such blocks. If they had not been available, Ms. O. could have used any uniform objects, such as washers, nails, or checkers.

3. MOTIVATION

Some sources call this part Motivation/Review. Review is an important way to focus pupils at the beginning of a lesson that is one of a continuing series of lessons. The balance lesson example was the first lesson on that topic, so there was no preceding lesson to review. Instead, the teacher used two other techniques to focus attention and set a meaningful context for what was to follow. First, she asked the children to recall a previous experience. She figured there was a good chance that most of the children had played on a seesaw because their small town had seesaws in the public park. An assumption of this sort is becoming less and less certain, however. As the United States becomes more urbanized and the school population becomes more diverse socioeconomically and ethnically, it becomes harder to be sure that all pupils share any particular experience from outside school. Ms. O. used another technique, just in case. She used an actual balance to show as well as tell.

In the example lesson, the use of a real balance for demonstration does not seem remarkable. Especially with young children, teachers use real objects often. In fact, in almost every lesson with learners of any age, real materials are highly effective as a motivational or focusing device. Many adults have a hard time remembering what it was like not to know about some common object or experience. For any new information to be meaningful, it must be "hooked on" to an older understanding. This is true even for adults, but adults have a rich store of previous experiences to form a context for understanding new information. The more removed from a person's past experience a bit of new information is, the harder it will be for that person to understand. Imagine how relatively poor a child's experience base is, compared to an adult's. There simply has not been time to build up many experiences. Because of a child's inexperience, a lesson is more effective if real things are used to provide a firsthand experience.

Once a teacher knows that all the children have had a certain experience, she can call up the pupils' memory with less tangible stimuli, perhaps even with words alone. In any case, the motivation part of the lesson should be short, and the pacing should be fast.

4. PRESENTATION

There are three characteristics of effective presentation: clarity, focus on the objective, and brevity (Smith & Land, 1981). One of the most consistent research findings is that students achieve more when teachers give clear explanations than when teachers offer vague, fuzzy, disconnected presentations. Teachers who interrupt themselves—who overuse "uh," "OK," "you know," and other such mannerisms—distract their pupils. The pupils shift their focus from the lesson objectives to the mannerisms. The following excerpt from a tape recording of a beginning teacher will illustrate the point:

> This lesson is—well—is going to be—about measuring liquids—*some* liquids, of course, not *all* liquids. We—well, actually, *you*, will measure the volume of liquids that—uh—I have prepared today. OK? First, though, I have to tell you what a liquid is—that is—if you don't already know.

Pupils cannot learn to do the lesson objective unless the teacher can create and maintain their focus on that objective. To do this, the teacher must maintain his or her own focus on the new skill or concept that constitutes the objective. Digressions (jumping ahead and backing up) and ambiguous phrases distract pupils from the main point and confuse them.

Brevity is especially important. If the teacher remembers while planning the lesson to keep the presentation as short as possible, clarity and focus will probably be maintained. Attention span is almost always shorter than one might think—better to underestimate than overestimate it.

With primary pupils, brevity and clarity are even more important. The teacher should directly tell and show with a minimum of asking. The pupils do not know how to do the objective; thus, time and clarity should not be compromised on trying to elicit answers during the presentation. (If pupils can already do the objective, then the objective needs to be revised.) Instead, show and tell directly and briefly; then move into the guided practice. These guidelines, partly developed from a summary of research (Rosenshine and Stevens, 1987), may be helpful:

- Start with an example or a demonstration, not with a definition. A definition is meaningless until some understanding of the skill or concept has been attained.
- Use examples or demonstrations that are simple. Above all, they should not be harder to understand than the skill or concept you are trying to teach. Examples must be concrete and must already be familiar and well understood.
- Present material in small steps. Stop frequently to check for understanding.
- Model the objective whenever possible—show your pupils what you want them to learn. Showing is always better than telling, though the combination of showing and telling makes things easier to remember than either showing or telling alone.

5. GUIDED PRACTICE

The main purpose of this part of a direct-instruction lesson is to provide an opportunity for pupils to practice a new skill in a controlled environment, where mistakes can be corrected and gaps in understanding can be identified. Consider guided practice in a piano lesson: the piano teacher shows the pupil how a passage should be played, the pupil tries it out while the teacher watches, the teacher gives feedback and corrects any mistakes, the pupil goes home to practice, and the pupil finally comes back to the teacher to demonstrate that he or she has learned how to play the piece. Guided practice in science in a classroom may not look like this example, but there are a number of similarities. In one class, the teacher asks questions, gives cues or help as needed, and gently corrects errors. In another class, pupils work problems at the board under the teacher's guidance or come to the front of the room to try out a new skill while the teacher gives help and feedback.

A secondary purpose of guided practice is to provide the teacher with feedback on how the presentation was understood, or rather, how it was misunderstood. By sampling the class for misunderstandings, the presentation can be refined and modified to correct those misunderstandings. Identifying incomplete or otherwise faulty comprehension of the presented content is a positive and desirable part of the lesson, as much a part of the learning as any other component of the lesson.

One of the fine points of teaching is learning to judge the most effective way to give feedback and correct errors. On the one hand, the teacher must provide clear, unmistakable guidance—a pupil must not be permitted to leave this part of the lesson with an uncorrected error. On the other hand, the teacher must be sure that the pupils are not embarrassed to make mistakes and be corrected. They must be guided toward the objective skill or concept in a manner that will ensure a high success rate. The objective is practiced until the teacher is satisfied that most of the pupils can do the work on their own with a reasonable expectation of success. Only then does the teacher move on to independent practice. This part of the lesson should not be as brief as the preceding parts but should not be any longer than absolutely necessary, because pupil involvement in this part is relatively low.

Although the guided-practice part is described separately from the presentation part, in actual practice there may be some overlap between the two. Most lessons have more than one important point. The lesson should be organized so that one point is practiced and understood before moving on to the next step. This means that there may be several periods of guided practice, questions, and discussion within one lesson. Notice how guided practice was used in the balance lesson. Also, when pupil responses show misunderstandings, the teacher often chooses to repeat the presentation in a shortened and modified form to clarify particular points needing more emphasis.

6. INDEPENDENT PRACTICE

Up to this point in the lesson, the pupil involvement has been relatively low. The teacher has been showing and telling, asking questions to the whole class (questions answered by only one child at a time), and having one pupil at a time perform guided practice. Independent practice provides a time for every child in the class to be involved to a much greater extent. In order to be effective, independent practice must provide each child opportunity to think about, try out, rehearse, apply, or otherwise internalize the new skill or concept set forth in the lesson objective. An independent practice that lets pupils practice the skill 10 times is more effective than one that lets them practice it five times. Practice means multiple applications or trials.

Before setting the class to work on this part of the lesson, the teacher must give clear directions and be sure that everyone understands what is to be done and what kind of general behavior is expected. At all times during a lesson, every pupil should understand what he or she is supposed to be doing, and this is especially true during independent practice. Depending on the complexity of the task and on the maturity of the pupils, procedural directions for going about the task may be presented as a series of steps during the guided practice part of the lesson. The teacher who does not think through the planning of this part will have to interrupt the pupils after they have started in order to clarify the procedure and give further directions. This is another example of distraction from the main objective and should be avoided if at all possible.

An example from the balance lesson may clarify the difference between the substantive learning tasks and the procedural tasks of going about the independent practice. The substantive task (in every lesson) is to practice the new skills or ideas; in this case, it is to put the balance together, learn the names of the parts, and recognize how to produce certain positions by placing objects in the pans (see the lesson objectives). The procedural task is how to go about doing the practice. A portion of directions given by the teacher might be something like this:

> Listen carefully so you will know what to do. Stay on the rug until I give the signal. First, you will return to your seats. Then you will work with your partner to put your balance together. Look at my balance to see how it goes together. [*Give each child a worksheet.*] Look at the pictures. Your job is to find how many blocks it takes in each pan to make the balance look like each picture. When you find out, write the number on your paper to show how many blocks you used. Let's do the first one together. [*Teacher shows with demonstration balance.*] Now, how many blocks are in this pan? [*one*] Fine. Now write a one there on your paper. How many blocks in the other pan? [*none*] OK. Then write a zero on that pan. You may talk quietly with your partner, but please do not leave your seat. If you need help, raise your hand. Who remembers the first thing you will do? [*and so on*]

In this example, the independent practice involved working with a partner using real objects. Sometimes the work will be only paperwork, and sometimes the work will be done alone or with larger groups. In every case, the involvement level will be high. Each pupil will be doing things directly and actively—more so than at any other time in the lesson. For this reason, independent practice should get the lion's share of the lesson time.

The teacher is also active during this part of the lesson—walking around, noticing who is having trouble, giving advice as needed, providing a word of praise here or there, and speaking to any pupil who is not being productive. Comments are made quietly to individuals and only as needed, without interrupting the whole class. The effective teacher knows when to be quiet and let the pupils work.

7. CLOSURE

To bring closure means to end the lesson in an orderly way, usually with a short summary or reminder of what the lesson was about. Time should be allowed for materials to be put away by the children, for things to be turned in if necessary, and possibly for questions and comments from the pupils about the lesson. If there is to be a related lesson at a later time, the teacher may choose to mention this briefly. Closure functions to "clear the decks" for the next lesson or activity in a logical and orderly fashion.

8. APPRAISAL

How does a teacher recognize a successful lesson? By whether the objectives were met. If, on the whole, the pupils can do the objective behaviors, then the lesson is a success. The importance of stating worthwhile objectives clearly and behaviorally becomes more apparent in this context. The clearer the statement of the objective, the easier appraisal is. It is often not possible to make a thorough and systematic evaluation of each student during the course of a lesson. The main need at this time is to determine whether enough of the pupils "got it" to continue with the next lesson of the unit or sequence, or whether the lesson "bombed" and needs rethinking, replanning, and reteaching.

Lesson appraisal is not so much evaluation of the pupils as it is self-evaluation by the teacher. If the lesson failed, what was the reason? Was it too hard for the pupils? Maybe it was too easy. Boredom with overly easy tasks can result in misbehavior. Was something overlooked? Were behavior standards appropriate for the type of activity? When a lesson fails, the teacher must take the responsibility to decide what went wrong and to correct the problem in the next lesson.

In the sample lesson, appraisal was done by informal observation and by checking the worksheets. Informal observation can be done fairly easily when the pupils are working with concrete materials. Ms. O. will notice which pairs are having trouble putting their balances together as she circulates during the independent practice. Seldom is it necessary to have an activity separate from the learning activities to decide whether the lesson was successful. In the balance lesson, Ms. O. is appraising at the same time that the pupils are learning. In this case, her informal observations are augmented by checking the worksheets. The pupils' responses there will tell her who understands how to get the balance to do various things.

There are times when it becomes important to do a more systematic evaluation. Situational tests, checklists, paper-and-pencil tests, and other forms of individual evaluation are described in later chapters.

▼ Mr. Newman observed the balance lesson in Ms. Oldhand's classroom, and the two discussed it after the pupils left for the day.

Mr. Newman:	I noticed that you laid out the balances on the desks before the children came back from lunch. Why didn't you just let them pick them up after the guided practice?
Ms. Oldhand:	Well, I do want them to learn to manage their materials eventually. I just thought it would be too much for them to handle this first time. I did have them take care of clean-up. Next time we use the balances, I'll let them do the whole thing. Today, the lesson was just about the right length of time. Any more would have taken too long, and they might not have had time to finish.
Mr. Newman:	Why did you have them come up to the front rug? Couldn't you show them just as well if they were in their seats?
Ms. Oldhand:	Not really. These children are only seven years old, remember. They wouldn't have the maturity to ignore the materials on

Ms. Oldhand: their desks while we did the first parts of the lesson. Something
(continued) I learned the hard way was never to expect children to pay attention or listen when interesting materials are within reach.
Come to think of it, that's pretty hard even for grown-ups.

A POSTSCRIPT ON PREPARATION

A postscript is usually an afterthought, but in this case, it is deliberate placement out of normal sequence. Now that you have thought about a particular lesson in rather specific ways, thinking about how to plan and prepare may be more meaningful. Preparation is crucial for all instruction. The comments here will be equally applicable for the higher autonomy levels introduced in Chapters 7 and 10.

Research shows that well-organized teachers are more effective than others. One of the most interesting and important studies of the relation of teacher behavior to pupil achievement was carried out in Texas in the early 1970s (Brophy and Evertson, 1976). Pupil achievement data for three consecutive years were obtained for a large sample of second- and third-grade teachers. Those teachers whose pupils consistently showed gains in achievement were studied through many hours of careful classroom observation as well as through individual interviews. Researchers found that these effective teachers were businesslike and task-oriented and that they demanded that their pupils spend their class time engaged in learning activities. They tended to maintain well-organized classrooms and to plan activities on a daily basis. Since their activities were well-prepared, the class ran smoothly with few interruptions and little time lost in confusion or aimless activity. In cases where some pupils found the activities too difficult or could not keep up, these teachers often prepared special materials for them. Likewise, the teachers provided additional activities for pupils who finished early. These teachers spent a minimum of time in getting the class started, in transitions, and in bringing closure at the end of the lesson. To sum up, these teachers were prepared to start on time, to move right into the lesson, to provide materials needed for pupils to engage in the learning activities, and to take care of special needs of individuals.

Time spent in preparation allows a teacher to spend class time in effective and productive teaching. Although this kind of preparation takes considerable time and energy, a well-prepared teacher is not as tired at the end of the day as one who is poorly prepared. Consider two teachers: one who is and one who is not well prepared. One has to rush around at the last minute gathering materials and making copies of worksheets for pupils who are left with nothing to do. One feels that the class is off to a poor start and that nothing seems to work right. One has more than the average number of behavior problems. The other one goes home tired but not entirely drained, satisfied that the class is doing well.

When a beginning teacher observes an experienced teacher conduct a lesson that flows smoothly with few interruptions and little off-task behavior, the novice is often unaware of the amount of planning and preparation that has gone into the lesson. Although experienced teachers seldom need the detailed lesson plans that student teachers are required to make, inquiry will reveal that the experienced teacher is clear

▼ The well-prepared teacher organizes materials needed for pupils to engage in interesting learning activities.

about what to do, how to do it, and what the expectations for the pupils are. The student teacher, because of inexperience, needs to think specifically about all these details in advance, to reduce the number of unpleasant surprises during the lesson to a minimum. The lesson plan helps to structure this specific thinking. A well-designed lesson plan, backed up by well-prepared materials, gives the inexperienced teacher a feeling of confidence and of being in control that is communicated to pupils and prevents many of the behavior problems that new teachers dread.

A LESSON ON LINE GRAPHING

▼ Ms. Oldhand is planning a lesson for her sixth graders to introduce them to line graphing. They previously have done many bar graphs and recently have learned about circle graphs. Ms. O. has carefully developed the pupils' understanding of how to make and use these types of graphs, and when to select one over the other for a particular purpose. They know, for example, that bar graphs are useful for showing distributions of things or events (such as how many of their birthdays fall on each month of the year) or for indicating which kinds of animals are most popular as pets. They also understand that circle or "pie" graphs are useful to show the percentages of different parts that go together to make up a whole object, class, or situation. For example, one of the circle graphs they constructed showed the different percentages of pupils in the class who walk to school, who ride bikes, and who come by private car, by schoolbus, and by city bus.

In this lesson, Ms. Oldhand will help the pupils learn to make line graphs. Because this is the first lesson on line graphs, she won't try to teach them everything there is to know about the topic. Many of the technical details will be simplified by the way the task is presented. Ms. O. doesn't expect the pupils to learn how to figure a scale (how many units of measure to represent by one square on the grid). She doesn't expect them to understand or remember the names for the kinds of variables (independent and dependent), and she doesn't expect them to use the terms *x-axis* and *y-axis* at this time. There are other details of this kind that Ms. O. will simply provide during this first lesson on line graphing, so that the amount of new material to master is not overwhelming.

As sixth graders, Ms. Oldhand's pupils already know a great many prerequisites for this lesson. In addition to knowing about other kinds of graphs, they are familiar with ordered pairs of numbers, number lines, and counting by twos, fives, tens, and hundreds. They also know how to use the metric system for simple measurements.

In a recent science activity, the pupils collected data on how high balls bounce when dropped from certain heights. Ms. O. plans to use that experience to make the introduction to line graphing more concrete. Her main goal for the lesson is for the pupils to see and appreciate the line graph as a powerful tool for communicating and predicting.

Three different situations are used for graphing in this lesson. First, during the presentation, Ms. O. shows the class how to make a line graph using data the pupils had collected earlier on the bounciness of a table-tennis ball. Then for guided practice, she shows them a setup for testing how much a rubber band is stretched when weights are added. With data previously collected on the stretching setup, Ms. O. guides the pupils to make a class graph using the overhead projector. Finally, a worksheet is distributed for independent practice. It consists of a labeled grid, a set of data for graphing, and some questions. The pupils are to graph the data on the grid and then use the graph to answer the questions. The subject of the graph, the growth of a plant, is new to the pupils.

Ms. Oldhand's lesson plan follows.

▼ LESSON PLAN 5.2 (Autonomy Level I)

GRADE LEVEL: 6

TOPIC: Communicating and Predicting with Line Graphs

GOAL: To see the usefulness of line graphs

PERFORMANCE OBJECTIVES

At the end of this lesson the pupil will be able to:

1. Locate points on a grid to represent pairs of observations.
2. Connect the located points with a smooth line.

3. Describe an unfamiliar system from a graph of that system.
4. Make predictions using a line graph.

MATERIALS

For the teacher:

- overhead projector
- grid transparencies (labeled but not plotted)

    a. Bounciness (see Figure 5.2)
    b. Stretchiness of Rubber Band (see Figure 5.4)

- transparency marker
- 2 meter sticks
- 1 table-tennis ball
- a rubber band stretcher (see Figure 5.3)
- bounciness data (see Table 5.1)
- rubber band data (see Table 5.2)

For each pupil:

- 1 plant growth worksheet (see Figure 5.5)
- 1 worksheet with questions (see Figure 5.6)

MATERIALS PREPARATION

1. Tape 2 meter sticks to the wall vertically, one above the other, to measure distances from the floor. Both sticks should have the low numbers below the high numbers. (Add 100 to readings of the upper stick.)
2. Set up a rubber band stretcher as shown in Figure 5.3. Add weights and record data for Guided Practice activity. Short rubber bands approach the limit of their elasticity sooner than long ones and are thus better for this lesson. This must be done well ahead of time, because this is where you get the data for making the transparency (Figure 5.4). Use the same setup and the same rubber band for the class activity.

MOTIVATION

Explain to students, "Yesterday you collected data on how high different balls bounce when you drop them from certain heights. Do you remember that I asked you to use only those heights on the chart and not to do any extras? Well, today you will find out why. I will show you how scientists are able to predict the future. Then you should be able to do it yourselves! You will check out your amazing new powers by predicting how high a ball will bounce from some of those drop heights you didn't try yesterday, and then we will test your predictions."

PRESENTATION

1. "We will be using a powerful tool called a line graph. The line graph is like the bar graph in some ways."
2. Turn on the overhead projector to show the grid labeled Bounciness (Figure 5.2). "I will show you how it works." Point to locations on the projection as they are mentioned. "A line graph has two number lines. The number line across the

bottom here includes all the values for the drop heights we want to consider. The other number line is a vertical one going up the left side. It includes all the bounce heights we are interested in, not only what we observed but also a range where our predictions will fall. Now take a look at this data table for the table-tennis ball. See how the observations go in pairs? For every drop height we observed, we also observed a bounce height. The line graph lets you show a pair of observations as a single point. To locate the point for this first number pair, we go across on the drop height number line until we come to 40 cm. Then we go straight up until we come to the line extending from the second number of the number pair, 27, on the bounce height number line. Where these two lines intersect is our point." Make a fat dot to mark the point. Continue in this manner for the other number pairs.

3. "When you find and mark a point like this, it's called 'plotting' the point." Continue to show and tell until all the points are plotted. "The points are sometimes called 'plots.' Let's look at the points we've plotted. Do they seem to have any pattern or regularity?" Pause. "Let's connect them and see." Draw a smooth curve through the dots. "You know about the bouncing ball system because you collected the data. But just looking at the data, can you describe the system?" Take a few comments but move on rather quickly, because this is not the time for a real discussion. Mention the following generalizations if they are not forthcoming:
   - The greater the drop height, the greater the bounce height.
   - The line looks straight at the beginning, but begins to level off at the end. This means that the bounciness of the table-tennis ball stays steady for a while and then begins to decrease.

4. Show them how to predict the bounce height for a drop height of 80 cm and 170 cm. "Find 80 on the drop height number line, from there go straight up until you reach the line we drew to connect plots, and then go directly left to the bounce height number line. The reading there should be the bounce height. Enter the drop heights in the blank spaces of the table of bounciness data [Table 5.1]. Then enter the values predicted from the graph on the table, but put parentheses around them."

▼ TABLE 5.1
Table-tennis ball
bounciness data

DROP HEIGHT (cm)	BOUNCE HEIGHT (cm)
40	27
60	40
100	54
120	63
140	72
200	85

▼ FIGURE 5.2
Bounciness of
table-tennis ball

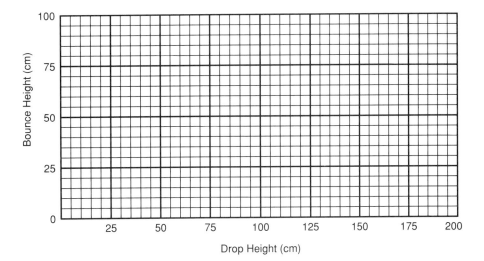

5. "Now for the moment of truth! Will our prediction work?" Hold the table-tennis ball 80 cm from the floor (next to the 80-cm mark of the two-meter ruler taped to the wall), release it, and observe the bounce height. Repeat the procedure at the 170 cm mark.

GUIDED PRACTICE

1. "Now we are going to try something new." Show the rubber band stretching setup. "I want you to see how this works. We have a rubber band attached to the support. There is a bent paper clip on the other end so we can hook a paper cup onto it. Into the paper cup we'll put equal weights—in this case, washers. With no washers in the cup, I'll set the ruler so the zero is at bottom of the rubber band. When I add a washer, the rubber band stretches down to [read measurement on the ruler]. I think you can

▼ FIGURE 5.3
A rubber band stretcher

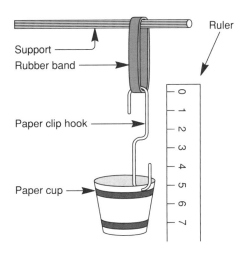

▾ TABLE 5.2
Rubber band
stretch data

NUMBER OF WASHERS	RUBBER BAND LENGTH (cm)
0	0.0
5	2.0
10	6.0
15	10.0
20	13.5
25	15.5
30	17.5
35	18.5
40	19.0

guess that if I add more washers the rubber band will tend to stretch more and more. But I'm not going to show you all of the data-collecting procedure just now. Instead, I'm going to put up a chart [Table 5.2] with the results I got when I did it last night. Then we will all make a graph together using the data."

2. Project transparency of the labeled grid (Figure 5.4) on the chalkboard. Lines and labels will be pale but visible. Ask a pupil to come up and plot the first ordered pair of observations on the projected grid by drawing on the chalkboard. Continue with other pupils for the remaining points. Be sure the pupils remember to move "over and up," and to locate points on lines rather than between them.

3. When all measurements are plotted, have the next pupil draw a smooth line to connect the points.

▾ FIGURE 5.4
Stretchiness of
rubber band

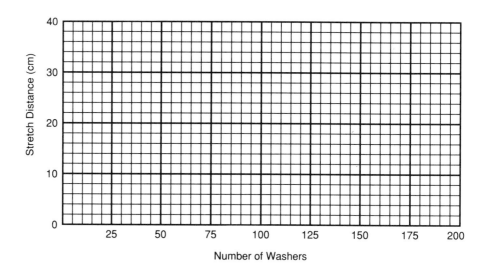

▼ FIGURE 5.5
Worksheet grid
and data

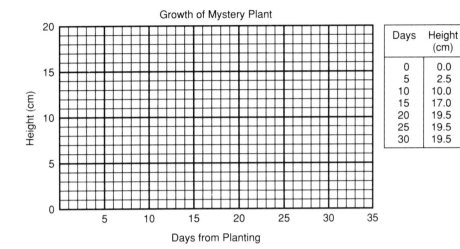

4. Get predictions from several intermediate points on the graph. Get a prediction for one point beyond the observations.
5. Discuss their predictions and then check predictions by demonstrating with the rubber band setup.

INDEPENDENT PRACTICE

1. Distribute plant growth worksheet (labeled Growth of Mystery Plant, shown in Figure 5.5) and give directions. Point out the Days number line across the bottom and the Height number line up the left side of the grid. Also distribute the worksheet with questions (Figure 5.6). "Your job is to plot the points, draw a smooth line to connect points, and answer the questions. You will have 15 minutes to do the worksheet. At 1:45 we will stop to discuss your results and ideas."
2. Circulate and help as needed.

CLOSURE

1. Compare a few results of the prediction questions. Emphasize a range of acceptable prediction values rather than a precise result, but try to identify the cause of any "wild" results.
2. Compare pupils' speculations about possible reasons for the shape of the curve.
3. "Next time you will learn how to choose useful number line values for the two variables."

APPRAISAL

Informal observation during the discussions and checking the worksheets.

▼ FIGURE 5.6
Worksheet Questions

1. A seed was planted on Day 0. What day did the plant come up? _____
2. How tall was the plant on Day 10? _____
3. How tall was the plant on Day 15? _____
4. Plot the points on your grid. Then use your graph to find how tall the plant was on these days:
   • Day 8 _____
   • Day 12 _____
   • Day 14 _____
   • Day 18 _____
5. Predict how tall the plant will be on Day 35. _____
6. Write a sentence to tell what happens to the plant's growth during the last two weeks shown on the graph.

▼ Ms. Oldhand asked Mr. Newman to study the lesson plan and decide whether he would like to actually teach it. After reading the plan, Mr. Newman had several questions.

Mr. Newman: I have studied your plan, and I understand most of it. I wanted to ask about the length, first of all. It seems kind of long. I'm afraid I won't be able to keep them interested that long.

Ms. Oldhand: Quite right. It is too long for one period. When I've taught it before, I have taken two or three forty-minute periods to do it all. And that's not counting the data collection. You look surprised.

Mr. Newman: I just never thought about a lesson being longer than a period. I guess I just thought lesson and period were synonyms!

Ms. Oldhand: Well, often they are, but they don't have to be. I find it makes more sense to keep all the learning activities with the set of objectives they go with and call the whole thing a lesson. I expect some people do it differently. There is no shortage of ideas on how to format a lesson plan.

Mr. Newman: OK, I see. I guess there is more to teaching than I thought. . . . Oh! I also wanted to ask you about the "fat dot." What difference does it make? Why not just make a normal dot?

Ms. Oldhand: It's just a way to avoid being over-precise. Our measurements weren't very precise, and there is no reason to try to make them more precise. Our measurements were just fine for what we were trying to do, which was to show the relationship between drop height and bounce height. If we made a very small dot, the line might look like it was taking a dip when actually it was just

Ms. Oldhand:
(continued) our measurements being off slightly. Elementary school children have trouble disregarding small differences. If they notice a difference, they figure it's a real difference, even when it isn't. Try talking them out of that idea sometime. You'll see what I mean. The fat dot avoids getting into that situation.

THE TEACHER'S ROLE AND THE PUPIL'S ROLE

Just as the nature of the teacher's responsibility is different when teaching a lesson from when doing other duties (lunch monitor or playground supervision, for example), it is different for different types of teaching. The role of the teacher consists of one set of responsibilities when teaching at Autonomy Level I, and another set when teaching at higher levels. The nature of the pupil's responsibility differs in various types of instruction as well.

When considering the roles of both teacher and pupil for the Autonomy Level I, try to keep in mind that some responsibilities will be different at higher autonomy levels. In general, the lower the pupil autonomy level, the more the decisions for the nature, direction, and pacing of the lesson are determined by the teacher. The pupils, at this lowest autonomy level, not only have little to say about lesson decisions but also are not given much latitude for movement or talking. More about how the roles differ at different autonomy levels will be explained in the appropriate chapters, and comparisons of the differences and similarities, as well as the advantages and disadvantages, will be drawn. Here are the roles of teacher and pupil in direct instruction.

Teacher's Role in Direct Instruction (Autonomy Level I)
- Set and enforce behavior standards and sanctions.
- Provide direct information by telling, showing, or by other means.
- Speak clearly and as briefly as possible.
- Listen carefully and check for understanding.
- Provide hands-on experiences whenever possible during independent practice.
- Estimate beforehand a time allocation for each part of the lesson.
- Plan carefully for smooth and efficient distribution and pick-up of materials, involving children when possible.

Pupil's Role in Direct Instruction (Autonomy Level I)
- Follow standards at all times during a lesson.
- Pay attention when others are speaking or demonstrating.
- Follow directions.
- Ask for help if anything is not clear.
- Answer questions when called upon.

BEHAVIOR MANAGEMENT

Management of pupil behavior is always a major concern of beginning teachers. In Chapter 3, some general guidelines for establishing a pleasant but productive classroom climate were described. Among the main points given were the following:

- Establish general rules (standards) and consequences (sanctions) at the beginning of the year.
- Teach direct lessons on the standards and sanctions during the first few weeks of the year.
- Review standards and sanctions as often as necessary thereafter.
- Be completely consistent in applying sanctions.
- Use "surface management" techniques as needed.

Those standards are the general standards used for most routine classroom situations, appropriate during most direct instruction, individual work, and classroom business. There are occasions, however, when the general rules need some amendments, such as when children are involved in activities outside the classroom. Different behaviors are expected at lunchtime, recess, physical education, library, assembly, and fire drills. When taught clearly and directly, children are not confused about appropriate behavior at these various activities. Another time that the usual behavior standards should be modified is when pupils are working with concrete materials, as, for example, in the individual practice part of a direct lesson. If you have ever seen children given the opportunity to work with concrete materials, you know how keenly interested they become. This natural motivation can be harnessed to the benefit of both the lesson and the children's growth in responsibility. Simply explain, before the materials are distributed, how the materials are to be used, and perhaps give a few examples of inappropriate use. Explain that children who cannot manage their behavior while working with the materials will be separated from the materials until they are in better control. Then enforce the rule strictly, or all is lost.

MATERIALS MANAGEMENT

Using concrete materials adds some logistical concerns that must be carefully planned, like any other aspect of a lesson. It is an absolute must for you to try out ahead of time the demonstrations and activities with the actual materials to be used. Attempting to "wing it" with untried materials or with last-minute changes is one of the most frequent causes of lesson failure among beginning science teachers. The method of distribution and clean-up must be carefully planned as well.

VERBAL TECHNIQUES

Giving information and giving directions are important techniques in every teacher's repertoire. Although the two tasks may seem different, they have many similarities.

Listening is hard work for children. The teacher should not rely on a child being able to thoroughly understand from the spoken word alone. Here is a short list of tips for giving information and directions:

- Keep comments brief. Attention span for spoken language is very short.
- Be clear. Think and plan ahead for clarity.
- Ask children to repeat instructions or information back to you. This is feasible when the comments are as brief as they should be.
- Model procedural information as well as lesson content. Use props and body actions to help children understand.
- For all but the youngest, list key words of the directions or information for the children to read and refer to later.
- Establish an atmosphere in which it is safe to ask questions. Then be sure to solicit questions before assuming everyone understands.

In other words, directions as well as lesson content should be taught rather than simply told. In summarizing a large body of teacher effectiveness research, Brophy & Good (1987) described the actions of good classroom managers:

> Effective managers not only told their students what they expected, but also modeled correct procedures for them, took time to answer questions, and, if necessary, arranged for the students to practice the procedures and get feedback. In short, key procedures were formally taught to students, just as academic content is taught. (pp. 220–221)

You may wish to review the detailed discussions of giving information and giving directions in Chapter 3. In the context of this chapter, note that giving directions for a new procedure should be taught directly, using elements of the direct-instruction model. For very young children, it may be necessary to prepare an entire lesson on the new procedure, with all of the lesson parts. Older children may be able to understand with just a few of the lesson parts. As a beginning teacher, you will need to decide how much teaching is needed for your pupils to learn a new procedure. To assume that children will be able to carry out new procedures without special instruction is risky.

MODIFYING THE DIRECT-INSTRUCTION FORMAT

Up to this point, only the standard model for direct instruction has been described and illustrated. The standard model is a useful starting point for beginning teachers. Once you get a feel for the function of each part, you can begin to consider modifications in certain situations. One way to modify the direct instruction model is to use an inductive rather than deductive presentation when the objective is a concept. In the usual presentation, the teacher presents the concept verbally, by stating a rule or generalization. Later, pupils are asked to give examples or specific applications for the generalization. In an inductive presentation, the teacher would present examples of the concept and then present nonexamples of the concept. Usually, the name of the concept is also given. The pupils are then asked to generalize—that is, find the rule that characterizes the set of examples and distinguishes them from the set of nonexamples.

This distinction between inductive and deductive presentations has itself been presented deductively. The same distinction can be presented inductively. Consider two examples of presenting the concept of symmetry. Can you decide which presentation is deductive and which is inductive?

Presentation 1

"Today we will learn about symmetry. We can say a shape has symmetry when it has two halves that exactly match. One way to decide whether a shape has symmetry is to see if you can find a place to fold it so that the two halves exactly match." The teacher demonstrates with her two hands. "Let's see which of these paper cutouts had symmetry." The teacher folds several shapes showing that some shapes have no symmetry and that some shapes have one or more lines of symmetry on which a fold results in two matching halves.

Presentation 2

"Watch what I'm doing. As soon as you notice a pattern or can figure out what I'm doing, raise your hand." Without speaking further, the teacher picks up a piece of paper, folds it, and cuts out a shape. She then unfolds the shape, recloses and opens it several times—demonstrating that the halves match—and places the paper on the left of her table. Then she takes another paper, cuts it, and then folds it. She opens and closes the fold several times to show that the halves do not match, and then places the paper on the right. She continues to fold first, cut, and place to the left, and to cut first, fold, and place to the right until most of the hands are raised.

If you picked Presentation 1 as deductive, or standard direct instruction, and Presentation 2 as the inductive modification, you are right! Think now about how this modified direct-instruction model affects the other parts of the lesson plan. Using the standard presentation, a teacher would have begun with some type of motivation. For example, a string of paper dolls or a paper snowflake might have been shown. The interest of the children would have been raised and a context developed to continue with the presentation. Although this same motivation could be used with the inductive presentation, it would have been less important because the puzzlelike presentation would have engaged interest and raised pupil involvement.

How do you think the other parts of the lesson plan would differ in these two variations of direct instruction? You may be surprised to learn that the other components would not change at all. Guided practice should always be used by the teacher to make sure that most, if not all, of the pupils have the idea or understand the task. Independent practice would also be the same in both cases.

Why would a teacher choose one method of instruction over another? What are the advantages and disadvantages? The advantage of the inductive modification is that pupils are more likely to be mentally involved right from the beginning. Instead of asking the pupils to watch and listen, the teacher begins by asking a question that requires figuring out a puzzlelike situation. Also, when a learner figures something out for himself or herself, the learner is more likely to understand and remember it than when simply told. At least three points are disadvantages: (1) the inductive modification is not equally effective for all kinds of objectives, (2) its use requires judgment that may be beyond the beginning teacher's ability, and (3) it usually takes more time than the standard model.

The method in Presentation 2 involves learning a concept (symmetry), and such learning has been called "concept attainment" by Joyce and Weil (1986). For learning concepts, the inductive modification of direct instruction is widely recognized as effective. But the method works poorly or not at all for procedural objectives. Examples of procedural objectives are how to line up for cafeteria, how to draw a graph, and how to focus a microscope. For other kinds of objectives, such as simple association of names or use of systems of notation, there is no easy rule. An experienced teacher can usually make effective judgments about when and when not to modify the way direct presentation is made. A beginning teacher may misjudge in similar situations. A common difficulty some beginning teachers have is in trying to get pupils to "figure out" names or procedures. Although the intention to increase involvement is a commendable one, asking pupils to guess names or procedures ("It starts with a *B*") simply slows down a lesson without providing any of the benefits described above. Furthermore, guessing names can be confusing to pupils because it emphasizes language rather than concept. The advantages for using the inductive modification of direct instruction for concept attainment generally outweigh the disadvantage of taking more time.

▼ SUMMARY

Basic skills such as psychomotor skills, facts, and straightforward concepts not requiring deep understanding have been shown by research to be taught effectively by direct instruction. This research link is best established for the early grades; continuing research may show a similar relationship at higher grade levels. There is a reluctance among some educators to use the term *teacher effectiveness* for this body of research because it looks only at pupil achievement and says nothing about affective and personal development, areas that are often included as educational goals.

The main strength of the direct-instruction model is its systematic treatment of elements known to be important in basic skill learning. Inexperienced teachers increase their success rate by using this model because it reduces the number of judgments and complex teacher behaviors required. Teaching is a complex business under any conditions; the direct-instruction model simplifies it a bit, with the result that new teachers have fewer lesson failures. With success comes confidence and the beginning of insight into the particular effects of particular teacher behaviors. With insight comes the beginning of conscious self-control of teacher behaviors to produce the pupil effects that are desired in a given situation. At that point, the teacher can begin recognizing some of the limitations of the direct-instruction model and considering some of the alternatives.

▼ DISCUSSION QUESTIONS

1. What is direct instruction and what are its main advantages?
2. What is teacher-effectiveness research and what does it say about direct instruction?
3. What types of science lessons work well in the direct-instruction method?
4. What is the difference between teaching by telling and direct instruction?
5. How can the degree of pupil involvement of a particular lesson activity guide the teacher's decision about pacing and time spent on the activity?
6. Sometimes it makes sense to have some overlap between the presentation and the guided-practice part of a lesson. Explain and give an example.
7. What should pupils always know before beginning independent practice? What can the teacher do to ensure that they know it?
8. What is the difference between individual pupil evaluation and lesson appraisal? Why not do thorough pupil evaluation for every lesson?
9. If a lesson fails, who is responsible and what is the next step?
10. Why spend time planning how to give directions? Why not just tell pupils how to do the procedure as it occurs to you?

▼ ACTIVITIES FOR THE READER

Some ideas for lesson plans are given here. Select one or more to develop using the direct-instruction model described in this chapter. Then form a discussion group in class with others who considered the same idea. Finally, present to the whole class your group's pros and cons of various ways to present the lesson idea.

1. *Planet Names.* Objective: The pupil will be able to name the planets in the order of their distance from the sun (Mercury, Venus, Earth, Mars, Jupiter, Saturn, Uranus, Neptune, Pluto). Use a mnemonic such as "My very educated mouse jumped suddenly under Nathan's pizza" (or make up your own). Include instruction to aid in remembering the order of planets whose names have the same initial letter.
2. *Observing Temperature.* Objectives: The pupil will be able to: (a) describe in words (cold/colder, hot/hotter, or cold/hot) the temperature of two objects of very different temperatures by touch alone, and (b) describe the effect of change in temperature on a thermometer as movement up or down (e.g., when it gets hot, the thermometer goes up). Materials could be chilled water from a drinking fountain, warm water from the hot-water tap, and a thermometer with label tape over the numbers. The label could be marked to show change.
3. *Classifying.* The first objective is to learn to pick a characteristic by which a set of objects can be sorted into two groups: those that have the characteristic and those that do not. The second objective is to reclassify the same objects by a different characteristic, and to tell what the characteristic is. Materials could be unshelled peanuts, flowers, leaves, sea shells, or buttons—any set of things that has sufficient

variety to permit multiple classifications. Pupils should be encouraged to use their own ideas for sorting, but must be able to defend their categories without switching them during a sort. For example, a first sort of buttons could be into groups of two holes and more than two holes. A second sort of the same set could be into blue buttons and nonblue buttons.

4. *Simple Concept Lessons.* Here are three ideas that can be taught by direct instruction (later you will get a chance to compare other methods of teaching these same ideas):

   a. Insects can be distinguished from other small animals by their six legs and three main body parts (head, thorax, abdomen).

   b. Although we cannot see air, it takes up space and can be felt when it moves.

   c. Water evaporates when not in a closed container.

▼ REFERENCES

Brophy, J., & Evertson, C. (1976). *Learning from teaching: A developmental prospective.* Boston: Allyn and Bacon.

Brophy, J., & Good, T. (1987). Teacher behavior and student achievement. In M. C. Wittrock (Ed.), *Handbook of research on teaching* (3rd ed.). New York: Macmillan.

Joyce, B., & Weil, M. (1972). *Models of teaching.* Englewood Cliffs, New Jersey: Prentice Hall.

Rosenshine, B., & Stevens, R. (1987). Teaching functions. In M. C. Wittrock (Ed.), *Handbook of research on teaching* (3rd ed.). New York: Macmillan.

Smith, L., & Land, M. (1981). Low-inference verbal behaviors related to teacher clarity. *Journal of Classroom Interaction, 17,* 37–42.

CHAPTER 6

BASIC SCIENCE PROCESSES

▼
_____

Science includes more than just facts and ideas that scientists of the past have discovered. The actions taken by scientists to find out those facts and ideas are also science. The modern elementary curriculum includes what scientists do (processes) as well as what they produce (content). In other words, the ways scientists notice things, figure out concepts, and try to explain them constitute the processes of science. Both content and processes, then, are important in the modern science curriculum. Science processes are sometimes called *inquiry skills* because they are the means of finding out about the world around us. Pupils must learn how to do science as well as learn about things scientists of the past have discovered. Everyone uses inquiry skills to some extent in everyday life, and scholars in fields other than science certainly use those skills as well. We will call them *science processes* not because they are unique to science but because doing science provides an opportunity to examine the processes directly and think about applying them in a scientific context.

Some of these processes may be called basic processes because they form a foundation of understanding and are components of the more complex processes. The basic processes are:

- *Observing.* Using one or more of the five senses to notice characteristics of objects or events.
- *Communicating.* Conveying information through language, pictures, or other means of representation. Using graphs can also be a means of communication.
- *Classifying.* Putting things into categories according to certain characteristics. Classifying includes creating and using new classification systems as well as using other people's systems.
- *Measuring.* Making quantitative observations by comparing things to one another or to a unit of measure.
- *Relating objects in space and time.* Using the relationships of space and time in describing and comparing shapes, locations, motions, and patterns.

Science for primary-grade children uses these basic processes. Children in the intermediate grades also use these basic processes, but because of their mental development, they can also begin to use more advanced processes. Among the advanced processes are predicting, inferring, and hypothesizing; these higher-order thinking skills lead towards the performing of controlled experiments. Advanced processes will be described in later chapters.

To become an effective science teacher, you must understand the meaning of each basic science process fairly thoroughly. The activities in this chapter were designed specifically to help you gain this understanding. (For children, understanding the meaning and use of science processes is developmental, often taking years to reach completion.) After these activities for teachers, there is a discussion of how to teach and use process skills with children. Although some of the activities in this chapter may be used with certain children without modification, most of the activities are not the best way for children to learn the processes. Whether and how to use these particular activities with children will be addressed later in the chapter.

OBSERVING

Observing, sometimes called the queen of the science processes, is essentially the same as noticing. In science there are special ways of noticing that help the observer become more sensitive to an object or system under study.

▼ OBSERVING ACTIVITY 1

Unknown Candy-Like Object

MATERIALS

- 1 hard candy or mint
- 1 cup of water
- 1 metric ruler

Pretend you don't know what the candy is. (It could be a refrigerator magnet that looks like candy.) Think of it only as "the object". Write down 10 things you notice about it. Then go back and decide which of your senses you used for each observation. Some items may have involved more than a single sense, and that is fine—just identify which senses were used. Did you use all of your senses? Perhaps you didn't listen to it. If not, hold it to your ear now. Did you hear anything? If not, you could record "makes no sound." Another way to observe with your ears is to do something with the object to make a sound and then describe that sound (if any). For example, you could drop the object on the table. Check your set of observations for the following:

- Did you notice any changes?
- Did you make any comparisons?
- Were any of your statements attempts to explain? If you listed "it is candy," you were making an inference—going beyond what your senses told you and using past experience to try to explain. Inferences should not be in your list of observations. "Tastes like candy" is acceptable as an observation because you described a taste by comparing it to something known; such a comparison does not imply any particular identity to the object.

Go back now and make a new set of observations. Use all of the materials, and improve your set of observations to be more informative.

▼ OBSERVING ACTIVITY 2

Moderately Rapid Changes

MATERIALS

- 1 birthday candle
- matches
- metric ruler
- clock or watch with second hand

Without reading further, record a set of observations about your candle. When finished, see how many of the following your set includes:
- height of the candle
- width
- color
- feel, smell, and sound
- all of the above both before and after lighting the candle
- all of the above after the candle went out (or was blown out)
- changes in the candle at measured time intervals

▼ OBSERVING ACTIVITY 3

Show Changes

MATERIALS

- 3 oranges (other fruit may be substituted)
- kitchen knife
- 4 large jars, with lids
- blank notebook

Cut one orange in half, and set up the four jars in this way:

Jar 1: whole orange, jar lid tightly closed

Jar 2: whole orange, jar open

Jar 3: half orange, jar lid tightly closed

Jar 4: half orange, jar open

A good set of observations makes use of all the senses reasonable to use. In this case, for reasons of safety, use only your sense of sight. Draw pictures of the four jars and a short description of each in your notebook. Record your observations by drawing and writing descriptions each day for two weeks. At the end of two weeks, look back over your observation records and answer the following:
- Which jar showed the most change? The least change?
- Which jar showed change first?
- Did changes continue throughout the two-week period, or did the specimens stabilize after a while and stay the same after that?
- Did you notice any changes inside the jars other than changes to the oranges themselves?
- Have you ever seen similar changes in everyday life? Compare.
- Were you able to avoid mixing inferences with your observations?

SUMMARY OF OBSERVING ACTIVITIES

One principle of scientific observing is to use as many of the senses as reasonable in any particular situation. In addition to noticing the appearance of an object, the observer increases the amount of information obtained if he or she also notices how an object feels and smells. Increasing the amount of information obtained is what careful observation is all about.

Another principle of careful observation is comparison. To notice that an object is big is one thing; to notice that it is bigger than your hand is a great deal more informative. To be even more specific, you could compare the object to a centimeter ruler and give its length as 15 cm. A third way to make your observations more useful is to repeat them over time and notice changes. Even if no change occurs, an observation of "no change" is much more informative than not noticing.

Finally, you always want to make sure that you have not confused your observations with inferences. An *observation* is a simple "reading" of an object by your senses, that is, a description rather than an explanation. It is natural to try to make sense of your observations in terms of past experience and a trial explanation of this kind is called an *inference*. An inference is based on observations but goes beyond the information reported by the five senses. Both observations and inferences are important, but you need to keep them straight. Inferring will be presented as an advanced process in Chapter 8.

COMMUNICATING

Communication begins with telling or showing, though it is much more. We all know people who are quite bright but who do not communicate well. In addition to having an adequate vocabulary, a good communicator must also be able to coordinate his or her viewpoint with that of the listener. Unless you can empathize with another's outlook and anticipate that person's questions and needs for clarification, you may not "get through" to the person. Activity 1 illustrates the viewpoint problem well.

▼ COMMUNICATING ACTIVITY 1

Describing Color Rod Construction

MATERIALS

- 2 identical sets of Cuisenaire® rods
- 1 baffle (tall book or box lid)

Two players sit side by side at a table with a baffle between so that they cannot see what the other is doing. One person builds with her set of rods and describes what she is doing. The object of the game is for the second person to construct the same thing with another set of rods from the spoken description alone. If this proves too difficult, add the following step to the game. When the second person is in doubt, he can ask to stop and look at her construction. At this point, the two players should talk briefly about how to improve verbal description of the problem situation, such as, "How could I have said that so you would understand better?"

▼ These children are practicing their verbal communication skills.

Even if this step is not used, the players should discuss their thinking at the end of the construction, addressing such questions as: "What was clear?" "What was confusing?" "How could I say that more clearly?" Players should alternate roles in order to develop appreciation of one another's difficulties.

USING GRAPHS

Complex quantitative data are more easily communicated when organized into visually intuitive forms. A graph is an example. Several kinds of graphs are widely used for a variety of purposes. In this section, several types of graphs are presented and described, and some rules for making graphs are given. In addition, information to help you decide what kind of graph to use for particular kinds of data is presented. You will then have a chance to test your understanding of the graphing information and finally will get a chance to construct some graphs yourself.

Graphs are a way of showing a relationship between two variables. A variable is simply something that varies. For example, height, age, weight, population, and your bank balance are all variables that could be graphed to show their relationship to time. In other words, these quantities can change over a period of time, and a graph could be used to show the nature of the change. Some variables are *continuous*, in that they can have intermediate values. All the examples just given, including time, are continuous. Other variables are *discontinuous*, meaning that there can be no intermediate values. States of the United States, kinds of zoo animals, and makes of cars are examples of discontinuous variables. For example, it makes no sense to talk about something halfway between a bear and a camel. An explanation of types of graphs should clarify these distinctions.

TYPES OF GRAPHS

Three main types of graphs will be presented in this chapter: the bar graph, the circle graph, and the line graph. Two variations of the bar graph—the pictograph and the histogram—will also be explained.

Bar graphs are used to show relationships between a discontinuous variable and a continuous variable. Figure 6.1 compares the normal annual precipitation of several cities. The discontinuous variable is city, and the continuous variable is amount of precipitation.

Pictographs are graphs that use pictures to represent quantities. For example, The Ace Ice Cream Factory showed its sales over the year with a pictograph (Figure 6.2). Notice the similarities and differences between this graph and the bar graph. Pictographs are actually a variety of bar graph.

▼ FIGURE 6.1
Normal annual
precipitation

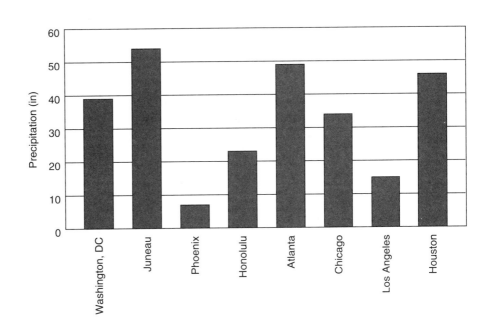

▼ FIGURE 6.2
Ice cream sales for
the year

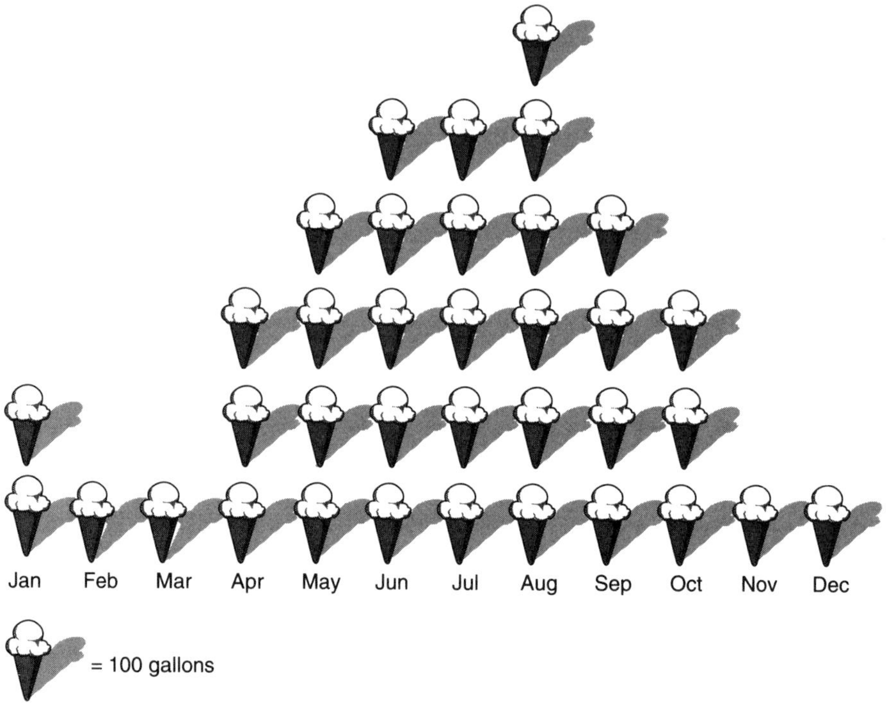

Jan   Feb   Mar   Apr   May   Jun   Jul   Aug   Sep   Oct   Nov   Dec

= 100 gallons

Histograms are graphs that show how often something occurs, or *frequency*, on the vertical axis. Ordinarily, each X (or whatever symbol is used) represents one occurrence of the object or event being studied. Histograms can sometimes be constructed as the data are collected, making unnecessary a record in another form first. For example, suppose you were studying the distribution of peas in their pods. You could start with a sheet of grid paper labeled with number of tallies on the vertical axis and number of peas per pod on the horizontal axis (Figure 6.3). Suppose the first pod you select has seven peas; then you make an X in the lowest position of the 7 column. If your next pod also has seven, you would make another X just above the first. When all the pods are counted and tallied, your histogram would look like the graph in Figure 6.3. The histogram has the same continuous and discontinuous variables as the bar graph, and may be considered another variation of it. Do you notice any differences?

Circle graphs, sometimes called *pie graphs*, are useful for comparing parts to a whole. If you planned a budget, your income would be the whole, and the percentages allotted to housing, clothing, food, entertainment, and so on would be the parts. The parts may be expressed as percentages or as fractions that combine to make up all of something. Examples of circle graphs appear in Figure 6.4 and 6.5; these graphs compare the percentage of religious affiliations in North America and in the whole world.

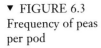

▼ FIGURE 6.3
Frequency of peas
per pod

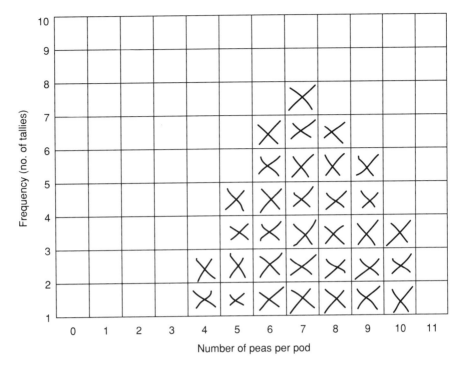

Circle graphs are like bar graphs in that they compare a continuous variable and a discontinuous variable. In Figures 6.4 and 6.5, the continuous variable is percentage of total population. The discontinuous variable is type of religion. The same data could have been displayed on a bar graph. One advantage of the circle graph is con-

▼ FIGURE 6.4
Major religions of
North America

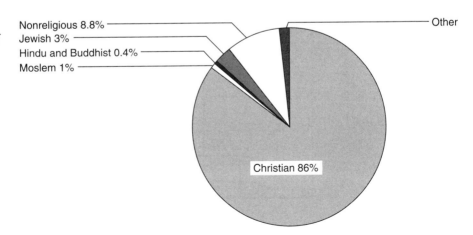

▼ FIGURE 6.5
Major religions of
the world

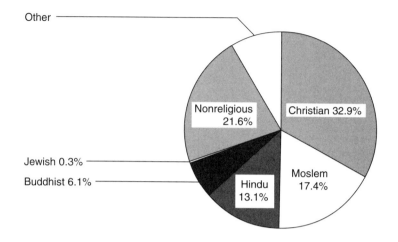

venience in comparing quantities that are very far apart. Notice in the North
America graph that several sectors account for only very small percentages, whereas
one sector is very large. These disparities would be hard to scale for a bar graph
without losing the distinctions among the smaller sectors.

Line graphs show the relationship between two continuous variables. In Figure 6.6,
the height of a growing tree is related to its age. Both height and age are continuous
variables because no matter what units are used to measure them, intermediate values
are easy to imagine.

▼ FIGURE 6.6
Growth of rain
forest tree

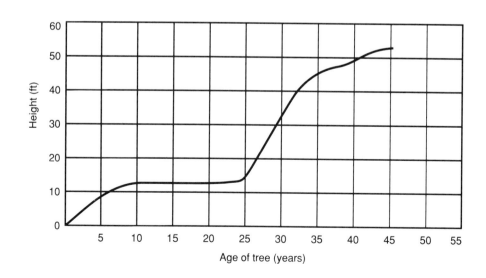

MECHANICS OF GRAPHING

Of the two variables on any graph, one can be identified as the *manipulated variable*, and the other as the *responding variable*. One way to think about the variables is this: You select something, and then you measure what happens in response to your selection. What you select is the manipulated variable; what happens and gets measured is the responding variable. A few examples may clarify. Table 6.1 classifies the variables in five graphs you have studied.

In the Bounciness graph (Figure 5.2) of Chapter 5, drop height was the variable selected, with centimeters as the units. Thus, drop height was the manipulated variable. Bounce height was the responding variable because that was what children measured as it responded to the drop height. In the Stretchiness graph (Figure 5.4) of Chapter 5, adding weights to a rubber band was someone's choice, with washers as the unit of weight. The manipulated variable was, therefore, added weight. In a graph involving growth (Figure 5.5 in Chapter 5), the manipulated variable was time. It may seem strange to think of manipulating time, but in fact, it was manipulated in the sense that two aspects of time were consciously chosen: when to begin measuring the height (the responding variable) and how often to measure it.

Notice that in every example, the responding variable is continuous. For any graph, at least one variable must be continuous, and that one is always the responding variable. The manipulated variable may be continuous also, as in line graphs, or it may be discontinuous, as in bar graphs. With these ideas established, now consider the conventions (rules) for drawing graphs.

Graphing Rules

1. The manipulated variable is graphed on the horizontal (or *x*-axis) with the numbers increasing from left to right.
2. The responding variable is graphed on the vertical (or *y*-axis) with the numbers increasing from bottom to top.
3. The graph is labeled with a descriptive name, communicating the relationship of the variables.
4. Each axis is labeled with the name of its variable.
5. Units of measurement are shown next to all names of continuous variables.

▼ TABLE 6.1
Variables of presented graphs

FIGURE	SHORT TITLE	GRAPH TYPE	MANIPULATED VARIABLE	RESPONDING VARIABLE
5.2	Bounciness	line	Drop Height (cm)	Bounce Height (cm)
5.4	Stretchiness	line	Weight Added (washers)	Stretch (cm)
5.5	Growth	line	Time (days)	Height (cm)
6.1	Precipitation	bar	City	Precipitation (in)
6.6	Growth, Tree	line	Time (years)	Height (feet)

6. The intersection of the *x*-axis and *y*-axis may be zero for both axes or zero for one axis or not zero for either axis. The range of each number line need not include values below or above those of interest.
7. The intervals along each axis should be evenly spaced.
8. The scale for the two axes does not have to be the same.
9. The scale should be chosen for convenience of drawing and clarity of reading.
10. Numerals on the axes are positioned *on*, rather than *between*, grid lines.

Rule 6 is included because people sometimes get the notion that both axes should begin with zero. Many of the examples in this book do begin at zero for both axes, but only because that range of the two number lines (axes) was of interest. If you were graphing the effects of high temperatures on the number of soft drinks sold, your temperature number line on the *x*-axis should begin with numbers quite a bit higher than zero.

Rules 7, 8, and 9 relate to the scale. You will have to decide what value to assign one space on your grid. Often, you will not have room to let one space represent one unit of your variable. In the graph of the rain forest tree, one space was chosen to represent 10 feet of height on the *y*-axis. Notice that the spaces are assigned regular intervals (0, 10, 20, 30, etc.) rather than irregular ones (0, 10, 30, 40, etc.). Be sure that the same length on an axis is labeled to represent the same amount of the variable throughout the whole number line. Deciding how to scale your graph is somewhat subjective but should reflect the guidelines given in Rule 9. Although you should try to avoid assigning some inconvenient number to a space just to make the graph cover most of the grid, you should also avoid making a graph that uses such a small fraction of the paper that it is hard to read and interpret.

A SPECIAL RULE FOR LINE GRAPHS

The line drawn through the plotted points should be a straight line or a smooth curve because you expect the relationship between the variables to be predictable. The changes that occur between points on the graph should ordinarily change in some regular way. Often, you need to "miss" the points a bit to get a smooth line. Such a line is called a *best fit* line. Some points may be "off" somewhat due to experimental error. An example of experimental error is an imprecise reading of a scale. Usually, you would expect to have about the same number of points above the curve as below, as in the graph of Figure 6.7. To draw straight lines precisely from one plotted point to the next—making a jagged line—would suggest that the relationship changes abruptly just at the observation points. If you think about the examples of line graphs you have studied—bounciness, stretchiness, and growth— you can see that the relationships continue in a regular way whether you are observing them or not. There is usually no reason to expect a relationship to change abruptly (for the curve to sharply change direction), especially just at an observation point. The reason the teacher in Chapter 5 suggested using "fat dots" when plotting a line graph was to make drawing a smooth, best-fit line through the dots easier.

▼ FIGURE 6.7
Best-fit line

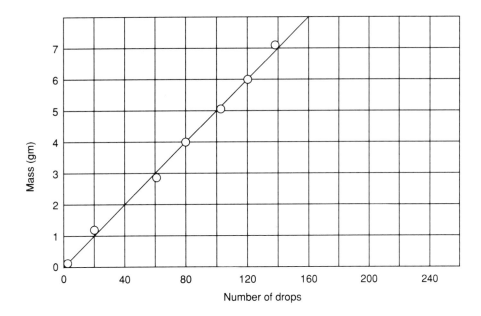

Number of drops

CONSTRUCTING CIRCLE GRAPHS

Constructing bar graphs and line graphs involves the use of a coordinate grid system. This is one of the many areas in which science overlaps with the mathematics curriculum. You may wish to refer back to Lesson Plan 5.2 in Chapter 5 to review details of making a line graph, though the construction of a circle graph is quite different.

Suppose you wish to make a circle graph to show the proportions of Ms. Oldhand's class that come to school by various means of transportation. A survey of the 30 children revealed that 15 walked, 5 rode bicycles, 8 came by schoolbus, and 2 were driven by car.

The first step is to find the fraction each group represents. It is unnecessary to reduce the fractions to lowest terms, though you may if you wish. Then multiply 360—the number of degrees in a circle—by the fraction. This gives the total degrees for each sector of the graph. The arithmetic can be done easily on a calculator:

$$15 \div 30 \times 360 = 180$$
$$5 \div 30 \times 360 = 60$$
$$8 \div 30 \times 360 = 96$$
$$2 \div 30 \times 360 = 24$$

Table 6.2 organizes the information for you.

Next, draw a circle with a compass, and use a protractor to measure the angle for each sector. The compass-and-protractor work can be tedious, however. It is a good exercise to do at least once because it will give you an appreciation for the signi-

▼ TABLE 6.2
How Ms.
Oldhand's pupils
get to school

HOW	HOW MANY	FRACTION	DEGREES OF CIRCLE
Walk	15	$^{15}\!/_{30}$	180
Bicycle	5	$^{5}\!/_{30}$	60
Bus	8	$^{8}\!/_{30}$	96
Car	2	$^{2}\!/_{30}$	24

ficance or insignificance of the various figures. Measuring angles with protractors is not particularly precise, and you may find you have trouble making the last sector drawn come out right.

A much easier way to make circle graphs is on the computer. There are many commercial programs for drawing graphs, but it is very easy to use the following simple Logo tools:

```
TO SETUP                TO LINE
CLEARSCREEN             FORWARD 100
FORWARD 100 RIGHT 90    BACK 100
CIRCLER 100 HOME        END
END


TO SECTOR :FRACTION
RIGHT 360 * :FRACTION
LINE
END
```

Enter those three procedures into your workspace. Then enter the word:

```
SETUP
```

You will see the turtle draw a line, turn right, and then trace a circle. Then it will turn left and return to the center of the circle. Then you can enter the specific data to complete the sectors of your circle graph:

```
SECTOR 15 / 30
SECTOR 5 / 30
SECTOR 8 / 30
SECTOR 2 / 30
```

As you enter each SECTOR command, you will see the turtle turn right and dart to the edge of the circle and then back to the center, drawing a very precise sector. It is actually unnecessary to enter the last SECTOR command, because the last sector will be the amount of the circle left over after the other sectors are drawn. Entering the last command is a nice demonstration, however, of how well Logo draws your graph; the last sector line will be exactly over the original line drawn by SETUP. Finally, you can print out a paper copy of your circle graph.

INTERPRETATION OF GRAPHS

Too often, graphing lessons end with the construction of the graph, as if the graph had a life of its own and just making one was enough. In fact, a graph is a tool for thinking and for communicating, and it is one of the most powerful tools of science that is easily accessible to elementary-age children. Graphs are made to be used, so use them!

Consider Figure 6.8. Notice that the plant grows about the same amount, .5 cm, during the first and second weeks. Then the rate of growth increases. Notice that the line curves up more steeply. This faster rate of growth, about 1.5 cm per week, remains fairly constant for a few weeks (as shown by the straight line) and then the rate decreases. A straight line indicates that the rate is constant; a line that curves up or down indicates a change of rate. During the last two weeks plotted, the plant continues to grow, but growth is slowing. This curve corresponds to the way many plants actually grow. At first, the plant is too busy developing a root system to gain much height above the ground. Then growth speeds up, continues steadily for a while, and finally begins to slow as it approaches its normal full height. Some other kinds of plants continue to grow throughout their lives as long as conditions are good. How would the graph of such a plant differ from the one in Figure 6.8?

Now look at Figure 6.9. Try to match the following descriptions with those graphs.

1. Circle study—x-axis = radius of circle; y-axis = circumference of circle.
2. Fish population in polluted lake—x = time; y = number of fish; each month, twice as many fish die as in the previous month.
3. Volume of a leaking water can—x = time; y = volume of water in can.
4. Bacterial culture—x = time; y = bacterial count; each hour, there are twice as many bacteria as previous hour.
5. Effect on can A of adding washers to can B—x = number of washers in can B; y = weight of can A.
6. Evaporation of water—x = time; y = volume.

▼ FIGURE 6.8
Growth of plant

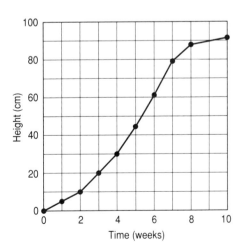

▼ FIGURE 6.9
Graphs to be identified

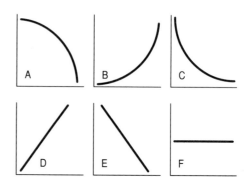

Put a piece of paper over the following list until you have thought about each graph and made an attempt to match them with their descriptions. When you are ready, look at these answers:

1. D. The bigger the radius, the bigger the circumference. This kind of relationship is called *direct*. It is also a straight line, indicating a constant rate.
2. A. The more time, the fewer fish; this kind of relationship is called *inverse*. It is not a straight line but a geometric relationship, because the decrease in fish speeds up with time.
3. C. The longer the can leaks, the less water is left in it. This kind of relationship is called *inverse*. It is not a straight line because the amount of water leaking out per unit time at the beginning is more than the amount leaking per unit time later. At first, the pressure of the water's weight causes the water to leak out faster. As the pressure decreases with the amount of water in the can, the rate of leaking decreases also.
4. B. Direct relationship, increasing geometrically.
5. F. Trick question! Adding weights to one container causes no change in another. There is no relationship.
6. E. The more time, the less water remaining. Inverse, straight line relationship.

The graph of the rain forest tree (Figure 6.6) also deserves a comment. Can you think of a scenario to explain the unusual growth curve? The curve indicates that the tree grew fairly rapidly for its first 5 years and then leveled off to a constant height for the next 20 years. At about year 25, growth "took off" again and continued

▼ FIGURE 6.10
Frequency of dice outcomes

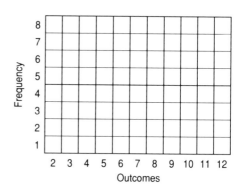

rapidly for 10 years before beginning to slow gradually. Even at the end of the data period, year 45, growth is still occurring, though at a slow rate.

Here is one explanation: The tree began growing in sunlight, but was outgrown by another tree, which shaded it. Without direct sun, the tree was only able to maintain itself, but not able to grow. At year 25, the other tree succumbed to disease and fell, opening up the canopy and allowing full sun to the tree, which then resumed its normal growth pattern.

▼ COMMUNICATING ACTIVITY 2

Dice Outcome Histogram

MATERIALS

- 1 pair of dice
- grid paper

In this activity you will roll a pair of dice repeatedly and record the total number of spots shown each time by placing an X on a histogram (Figure 6.10). Set up your grid with the numbers 2 through 12 on the x-axis; these are all the possible outcomes of rolling two standard dice. Each time you roll, place an X in the appropriate column.

Before you begin, which column or columns do you think will have the most Xs at the end? Which do you think will have the least? Do you think the shape of the bars (columns of Xs) will change as you continue? Why or why not? To give this last thought a chance to develop, you should roll the dice as many times as you can. If possible, work in a group, recording the outcomes of several people rolling dice at the same time.

▼ COMMUNICATING ACTIVITY 3

Circle Graph of Coins

MATERIALS

- 1 compass
- 1 protractor
- small change on hand

Reach into your purse or pocket and produce all your available coins. Record the frequency of each coin in a table, such as:

COINS	NUMBER
Halves	1
Quarters	3
Dimes	4
Nickels	6
Pennies	12
Total	26

Use these data to construct a circle graph showing the proportion of your coins for each denomination. A drinking glass or other cylindrical object can be substituted for the compass to draw the circle, but a protractor is essential for measuring the angles.

Alternative: Draw your circle graph on the computer using the Logo tools presented.

▼ COMMUNICATING ACTIVITY 4

Line Graphing a Rolling Object

MATERIALS

- 1 meter stick or yard stick
- 1 ruler (cm or inches)
- 1 spool of thread (with or without thread)

Set up as shown in Figure 6.11. Prop the ruler on books or some other object to make a gently sloping ramp. Be sure the zero end of the ruler is the low end. Allow the spool to roll down the ramp, noticing the path it takes on the table. If the spool runs off the table, lower the ramp or place a towel on the table to reduce the distance rolled. Make adjustments so that a high release point on the ruler causes a roll distance near the far end of the meter stick. Lay the meter stick parallel to the spool's path, with its zero end even with the end of the ramp, but at an offset so the spool will roll alongside the meter stick rather than on it. Hold and then release the spool from the 1-inch mark on the ruler. Read the distance rolled on the table from the meter stick. If the spool rolls away from the meter stick, you can measure the distance rolled by moving the meter stick. Continue for other release points until you have at least 10 data points to graph. Then answer these questions:

1. Were you able to draw a best-fit line?
2. Did you roll several times at each release point and plot the average to reduce experimental error?
3. Did you follow all the graphing conventions?
4. How would you describe the relationship between release point and roll distance?

▼ FIGURE 6.11
Spool roll setup

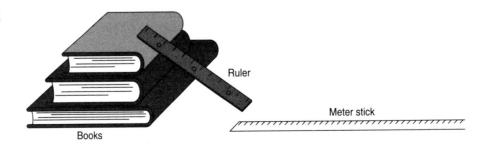

Ruler

Meter stick

Books

SUMMARY OF COMMUNICATING ACTIVITIES

Communicating clearly and effectively is a pervasive need in every activity involving two or more people. In science, some ways of communicating have been developed that are useful throughout the day and the curriculum. Communicating involves empathizing with listeners and anticipating their questions, and it is not limited to simply using expressive language. Graphing is a particularly effective way to communicate certain kinds of information.

CLASSIFYING

Observing may be thought of as reporting what you notice about particular objects. Classifying, on the other hand, has to do with abstracting similarities and differences from the objects observed.

▼ CLASSIFYING ACTIVITY 1

Two-Difference Trains with Attribute Pieces

MATERIALS

32 attribute pieces, 1 each:
- large triangles: red, blue, yellow, green
- small triangles: red, blue, yellow, green
- large circles: red, blue, yellow, green
- small circles: red, blue, yellow, green
- large diamonds: red, blue, yellow, green
- small diamonds: red, blue, yellow, green
- large squares: red, blue, yellow, green
- small squares: red, blue, yellow, green

These pieces can be made from construction paper or tagboard. If you have never worked with attribute pieces before, spend some time exploring the set. How many ways can you sort them? Place all the pieces into two groups according to some characteristic. What is alike for all the pieces in one group that is different from all the pieces in the other group? Now shuffle the pieces and sort into two groups again, but this time by a different characteristic. The word *attribute* simply means "characteristic." How many different ways can you sort into two groups?

The object of the Two-Difference Train Game is to place all the pieces in a row so that each piece is different from its neighbors in exactly two ways. With this set of attribute pieces, each piece has three characteristics: size, color, and shape. For two pieces to be different in exactly two ways means that they must be alike in one way. For example, the large green triangle is different from the large blue circle in two ways: color and shape; size is the same. The small yellow square is different from the large yellow circle in size and shape and alike only in

▾ Mr. Newman shows children a classification game.

color. The small blue diamond, however, is like the small blue triangle in two ways and different only in one way. See if you can place all pieces of the set into a two-difference train. If you get stuck, you may need to go back and undo some pieces that are already in place. Hint: Each time you place a piece in the train, state aloud how it is different and how it is like each of its neighbors. This will force you to think about each characteristic in turn and will reduce the likelihood of oversights.

Variations on this game include: One-Difference Train, Three-Difference Train, Make a Loop instead of a Train, and Make a Figure-eight instead of a Loop.

Attribute pieces can be used for many fascinating activities. For additional ideas, see the teacher's guide for *Attribute Games and Problems* (Elementary Science Study; 1984) or Chapter 1 in Fuys & Tischler (1979).

▾ CLASSIFYING ACTIVITY 2

Single-stage and Multistage Systems

Another way to think about sorting is to construct classification systems with stages. You could easily make a one-stage system for the attribute pieces described in Classifying Activity 1 that would look like Figure 6.12.

▼ FIGURE 6.12
One-stage classification system

To construct or use the system, it is convenient to begin by actually placing all attribute pieces in the rectangle labeled ALL. Then think about how the pieces could be sorted into two groups. Consider how size could be used for the sort; all the large pieces would then be moved from the ALL rectangle to the LARGE rectangle. Similarly, the small pieces could be placed into the SMALL rectangle. There would still be many pieces in each of the two lower rectangles. To isolate each item, you would need several more sortings, or stages. To simplify the problem, limit yourself to the red pieces and see how many stages it takes to isolate each of them.

Look at Figure 6.13. To save space, the pieces are named by initials. For example, LRC means large red circle. In each case, the size is given first, then the color, and finally, the shape.

Looking at Stage 2 of Figure 6.13, you will notice that the attribute—or *criterion*—chosen was whether the piece had four sides or not. This criterion separated the pieces into two groups. You may have seen classifying systems in which

▼ FIGURE 6.13
Three-stage
classification
system

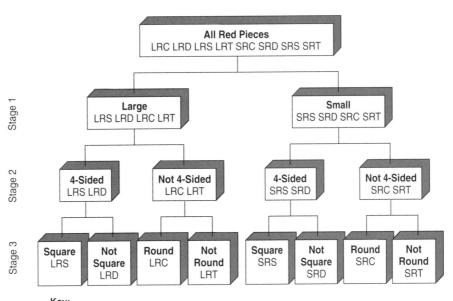

Key:
LRC/SRC = Large/small round circle
LRD/SRD = Large/small round diamond
RND = Round

LRS/SRS = Large/small round square
LRT/SRT = Large/small round triangle
SQ = Square

a sorting involved separation into more than two groups. For example, instead of four-sided versus non-four-sided, you could choose specific shape as the criterion and divide the pieces directly into the four shapes: circle, diamond, square, and triangle. There is nothing "wrong" with sorting into more than two groups, but there is a special advantage to using two groups only.

The criterion for sorting into two groups can be thought of as a yes-or-no question. All possible items, even those not in the current set of items being classified, could be placed into one or the other category. Suppose someone came along later with new attribute pieces: large red hexagon and small red semicircle (the color is kept constant, still limiting the whole system to red only). Would you be able to find a place for the new pieces on the system shown in Figure 6.13? Yes, the large red hexagon would fall into the following categories, beginning with Stage 1: large, not four-sided, not round. The small red semicircle would fall into these: small, not four-sided, round. If you had a system where Stage 2 was shape and had four possible categories, you would be unable to place the new pieces at that level because neither belongs to any of the existing categories. When the "question" asked can be answered with a yes or a no, finding a place for all possible items is much easier.

Another situation in which it may be hard to place an item is when the criterion for the sorting is not clear. In Stage 1 of our attribute-pieces system (Figure 6.13), the criterion size was used, with large and small as its values. This will work easily with the set of attribute pieces developed in Classifying Activity 1 because there are only two sizes. But if you were to add new pieces to the system that were intermediate between the original pieces—or larger than the original large or smaller than the original small—then you would be in serious trouble. *Large* and *small* are not very good words for describing size unless you are working with a known, limited set of objects or a set of things with a known range of possible sizes. Notice that in both of these cases of "known" things, the assumption is that someone "knows" something, and clear communication depends on that assumption being valid. It is better practice when striving for clarity to specify the size by a standard unit of measurement. For example, categories might be "larger than 3 cm in diameter" and "3 cm or smaller". This would make the sorting of new, currently unknown objects much easier.

Look at a different kind of set to use in a multi-stage system, 10 living things:

a mature red oak tree

a mature date palm tree

a blooming daisy plant

a tuft of rye grass

a carrot plant

a domestic cat

a rainbow trout

a house sparrow

an anole lizard

a bullfrog

Each of these things is a distinct species of living organism in the real world. If you need to find out more about any of them, you could look them up in reference books or ask other people who know more about them. A classification system with two stages is shown in Figure 6.14. In the example shown in Figure 6.13, the two sides of the system tended to be symmetrical. Symmetry is neat but unessential. It often does not fit well, as in this case. Notice that Stage 2 in Figure 6.14 has different criteria on the two sides of the system.

The activity for you to try has two parts. For Part A, complete the system for classifying the 10 living things. What will you choose for your criteria in Stage 3? Although it is possible to choose functions or purposes, observable properties make better criteria. For this exercise, limit yourself to characteristics that can be observed. For Part B, collect two or more identical sets of common small objects. About 10 or 12 different items make a good problem. Here is a list of items to jog your imagination; feel free to substitute for convenience:

rubber band

small paper clip

large paper clip

pencil

ball-point pen

thumbtack

nail

pipe cleaner

▼ FIGURE 6.14
Two-stage
classification
system

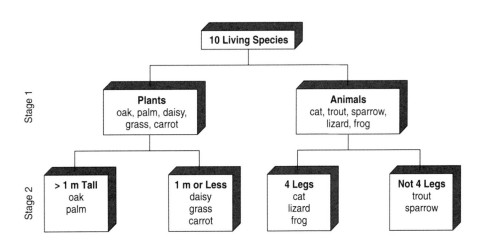

stick of chewing gum

buttons (different colors, sizes, or styles)

beads (different colors, sizes, or styles)

spool of sewing thread

art gum eraser

This activity works better with two or more people. Each person or team gets an identical set of items and a large sheet of chart paper. Everyone works to construct classification systems with enough stages to isolate every item in the set. When done, individuals or teams exchange chart papers and try to find where all the items go in the other people's classification system. If you have trouble, discuss the problem with the person who made the system. Try to come up with a solution that solves the problem.

▼ CLASSIFYING ACTIVITY 3

Using Computers in Sorting

There is a BASIC program in public domain called "Animals" that is similar to the old 20-questions game. The player is asked to think of an animal and then respond to the computer's yes-or-no questions as it tries to guess the animal. At first, the computer knows only two animals. If the player's animal is not one of these two, the computer asks the player to type in a question that would distinguish between the player's animal and the one the computer just guessed. Here is a sample run:

```
DOES IT LIVE IN THE WATER?
NO
IS THE ANIMAL YOU'RE THINKING OF A MOOSE?
NO
ALL RIGHT, I GIVE UP. WHAT ANIMAL WERE YOU THINKING OF?
RHINO
PLEASE TYPE A QUESTION THAT WOULD DISTINGUISH BETWEEN A
MOOSE AND A RHINO.
DOES IT HAVE A HORN ON ITS NOSE?
WHAT WOULD THE CORRECT ANSWER FOR A RHINO BE?
YES
I NOW KNOW 3 ANIMALS!
WANT TO PLAY AGAIN?
```

Each time new animals are added in this way, the program stores them in a data file, which it accesses during play. The player can erase all the learned animals at any time. This often becomes desirable when players use vague or confusing questions.

Software in public domain is free and widely available. Ask your instructor or a friend who is a computer enthusiast to help you find "Animals." School-district computer specialists are another possible source.

Once you have located the program, play it several times to increase the number of animals in the data file. Then see if you can construct a multistage classification system to fit the animals and the criteria. Study the chart you make and decide whether the system can be improved. For example, a criterion that distinguishes between two fairly equivalent-sized groups is convenient because it reduces the number of stages necessary to isolate all the items. If a criterion separates only 1 item from a group of 20, it is less convenient than a criterion that separates 9 or 10 from 20. Clarity is another point to look for in critiquing your multistage system. Does the question need to be rephrased? Does the whole criterion need rethinking?

Another computer application involving the process of classifying is using a database management system. A database management system is a software program that allows you to set up your own filing system, fill it with your own data, and retrieve the data in a selective manner. A set of organized data that is made in this way is called a *database*.

Although commercial software companies offer preconstructed databases containing information on various topics, you should make some of your own to become familiar with this application of classifying. Set up a simple database of the animals you used in the "Animals" program. For each animal, decide on four or five types of information, such as weight, length or diet. These headings are called *fields*. Each animal name and all its related data is called a *record*. A sample arrangement is shown in Figure 6.15. The records are shown in horizontal rows, the fields in vertical columns. Once the data are entered, you can retrieve information selectively. For example, which animal(s) that weigh over 500 pounds eat plants?

Even if you do not have access to database management software at this time, try filling out a paper one, such as the outline shown in Figure 6.15, or make your own set of categories.

▼ FIGURE 6.15
"Animals"
database

ANIMAL	HABITAT	DIET	WEIGHT	LENGTH
Moose				
Frog				
Rhino				
Hippo				
Trout				
Cat				

SUMMARY OF CLASSIFYING ACTIVITIES

Three important concepts involved in classifying are: (1) classification is meant to be useful, (2) classification is arbitrary, and (3) any group of objects can be classified in more than one way. Because of the way classification is often taught, many people sometimes get the notion that classification systems have some internal logic that was simply "discovered" by scientists of the past, and is now passed on in school. Actually, systems of naming and classifying animals, plants, rocks, and other things were devised to make it easier for scientists to communicate with each other. The categories could just as well be classified by different criteria. In fact, many systems and names of things in science change rather often as new knowledge becomes available, or as the animals themselves (or other things being classified) actually change.

In the example systems you worked with in this chapter, you saw that a set of objects could be classified differently. The attribute pieces could have been sorted by shape first and size later. The first criterion chosen could just as well have been size for the living things, rather than plant/animal kingdom. The criteria you chose for the third and fourth stages were probably different from those chosen by another student in your class. This points out the arbitrary nature of classification systems. Criteria and their sequence become standardized in some situations not because other possibilities are unavailable, but simply as a way to clarify communication.

MEASURING

Measuring has been defined as the process of finding out the extent, dimensions, or quantity of something, and of making quantitative observations by comparing things to one another or to a unit of measure. The main theme of measuring and learning to measure is *iterating* (physically repeating, or placing over and over again) a unit until a mental picture of that unit is thoroughly established.

▼ MEASURING ACTIVITY 1

Premeasuring: Simple Comparison ($<$, $>$, $=$)

Cut a strip from an index card or similar material to match the length of the rectangle shown in Figure 6.16. Then make a list of things in your home that are the same length or close to the same length. For example, you may notice that an electrical switch plate is very close to that length. Find other objects to bring your list to about 10 items. Share your list in class. Which things named by your classmates did you also have on your list?

▼ FIGURE 6.16
A rectangle of a certain length

▼ MEASURING ACTIVITY 2

True Measuring: Iterate a unit and count the iterations

Because of the way *area* is sometimes taught in school, it is often thought of as something figured out by multiplying linear measurements. This multiplying procedure is a shortcut for finding area, but it does not help in the understanding of the meaning of *area* or the meaning of *measurement*. Measuring Activity 2 is designed to make these meanings clearer. Area is the extent of a surface. Choose a surface whose area you will measure. A table or small "area" rug would be convenient. Next, choose an area unit, also for convenience. For a unit, choose something that possesses area itself. Also you will want multiple copies of the unit. A string or a pipe cleaner will not do as an area unit because each only has length. You could use playing cards, small index cards, or pages from a small tablet. First, look at the surface to be measured—say, a card table. Just by looking, estimate how many of your units—say, playing cards—it will take to cover the table. Write down this estimate. Then check your estimate by actually covering the table with cards. Finally, count the cards. How close did you come to your estimate?

▼ These children practice predicting and measuring liquids with the metric system.

▼ MEASURING ACTIVITY 3

Metric System

Select a group of containers in your kitchen. Here is an example of things you might easily round up:

sauce pan   pie pan
drinking glass   mixing bowl
coffee mug   cereal bowl

You will also need a measuring cup. It can be 1-cup, 2-cup, or 4-cup capacity. Turn the cup around and look at the markings on the side opposite the cup and fractional-cup markings. Unless your measuring cup is an antique, you will find milliliter (ml) markings. Now follow these steps:

1. Look at the containers you have gathered. Which do you think will hold the most? Which will hold second most? Arrange your containers in the order you think will be from least to most volume. This may not be as easy as you think. Containers of different shapes may be hard to compare without pouring, but for now do not do any pouring. List your containers on a sheet of paper in the order you estimated.
2. Check your estimated volume sequence this way: Fill with water the container you think is the smallest. Pour it into the next largest container. Did the second container still have room for more water? If not, rearrange the order. Continue in this way until you have checked all the containers and are sure that they are correctly ordered by volume.
3. Find another container that is smaller than the smallest container you listed. It might be a small paper cup, a spray can lid, or a demitasse. Make your list into a worksheet, as in Table 6.3. If your small additional container is not a lid, substitute its name in your worksheet.

▼ TABLE 6.3
Metric worksheet

CONTAINER	LIDS		MILLILITERS	
	ESTIMATE	MEASURE	ESTIMATE	MEASURE
drinking glass				
coffee mug				
cereal bowl				
pie pan				
sauce pan				
mixing bowl				

4. In the Estimate column under the heading LIDS, write the number of lids you think each container will hold.

5. After you have entered all your "lid" estimates on the worksheet, use the lid to measure each container. Pour and count the number of lidfuls necessary to fill each container to the brim. Enter your results in the worksheet.

6. Fill the measuring cup to the 1-cup mark. Turn the cup around and notice the ml equivalent. If you have a larger measuring cup, fill it to 2 cups and 4 cups, noticing the ml equivalents.

7. Without pouring, look at the drinking glass (or whatever is first on your list), and estimate the number of ml needed to fill it to the brim. You may look at your ml measuring cup as a reference, but don't touch. Enter your estimated ml on the worksheet. Continue for each of the items on your list.

8. Now, measure the volume in ml of each container using your measuring cup. Write your results in the far-right column. Are you getting better?

SUMMARY OF MEASURING ACTIVITIES

The learning and teaching of measuring is a topic much too extensive to cover in this section. Many short accounts of measuring stop with length measure and limit activities to those confined to the size of a desk top—or worse, a single sheet of paper. There are so many terrific, fun, and valuable activities possible that you should continue to search them out and to invent your own. Four resources to get you started are Cunningham (1976), Fuys and Tischler (1979, Chapter 6), *Match and Measure* (ESS, 1985), and *Measurement in School Mathematics* (NCTM, 1976). Measuring is one of those topics that is so universal that it can be used to integrate many areas of the curriculum and school life and should not be limited to science and mathematics.

You may not realize it, but by virtue of having done Measuring Activity 1, you now have a mental picture of a decimeter in your head! Although the activity was presented to illustrate the pre-measuring idea of simple comparison, the strip of tag board you made to match Figure 6.16 is exactly 10 centimeters—1 decimeter—long. You did not need to know that until now. The idea of the activity was to establish the beginning of confidence in you as a measurement teacher and a user of the metric system. Try to avoid translating metric units into units in the U.S. Customary System (i.e., the foot-pound system). Because Americans grow up with the customary system, most already have mental images of many of its units. The way to feel comfortable with the metric system is to experience its units and build up mental pictures. It is much like learning a foreign language. If you have to translate word-for-word into and out of English, you will never approach fluency. Just live with the new language through firsthand experiences, and you will pick it up before you realize it.

Another important idea in the learning and teaching of measurement is to avoid using shortcuts until the mental unit is established. Many shortcuts are used in real-life measuring, including indirect methods followed by computation and use of tools, such as trundle wheels. If the objective of an activity is to learn the concept of measuring or the concept of the quantity (e.g., area), then measuring should be the most direct means possible of reiterating the unit. You did this in the activity that involved covering a table with cards. It would have been more efficient to use a ruler and measure the length and width of the table and then multiply. It would have been better to do it that way if your objective had been to quickly get a measurement. The objective, however, was to learn; so you did it the hard way.

RELATING OBJECTS IN SPACE AND TIME

Space and time are the two most basic concepts in physical science. Relating objects in space and time involves describing and comparing objects and events by describing shapes, locations, motions, and changes in shapes and patterns over time.

▼ SPACE/TIME ACTIVITY 1
Drawing Three-Dimensional Shapes

MATERIALS

Several models of three-dimensional shapes such as:
- 1 cube (wooden block or die)
- 1 noncubic rectangular prism (brick, cereal box)
- 1 cylinder (food can)
- paper and pencil

Set the cube where you can observe it as a model, with one face towards you. Follow these directions along with the steps in Figure 6.17.

▼ FIGURE 6.17
Drawing a cube

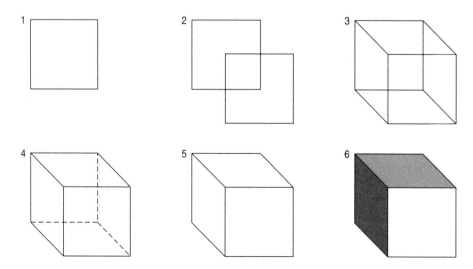

▼ FIGURE 6.18
Drawing a
cylinder

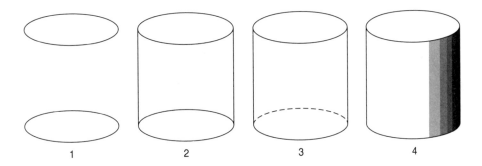

1. Draw a square to represent the face closest to you.
2. Draw a second square of the same size, overlapping in the way illustrated in Figure 6.17. This second square represents the back face of the cube, which is parallel to the first one you drew.
3. Connect the vertices of the two squares.
4. Replace the solid line with dotted lines in the positions that you cannot actually see on your cube model. You may choose to stop here, since you have drawn a cube the way it is usually shown in mathematics books.
5. Proceed, if you prefer, to erase the lines not actually visible on the model.
6. Shade two faces, if you wish, for a more realistic drawing.

Notice that the lines in the second square of Figure 6.17 are parallel to the lines in the first square, and notice that all the connecting lines are parallel to one another. Rectangular prisms other than cubes can be drawn in this same manner. Experiment with a rectangular prism, such as a cereal box, that has three differently shaped pairs of faces. Draw it with one face forward, then another. Also experiment with making the rear face somewhat smaller in order to produce perspective.

Drawing a cylinder requires a somewhat different technique. The only surfaces of the cylinder that are truly two-dimensional are the circles at either end. In order to see any of the curved surface connecting the two circular ends, it is necessary to view the circles at an angle. When a circle is viewed at an angle, it takes on the appearance of an ellipse. Look now at your cylinder model. As it sits on one circular end, the other should look elliptical. Try drawing two ellipses, as shown in Figure 6.18. After you get the ellipses, connect the ends in much the way you did with the rectangular prisms. The only hidden edges will be those where the circular ends meet the curved surface. Again, use dotted lines or shading to finish your drawing.

▼ S P A C E / T I M E   A C T I V I T Y   2

Making 3-D Shapes by Spinning 2-D Shapes

MATERIALS

- Cardboard
- Scissors
- String

▼ Spinning two-dimensional shapes helps children visualize three-dimensional shapes.

Most of us are familiar with a simple toy made by threading a looped string through a button, winding the string, and then pulling the string taut to cause the button to spin as the string unwinds. This activity is a variation on that toy. Cut several two-dimensional shapes from cardboard, such as those shown in Figure 6.19. Punch two holes on opposite ends of each shape and thread string through the holes. Tie each string into a loop as shown. (Item F in Figure 6.19 is an enlargement to show how the string is attached.) Wind up the strings while holding both ends. Pull the strings, causing the shape to spin. What three-dimensional shape do you see as the two-dimensional shape spins? Can you predict before actually spinning? In Shapes A and E, how would the generated 3-D shape be different if the strings were attached near the check marks?

▼ SPACE/TIME ACTIVITY 3

Animation (Extension with Logo)

Have you ever thought about how motion pictures are made? Perhaps, as an adult, you know that each frame of movie film has a picture that is slightly different from

▼ FIGURE 6.19
Two-dimensional
shapes

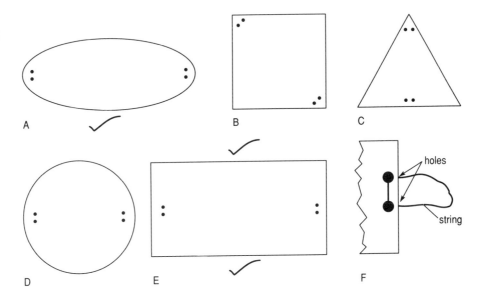

the one before. When these pictures are projected rapidly, the mind of the viewer perceives motion rather than a series of still photos or drawings. You can create your own motion picture with very little expense. All you need is a blank note pad or even an old book you don't mind marking up. In the series of "frames" shown in Figure 6.20, a worm is represented by shading in several small squares of a grid. In each successive frame, the worm moves one grid square farther along. If these frames were cut out and taped on the corner of the pages of a book, you could perceive motion by flipping through the pages.

▼ FIGURE 6.20
A worm moves

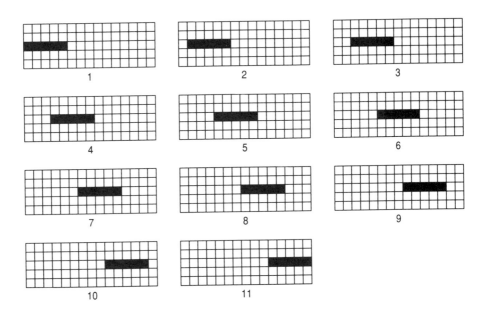

Because the drawing is so simple, you won't have to cut up this book to get the effect; you can just draw it. The grid is only for your reference, to get the idea of progressive position change even while you are not flipping. You can draw your worm in the corner of a book or on a note pad. Check that each page is right in relation to the preceding one by flipping that page back and forth. You will find that you can produce much more complex movies than the marching worm illustrated in Figure 6.20. Once you catch on, you will be able to make stick figures that do aerobics or faces that change their expressions.

EXTENSION OF ANIMATION ACTIVITY

The marching worm shown in Figure 6.20 can be produced on the computer using the programming language Logo. On the left, the lines of the program are given; on the right, each line is explained:

```
TO WORM                      (Title line of main procedure)
HIDETURTLE                   (Turtle may eat our worm!)
REPEAT 80 [INCH]             (Run subprocedure, INCH, 80 times)
END                          (End of main procedure)

TO INCH                      (Title line of INCH subprocedure)
FORWARD 5                    (Draw a line 5 units long.)
PENUP BACK 5                 (Pick up the pen and back up 5 units.)
PENERASE FORWARD 1           (Deploy eraser and move forward one unit.)
PENDOWN                      (Put the pen down.)
END                          (End of INCH subprocedure)
```

Enter the two procedures into your computer's memory. Then enter the name of the main procedure, WORM, and press Return. Although you have hidden the turtle, it is doing its job invisibly. It draws a line 5 units long, picks up its pen, and goes back to the beginning of the worm. Then it erases one unit. This completes one cycle of the INCH procedure. When it repeats, a new worm is drawn starting from the place it quit erasing, so the worm extends one unit further. In this way, each repeat causes the worm to progress one unit to the right and to be erased by one unit on the left, producing the perception of motion.

SUMMARY OF SPACE/TIME ACTIVITIES

Visualizing and thinking about movement through space and time are skills that need cultivation. Although some people seem to be born with special ability in these areas, everyone improves with practice. These activities have been presented to help you appreciate some aspects of space and time relationships that you may not have otherwise thought about.

Only a small sampling of space/time activities has been presented. Other topics appropriate to this process include shapes, symmetry, flips, slides and rotations, light and shadows, map skills, vectors, relative position and motion, speed, and acceleration.

COMMENT ON BASIC PROCESSES

It is useful to be able to talk about each of the basic processes in turn, and to plan and carry out activities to teach the meaning of each, as well as to do other science activities in which the processes are used as tools. In reality, however, it is difficult or impossible to completely distinguish among them. When you make a list of your observations, aren't you communicating? When you communicate the position of color rods to your partner, aren't you relating objects in space? When you tell what is alike about two observed objects, aren't you classifying? These comments are not meant to confuse you, but to put you at ease when concerns arise about telling processes apart. Ordinarily, there is no need to draw too fine a point on keeping processes completely separated in your mind.

USING PROCESS ACTIVITIES WITH CHILDREN

The activities in this chapter were designed to help you, as an adult, understand the meaning of each of the basic processes in a somewhat global way. Each process can be thought of as a tool. In that sense, the activities given were for you to learn about the tools. Generally, you will want your pupils to use the tools in a context rather than just learn about the tools. Because you are an adult, you can understand the processes at a fairly sophisticated level after experiencing the activities, reading the text, and discussing them in class. Children will usually need much more experience with each of the processes. Older children may be able to benefit from activities such as those described—if the activities are developed into carefully structured lessons. Learning the processes is developmental in nature, and thus children need many experiences with science processes over a long period of time. The experiences should extend over the entire range of the elementary years and beyond.

Did you notice that many of the science processes are used as means to determine a child's mental maturity? The abilities assessed by Piaget's tasks depend on science processes such as classification and measurement. Young children whose abilities in these areas are limited will naturally need a different kind of experience—with measuring, for example—than older children. Because of this, younger children can begin practicing the use of processes under careful guidance but should not be expected to appreciate the overall nature of a process in the way adults should and older children may. For example, young children should not be taught directly that the meaning of measurement is comparison and unit iteration. They can simply be given tasks in which they perform matching and unit iteration.

In this section, the activities presented in this chapter are analyzed regarding whether and how they can be used or adapted for teaching children.

OBSERVING

OBSERVING 1: UNKNOWN CANDY-LIKE OBJECT; OBSERVING 2: MODERATELY RAPID CHANGES

Both of these activities were designed to help you understand what observing is and what it is not. Upper-grade pupils (grades 5, 6, and perhaps 4) could use these activities. Younger children should simply do the observing in the context of studying mealworms, for example, or other objects to be observed. Lessons that emphasize using all of the senses are accessible to children of all ages, but the distinction between observations and inferences is better left until the upper grades.

OBSERVING 3: SLOW CHANGES

The idea for this activity was taken from the ESS unit *Changes* (ESS, 1968), which was designed for primary pupils. Although the activity is interesting to people of all ages, young children especially benefit from drawing pictures of their "change jars" every day and then looking back over them at a later time when a fair number of pages have accumulated. The drawings serve not only to telescope the time, but also to encourage the child to "go back" in time, or reverse his or her thinking, a developmental ability that is just becoming possible for the child during the primary grade years.

COMMUNICATING

COMMUNICATING 1: DESCRIBING COLOR ROD CONSTRUCTION

This activity is perfect for upper-grade children, though you may wish to try it with younger ones as well. The optional step of allowing the player to "peek" when he or she gets stuck makes this activity possible for younger children. You will have to decide at what level it is too hard. Teacher intervention in the form of focusing questions may be helpful with younger pupils. The step in which a discussion is held to establish better communication should be especially emphasized with children of any age.

USING GRAPHS

Young children can start with real graphs, or with arrangements of actual objects. For example, each child receives a random handful of colored blocks. A stack of each color is made, resembling a histogram. Questions for discussion would be: "Which color did you have most of? Least of? Did you have any colors with just the same number of blocks?" An amusing real-graph activity is type of shoe. Have everyone take off one shoe and place it in a pile in the middle of the room. Then have selected pupils arrange the shoes into histogramlike positions according to categories; for example, fasteners: buckles, strings, velcro, other, none. Discussion can center on popularity of types, functions, and so on. Pictographs, histograms, and other bar graphs are perfect for children of all ages, as soon as they understand the real graphs. Circle and line graphs can be introduced to upper grades. There are many graphing activities in most mathematics curricula, but graphing should be used in every possible subject, not limited to science or mathematics. In the upper grades when line graphing is introduced, a natural extension of the ideas involved is the coordinate system in Logo. Logo has a full four-quadrant coordinate system built in. Learning activities with Logo can be very useful in this connection.

CLASSIFYING

CLASSIFYING 1: ATTRIBUTE GAMES

There are attribute games appropriate for school children of any grade level. See references for ideas. The two-differences game may be too hard for most primary pupils, but if you think yours could manage it, do not hesitate to try.

CLASSIFYING 2: SINGLE-STAGE AND MULTISTAGE SYSTEMS

Laying out classification systems in this formal way should probably be left until fifth or sixth grade. Younger pupils should be encouraged to think about how objects or events can be grouped and regrouped according to common characteristics, however. "What's alike about these countries? What's different?" Any kind of groupings and sets should be thought about in this way, as such activity assists in the development of abstract thinking.

CLASSIFYING 3: USING COMPUTERS IN SORTING

By all means, involve all children who are able to read to the extent necessary and who show any interest at all, in using the "Animals" program and others of the type. Difficulties should be discussed in groups to help in clarifying any misunderstandings. The use of database management systems is appropriate for upper-grade children, but even younger ones can be helped to organize and interpret data in tabular form.

MEASURING

All three of the measuring activities could be used with upper-grade pupils with little or no modification. But you may be interested in some activities designed specifically for children of different ages. Measurement is one of the most sensitive areas of the curriculum to the mental development of children. For example, young children who do not conserve length will not be able to measure length in any way that involves understanding. The same is true with the other quantities that are measured—weight, area, volume, and so on. The development of a child's ability to understand these quantities takes years, however. Is the teacher to wait until everyone in the class can understand a quantity before introducing measurement activities? There is no simple answer to this dilemma. Most Piagetian scholars would agree, however, that children need to engage in activities that call their attention to these quantities, so they can begin thinking about them. Whether such activities accelerate acquisition of the concept of conservation is debatable, but they are felt to be important to keeping a child on his or her normal schedule for acquiring conservation.

An example of a primary (kindergarten, first grade) activity that helps a child think about length involves the use of color rods. The child is given a picture or pattern that was made by tracing around color rods. The rectangular outlines can be arranged into a monster, a flower in a pot, or any kind of picture. The child finds a rod to fit each rectangular outline and then uses crayons to color in the outline to match the color of the rod. This allows the teacher to check the work. Far from "busywork," this task requires the child to look at a rectangle, and then holding the size of it in mind, look at the pile of rods and search for one whose size matches that of the rectangle. Finally, the child has to move the rod to the paper and actually try the size for a match. All of these actions involve thinking about length. Consider the actual rod as it moves through space in the child's hand. Depending on the rod's orientation relative to the child's eyes, its length appears to change—shorter as it is viewed end-on and longer as viewed from the side. These perceptions, together with the task requiring conscious thought about length, are exactly the kind of experiences necessary for the child to construct a personal meaning to the idea of conservation of length.

After learning about the balance (see Chapter 5), pupils in second and third grade can use it to weigh objects of interest in science activities. A convenient nonstandard unit can be used, such as uniform blocks, tiles, washers, or paper clips. Cage animals could be weighed in this way every day to provide data for graphing growth patterns.

After suitable instruction in the meaning of measurement, in metric units and various measuring devices, children in fourth through sixth grade can use measuring as the tool it is, to collect more precise data, and to use the data in more interesting ways. To stop after just learning to measure is as undesirable as stopping with the construction of graphs before getting to the interpretation. Teach pupils to measure, and then find ways for them to apply what they have learned, through using measurement as a tool.

RELATING OBJECTS IN SPACE AND TIME

SPACE/TIME ACTIVITY 1: DRAWING THREE-DIMENSIONAL SHAPES

Upper-grade pupils can draw three-dimensional shapes easily. An extension would be to make wire outlines of two-dimensional and three-dimensional shapes and use them to cast shadows. Pupils could trace over the shadows cast onto the chalkboard. A motivational variation is to have one set of pupils draw shadow outlines, and another set of pupils try to find the model used to cast the shadow and the orientation necessary.

SPACE/TIME ACTIVITY 2: MAKING 3-D SHAPES BY SPINNING 2-D SHAPES;
SPACE/TIME ACTIVITY 3: ANIMATION

Both of these activities can be done with all but the very youngest pupils. A set of solid geometric shape models is useful to have handy in the case of Activity 2. One child could spin a two-dimensional form and a partner could try to pick out the three-dimensional model that is like the generated shape.

COMPUTERS

We begin with the assumption that the reader of this book has had or will soon have some understanding of the rudiments of computer use. Some of the ways that computers may be used to provide practice in basic processes or as a means of enhancing direct instruction lessons are:

1. *Instructional Software.* If appropriate games or other instructional activities are available, they can be used as an extension of independent practice for lessons on the topics involved. The BASIC program in public domain, "Animals," was described as an example of this kind of software.
2. *Computer Tools.* Word processors, database management, and spreadsheets can be used to support instruction. Use of database management systems for sorting by attributes has been mentioned in the section on classifying.
3. *Programming.* Programming in Logo or BASIC can be used to support direct-instruction topics in the following ways.
   a. Teaching children to program is wonderful but does not support the usual sense of goals of direct instruction. This area of educational computing will be described in later chapters because it is more appropriate to higher levels of pupil autonomy.
   b. Using simple programs written or copied by the teacher can be useful.

   This is the application utilized by the various Logo tools presented in this chapter. A teacher does not have to be an expert programmer to use simple tools of this type, and the pupils need only the most rudimentary skills of computer literacy to interact with the tools.

▼ SUMMARY

An important part of teaching science to children is being able to use science processes yourself and to teach children how to use them. As they develop ease and skill in the use of these processes they will begin to use them as tools for further learning. The processes that you have practiced in this chapter are observing, communicating, classifying, measuring, and relating objects in space and time. The activities were designed to help you learn what the processes are and how to use them. You have also been given some ideas about adapting these activities for use with children.

These processes will form a permanent part of your repertoire of teaching skills. As you begin to plan science lessons, you may want to return to this chapter to keep these five basic processes in mind and use one or more of them in all of your lesson planning.

▼ DISCUSSION QUESTIONS

1. Describe three situations in which hands-on activities could be a part of direct instruction.
2. Identify the following variables as continuous or discontinuous. Could any of them be categorized both ways? Under what circumstances?
   a. Drop height
   b. Wavelength of visible light
   c. Grade points
   d. Grade point average
   e. Total credit units (e.g., semester hours)
   f. College student classification (freshman, etc.)
   g. Population
3. The graph in Figure 6.21 has several problems. How many graphing convention errors can you find?
4. Why do you multiply fractions by 360 in making circle graphs?
5. Here is the beginning of a one-difference train using the 32-piece set of attribute pieces described earlier in the chapter. List all the possible remaining pieces that could replace the question mark:

   LBS LBC SBC SGC LGC ?

▼ FIGURE 6.21
A graph with problems

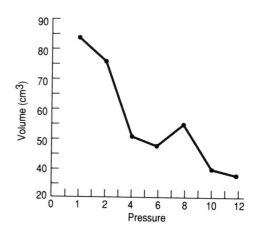

6. Estimate the length of your desk or table in decimeters. Then measure using the comparison strip you used in Measuring Activity 1. How well did you do? In class, make a list of everyone's decimeter estimate for the width of the classroom. Then use the estimate to construct a histogram. What was the most frequent estimate? How does it compare with the actual measurement? Are most people coming close?

7. Which of the following lesson objectives would be appropriate to present by modified (inductive) direct instruction? Why do you think so?
   a. A graph should be scaled to include all points of interest.
   b. A bird is an animal having certain characteristics such as feathers, warm-bloodedness, and egg-laying.
   c. All materials must be cleaned up and put away before we line up to go home.
   d. Any set of objects can be classified in more than one way.

8. During which lesson element should hands-on experience be used? Why not use it in other lesson elements?

9. React to this teacher's statement: "It is important for children to learn to listen; rather than worry about always keeping my telling and explaining short, I intend to teach my pupils to be better listeners."

10. What are some things that could go wrong when the teacher has not planned well enough in regard to using concrete materials? Perhaps you have a personal "horror story" to share with your classmates.

▼ REFERENCES

Cunningham, J. (1976). *Teaching metrics simplified*. Englewood Cliffs, NJ: Prentice Hall.

Elementary Science Study (ESS). (1968). *Changes*. New York: Webster Division, McGraw-Hill.

Elementary Science Study (ESS). (1985). *Match and measure*. Nashua, NH: Delta.

Elementary Science Study (ESS). (1984). *Attribute games and problems*. Nashua, NH: Delta.

Fuys, D., & Tischler, R. (1979). *Teaching mathematics in the elementary school*. Boston: Little, Brown.

Good, T., & Brophy, J. (1987). *Looking in classrooms* (4th ed.). New York: Harper & Row.

Joyce, B., & Weil, M. (1986). *Models of teaching* (3rd ed.). Englewood Cliffs, NJ: Prentice Hall.

National Council of Teachers of Mathematics. *Measurement in school mathematics*. (1976). NCTM Yearbook. (D. Nelson & R. Reys, Eds.) Reston, VA: National Council of Teachers of Mathematics.

GUIDED DISCOVERY

CHAPTER OUTLINE

▼
_____

Guided discovery is an instructional method that allows and requires more pupil autonomy than direct instruction. This method is the one most often recommended by science educators, but it has proved to be difficult to implement as a regular method of instruction for many teachers and in many schools. The explanations and descriptions in this and the following chapters are designed to lead you step by step through the process of planning, conducting, and evaluating guided-discovery lessons and to help you sidestep some of the pitfalls that unsuspecting teachers have fallen into.

WHY DISCOVERY?

You have already learned about an initial teaching method called direct instruction. The method introduced in this chapter, guided discovery, can be described as an indirect method. Indirect teaching methods are harder for teachers to learn and take more time and energy to use in the classroom than does direct instruction. But there are special reasons for choosing such a method that more than compensate for the difficulties. Jerome Bruner, in his article "The Act of Discovery" (1961), describes how practicing at discovering results in several positive effects. In addition to learning facts and generalizations in an interesting context, children learn a great deal about problem solving itself:

> I would urge now . . . that emphasis upon discovery in learning has precisely the effect upon the learner of leading him to be a constructionist, to organize what he is encountering in a manner not only designed to discover regularity and relatedness, but also to avoid the kind of information drift that fails to keep account of uses to which information might have to be put. . . . Practice in discovering for oneself teaches one to acquire information in a way that makes that information more readily viable in problem-solving. (p. 27)

In elementary school, when science is taught at all, it all too often is taught with reading as the main source of knowledge. The cognitive result is what Papert (1980) calls *dissociated* learning—isolated facts having little or no connection to the learner's life. In the affective domain, this results in attitudes toward science that range from neutral to negative. There is an undercurrent of feeling in American society that learning and fun are incompatible—that learning is drudge work and that the only fun is getting out of learning. One reason for this feeling is that much of the school curriculum is inappropriate for children or is presented in an inappropriate way. In fact, children love learning when it is meaningful. Play is not just a "childish" pastime but the way children learn their world. Hands-on science capitalizes on the child's natural curiosity about interesting objects. It results in a type of knowing, physical knowledge, that is not just disembodied words from a book but a fully integrated part of the learner. The difference between knowledge derived from action on objects and knowledge derived from a book is the difference between knowing something as opposed to knowing about something.

Guided discovery is more than just hands-on experiences, however. Another essential step is thinking about the experience. Through guided discussion and other methods, the child is led into reflecting on the activity by comparing, looking for patterns, predicting, and making trial explanations. The physical knowledge acquired from objects becomes the building blocks with which the child constructs personal logical knowledge. Both of these aspects of guided discovery are taught indirectly, in that learners are not told the expected outcome of a lesson at the beginning.

WHY GUIDED?

Many attempts at teaching discovery science have failed because there was not enough teacher guidance. In reaction to the excesses of traditional direct instruction, reformers have sometimes overcompensated in the direction of "anything goes." Guided discovery is an attempt to avoid both extremes. By indirect guidance, the teacher increases the likelihood of outcomes that are both worthwhile and interesting. Guidance is accomplished through the initial selection of materials, the type of data children are asked to collect, and, most especially, through skillful use of discussion techniques.

Another aspect of guidance that is also essential to the success of guided-discovery teaching involves helping children become more responsible for their behavior and their own learning. Children who are accustomed to direct instruction as the main or only classroom method will not automatically function well at this higher level of autonomy; they must be taught how. Ironically, the most effective instructional method for teaching children to behave more responsibly is direct instruction. Behavior standards provide the child a means to decide for him- or herself whether a behavior is acceptable. Although not mature enough to judge without a standard, having a standard allows each child to practice regulating his or her own behavior.

Teaching new behavior standards can be done in a direct-instruction format. Once the standards are learned, the child practices applying them to his or her behavior in the limited freedom of the guided-discovery lesson. How to do these things will be explained later in this chapter.

KINDS OF KNOWLEDGE AND METHODS OF TEACHING

The rationale for using discovery learning is based in part on the work of both Bruner and Papert. A third theoretical underpinning for the method not only justifies the use of discovery methods in certain circumstances, but also allows teachers to make rational choices between teaching methods according to the type of knowledge to be learned.

In Chapter 1 you learned about four kinds of knowledge, based on Piaget's ideas as elaborated by Kamii & DeVries (1977, 1978). Consider the four kinds of knowledge again and compare their characteristics.

Social-arbitrary knowledge includes the learning of rules, stepwise procedures, customs and conventions, names, other symbols, and the mechanical aspects of language use. It is normally derived through language, either spoken or written. These are things that require no great depth of understanding and that can be memorized. Direct instruction may be the most appropriate method for teaching this kind of knowledge. Examples of social-arbitrary knowledge include:

Names of parts of the balance.

How to assemble a balance.

How to apply the long division algorithm.

How to construct and interpret a graph.

How to use a measuring device.

Words and music of a new song.

Basic math facts.

Mechanical aspects of language such as decoding, spelling, and grammar.

Procedural parts of lessons.

Physical knowledge is derived from direct experience with concrete objects. It consists of characteristics or properties of particular objects and events, or, in other words, information derived from observing things with the senses. The best way to teach physical knowledge is to arrange such experiences for pupils, in what is usually called "hands-on" activities. Examples of physical knowledge include:

The feel and sound of a mystery box.

That particular objects sink or float in water.

That some arrangements of battery, bulb, and wire cause the bulb to light, that some cause the wire to get hot, and that some do neither.

That baking soda fizzes when mixed with vinegar.

That hexagons (but not pentagons) fit together to tessellate (tile) a surface.

That ripe bananas are yellow and have a certain odor.

Logical knowledge includes concepts, generalizations, conclusions, and other higher-order ideas derived from thinking about observations. It is knowledge that must be constructed (put together, thought up) by each knower. Logical knowledge has to be figured out; it cannot be memorized. Although the words used to describe these concepts can be memorized, such learning is superficial and disconnected from operational meaning in the memorizer's thinking. Cognitive development limits the kinds of logical knowledge that can be learned. In general, preoperational learners are quite limited in their ability to acquire logical knowledge (the word *preoperational* is a synonym for *prelogical*). Concrete-operational learners can learn considerable logical knowledge through skillfully guided discussion about firsthand experiences provided by the teacher. Formal-operational learners can grasp logical knowledge through language alone—without the immediate hands-on experiences—if their past experiences have come close enough to permit them to think about the idea in question. Even formal thinkers, however, learn logical knowledge much more easily if pertinent experiences are provided. The best teaching method is high-involvement discussion leading to critical thinking and reflection about physical knowledge that has previously been established. Such discussion may happen in small groups of peers, or in a whole class with teacher guidance, or both. Although logical knowledge can be constructed in solitude, most people do it better with help. Examples of logical knowledge include:

The electrical circuit.

That drop height and bounce height of a ball have a straight-line relationship.

The laws of buoyancy.

How aircraft keep from falling.

The concept of center of gravity.

That five things are still five regardless of arrangement.

Social-interactive knowledge includes getting along with others and being capable of productive and pleasant group work. It is more complex than simply suppressing individual egos for the benefit of the group; also involved is learning to disagree amicably. This kind of knowledge is learned only through interaction with others, especially peers. It is closely related to social-arbitrary knowledge but has more to do with group ethics, whereas social-arbitrary knowledge has more to do with verbal information. Social-interactive knowledge must be taught by group experience and guided discussion about the group experience. Examples of social-interactive knowledge include:

Take turns.

Share.

Consider other's feelings.

Two heads are better than one.

"I see your point, but I have a different one."

"That's one way to think about it; another way is. . . ."

Notice that it is not the content of the knowledge that determines its type, but the way in which it was learned. It is possible for two people to "know" the same content in different ways. One person can know it by having figured it out (logical knowledge) while another person knows it only as a rote formulation (social-arbitrary knowledge).

AN EXAMPLE SCIENCE ACTIVITY

A single science activity or lesson may involve more than one type of knowledge among its objectives. All four kinds can be identified in the following activity, which was introduced in Chapter 5.

Working in small groups, children release balls from a given height and observe how they bounce. They record the data—drop heights and corresponding bounce heights—on data sheets. After the teacher shows them how to plot the data in graph form, the groups construct their own graphs of their data. Finally, the whole class discusses the graphs. Through careful questions, the teacher guides the class in thinking about the relationship of bounce height to drop height. Then they use the graphs to predict the bounce heights for certain drop heights they had not experienced earlier, and finally, verified their predictions through a teacher demonstration.

In this lesson, the actual bouncing of the balls and measuring both drop and bounce height are examples of learning physical knowledge. The direct experience gained provided a way of knowing about balls and bouncing that no amount of reading or listening could give. When the teacher showed the children how to make a graph, the teacher was transmitting social-arbitrary knowledge. Showing and telling directly is a good way to teach this kind of knowledge. The guided discussion led the children to reflect on their observations and on how the graph suggested a certain kind of relationship; this is the way logical knowledge is constructed internally by each learner. Finally, the group work was designed in a way to maximize an increase in social-interactive knowledge.

SUMMARY OF KINDS OF KNOWLEDGE

Can it be found out by observing? (Physical knowledge)

Can it be figured out by thinking about physical knowledge? (Logical knowledge)

Can it be memorized without understanding? (Social-arbitrary knowledge)

Does it involve getting along in work groups? (Social-interactive knowledge)

Consider the bouncing ball lesson again. How would the kinds of knowledge acquired be affected if the lesson had been presented differently? Suppose the teacher had just presented a table of data without having the pupils collect their own data from direct experience. The teacher would be substituting social-arbitrary knowledge (data as a list of numbers collected by others) for physical knowledge (data the pupils collected themselves). Some children may possibly have had the right kind of previous experience with bouncing balls to make the rest of the lesson meaningful for them. Notice the words *possibly*, *some*, and *right kind*. For those children not having the right kind of previous experience, the rest of the lesson would have been meaningless. In addition to taking a chance that many pupils would be unable to understand, the teacher who skips the hands-on part of the lesson also omits a source of great motivation and attitude building.

Consider also what differences would occur in a lesson in which the teacher presents the conclusions directly, rather than indirectly guiding pupils to draw their own conclusions. The teacher would be substituting social-arbitrary knowledge (other people's conclusions) for logical knowledge (conclusions drawn by the pupils). In a well-guided, indirect discussion, the pupils get a chance to think through the steps of logic involved at their own pace and to draw their own conclusions in their own roundabout way. All this is necessary for building true understanding. When a teacher presents conclusions directly, the teacher prevents the pupils from building their own. The type of knowledge that results is social-arbitrary rather than logical. Because traditional education has not distinguished between the kinds of knowledge, teachers tend to teach everything as if it were social-arbitrary knowledge (Kamii &

DeVries 1977, p. 384). Many of us have had the experience—in high school, college, or later—of finally understanding something that we learned as social-arbitrary knowledge during childhood—so *that's* what Miss Thompson was talking about! How much better our attitude toward school and learning would have been if Miss Thompson had helped us to understand or construct personal meaning, in the first place.

Now consider a guided-discovery lesson in which children are introduced to mealworms. A formal lesson plan (Lesson Plan 7.1) for this lesson will be presented later in the chapter.

Ms. Oldhand's Mealworm Lesson

▼ "Today we will begin a new science unit," Ms. Oldhand told her pupils, "but first we must discuss behavior standards for science." Ms. O. brought out a chart on which was written:

Science Activity Standards

1. You may talk quietly.

2. Stay in your seats.

3. Raise your hand if you need help.

4. Stop, look, and listen at the signal.

Ms. O. explained the standards to her third graders and checked to make sure that each pupil understood. For standard 4, she said that when she needed to speak to them, she would sound the chime. This signal was already known by the class and had been used in similar circumstances. "Working directly with the materials is a privilege for those who are grown up enough to remember the standards," she said. "If you forget, I will have to take away your materials until you are ready to be more responsible."

Ms. O. took a mealworm from the container on her desk. "Look at what I have in my hand. It isn't harmful in any way, but it is a living creature with feelings, so we must be careful not to hurt it. It is called a mealworm, and each of you will have one to observe. See what you can notice. After a while, I will give the signal and then we'll discuss what everyone noticed about their mealworms."

She passed among the children, placing a paper cup containing a mealworm on each pupil's desk. There was a great deal of interest, but some of the children seemed reluctant to touch their specimens. Ms. O. did not insist that they do so, and after a few minutes of poking their worms with pencils, the reluctant children gradually became confident enough to touch and handle them directly. Ms. O. walked among the pupils, sharing their excitement and listening to their comments.

The room was arranged in groups of four double desks, with eight pupils to a "table." After about 15 minutes, she sounded the chime. Most of the class remembered to look up from their mealworms to see what Ms. O. had to say. The others did so as soon as they heard her begin to speak. "Thank you for remembering the special science standards so well! Please take a minute to place all your mealworms in the paper cup and then put the cup back in the center of your table." Ms. O. then asked the table monitors to collect the cups and place them on her desk.

▼ As their confidence increases, children begin to handle the mealworms directly.

"What were some things you noticed?" Ms. O. called on several pupils to share their observations. "Did anyone notice how many legs there were?" Some thought there were one number, some another. "Well! Do you suppose all mealworms have the same number of legs, or that maybe some are different? Let's think about how we could find out. Did anyone notice other things?" Discussion along this vein revealed that most of the children did not notice fine details, but were more interested in how the mealworms moved and how they reacted to pokes and other stimuli. "What are some things you'd like to investigate with your mealworms next time?" Ms. O. asked. Several ideas were offered, and Ms. O. listed them on chart paper. "Fine," she said. "Let's be thinking about how we might find out some of these things. Tomorrow we will decide what to do next."

Ms. Oldhand:	I wanted you to know that I included the strict behavior standards for your benefit. When I am just teaching my pupils without you here, I can be a bit more relaxed. I even let them move around the room. Student teachers usually need more structure, though.
Mr. Newman:	Thanks. I appreciate seeing how you did it. I feel really insecure trying to think about how to present this method and how to prevent behavior problems at the same time.
Ms. Oldhand:	[*smiling*] You will soon internalize how to keep order and forget that you ever needed this technique.
Mr. Newman:	When I looked at what was happening as a pupil, it was fun, but when I think about teaching it, I get nervous because I don't understand how it works. Like the questions about the number of legs. If it's important for them to know, why didn't you just tell them, or settle it in some way? It seemed like a lot of questions came up that didn't get settled.
Ms. Oldhand:	The main goal of this lesson was just to get started—to get the "new" off of the mealworms. In particular, I wanted everyone to get comfortable with handling the mealworms. Now they all know that the worms don't bite, and that they don't move suddenly. In fact, mealworms don't do much of anything that is very startling. Now that they know that from their own experience, they will be able to turn their attention to more specific observations and tasks. Later in the unit, we will decide together how to answer some of the questions. What they find out by observing, like the number of legs, is less important than the act of finding out for themselves.
Mr. Newman:	I'm not sure I know how to decide what's more and less important.
Ms. Oldhand:	This lesson was more process than content. I wanted them to work on the process skills—observing and communicating.
Mr. Newman:	I remember hearing something about processes, but I'm pretty rusty on them.
Ms. Oldhand:	[*reaching for a book on her desk*] Why don't you skim through this chapter on processes tonight and we can talk more about them tomorrow.

PLANNING AND PRESENTING
A GUIDED-DISCOVERY LESSON

Guided-discovery lessons, like Direct-instruction lessons, can be structured into lesson plan parts, each with its specific function. Some of the parts are the same in both methods, but some are new, reflecting the special characteristics of discovery. Content appropriate for direct instruction can easily be presented by direct means, such as telling and showing. Content that is more appropriate for a discovery method often involves more mental construction by the learner. The skill of making careful and critical observations and accurate representation of observations cannot be transmitted through telling or showing. Although the objective of learning the parts of a mealworm could quite easily be presented by direct instruction, that objective is not very important in itself. There is, furthermore, a special motivational aspect in finding out something for oneself. That motivation is an important rationale for using a discovery approach. The most important reasons for doing a discovery lesson of the type described here lie more in the cognitive-process, affective, and social domains than in the cognitive-content domain.

COMPARISON OF LESSON PLAN PARTS

In Chapter 5 you learned to structure a lesson for direct instruction. Several specific learning activities were prescribed: motivation, presentation, guided practice, and independent practice. Guided discovery lessons also need to be structured, but there are more options to choose from, based on the particular goals of the lesson. Consider a generic lesson-plan format:

All-Purpose Lesson Plan Format

1. Performance objective
2. Materials
3. Learning Activities
4. Appraisal

Every lesson plan needs objectives, materials, and an appraisal. Every lesson plan also needs learning activities, but their type and sequence depend on the method to be used and the nature of the lesson goals. Now examine the differences in the type and sequence of learning activities in direct instruction and guided discovery:

Direct Instruction

1. Performance objective
2. Materials
3. Learning Activities
   a. Motivation
   b. Presentation
   c. Guided Practice
   d. Independent Practice
   e. Closure
4. Appraisal

Guided Discovery

1. Performance objective
2. Materials
3. Learning Activities
   a. Motivation
   b. Data Collection
   c. Data Processing
   d. Closure
4. Appraisal

DESCRIPTION OF GUIDED-DISCOVERY LESSON PLAN

Notice that everything in the two outlines is the same except for the central section of the learning activities. The new parts that make guided discovery possible are described in this section.

DATA COLLECTION

Data collection simply means gathering information about a situation. The information may be recorded as a list of words describing an object or event or as numbers representing measurements. Data may be recorded in many different ways, not only as words or numbers. Data can be collected as sound recordings, as pictures, as impressions in stone, or in countless other ways. In any case, data collecting involves making and (usually) recording observations. *Data* (singular, *datum*) are records of observations, that is, information from the senses: sounds, feels, tastes, smells, and sights. In some situations, especially with younger children, data may not be physically recorded but simply reported during discussion. Guesses, predictions, specula-

▼ Ms. Oldhand explains to Mr. Newman how to write a lesson plan.

tions, inferences, conclusions, and other mental constructions go beyond observation and are, therefore, not examples of data.

DATA PROCESSING

Most desirable learning outcomes do not result from just hands-on activities alone. Now that the data have been collected (that is, the observations have been made), what happens to the data? Teachers must guide the children in using this information to arrive at inferences, speculations, generalizations, and other higher-level thinking. Guided discovery needs to stimulate thinking that goes beyond simple observation. Once the observations are made and recorded, the pupils need guidance in thinking about those observations. Usually this is done through guided discussion. With younger children, the discussion may be limited mostly to describing and comparing the objects that were observed. Older children can begin to do more powerful thinking. Leading a discussion indirectly to help children think about observations and connect these observations logically with prior knowledge is a higher-level skill itself. The idea, after all, is for the children to reflect on their recent experience—not to "read" the teacher's face. Discussion techniques will be introduced in this chapter and presented in more depth in Chapter 9.

Another way to think about this part of the lesson is in terms of the type of knowledge it is designed for. Whereas data collecting involves acquiring physical knowledge, data processing should lead toward the construction of logical knowledge.

▼ *Mr. Newman*: Thanks for lending me this book. Reading about the science processes helped. I still don't understand exactly how to use them in lessons, though.

Ms. Oldhand: That's OK. I'll help you see them in action. Thinking about processes helps me remember that science is something for children to do. Otherwise, I might just tell them things—like the mealworm has six true legs. Sometimes the particular information they discover is less important than the fact that they are learning to observe, communicate, and so on.

Mr. Newman: I want to get involved in doing guided discovery, but it's still sort of vague to me.

Ms. Oldhand: I wrote out a plan for the lesson you watched yesterday. Also, here is the beginning of my plan for the second lesson. I have the topic and a set of objectives. Why don't you try writing the rest of the plan? You better take a couple of mealworms and a magnifier with you tonight, too.

Mr. Newman: Really?

Ms. Oldhand: You have about a two-hundred percent better chance of planning a successful lesson if you have thoroughly experienced what you want the pupils to do and have tried out everything with the specific materials you plan to use.

Ms. O.'s plan for the first lesson of the mealworm unit follows.

▾ LESSON PLAN 7.1

GRADE LEVEL: 3

TOPIC: Getting to Know Your Mealworm (Lesson 1 of unit)

PERFORMANCE OBJECTIVES

By the end of these activities, the learner should be able to:

1. Demonstrate confidence in handling a mealworm.
2. Describe the general appearance and behavior of a mealworm.

MATERIALS

For each pupil:

- 1 mealworm in a paper cup

LEARNING ACTIVITIES

MOTIVATION

"Look at what I have in my hand."

NEW STANDARDS

A mini-lesson.

DATA COLLECTION

1. Give directions for data collection: "See what you can notice."
2. Allow 15 minutes.
3. Collect materials.

DATA PROCESSING

Ask:

"What did you notice about your mealworm?"

"Did anyone notice something different?"

"What else would you like to find out about your mealworm?"

Write several of the ideas on chart paper.

CLOSURE

"Tomorrow we will take a closer look at our mealworms."

APPRAISAL

Informal observation

THINKING ABOUT WHAT COMES NEXT

The topic of instructional units has not yet been introduced here, but the idea should not be totally unfamiliar. Ms. Oldhand plans to present a series of lessons, all on the topic of mealworms. She wants the lessons to relate to one another in a logical way, with the skills and concepts developed in the earlier lessons to be used and further developed in the later lessons. To begin thinking about lesson sequence and learning activities to provide instruction for given objectives, you are invited to try your hand at the following task.

Here is the beginning of Ms. O.'s plan for the second lesson of the unit. How would you complete it?

Topic: A closer look at mealworms
(Lesson 2 of unit)

Performance Objectives

By the end of these activities, the learner should be able to:

1. Use a magnifier to examine details of mealworm anatomy.

2. Describe specific details of mealworm anatomy, such as number of legs, number of segments and appearance of mouth parts.

3. Describe or enact the way a mealworm walks.

4. Construct an enlarged drawing of a mealworm.

5. Compare his/her own drawing with an enlarged photograph of a mealworm and explain how to resolve disagreements between the two (by rechecking the real mealworm).

MODIFYING THE FORMAT

Because guided discovery is so much more complex to plan and teach than direct instruction, it may be desirable at times to take certain liberties with the suggested format. Even then, there are points that should always be considered. What are the essential features of planning a guided-discovery lesson? Consider these thoughts on the parts of a guided-discovery lesson plan:

▼

PERFORMANCE OBJECTIVE(S)

You will always need a statement of objectives; this is the heart of any lesson plan.

MATERIALS

Always include a materials list. It may be simplified in a unit if a set of materials is used repeatedly. In that case, the objects can be listed once and referred to afterwards by name, such as "Pupil Kit."

LEARNING ACTIVITIES

MOTIVATION

Always consider whether "special" motivation is needed. Sometimes the materials themselves are sufficient motivation.

DATA COLLECTION

Always include, except in a situation where you are sure that all the pupils have had previous firsthand experience with the particular objects and type of observations involved. An obvious example is when more than one data-processing session is used to stimulate thinking about a set of observations collected earlier. The time between data collection and data processing should be short, especially for younger pupils.

DATA PROCESSING

Always include this essential part of a discovery lesson. There may be times when it is necessary to hold a discussion on a different day from the day the observations were made. In that case, the lesson is considered to extend over that period of time. Ideally, data processing takes place immediately after data collection, while the details of the hands-on experience are still fresh in the pupils' memory.

CLOSURE

Always decide how the lesson is to end. Sometimes it will be appropriate to ask pupils to summarize their conclusions. Other times, you may choose to leave the ideas open so pupils will continue to think about them after the lesson. In that case, you may want to close with a question.

APPRAISAL

Always include a statement of how you will judge whether the lesson objectives have been met. Although this may sometimes be through informal observation, you should always decide and state your decision.

Perhaps you are thinking that there is not much difference between the essential aspects of the modified format and the original description of lesson plan parts. That is true because most of the flexibility comes in adding to the standard format rather than in subtracting from it. Think about giving directions, for example. Because directions for a procedure can be classified as social-arbitrary knowledge, it is appropriate to use direct instruction for giving directions. If the directions are fairly simple and the children are fairly mature, you can usually manage with just telling. The less mature the children and the more complex the procedure you are teaching, the more your directions will begin to resemble a direct instruction mini-lesson within the main guided discovery lesson. When simply telling is not sufficient, you will need to incorporate additional parts of the direct-instruction model. You could easily have guided practice by having pupils recite back to you the steps of the procedure. You might also ask questions to assure that complex directions have been understood. The independent practice will be taking place simultaneously with the data-collection part of the main guided-discovery lesson. In carrying out the procedure, pupils are practicing the directions you gave as well as collecting their data.

In summary, two types of justifiable lesson-plan format modification have been described. One type involves modification to the data-collecting part. Data collected previously by the pupils or, in rare situations, data collected by others may be substituted for immediate hands-on activities. Data processing may be done on a different day from that when the data was collected, but this is not really a format modification since the lesson is considered to extend over more than one day. A second justifiable format change is the addition of direct instruction elements for teaching procedures (giving directions) and for teaching or reviewing behavior standards.

▼ THE SECOND MEALWORM LESSON

Ms. Oldhand picked up a magnifier and a mealworm from her desk. "Today we will be looking at our mealworms with magnifiers." She held the mealworm in the palm of one hand and used the magnifier to peer at it. The pupils watched with interest.

Ms. O. congratulated the pupils on what good scientists they had been. She thanked them for making science period pleasant by remembering the special behavior standards. She then reviewed the standards with the class and asked them if they remembered what would happen if they forgot to stay seated. "You have to lose your mealworm for a while," replied one child. "And what happens if you forget to keep your talking quiet?" she asked. In this way, she went through all the special standards with the children so they would have a better chance of remembering. Then she went on to give directions for the day's activity.

"The next thing we will do with our mealworms is something very interesting. Yesterday you noticed certain things about your mealworms. Today, using magnifiers will help you notice new things. In a few minutes I will also give you some drawing materials so you can record your observations by making a picture of your mealworm. Make your drawing big enough to cover most of the page. Your picture should be much bigger than the actual mealworm. Notice every detail you can and show it in your picture. How many legs? How many segments? How does the mouth look? Look very carefully at your mealworm and then draw what you notice. Then look again and draw what you notice. Keep looking back at your real mealworm and then using what you see to make your picture more realistic. Compare your picture with your partner's picture. If they are different, look back at your mealworm to see if that will help.

"Now, before we begin, who can remember today's procedure?" Ms. O. made sure that they remembered to make their drawings large, and that they would include details in their pictures.

Before the lesson began, Ms. O. had assigned one monitor from each table to pick up materials. "Would the materials monitors please come get the things for your tables?" She gave each of the monitors a box-lid tray with mealworms in cups and plastic magnifiers, which they then distributed.

The children went right to work, looking at the mealworms with their magnifiers. Ms. O. then passed out the drawing paper and crayons without interrupting

▼ Drawing the specimen larger than life is a step toward careful observation, even when some details are fanciful.

or interfering. As they worked, she walked around and answered questions that some children had.

After about 15 minutes, she rang the chime for attention and asked the monitors to pick up the mealworms, magnifiers, and crayons. There were a few groans from the pupils as the mealworms departed.

"What new details did you notice today?" The discussion first involved comparing observations. "How many legs?" "How many segments?" "Shall we count the head as a segment or not? Let's decide and then all use the same rule." Next, she asked about how the legs moved. This proved hard to describe, so she asked for three volunteers to come forward to act as the three pairs of legs on a mealworm. Several groups of three demonstrated their versions of the gait of their specimens. Afterwards, they debated which rendition was the most realistic. Finally, Ms. O. revealed a large photographic enlargement of a mealworm. She asked them to compare the photo with their own drawings and to notice any differences. Discrepancies the pupils pointed out were listed by Ms. O. on a large chart paper. "Fine," she concluded, "We will use this list next time as a guide to find out more. How do you think we will do it?" A look at the real mealworms would help decide. "Thank you for being such good scientists today. Please pass your drawings up and let's get ready for lunch."

Ms. Oldhand's plan for the second lesson follows. Compare it with the plan you developed for Reader Activity 1. Also, do you notice any modifications in format?

▼ LESSON PLAN 7.2

GRADE LEVEL: 3

TOPIC: A Closer Look at Mealworms (Lesson 2 of unit)

PERFORMANCE OBJECTIVES

By the end of these activities, the learner should be able to:

1. Demonstrate use of a magnifier to examine details of mealworm anatomy.
2. Describe specific details of mealworm anatomy, such as number of legs, number of segments, appearance of mouth parts.
3. Describe or enact the way a mealworm walks.
4. Construct an enlarged drawing of a mealworm.
5. Compare his or her own drawing with an enlarged photograph of a mealworm and explain how to resolve disagreements between the two (by rechecking the real mealworm).

MATERIALS

For each pupil:

- 1 mealworm in a paper cup
- 1 magnifier
- 1 sheet drawing paper

For each 4 pupils:

- 1 set of crayons

For the teacher:

- Enlarged photo of a mealworm

LEARNING ACTIVITIES

MOTIVATION

"Today we will be observing our mealworms with magnifiers."

REVIEW STANDARDS

A mini-lesson.

DATA COLLECTION

1. Give directions for data collection: "See what new details you can notice."
2. Distribution of mealworms and magnifiers by monitors.
3. Allow 15 minutes.
4. Monitors collect mealworms, magnifiers, and crayons.

DATA PROCESSING

1. (Description of findings) Ask: "What new details did you notice?" "How many legs?" "How many segments?"
2. Ask volunteers to act out how a mealworm walks. Discuss.
3. Comparing drawings with photo, ask pupils to notice discrepancies between their drawings and the photo. List on chart paper to refer to at next lesson.

CLOSURE

"We will use this list next time as a guide to find out more. How do you think we will do it?" Look at our real mealworms to decide.

APPRAISAL

Informal observation

WORKING TOWARDS GREATER AUTONOMY

In both of these lessons, the pupils were given only limited freedom, and that within specific bounds. They were not permitted to move freely about the room, and the activities were relatively simple without a great many choices for them to make. Ms. Oldhand was demonstrating for Mr. Newman how to begin a unit with third-grade children whose experience with guided discovery is limited. In order to demonstrate techniques that could be used by a less-experienced teacher such as

Mr. Newman, Ms. O. was more conservative in allowing pupils freedom than she might have been otherwise. Nevertheless, Ms. O. was using several techniques intended to help the children increase their learning independence. They were allowed to talk quietly as long as they kept the volume down. In this way, they were practicing being responsible by exercising judgment. The distribution and pick-up of materials used in this case was easy and quick. Monitor duty will rotate each week so that everyone gets a chance to practice this kind of responsibility. In cases where more or messier materials are involved, every child would participate more actively in clean-up.

CAUTION POINTS

When a relatively inexperienced teacher does a guided-discovery lesson, there are several areas of potential difficulty that can usually be avoided with a bit of foresight.

Keep directions short and clear. Motivation is lost and management becomes a problem if directions are too long. On the other hand, children get lost and into trouble if they do not know what they are supposed to be doing. Review the section on giving directions in Chapter 3.

Minimize interruptions during data collection. It is very hard to get children's attention to give more directions after they are engaged in hands-on activity. Try to give all the directions at one time so that further announcements to the whole class are unnecessary until you are ready to conclude the data-collection activity. Try to remember not to interrupt children to give directions or ask questions unless they need help. Sometimes teachers grow used to being the center of attention and feel somehow uncomfortable just watching pupils work on their own without immediate controlling influence. Try to resist this feeling. One important objective of guided discovery is to help pupils become more independent in their learning. When they are doing what they are supposed to do, try not to interfere!

Plan materials distribution and clean-up carefully. The idea is to accomplish these housekeeping chores quickly and smoothly. An operation that took two minutes for you when you were trying out the activity at home may take an hour when multiplied by 30 children. Not only is it desirable to spend most of the time doing the interesting part of the lesson, but making children wait idly for extended periods while materials are being passed out usually leads to behavior management problems.

Enforce behavior standards strictly. Once a child or two start to lose self-control, chaos spreads rapidly to the whole class. Review the section on behavior management in Chapter 3.

Limit novelty. Children can easily be overwhelmed by too much novelty. Whenever new elements of learning are to be introduced, the teacher must find ways to limit the amount or number of new things that happen at the same time. New procedures, new locations, new ideas, new tools, or new objects to study should be introduced gradually. Some teachers have been known to avoid novelty as much as possible: "The children can't handle that." "That activity would be too stimulating."

"The pupils won't like that because they are not used to it." This is an unfortunate attitude; learning by its very nature involves novelty. Novelty is the essence of learning. To avoid novelty is to take the interest and life out of learning.

The trick, then, is not to avoid novelty, but to spread it out in time so it does not all happen at once. Exploration is a preliminary examination in which a person finds out the general nature of the unknown object, place, or situation. In the case of children, exploration can help them learn the main characteristics of the new thing, and it sets the stage for more systematic examination. Exploration also reduces the degree of novelty to the point where children are not overwhelmed by additional novelty. Any time there is a new physical object in a lesson, problems in management will be minimized by allowing some time for exploration. New things are intensely interesting to children. Before they are able to work systematically with or upon the object, they must be allowed to "play" with it and "get some of the new off." Although the novelty-reducing aspect of exploration is essential for children, exploration also serves as a legitimate first step of investigation used by scientists and other adults in new situations.

Separate pupils from materials before a discussion. Spoken language is much less engaging for children than hands-on activities. If you try to compete for their attention with attractive materials, you will probably lose. There are several ways to separate pupils from materials. Collecting the materials while the pupils remain

▼ Moving pupils to an area away from the materials is one way to enhance discussions.

seated is one way. Moving the children to a discussion area away from their activity tables is another. In extended units where pupils have time to get accustomed to the materials, you may be able to get by with the following: Each child or team has its own container for storing materials. If the container is small enough (and opaque), have them put materials in the container and move it to the center of the table, out of touching range. When pupils are mature enough to manage it, this method has the advantage of reducing the interruption of thinking between activity and discussion.

HOW TO LEAD INTERESTING DISCUSSIONS

Learning to give directions, manage materials, manage behavior, and monitor progress during the data-collection phase of the lesson is relatively easy. A little practice and some feedback from an experienced teacher will do wonders for your confidence and competence. Learning to lead good discussions, however, takes time. Most teachers continue to show room for improvement in this area for a very long time. Still, every teacher can make a good beginning by just thinking about the goals of guided discovery and how it differs from direct instruction.

Rowe, in her classic book, *Teaching Science as Continuous Inquiry* (1978), characterizes the difference between discovery teaching and more traditional methods as "inquiry versus inquisition." Everyone is familiar with the traditional discussion where the main focus is reciting correct answers and getting lots of praise. Learners are often intent on studying the teacher's face for clues for whether answers are acceptable. What children learn in this situation is a game of remembering and, to an even greater extent, of reading the teacher's face. Thinking has little or no place in this game. An inquiry-style discussion, by contrast, has everything to do with pupils' learning to think and with learning a whole new set of "rules" for doing well. These discussions are more like normal conversations about things that all parties, including the teacher, are really interested in. The teacher's role in inquiry is to stimulate and encourage thinking. But how?

One rule of thumb for beginners is to keep the discussion pupil-centered. That is, keep teacher talk to a minimum. Ask questions that elicit longer pupil responses. These should be thought about in advance, and some key questions should be written down in the lesson plan. It is a good idea to begin with a few questions of description, such as, "How many legs did you count?" Begin at a fairly low level, but move on quickly to questions requiring more thought, such as, "What kind of food do you think mealworms like?" Open-ended questions are desirable for eliciting several different hypotheses quickly. Then, pupils can be asked to justify their points of view in terms of their observations: "What evidence do you have to support your idea?" "Have you noticed something that leads you to think that?" Further investigations can be planned together to get more evidence for some of the ideas, such as by asking, "How could we find out about what mealworms eat?"

Another rule of thumb is to avoid using excessive praise for pupil responses if you want to establish a trusting, inquiring atmosphere. Think about when praise is used in noninstructional situations. When you are having a conversation with equals, you seldom use praise. When you do use praise in informal situations, it is seldom effusive, but usually more natural. For example: "That's an interesting idea", or "good work!" Rarely if ever would you tell a friend that he is a good boy for answering something well. Overly energetic and repetitious praise is a mechanism to keep the atmosphere teacher-centered. By stressing verbal rewards—given, incidentally, only by the teacher—the teacher keeps control of the game. To limit praise, practice listening carefully and responding to the content of a child's idea rather than to its "correctness." A traditional classroom discussion is usually characterized by a series of single exchanges of this type: teacher question, short pupil response, teacher praise (or request for help of another pupil). In an inquiry discussion, there is much more variation. Much less of the total amount of time is occupied by teacher talk (giving directions, giving information, asking questions, giving praise or criticism, etc.). Total pupil talk is much higher. Interchanges involving pupils speaking directly to other pupils during formal discussion occur frequently (almost never in traditional discussions). Also, teachers stay with a single pupil longer. Instead of moving to another pupil after one short response, teachers in inquiry discussions often ask further questions probing for detail, reasons, or additional thoughts related to the child's responses.

Many of these ideas may be new for you. They will be developed more fully in the next two chapters.

▼ *Mr. Newman*:   I'm beginning to catch on to the way you get them started and then keep quiet while they are working, but I was wondering about the groans I heard when the materials were collected.

Ms. Oldhand: It's better to stop the activity while interest is still high than to wait until they are starting to get bored. The groans just show that they would rather work with actual things than have a discussion. That's natural; it's why I engineer the transition so carefully. Once they get into a discussion, they like it well enough.

WORKING ARRANGEMENTS— ROTATING STATIONS

In the mealworm lessons, the children worked individually in that they each had a complete set of materials, and each collected data in the same way. You could also say that they worked in groups, since they were permitted to talk quietly and they exchanged interesting observations and questions. For simple activities of this type, the distinction between individual and group work is not very important. In a more complex activity, groups could work in a more formal way to collect data together.

Individuals or pairs within a group might divide up the collection of data in a particular situation and then compare and share with others in the group prior to the discussion with the class as a whole. Or the members of each group may have different roles in the collection of their data. Many variations make sense for particular activities and situations. In all of these arrangements, however, all of the groups were using the same kind of equipment and doing essentially identical tasks.

Another distinct working arrangement may be called *rotating stations*. Groups of children are given a period of time to work at a station and are then rotated to the next station. Each station can provide a different set of materials and a different task. This arrangement is convenient when planning several short activities. There can be as many different activities as there are groups, or as few as two different activities. The main advantage is efficient use of class time and materials. Normally, the stations have materials and tasks that relate to one another so that when the pupils finish all the stations, a class discussion on the total experience may be held for data processing.

One example of rotating stations might be six different caged insects on six different tables. If a data collection period of 30 minutes were desired, groups could spend 5 minutes observing the insect at each station before moving to the next. Another application of the stations idea could be used for presenting two different liquids in which to test sink-or-float objects. Half of the tables could be set up with containers of one liquid, half with the other. In this way, the pupils could spend 15 minutes at each task before moving to the next.

Notice that the rotating-stations plan is simply a variation in the data-collection part of the lesson. The data-processing part, or discussion, remains an essential part of every lesson. Hands-on is not enough; children need minds-on as well. Related short activities fit well in this arrangement when they serve as input for comparisons during the discussion. At first glance, this arrangement looks very attractive, especially in regard to obtaining materials—it is usually easier to get 5 or 6 of something than 30 of them. But there are some conditions in which rotating stations should not be used: (1) when the activities are so different from one another that they cannot be thoroughly discussed, compared, and reflected upon during data processing; (2) when any station activity is too complex or involved to be completed satisfactorily in the relatively short time allotted to it; and (3) when a particular sequential order of the activities is important.

GROUPING FOR INSTRUCTION— COOPERATIVE LEARNING

A teaching strategy generally referred to as *cooperative learning* has become very popular with teachers during the past decade. This is a way of structuring learning groups in the classroom so that children develop the ability to work cooperatively and productively with other children on learning tasks. Everyone has seen pupils working together in groups in which one person did most of the work; this happens in adult life as well as in school. In some groups, one child is effectively excluded and not given the opportunity to contribute. On the other hand, for other groups, the outcome is much better than anything that could have been accomplished by individuals working alone. Groups of the last kind are, of course, what you would like to have in your classroom.

Cooperative-learning groups are formed by the teacher; that is, pupils are assigned to groups rather than choosing those they wish to work with. Groups of four or five pupils seem to work best. The groups should be as heterogeneous as possible. This means a mix of male and female, students with special problems, low-ability pupils and high-ability pupils, and, of course, pupils from the various racial and ethnic groups in your class. Research on the effects of using cooperative learning has shown that this strategy is effective in promoting better working relationships between boys and girls, handicapped and nonhandicapped children, and minority and nonminority children (Slavin, 1980). Children usually remain in one group for about six weeks; then the groups are changed. Groups work best when the whole group has one task that must be performed by the group. For example, in data collecting, each group will collect one set of data that "belongs" to the whole group. Each child contributes to the collection and display of data but no child has his or her own set. Thus, if the observations are incomplete or the report is below expectations, the whole group has fallen down on its responsibilities. Conversely, a good result is something for all members to be proud of.

In cooperative learning, you start by explaining the process, forming groups, giving each group a problem or task, and monitoring both the attention to the task and the group behaviors. Johnson and Johnson (1987), who have worked for years with teachers and pupils in many kinds of classrooms, have developed guidelines for the formation of cooperative-learning groups. The four basic elements they believe must be included are:

1. *Positive interdependence.* Students must perceive that their own success in the task at hand is dependent on others and vice-versa. They will "sink or swim" together.
2. *Face-to-face interaction.* The perception of interdependence leads to discussion, aguments, and attempts to persuade. It is this interchange that produces learning.
3. *Individual accountability.* Each group member is responsible to learn as well as to participate. Participation for its own sake is not the point. A student participates in order to learn.
4. *Appropriate use of social skills.* Pupils must be taught the social skills needed for collaborative work and motivated to use them.

The important things to remember at this time are to set up groups across gender and ethnic lines and to teach and promote the social-interactive skills needed to work effectively in groups. In setting up groups, assign a role to each pupil; for example, one will be recorder, another will see that each pupil has a turn to present ideas, one will report results.

Cooperative learning will be described in detail in Chapter 10 but you may decide to use some of the ideas as you begin to plan guided-discovery lessons.

INFLUENCE OF AGE AND MATURITY ON METHOD

In this chapter you have been learning about guided discovery, a method developmentally accessible to all pupils, including the youngest. A teacher using the management techniques and teaching tips described here should normally be able to use the method successfully with any age level. The difference between primary-grade and intermediate-grade children will show up in several ways, however. Young children may need to stick to fairly simple procedures, whereas older pupils have the potential to keep a multi-step set of directions in mind. The main difference between age groups shows up in the data-processing part of the lesson. Discussions with younger children should stress description and comparison of the objects and events they just observed. Older children should begin their discussions in the same way, but are able to move into higher-level thinking skills, such as inferring, predicting from graphs, and even planning experiments. Another way to think about the level of thinking skills is as science processes. The basic processes, introduced in Chapter 6, are generally appropriate to use during discussion in guided discovery. In Chapter 8 you will learn about using the more advanced processes, such as predicting, inferring, controlling variables, and hypothesizing. Primary pupils will be limited in their ability with these advanced processes, but older children will be able to begin learning to use them.

STEPS FOR GETTING STARTED WITH GUIDED DISCOVERY

Each of the following steps has been or will be described in detail, either in this chapter or in others. You will find it useful to refer to this list from time to time as you gain experience and become more aware of the subtle aspects of guided discovery.

1. Set or review behavior standards.
2. Do not tell pupils the objective of the lesson or present the concept. That would give away what they are supposed to discover for themselves, robbing them of the fun and destroying the discovery rationale.
3. Give clear, brief directions for the procedure to be used. Pupils should not be expected to invent their own procedures in this method. Although the mealworm lessons in this chapter have simple procedures, such will not always be the case. Directions for more complex procedures should be made clear before the pupils begin working.
4. Introduce new vocabulary only as needed in context—that is, when it arises naturally in the lesson. Words taught before contextual meaning has developed are not useful and can actually block development of meaning at a later time.
5. When pupils are working productively during the data-collecting part of the lesson, do not address the class as a whole. Don't interfere when they are doing what they are supposed to be doing.

6. Speak softly to children as needed, only to prevent serious boredom or terminal frustration. Mild, occasional frustration and limited boredom are to be expected in any worthwhile endeavor, including guided-discovery lessons.

7. Separate pupils from materials before trying to hold a discussion.

8. During the data-processing part of the lesson, first ask pupils to report their data, that is, to describe their observations.

9. When possible, continue the discussion beyond description by asking for higher-level thinking such as inference, justification, generalization, and speculation about related systems not yet experienced.

10. Do not summarize the lesson for the pupils. Ask them to do it.

▼ SUMMARY

A method of instruction in science has been presented that differs from direct instruction in that the content to be learned is presented indirectly. The presentation and practice parts of direct instruction have been replaced by data collection and data processing. Data collection consists of hands-on activities in which pupils observe and use other basic science processes to learn directly from interaction with the materials. Data processing normally occurs in a class discussion led by the teacher to guide the pupils to reflect on the experience they just had. Discussions are begun with questions of a relatively low level to elicit description and comparison of the objects and events studied. Gradually, the teacher increases the cognitive level of the questions to help pupils construct higher-level ideas and deeper understanding. The age and maturity of the children determines how far this process continues, with older pupils being expected to move to greater abstraction than younger pupils.

Cooperative learning was suggested as a way of organizing pupils in learning groups during guided-discovery lessons. The purpose of this method is to ensure that all pupils participate in a constructive, cooperative process of sharing ideas and learning with and from one another.

Four kinds of knowledge derived from Piaget's work were described in this chapter. Social-arbitrary knowledge is knowledge that is possible to memorize without understanding. Physical knowledge, the outcome of direct experience with objects, involves firsthand observation of characteristics of the objects and the result of interacting with the objects. Logical knowledge is the outcome of reflective thought about physical knowledge and other kinds of knowledge already possessed by the knower. By reflecting, the learner establishes connections between new ideas and personal preexisting knowledge. In other words, logical knowledge results when the learner actively constructs personal meaning from new input and his prior knowledge. A fourth knowledge type, social-interactive, has been construed from Piaget's work. It pertains to knowledge constructed as a result of group interaction and serves as adaptation to social cooperation.

The usefulness of the idea of kinds of knowledge is that it allows you to choose the best way to teach for a particular objective. Because this idea has not been widely available in the past, teachers in traditional education have tended to teach everything as if it were social-arbitrary knowledge. When new teachers first begin trying out guided discovery, they sometimes go to the other extreme—teaching everything as if it were either physical or logical knowledge. Pupils should not be expected to "discover" names, procedures, preexisting classification schemes, or established systems of notation. These are examples of social-arbitrary knowledge, best presented directly.

▼ DISCUSSION QUESTIONS

1. Describe your understanding of guided discovery. Why should a teacher take the extra trouble to present lessons this way?
2. What is the difference between guided discovery and guided practice?
3. Is there a difference between hands-on science and discovery science? One often hears the terms used more or less synonymously.
4. How would the mealworm lessons be different if all the objectives were to be achieved at the level of social-arbitrary knowledge?
5. How much behavior management structure do you personally prefer? How much do you think is ideal for achieving the lesson objectives? For helping pupils to become more independent learners?
6. Bruner holds that one of the benefits of discovery learning is enhanced memory of the outcome. Share something you remember from your elementary school science instruction. Do you think it was presented in a discovery method?
7. How can a pupil be moving toward greater autonomy and independence and at the same time participate in a learning group in which interdependence is an important aspect?

▼ ACTIVITIES FOR THE READER

The following activities can best be done in groups, and then discussed by the class as a whole.

1. In the body of the chapter, you were asked to complete Ms. Oldhand's second lesson plan for the mealworms unit. Share and discuss your results with your classmates.
2. Look back at the performance objectives for Lessons 7.1 and 7.2. Classify them according to knowledge level.
3. Examine an elementary science textbook on a topic such as insects. Try to list the main objectives of the section. Then classify the objectives according to knowledge level.
4. Select a small part of the insect (or other topic) section from the elementary science textbook and develop a guided-discovery lesson plan for it.

▼ REFERENCES

Bruner, J. S. (1961). The act of discovery. *Harvard Educational Review, 31,* 21–32.

Johnson, D., & Johnson, R. (1987). *Learning together and alone: Cooperative, competitive and individualistic learning* (2nd ed.) Englewood Cliffs, NJ: Prentice Hall.

Kamii, C., & DeVries, R. (1977). Piaget for early education. In C. Day & R. Parker (Eds.), *The preschool in action: Exploring early childhood programs* (2nd ed.). Boston: Allyn & Bacon.

Kamii, C., & DeVries, R. (1978). *Physical knowledge in preschool education: Implications of Piaget's theory.* Englewood Cliffs, NJ: Prentice Hall.

Papert, S. (1980). *Mindstorms.* New York: Basic Books.

Rowe, M. (1978). *Teaching science as continuous inquiry: A basic* (2nd ed.). New York: McGraw-Hill.

Slavin, R. (1980). Cooperative learning. *Review of Educational Research, 50,* 315–342.

8

ADVANCED SCIENCE PROCESSES

▼

In this chapter, you will learn more about science processes, especially the more advanced ones. Some lessons that use these processes in the guided-discovery method are presented so that you get a feel for their usefulness. The lessons have a new element not previously developed in this book. In the data-processing part of the lesson, the teacher helps the pupils go beyond simply describing to apply higher-order thinking that approaches what is done by scientists. Before going further, take a brief look at the advanced processes presented in this chapter:

- *Predicting*. Using previous observations to make an educated guess about a future event or condition.
- *Inferring*. Making a tentative or trial explanation for a set of observations.
- *Controlling Variables*. Identifying attributes that could vary in a system and holding all but one constant.
- *Defining Operationally*. Setting specific limits to the meaning of a term for the purpose of dealing with a particular situation.
- *Experimenting*. Applying all the science processes, as needed, to design and carry out as well as to interpret a test of a question or hypothesis.

As children grow mentally, they become able to use the more advanced science processes. Figure 8.1 shows this general relationship. As you can see from that table, the basic processes (described in Chapter 6) may be introduced with the youngest children and used in every grade thereafter. Predicting and inferring should first be introduced in the middle elementary grades, and the other advanced processes should be introduced in the last two elementary years. Each process, once introduced, should continue to be used in the subsequent years. The reason for this gradual introduction is to match the child's developing mental abilities. Perhaps you noticed that some of the processes parallel certain classical Piagetian diagnostic tasks: there is a relationship between the average age at which certain cognitive abilities are

▼ FIGURE 8.1

Approximate sequence for processes; kindergarten through grade 12

PROCESS	K–2	3–4	5	6	7–12
Observing	•	•	•	•	•
Communicating	•	•	•	•	•
Classifying	•	•	•	•	•
Measuring	•	•	•	•	•
Relating Objects in Space & Time	•	•	•	•	•
Predicting		•	•	•	•
Inferring		•	•	•	•
Controlling Variables			•	•	•
Defining Operationally			•	•	•
Experimenting				•	•

acquired and the grade levels at which certain processes may be most effectively introduced.

You may recall that most primary children do not understand conservation of length, area, weight, or volume—four quantities most often associated with the process of measuring. Yet, as Figure 8.1 suggests, measuring should be introduced in the earliest grades. Is there an inconsistency here? Should teachers wait to introduce a topic until the learner is completely ready to deal with it? If teachers always waited, then science in elementary school would be very limited. The ideas of two other learning theorists come into play here. Bruner, in what he calls a spiral curriculum, recommends multiple introductions of a topic at increasingly sophisticated levels as the child matures mentally. Vygotsky proposes that topics should be introduced slightly before a child is totally "ready" for them, with much of the structure for introducing those topics provided by the teacher.

The last three processes listed in Figure 8.1—controlling variables, defining operationally, and experimenting—require special comment. These advanced processes are generally thought to require formal operational thought. Some tests of formal operational thinking, in fact, consist of asking a person to perform tasks that involve controlling variables and aspects of experimenting. Although some older elementary-age children may be ready to think about these processes, teachers should probably not expect mastery or even consistent performance from those students. It is enough for the teacher to introduce these three processes and to provide the necessary logical structure for the processes that the children are not yet ready to construct on their own.

PREDICTING

At a basic level, predicting can be used as a motivational device. Pupils can be encouraged to consider what they already know when making predictions, but formal data processing need not be used. Asking pupils to predict what will happen encourages growth of reflective thought and creates interest in the outcome of some manipulation. Making a prediction requires a mental construction by the pupil. Having made it, the pupil then "owns" the prediction and thus is personally involved in how it turns out.

Consider some examples of this type of "early" predicting. In Chapter 6, measuring activities involved making estimates before actually measuring. Estimates are a type of prediction. Compare these two situations involving use of a trundle wheel, as shown in Figure 8.2.

1. The teacher says, "Let's measure off twenty meters. Raphael, please take the trundle wheel and roll it down the playground until it clicks twenty times." Raphael does so and then stands there. Everyone can then visualize the distance of 20 meters.
2. The teacher says, "Here is a beginning mark." She chalks a line on the blacktop. "Raphael you stand here with the trundle wheel. Everyone else, walk toward the

▼ FIGURE 8.2
Using a trundle wheel

flagpole until you think you have walked twenty meters. Then stop. Raphael will then roll the trundle wheel and measure off twenty meters. We will see how well we can estimate."

By estimating how many meters away from Raphael they are standing, the pupils are making a prediction of what the measurement will be. By estimating, they not only are making a mental reiteration of the unit but also are becoming personally involved with the eventual outcome. When the real measurement is eventually performed, they really care what the measurement is. Therefore, situation 2 is a richer and more involving experience.

In another example, pupils might be asked to predict whether an object will sink or float before testing it by putting it in water. At the beginning of such an activity, the "prediction" may be nothing more than a guess; as more observations are made, some kind of pattern or rationale starts to occur to the observer. Asking pupils to predict in this way encourages them to be more active mentally and creates more interest in the outcome.

To get a feel for this type of predicting, fill a drinking glass or small box with dried beans. First, make a guess—just off the top of your head. Then devise some sort of procedure to refine the guess without actually counting all the beans. Figure 8.3 shows how you might organize this activity.

At a more advanced level, predicting is usually associated with tables of data and graphs. Lesson plan 5.2 in Chapter 5 was a direct-instruction lesson on how to construct and predict from a line graph. The broader implied lesson was actually a guided-discovery lesson on predicting the bounce height of dropped balls. The relationship of bounce height to drop height of balls graphs as a straight line over most of its range. In straight-line relationships of this kind, quite good predictions can usually be made from simply looking at tabular data without the trouble of constructing a graph. More complex relationships are examined in studies presented later in this chapter. The usefulness of graphs in predicting complex relationships is much more dramatic than is the case with bouncing balls.

▼ FIGURE 8.3
Predicting number of beans in a jar

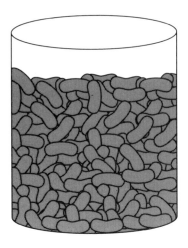

○ Predicting Number of Beans

My Guess _____
My Procedure _____
_____
_____
○ _____
_____
_____
_____

My Prediction _____
○ Actual Count _____

▼ A LESSON ON PREDICTING THE SHORTEST DAY

Ms. Oldhand started a discussion with her sixth graders. "Now that the year is getting along into November, have you noticed anything about the time it gets dark in the evening?"

Several children remarked that the time of sunset was getting earlier. One had noticed that for his after-school softball program lights were now needed, whereas a few weeks ago they were not. Another said her parents did not allow her to stay outdoors after dark and that her afternoon play time was getting shorter and shorter. Other students offered several more responses of this type.

"Have you noticed anything about the time the sun rises in the morning?" asked Ms. O.

Few children had noticed changes in sunrise on their own, but most agreed that they had to get up before it was completely light now and that last month this had not been the case.

"Does anyone know when the shortest day in the year is?" Ms. O. asked. "There is a day that has the shortest time between sunrise and sunset. Before it comes, the days get shorter and shorter. After it is gone, the days begin to get longer again. The shortest day is called the winter solstice. Does anyone know the approximate date it falls on?" Several volunteered that it was late in December.

Continuing in this way, Ms. O. established that the pupils had all noticed to some degree or other that the time of sunrise and sunset changes throughout the year in a regular and predictable way. Then she posed a problem. "I like to go for a walk after school. I walk a certain distance from my house through the park and back home again. It is about five o'clock when I get home. I have noticed that the sun is setting when I get home and that it gets dark very soon afterwards. I don't like to be out walking after dark. Do you think I will be able to continue taking my usual walk throughout the winter, or will I have to cut it short in order to get home before dark? Will sunset continue to come earlier and earlier until the winter solstice?"

After some discussion by the class, Ms. O. suggested a way to find out. "Let's see what patterns show up when we graph the data. First, let's look at this data sheet. I got the sunset time for three months from an almanac. Maybe that will

▼ FIGURE 8.4
Sunrise/sunset data sheet

SUNRISE AND SUNSET TIMES FOR LATITUDE 30°			
DATE	SUNRISE A.M.	SUNSET P.M.	DAYLIGHT (Hrs, Min)
11–01	6:13	5:14	
11–04	6:16	5:12	
11–07	6:18	5:09	
11–10	6:21	5:07	
11–13	6:23	5:05	
11–16	6:26	5:04	
11–19	6:28	5:02	
11–22	6:31	5:01	
11–25	6:33	5:00	
11–28	6:36	5:00	
12–01	6:38	5:00	
12–04	6:40	5:00	
12–07	6:42	5:00	
12–10	6:44	5:00	
12–13	6:47	5:01	
12–16	6:49	5:02	
12–19	6:51	5:03	
12–22	6:52	5:05	
12–25	6:54	5:06	
12–28	6:55	5:08	
12–31	6:56	5:10	
1–03	6:56	5:13	
1–06	6:57	5:15	
1–09	6:57	5:17	
1–12	6:57	5:20	
1–15	6:57	5:22	
1–18	6:56	5:25	
1–21	6:55	5:27	
1–24	6:54	5:30	
1–27	6:55	5:33	
1–30	6:52	5:35	

Source: The New World Almanac, 1990. This and similar references give sunrise and sunset data for various latitudes; when using the information for a class, choose the times for the latitude closest to your location.

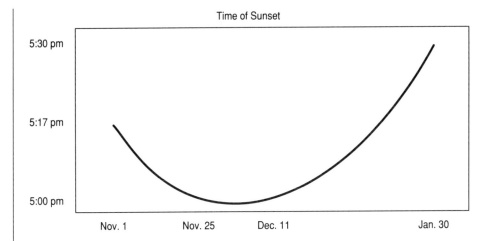

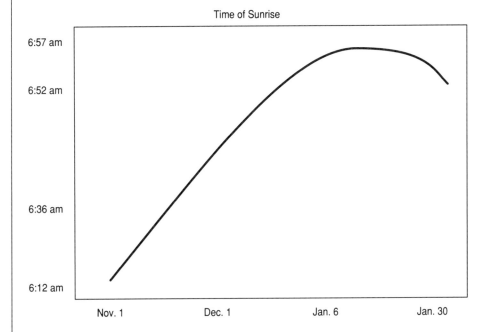

▼ FIGURE 8.5
Times of sunset and sunrise

help you decide whether I will be able to continue my evening walks." Ms. O. provided the students with the data shown in Figure 8.4. After a few days, the class had completed two different graphs, time of sunset and time of sunrise, as shown in Figure 8.5. Then the discussion continued. They found that sunset got earlier for a while, then stayed the same for a few days around the end of November. Then in early December, sunset began getting later. Sunrises continued to get later until January 6th, when it reached 6:57 A.M. Then they stayed the same for several days, and on January 21st they began getting earlier.

Ms. O. asked how they could find the day with the shortest amount of daylight. Someone suggested finding the difference in the times of sunrise and sunset. She agreed that this would work, and they briefly discussed how to compute between A.M. and P.M. times. She also suggested an easier way: "Hold your two graphs together, up to the light, so that the dates on the x-axes coincide. Then slip the papers up and down until you find where the two curves just barely touch." This place turned out to be several days in late December (see Figure 8.6).

Then Ms. O. suggested that they look back at the data sheet she had given them and actually compute the number of hours and minutes between sunrise and sunset for those days that "touched" on the graphs. When they did this, they found that December 22 was the day having the least sunlight, or the shortest day of the year.

To give everyone an opportunity to think about these discoveries, and to relate them to their own lives, Ms. O. asked the children to write in their science journals, telling in their own words about the shortest-day lesson and what effect the changing amounts of sunlight had on them personally.

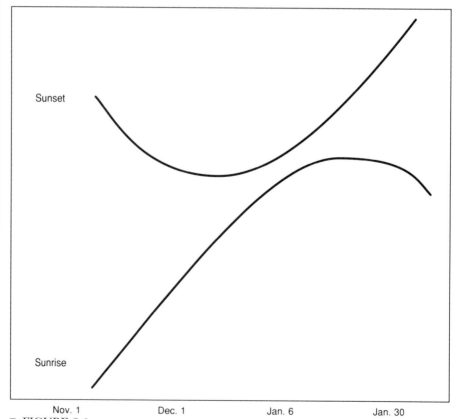

▼ FIGURE 8.6
Sunset and sunrise composite graph

▼ L E S S O N   P L A N   8 . 1

GRADE LEVEL: 6

TOPIC: Predicting the Shortest Day

PERFORMANCE OBJECTIVES

By the end of these activities, the learner should be able to:

1. Construct line graphs from provided data.
2. Predict from graphs the day with the earliest sunset, the day with the latest sunrise, and the day with the shortest period of daylight.
3. Describe effects of changes in time of sunrise and sunset on their lives.

MATERIALS

For each pair of pupils:

- sunrise/sunset data sheet (Figure 8.4)
- 3 sheets of graph paper

LEARNING ACTIVITIES

MOTIVATION/REVIEW

1. "Has anyone noticed when the sun is setting recently?" "How did you happen to notice?" Repeat for sunrise. Tell name for shortest day—winter solstice.
2. Pose problem: "Can I continue walking after school, or will it soon be dark too early?" If date of winter solstice (December 21 or 22) was mentioned earlier, ask: "Will sunset continue to get earlier and earlier until winter solstice in December? Let's find out."

DATA COLLECTION

[In this lesson, the data are not collected firsthand by the pupils, but are presented by the teacher from a reference source. Because every child has experienced many sunrises and sunsets and because personal collection of three months of data would not be feasible, this procedure is acceptable.]

Pass out data sheet and discuss briefly. Point out that only every third day is given. This does not affect the shape of the curve, and will make constructing the graphs quicker. Briefly review graphing procedure. Have pupils work with a partner. One partner can read data from the data sheet and the other can plot the points. Partners should alternate occasionally and check each other. Allow at least two days. Don't try to do all the graphing in one sitting.

DATA PROCESSING

1. Ask pupils to report earliest sunset and latest sunrise (roughly, November 28 and January 9). "Are you surprised? Did you expect them to fall on the same day?"
2. "How could we find the shortest day?" (We could compute difference between sunrises and sunsets on the data table.) "That would work, but even easier is this method . . ." Explain how to hold graphs up to light, slide up and down, and find where curves touch. After days that "touch" are located, ask pupils to compute difference for those days only.

CLOSURE

Ask pupils to write in journals (1) their results and (2) how the changes in daylight have affected their lives.

APPRAISAL

Informal observation during discussion, graphs, and reading journals.

SUMMARY OF PREDICTING

Two types of prediction activities have been described: early predicting and predicting from organized data such as tables and graphs. Early predicting, in which the learner predicts a possible outcome, may be based on previous knowledge and current observations or may be little more than a guess. The main functions of early prediction are motivational in nature. It is especially useful in measuring or other activities that involve development of techniques or skills, when such activities may not be highly interesting in and of themselves. But early prediction is more than just window dressing to "jazz" up tedious activities. By thinking ahead, the learner takes an early step in assuming responsibility for his or her own learning. To make a good prediction—that is, one that has a reasonable chance of approximating the actual outcome—critical thinking must occur. The steps or concepts of the activity must be rehearsed mentally and anticipated. The learner takes a more active role in the learning process. Early predicting is appropriate for learners at all levels—the youngest as well as the oldest.

Predicting with graphs is one of the most powerful processes available to elementary school children. Graphs allow abstract relationships to be seen and analyzed at a semiconcrete or pictorial level. Young children should learn to make and interpret graphs in ways appropriate to their developmental level. For these young children, the main emphasis is graphing as a means of communication. The use of various types of graphs for communicating was presented in detail in Chapter 6. An especially rich source of graphing activities for primary pupils is Chapter 6 of Baratta-Lorton's *Mathematics Their Way* (1976). In the upper elementary grades, it becomes possible to use graphing as a tool to make predictions of complex relationships; the pupils used graphs in this way in the shortest-day lesson.

A number of computer programs for constructing graphs are available commercially. Generally, the user enters the data at the keyboards; the program works out the scaling and then draws the graph, which can be hard copied on paper. Even more exciting is a concept called *microcomputer-based laboratory*, or MBL. When electronic probes or sensors are plugged into the game port of the computer, data can be collected directly from the system being studied. For example, temperature probes can be placed in cold water to study the nature of warming under various conditions. Other types of probes can be used to measure light intensity, motion, pressure, and many other factors. The computer uses input from such sensors to produce a graph in real time, as the experiment is taking place. Mokros and Tinker (1987) have reported that this immediate connection between the phenomenon and the graph greatly improves understanding of the concepts involved and of how to interpret graphs in general.

INFERRING

In the section of Chapter 6 on the process of observing, inferring was mentioned, mainly as something to avoid confusing with observations. Scientists use both processes—observing and inferring; neither is better than the other, only different. Learning to think critically necessarily entails learning to distinguish observations from inferences.

In everyday life, people of all ages confuse observations and inferences, sometimes getting into trouble by assuming that something (an inference) was the case, when in fact it was only a possible explanation of one or more observations. For example, a California woman was speaking of her dog's behavior. There had been an earthquake a few weeks earlier, and frequent aftershocks had continued to keep nerves on edge. "Every time there is an aftershock," she explained, "Trixie runs to the door to see who is shaking the house." In this statement, "Trixie runs to the door" is an observation. That Trixie thinks someone is shaking the house or that Trixie runs in order to see that person are both inferences. A counter-inference is that Trixie runs to the door to escape from the shaking house.

In science, inferences can be very important in helping clarify what is known as a fact (observations) and what still needs to be verified.* When considering a set of observations, a person normally tries to make sense of them by thinking of a trial explanation, or inference. An inference often suggests additional observations to be made: "If this is true, then x and y should be there." Two different sorts of inferring activities are presented in this section. Working through them will help you consolidate your understanding of the process of inferring.

▼ INFERRING ACTIVITY 1

Analyzing Tracks

The three panels in Figure 8.7a represent a continuous trail of tracks observed on the beach. The tracks begin in panel 1 and continue in the other panels, as if the panels were laid out in a single line. The dots around the tracks in the first panel indicate especially deep tracks. On a separate sheet of paper, make a list of observations and inferences based on your observations for each panel. Remember that more than one inference can be made from a single observation. Check your inferences with those of a classmate. Many are possible. A few possibilities are given in Figure 8.7b. Yours may be different and equally defensible.

---

* There are situations in which perception can be misleading; seeing is not always believing. For purposes of establishing the difference between observation and inference, the discussion here simply accepts observation as fact.

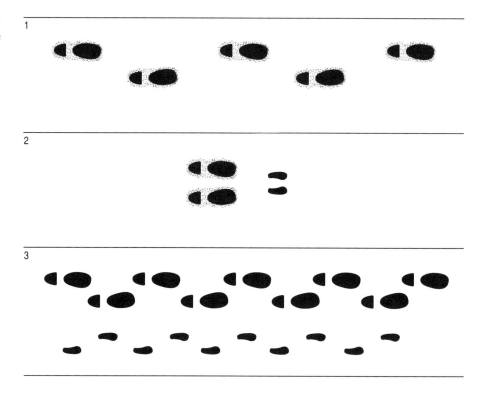

▼ INFERRING ACTIVITY 2

Mystery Boxes

MATERIALS

Small boxes containing one or two objects each, such as: nail, screw, washer, marble, chalk, button, wooden ball, wooden cube, dice, checker, poker chip, rubber eraser.

If you are doing this activity at home, try to get someone else to put an object in a box for you—this activity is not much fun if you know what is in the box. The idea is to try to figure out what might be in the box without opening it. Observe the sounds and touch sensations that result when you move the box in various ways. Then try to infer what sort of thing could produce those observations. You do not have to know the function of the enclosed object to play this game. You can simply speculate about the material and its shape. The idea for inferring is not necessarily to get one right answer but to come up with as many different possible explanations as you can. As long as an inference is a reasonable way to explain a set of observations, it is a good inference.

Jot down a list of your observations. The difficulty you experience in doing this is an indication of how hard it would be for children. A teacher can take advantage of science activities to help children improve their descriptive vocabulary. When

▼ FIGURE 8.7b
Observations and
inferences

Observations		Inferences
Panel 1		
1. Prints look like feet with men's shoes.	a.	A man was walking on the beach during his lunch break from the office.
	b.	A woman wearing men's shoes was walking on the beach.
2. The prints are deep in the sand.	a.	The person was obese.
3.	b.	The person was carrying something.
Panel 2		
1. The left and right prints are even with each other.	a.	The person stopped walking.
	b.	The person hurt his foot.
2. Two small prints appear, even with each other.	a.	The adult put down a child he had been carrying.
	b.	A small adult jumped out of the water.
Panel 3		
1. Two sets of alternating prints, one large, one small, lead off to the right.	a.	Two people, an adult and a child, were walking together.
	b.	Two people walked the same way at different times.
2. The large prints are not as deep as before.	a.	The adult was no longer carrying the child.
	b.	The sand was harder than in Panel 1.
3. The large prints are not as far apart as before.	a.	The man was walking slower than before.
	b.	The man has sore feet.

left to their own devices, children describe everything that is new to them as "weird." A mini-lesson to generate some "observation" words may be called for. When words useful for each of the senses are made available, the quality of the observations as well as the quality of the descriptions increases! In the case of a mystery box, the senses are essentially limited to hearing and touch.

Consider this sample list of observations for a mystery box. Can you infer the hidden object?

- Heavier than a pencil.
- When shaken, it makes a "double bump" (ka-bump rather than just bump).
- When box is tipped end-to-end, the object slides.
- When box is tipped side-to-side, the object rolls.

"What's in the Sock?" is a mystery-box variation using a large sock. The sock may contain one or two objects of the sort listed at the beginning of the activity or objects having distinct odors, such as food or scented things. Because shapes can be felt directly, objects with distinctive shapes may be too easy. For example, a tooth brush or a pencil may be a dead give-away.

Another variation uses a duplicate set of all objects used in the first mystery box plus some detractors and empty boxes. After pupils have inferred an object in a sealed box, let them compare the sealed box with models they construct using open boxes and objects from the duplicate bin. For example, if they infer that the mystery box contains a marble, they could select a marble from the duplicate bin, place it in an empty box, and compare the sounds and touch sensations with those of the unknown box.

This variation is quite similar to what scientists do in real scientific research. Such problems are called *black box* problems. There is usually no way to "look" into the black box in nature to check on inferences, so scientists build models of their inferences and then compare the models with the black box. Whether you allow pupils to look in their mystery boxes is your decision. Motivation for this activity runs high until the contents of the box are seen. After that, the window of learning opportunity slams shut. Many science educators feel strongly that in order to simulate a real science situation, learners should not be allowed to open the boxes. This may seem hard, but consider the possible benefits of at least deferring the revelation for a day or more.

▼ A LESSON ON INFERRING HIDDEN CIRCUITS

"Today we will continue with our electricity unit," said Ms. Oldhand. "Let's review what we have done so far." Hands went up, the main accomplishments were recalled and briefly reviewed. The pupils knew how to make simple circuits with one battery, one bulb, and one wire. They also had used simple holders for the batteries and bulbs and understood how those materials worked. The last thing they had done was to make circuit testers, as shown in Figure 8.8; they had used the circuit testers to identify objects that would complete or would not complete a circuit. In other words, the pupils were able to decide whether an object was a conductor or a nonconductor by testing it. These understandings were essential prerequisites for today's lesson.

Ms. O. clipped a large demonstration circuit board on the chart rack. These circles are brads—brass paper fasteners. On the inside of the board, some of the brads are connected by copper wires and some are not. She opened the circuit board to show the wires inside. Figure 8.9 shows four such circuit boards. "Our job will be to figure out how the wires are connected without looking at them directly," she said. "The boards you will be testing will be wired differently, and you aren't allowed to look inside. Scientists work on puzzles like this sometimes. First, let's review how the circuit tester works. What will happen when I bring the contact points together?" (The bulb should light.) She held the contacts of her circuit tester close together. "Let's see," said Ms. O. as she touched the contacts to demonstrate. "What if it doesn't light?" (Shows your tester isn't work-

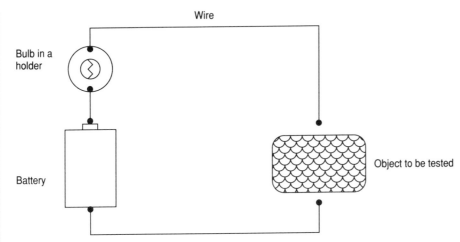

▼ FIGURE 8.8
Circuit tester

ing.) "So it's a good idea to check the tester before using it. Yesterday, I saw someone trying to test an object by touching the tester contacts to the object, but the contacts were also touching each other. Is there a problem with this procedure?" (Yes, it only shows that the tester is working. The electricity is going through the tester wires only and is not forced to go through the object being tested.)

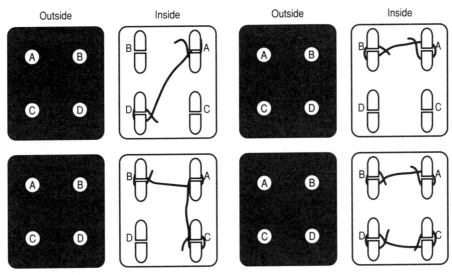

▼ FIGURE 8.9
Four circuit boards, outside and inside

"This is how you can test for hidden connections," said Ms. O. as she placed her two circuit tester terminals on points A and B of the demonstration circuit board. "Aha!" said Ms. O., "the circuit tester light did not come on when the ends touched A and B. What does this tell us about a wire connection between A and B?" (There is none.) Ms. O. wrote a negative sign after AB on the chart. "A negative sign means no reaction—no light." Ms. O. then moved a terminal to point C, leaving one on point A. "Again, a negative result means no connection." For points B and D, she elicits the response that a positive result (light turned on) means that there is a connection. Ms. O. continued in this manner until every possible pair of contact points had been tested and the result recorded. Figure 8.10 shows the results.

"Let's show the result by drawing a line between the points on the diagram," said Ms. O. She then made a diagram for the six results, drawing connecting lines between points when the data table showed a positive result. At the end, her diagram looked like Figure 8.11a. "Does the real circuit board have to look like this . . . or could there be any other arrangements of wire connections that would give these same results?" The pupils were not sure about this, and no one suggested any other arrangements. "What would happen if this wire were missing?" She put her hand over the connecting line between Terminal C and Terminal B on the diagram, making the diagram now look like Figure 8.11b. Then Ms. O. touched points B and C again. "Would the circuit tester light up? Natalie?" After a few seconds, Natalie replied, "Oh! I see! Yes, the electricity doesn't mind turning the corner!" Ms. O. smiled, and said, "These are ideas you can check for yourselves. You will have some unwired practice circuit boards to test your inferences. If you are not sure that one of your inferences

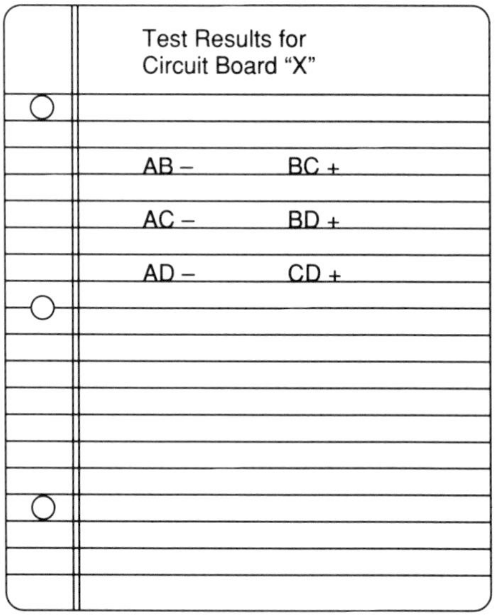

▼ FIGURE 8.10
Test results

Test Results for
Circuit Board "X"

AB –	BC +
AC –	BD +
AD –	CD +

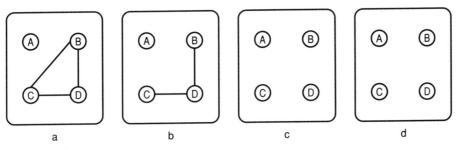

▼ FIGURE 8.11
Wiring diagrams for a four-circuit board. [There are four possibilities for wiring a four-point circuit board to give the results shown in Figure 8.11. Can you find the other two?]

will work, wire up a practice board and test it. We will talk more about this later, but for now, I'll just say that there are several wirings that will work. Try to think of as many as you can that will give the results you get with your testers, and record your inferences on the data sheet. Now," said Ms. O., "would table captains please come up for your materials? When you have your supplies, you may begin working."

Each team of four pupils at a table received a duplicate set of three circuit boards and a data sheet like the one in Figure 8.12. The boards were made of corrugated cardboard with labeled brad heads showing on one side and wires connecting some of the brads on the other side. Pupils could not see the wiring, however, because another piece of cardboard covered the wires (making a "sandwich" held together with rubber bands). Team members worked together: testing with circuit testers, recording results, and trying to figure out all the possible wirings that might give those results.

As the pupils worked, Ms. O. walked about from table to table, helping with procedural questions and equipment problems. Occasionally, a child would show her a data sheet with an inferred wiring and ask, "Is this right?" Ms. O. would always turn such questions back to the pupil: "How can you decide?" or "Have you tried wiring your inference on your practice circuit board?" or "Have you discussed it with your partners?" or "Do your best for now and we will talk about it in the whole group later."

When most of the pupils had finished, Ms. O. signaled for attention and asked the monitors to collect the materials. Then she asked the class to get ready to discuss their results. Each of the circuit boards was discussed in turn. The results were reported, and volunteers checked with a tester to verify in cases of disagreement. The pupils then shared the various inferences they had made. Pupils explained why they thought some inferences would be impossible and came to the conclusion that there was no way to decide among the defensible inferences, given the limited materials of the activity. Finally, the insides of the three circuit boards were revealed. [Some teachers would choose not to allow pupils to look inside. See earlier comments about revealing black-box contents.]

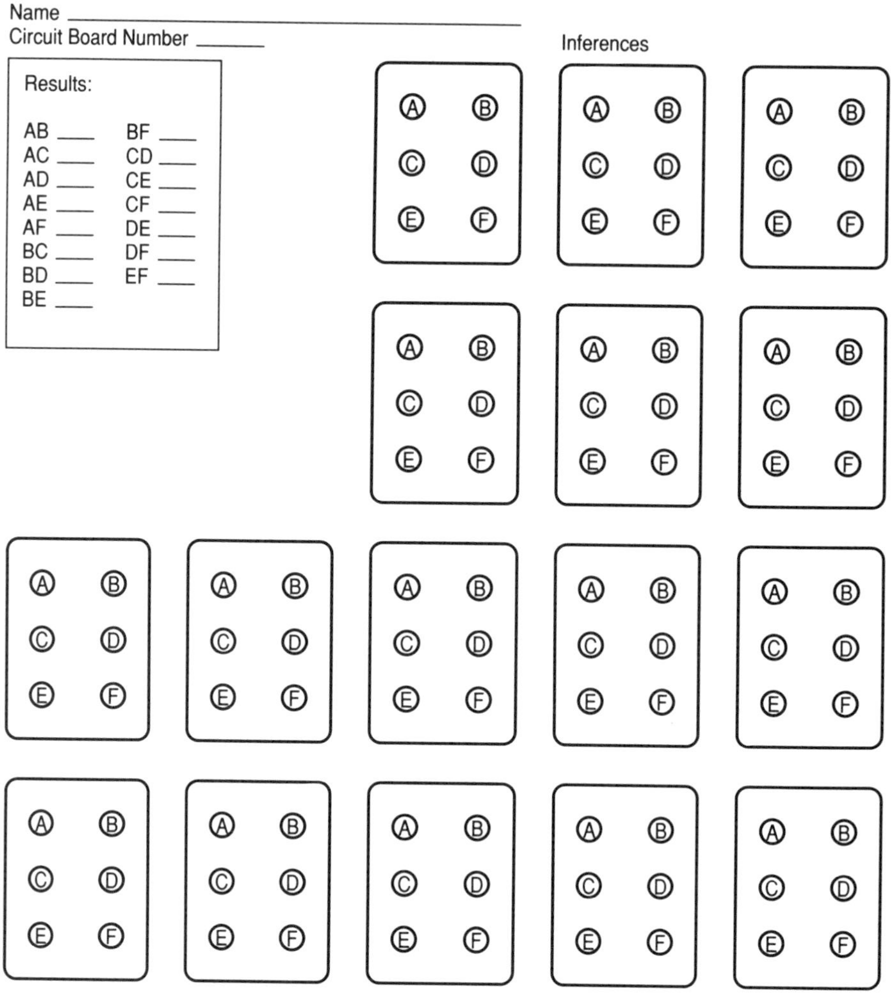

▼ FIGURE 8.12
Data sheet

▼ LESSON PLAN 8.2

GRADE LEVEL: 5

TOPIC: Inferring Hidden Circuits

PERFORMANCE OBJECTIVES

By the end of these activities, the learner should be able to:

1. Recognize that a set of results can be logically explained by more than one inference.

2. Construct inferences of possible wiring to account for results of testing all possible pairs of terminals on a circuit board.
3. Distinguish between possible inferences and impossible ones.

MATERIALS

For the teacher:

- A data sheet similar to Figure 8.12
- 1 large demonstration circuit board
- 1 circuit tester
- prestructured transparencies for overhead projector (similar to pupils' data sheets)
- unwired circuit boards (3 or 4)
- copper wire and wire cutters

For each team of 4 pupils:

- 3 hidden circuit boards
- 1 unwired "practice" circuit board
- 6 short insulated copper wires with ends stripped
- 2 circuit testers
- 4 data sheets

LEARNING ACTIVITIES

MOTIVATION/REVIEW

Briefly review previous activity on using circuit testers to distinguish conductors from nonconductors.

▼ Methods students learn to infer hidden circuits.

DIRECTIONS (DIRECT-INSTRUCTION MINI-LESSON)

Using chart, show how to test circuit boards for connections, and how to record observed results on data sheet. Lead a short discussion to establish that several arrangements of the wiring are possible for a single set of results. "What would happen if this wire were missing?" "Are there any other ways the wire could be connected to give the same results?"

DATA COLLECTION

Ask table captains to distribute materials. Allow about 20 minutes, or longer if needed and time permits. Ask table captains to collect all materials except data sheets.

DATA PROCESSING

1. Ask pupils to report results for each hidden circuit board in turn. Record results on the overhead projector using prestructured transparencies. Ask whether anyone got different results. Ask for volunteers to come up and retest circuit boards that are disputed.
2. Ask pupils to report their inferences. Wire locations can be described as A to B, B to C, etc. Record on prestructured transparency. Collect as many inferences as possible for each set of data. Ask: "Are all of these inferences possible?" "Are there any that just wouldn't work?" If there is any disagreement, ask volunteers to come up and test the inference by constructing the wiring arrangement on an unwired circuit board. Ask, "Is there any way we could decide which of these possible circuits is the one in the circuit board—without looking in and with only our circuit testers?" (No)

CLOSURE

"Should we look inside the circuit boards?"

APPRAISAL

Informal observation during discussion and looking at the data sheets.

▼ *Mr. Newman*: I see you're adding a section in your lesson plan called Directions just before the Data Collecting. Should I start doing that all the time?

Ms. Oldhand: Only if you need it. I have learned the hard way that fifth graders need extra help with the idea of several possible wiring arrangements for each set of data.

Mr. Newman: To tell the truth, it was a new idea to me, too. Maybe I would have figured it out during the testing, but I'm not sure.

Ms. Oldhand: I have learned that when a procedure is complex or when a certain concept is important to carrying out the hands-on part of the activity, I add a little structure in this way. It is called guided discovery, don't forget.

SUMMARY OF INFERRING

Inferring activities such as mystery boxes and socks can be used with primary-grade children, though it is hard for pupils below third or fourth grade to grasp the distinction between observing and inferring. At this point, you should look back at the observing activities in Chapter 6, paying special attention to the sections dealing with the distinction between inferences and observations.

Children tend to "jump to conclusions," that is, infer causation or identity based on insufficient data. Withholding judgment—recognizing that an inference is a tentative explanation—takes a certain mental maturity and self-discipline that young children do not have. Even adults sometimes jump to conclusions, so helping older children practice making the distinction between observations and inferences is important.

Sometimes particular inferences can be eliminated on the basis of the first set of collected data, but usually a person cannot decide which of the inferences (if any) match reality without making further observations. This points to the great usefulness of inferring in helping a person think about what to investigate next in order to learn more about a situation.

CONTROLLING VARIABLES

Controlling variables is one of the tasks by which formal operational thinking is diagnosed. You might think that using this process would be too hard for all but a small percentage of sixth graders. In a sense, this is true, but with some careful structuring, even children younger than sixth grade can begin to think about controlling variables. As a result of past experience with games and contests, most children in the upper elementary grades have some concept of a "fair test" or "fair contest." Such background will go a long way toward understanding this and the other advanced processes. Before a teacher helps pupils think about how to plan an experiment, an example such as the following could help.

Suppose Mr. Williams' sixth-grade class challenges Ms. Oldhand's sixth-grade class to a basketball free-throw contest. Each class chooses its best shooter to represent it. Justin from Mr. Williams' room gets 10 shots and is able to make 6. Aaron from Ms. Oldhand's room is allowed only 5 shots, has to stand further from the basket than Justin, and has to use a ball that contains too much air. Aaron makes 4 free throws. Who is the winner, Justin or Aaron?

At this point, there are plenty of complaints from the children in Ms. Oldhand's class. If asked to set up another game that would be a fair test of basketball skill, they might mention factors such as these:

- Both players get the same number of throws.
- Both players use the same equipment.
- Both players stand the same distance from the basket.

At this point, Ms. Oldhand might point out that the factors they named—number of throws, type of equipment, distance from the basket—are all *variables*, factors that can be changed or varied. To make a fair test of which boy was the better free-throw shooter, all these variables have to be the same for each. Ms. Oldhand might also point out that there are two other factors to consider: the player (Justin or Aaron) and the scores they make. These two factors are also variables.

In most experiments, the experimenter has two variables that are of interest and usually asks, "What effect does variable *x* have on variable *y*?" In the case of this contest, the question is, "What effect does the person who is shooting have on the score?" or "Does it matter who is shooting—Justin or Aaron—on the final score?"

▼ CONTROLLING VARIABLES ACTIVITY 1

The Battery Contest

Different brands of batteries advertise that their batteries last longer than competing brands. Before looking ahead, think about how you would set up a fair test to compare the lasting power of three brands of batteries. First describe the test and then list all the variables you can can think of. When you have finished, read on.

In this "contest," you could set up three circuits, each with a different brand of battery, place them in a prominent place in the classroom, and look at them periodically to see if any bulbs have gone out. You would have to open the circuits before leaving school because if more than one bulb went out while you were away, you would not know which went first. When a bulb does go out, you would check all the elements in the circuit to make sure it was the battery that died rather than some other part. You would continue until only one battery is left. Some possible variables are listed here. You may have thought of others.

- Brand of battery
- Kind and size of wires
- Kind and size of bulbs
- Kind and size of connectors
- Location of circuits kept in the classroom
- Time of afternoon disconnection
- Time of morning reconnection

Should all of these variables be kept constant? No—in order to have a contest, you must have different brands of batteries. All the others listed would need to be constant in order to have a fair test. The variable that you choose to vary—in this case, the brand of battery—is called the *manipulated variable*. The variables that kept constant are called *controlled variables*. The lifetime of the battery is a variable, too, called the *responding variable*.

▼ Let's test Brand X and Brand Y to see which lasts longer.

▼ CONTROLLING VARIABLES ACTIVITY 2

Pendulums

MATERIALS
- Spool of sewing thread
- paper clip
- several washers of the same size
- 1 ruler or short stick
- tape
- 1 meter stick
- clock or watch with second hand

For this activity, you will investigate the behavior of simple pendulums to see if you can determine the effects of certain manipulated variables on how long it takes to swing from one point back to that point. This amount of time is called the *period*. Using the materials listed, make a pendulum like that in Figure 8.13. These are some variables that may be considered:

- Period of pendulum
- Weight of pendulum bob
- Length of pendulum
- Angle of release
- Method of release
- Nature of support

Can you classify these variables as manipulated, responding, and controlled? The period will be the responding variable, but which of the others is the manipulated variable will depend on which you are testing. If you choose weight as your manipulated variable, then length, angle of release, method of release, and nature of support will all be controlled variables. If you choose length as your manipulated variable, then weight, angle of release, method of release, and nature of support will be your controlled variables. Although you can certainly check all of these variables for their effect on period, the last three are somewhat difficult to measure and are also difficult to manipulate in a consistent manner. At this time, simply control those factors, and test first weight and then length as your manipulated variables. In order to control the last three factors, use the following procedures.

Cut a piece of thread somewhat longer than a meter. Open a paper clip into a hook and tie it to one end of the thread. Put one washer on the hook. Measure the desired length of the entire pendulum, from the bottom of the washer to the pivot point of the string. Tape the string at the pivot point to the end of a ruler or thin stick. Hold the ruler steady against a tabletop or other stable platform, with the thread hanging over the end of the ruler. This is shown in Figure 8.13.

▼ FIGURE 8.13
Pendulum setup

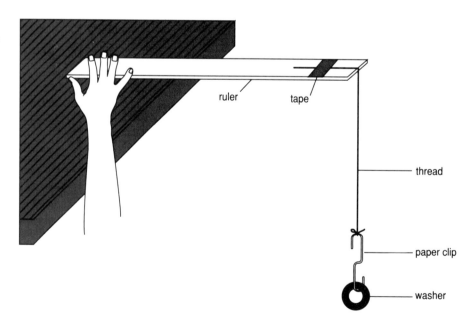

▼ FIGURE 8.14
Pendulum data
sheet

LENGTH TRIALS	
Length (cm)	Swings/15 sec.

WEIGHT TRIALS	
Weight (washers)	Swings/15 Sec.
1	
2	
3	
4	

Pull the washer back slightly—15 degrees or less from vertical. Release the washer so that it swings smoothly without bouncing. The pendulum may change the direction of its swing from parallel to the table edge to somewhat perpendicular. Don't worry about this; just keep counting. Count twice for each trial, to be sure everything is normal. If the two counts are different, continue trials until you get two that are the same.

To check for weight as the manipulated variable, keep the length constant, and simply add a second washer on the hook for the next trial. Continue for washers three and four. To check for length as the manipulated variable, keep the weight constant and vary the length for successive trials. It is easier to start with the longest pendulum and work toward the shortest.

In order to simplify the timing of the period, count the number of complete swings during 15 seconds and record your results in tables similar to those in Figure 8.14. It is easier if you have a partner to tell you when to begin and when to stop counting. The measurement you get is not strictly called the period, but it will have a regular, inverse relationship to the period.

DEFINING OPERATIONALLY

Communicating clearly is not an easy job. Almost every word or expression in the English language has several meanings, leaving considerable room for different interpretations. Consider Matthew's dilemma. His father was inspecting Matthew's room. "I thought I asked you to make up your bed," said the father. "But I did," replied Matthew. The father pulled a coin from his pocket and tossed it on the bed and said, "See? The quarter didn't bounce. The bed is not made up."

Although Matthew was not exactly delighted with this definition of a made bed, at least he knew what was expected and had a clear way to check whether the job had been done satisfactorily. This is a good example of an operational definition: it narrows the possibilities of interpretation and provides a criterion in the form of an operation, or action.

Operational definitions are often used in law. To make sure everyone drives at a safe speed, most states and cities have specific speed limits for particular stretches of road. You may feel inclined to argue with the officer who gives you a ticket for driving at an unsafe speed. You could try to make a case for driving quite safely. For example, if it is 3 AM and there is no traffic, you may be entirely safe driving at 40 mph. But if the law says that the safe speed for that stretch of road is 30 mph, you are legally unsafe.

Scientists use operational definitions to communicate exactly what some variable in an experiment is. Given a single question to be investigated, consider how different people might set up their experiments. The question is, "How does exercise affect pulse rate?" Investigator A has people take their pulses, do 10 situps, and then take their pulses again. Investigator B has people take their pulses, run up a flight of stairs, and then take their pulses again. Each of the investigators has the subjects count pulses, but each interprets exercise in a different way. One uses situps whereas the other uses running up a flight of stairs. Would it be valid to compare one of these experiments with the other?

▼ DEFINING OPERATIONALLY ACTIVITY 1
What is a Good Conductor?

Using simple electrical materials, how could you determine good conductors, poor conductors, and nonconductors? When you tested objects with a simple one-battery circuit tester, you said an object or material was a conductor if the bulb came on and a nonconductor if it did not. Can you think of a reasonably simple way to measure degrees of "coming on"? If your bulb was shining dimly even with a copper wire (a good conductor), then it may be useful to place one or more additional batteries in your circuit tester. With multiple batteries, you would have a fairly bright light with a good conductor but you would still be able to see a dim light even with conductors that were not so good. To add more precision to your measurement, you could make a brightness meter from 10 pages of white paper fastened together. The number of pages through which the light is visible is the measure of brightness. Using this brightness meter, you could operationally define "good" conductors as those giving a reading of 8 to 10 on the meter, and so on. Figure 8.15 shows how you could use this brightness meter to classify a number of objects with operational definitions. Every investigator has a right to define a "good conductor" any way he or she pleases, as long as the operational definition is clearly stated.

MATERIALS
- Circuit tester (see Figure 8.8)
- #32 Nichrome wire (available in hardware stores)

▼ FIGURE 8.15
Operationally
defining
conductors

BRIGHTNESS READING	CONDUCTIVITY OF TEST OBJECT
0	nonconductor
1–4	poor
5–7	moderate
8–10	good

▼ FIGURE 8.16
Nichrome-wire
board

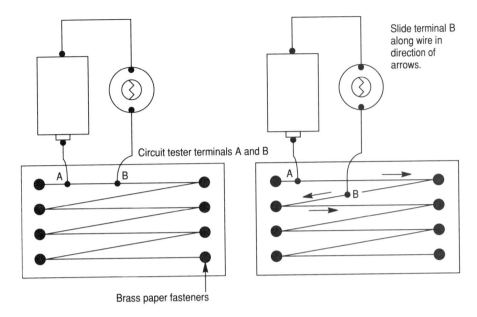

• pencil, paper
• 1 pencil without eraser, sharpened on both ends
• assorted common objects such as: aluminum foil, gold or silver (rings, watch case, tableware), lead (fishing sinker, tire balance weights), plastic, cloth, rubber, wood, paper, nail, paper clip, and mixed material objects such as twist ties, painted metal

Optional materials: liquids such as water, cooking oil, coffee, cola, vinegar; various solutions of salt, baking soda, sugar, etc.

Test these materials with your circuit tester and classify them as good, moderate, poor, or nonconductors. Use the operational definitions given in Figure 8.15 or define your own. The number of batteries needed in your circuit tester will depend on the type of materials you choose to test. Consider these notes before you begin your tests:

• Nichrome wire can be mounted on a piece of cardboard to make the testing of increasing lengths easier. A diagram of a Nichrome-wire board is shown in Figure 8.16.
• Pencil lead as a possible conductor may surprise you. After testing the pencil sharpened at both ends, test pencil marks on paper. Make some marks thick and heavy, others thinner and lighter. Try different lengths of mark as well.*
• You may need several batteries in your circuit tester to see any conductivity in liquids. Try moving the tester terminals different distances apart.

---

* Pencil lead is not lead at all, but graphite, a form of carbon. Long ago, metallic lead was used for marking, but someone discovered natural graphite to be much better. Eventually, wooden pencils with graphite cores were invented, but the name *lead* stuck for the black core material.

Test Material	Brightness	Conductivity
1. Nail	10	good
2. Paper	0	nonconductor
3. Nichrome wire, 20 cm	7	moderate
4.		
5.		
6.		

Record your results in a table such as that in Figure 8.17. Classify test materials from *good* to *nonconductor*.

EXPERIMENTING

Pupil autonomy should increase gradually through the school years. In other words, as pupils grow mentally and emotionally, they should be taught to take more responsibility for structuring their learning activities. Generally, this shift in the source of structure occurs as the teacher presents and guides practice in new methods of operating, just as teacher presentation and guidance is used to teach content. As pupils gain understanding and facility with the methods, less and less presentation and guidance by the teacher are needed. As teacher, your role is to decide how much outside structure your pupils need and how much structuring they are ready to manage for themselves in any particular activity. This section on the science process of experimenting examines how teachers can introduce pupils to taking all or almost all of the responsibility for structuring. Obviously, there must be some degree of structure provided while pupils are learning how to carry out all the steps of this process. The ideal, however, is for them to reach a point where they can experiment on their own.

All or most of the various steps in experimenting should be familiar to pupils before anything approaching fully autonomous experimentation is possible. The steps themselves are open to some variation, but in general, an experimental procedure includes these:

1. Stating the question (sometimes called "the problem")
2. Formulating the hypothesis (optional)
3. Identifying variables (using operational definitions as needed)
4. Designing a test of the question or hypothesis (using operational definitions as needed)

5. Setting up the test and collecting data
6. Organizing and interpreting the data (tables and graphs)
7. Stating a conclusion in terms of the question or hypothesis
8. Writing a report of the experiment

In the following example experiment, each of these steps is explained.

▼ EXPERIMENTING ACTIVITY 1

Is This Fertilizer Any Good?

The question "Is this fertilizer any good?" is one that might arise spontaneously in conversation between gardeners. Before it could be tested, however, some critical thinking is needed. What is meant by "any good?" What is fertilizer expected to do? And how could you decide whether it does this function "well"? When people buy fertilizer, they must expect some kind of improvement in their plants—otherwise, why buy it? Actually, there are different kinds of fertilizer to correct different kinds of plant problems or to improve different aspects of plant growth. Consider one function for study, whether a fertilizer causes plants to grow faster. The question could be restated more specifically now:

How does Fertilizer X affect the growth of corn plants?

A *hypothesis* is a formal statement of the experimental question. It is general in nature; that is, it includes all objects and events in the class of each main variable. And it is stated as a declarative sentence rather than a question. An example of a hypothesis for a plant study is:

"Corn plants treated with fertilizer will grow taller than nontreated corn plants during the same length of time."

The experimenter does not know yet whether the hypothesis is true. The purpose of a hypothesis is to guide an investigation. If the corn grows taller with fertilizer than without, then the experimenter can conclude only that the hypothesis is supported. "Proving" the hypothesis is true would entail testing every kind of corn plant with every kind of fertilizer. Obviously, that would be impossible. In fact, no one can ever say that a hypothesis is proven—only that it is supported or not supported. If lots of corn plants and lots of fertilizers are tested and the corn grows taller in every case, then the experimenter can have strong confidence in this hypothesis. Theoretically, it would take only one experiment in which the fertilized corn did not grow taller to disprove the hypothesis. Actually, when negative results occur, scientists usually use the new data to modify the old hypothesis rather than throw it out and start all over.

Formulating a hypothesis is more abstract than simply stating a question. A clearly stated experimental question is often sufficient to guide the relatively simple experiments appropriate for elementary children. You can be the judge of whether or not to include formulating hypotheses in your pupils' experiments.

Next, consider identification of variables. By stating the question clearly, you have already identified the manipulated variable (fertilizer or not) and the responding variable (growth of corn plants). Do either of these variables need operational definitions? You could decide to compare several different amounts of fertilizer, or you could compare plants with the amount of fertilizer recommended on the label to plants with no added fertilizer. For simplicity, do the latter. You have operationally defined *fertilizer* as Fertilizer X in the amount recommended on its label. What about "growth of corn plants"? Growth sounds like something that should be measured. How could this be done? There are a number of different ways, but since corn plants generally grow straight up and fairly stiff, it should be easy to measure height of the plants with a ruler. If a different sort of plant had been chosen, you may have needed a different way to operationally define "growth of corn plants." For a vine or a shrubby branching plant, you might decide to count leaves or measure in some way the total surface area of the leaves. In any case, you would need an operational definition for growth.

Now think of other variables that you are not especially interested in, so that you can be sure that none of them is a factor in any plant growth differences you may see later. These other factors include: amount of light, amount of water, temperature, type of corn plants used, type and size of containers for the plants, and kind and amount of soil. Your list may include other factors as well. There is no way such a list is ever complete, because there is no end to other factors that might be involved. These other factors are called controlled variables. You should try to keep them the same for all plants. The more of them you name, the more sure you can be that they do not influence any differences we may observe later in the growth of our plants.

The next step of the procedure is to design a test to answer the experimental question. There is no formula that tells how to design a test. You must consider the variables and make a number of judgments. How many plants are needed? What kind of containers, soil, and so on. How often should you water? How should the fertilizer be applied? Should you start with seeds, or could some corn plants be purchased at the nursery? How often should the seedlings be measured? Perhaps you can think of other decisions to be made.

Before deciding on the details of the experiment, keep in mind that one or more corn plants will receive fertilizer and one or more corn plants will not receive fertilizer. Conditions for both groups should be as much the same as possible—except for the fertilizer. All plants should have the normal amount of the other factors—water, light, and so on—because you want to test normal plants. If the plants were stressed by lack of water, for example, they might react differently to fertilizer. This means you need to know how to provide normal care for the plants. You might ask an expert or get information from a resource book about how to best maintain the plants in normal good health. Both sets of plants should receive all this good normal care in exactly the same way, except for fertilizer.

Sometimes plants die for reasons no one can control. Also, plants receiving exactly the same care may not all grow exactly the same. It is usually a good idea to have several trials or multiple data to provide a more typical result by averaging. The following is one way to design the experiment; others could be equally valid.

   Plant several shallow boxes (flats) of corn seeds—say, about 100 seeds. When the seedlings have grown to a height of about 10 cm, choose 20 seedlings that are as much alike as possible. Carefully transplant these seedlings to individual 1-liter containers, each having equal amounts of potting mix from the same bag. Place all the containers on the window sill, and water each 100 ml. After three days, eliminate any plants that do not look healthy. Divide the remaining plants equally into the fertilizer group and the no-fertilizer group (also called the experimental group and the control group). Decide on a watering schedule—how much and how often will depend on what you learn from the resources you consult. All plants should be watered the same amount at the same time. In the water of the fertilizer (experimental) group, dissolve the recommended amount of fertilizer.

   Set up the experiment physically in the way you have planned. Measure and record the height of each plant periodically—say, every Monday, Wednesday, and Friday for a month. Design a data table to record the measurements. Figure 8.18 is an example of a data table.

   Construct a graph to show the pattern of growth for each of the two groups. Look at the overall growth of plants in the two groups. Figure 8.19 is a graph of the data in Figure 8.18. Can you draw any conclusions? Do the graphs give any information not provided by simply comparing the final average heights of the two groups? The data table and the graphs show that there is no consistent difference between the growth of the two groups of plants. This conclusion could be stated in two ways, depending on whether it is in response to the question or the hypothesis. To the question "How does Fertilizer X affect the growth of corn

▼ FIGURE 8.18
Average height of
corn plants (cm)

Day	Fertilizer	No Fertilizer
1	10	10
3	10	10
5	12	13
8	18	17
10	25	25
12	33	31
15	45	44
17	55	55
19	68	69
22	84	83
24	89	91
26	92	93
29	95	95
31	95	95

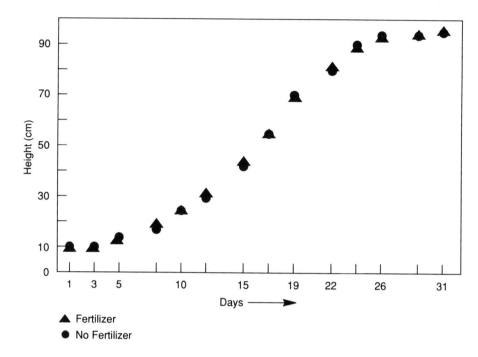

▲ Fertilizer
● No Fertilizer

plants?" the conclusion could be stated in this way: Fertilizer X does not seem to have any effect on the growth of corn plants. To the hypothesis "Corn plants treated with fertilizer will grow taller than nontreated corn plants during the same length of time"), the conclusion could be stated in this way: The hypothesis is not supported.

Writing a report on this experiment would be brief—and easy if the previous steps were all taken. A report of an experiment should have the following parts:

1. Title of report
2. The question (or problem)
3. The hypothesis (if used)
4. Variables (manipulated, responding, controlled)
5. Design and procedure
6. Results (data, including tables and graphs)
7. Conclusions (Was the question answered? Was the hypothesis supported or not supported?)

An example of such a report is shown in Figure 8.20.

When an experiment gives negative results, there is just as much opportunity to think and learn as when the results are positive. When the results are unexpected (as in this case), it is a good idea to check that the procedure was carried out as originally stated and then to check for any possible measurement errors. If no such problems occurred, then the experimenter must examine whether the question or procedure needs rethinking. All of these steps are a part of real science and

---

TITLE

A Study of the Effect of Fertilizer on Corn Plants

THE QUESTION

How does Fertilizer X affect the growth of corn plants?

THE HYPOTHESIS

Corn plants treated with fertilizer will grow taller than nontreated corn plants during the same length of time.

VARIABLES

manipulated = fertilizer or no fertilizer
responding = height of corn plants
controlled   = soil, light, temperature, type of corn plant, type and size of container, water

DESIGN AND PROCEDURE

Twenty young healthy corn plants 10 cm tall were selected from a flat on basis of looking alike. Each plant was transplanted into equal volumes of planting mix in identical one-liter containers. Plants received normal care for three days, then unhealthy plants were discarded. The remaining 14 plants were divided into two groups. The experimental group received fertilizer (amount stated on label) in its water. Otherwise, all care was identical. Height of all plants was measured three days a week for one month. Average height for each group was graphed.

RESULTS

Data recorded in tables and graphs.

CONCLUSIONS

Added fertilizer appears to have no effect on the growth of corn plants. The hypothesis was not supported.

▼ FIGURE 8.20
An example report

are valuable in practicing critical thinking. In this experiment, you might consider these two alternatives:

1. Fertilizer X is worthless, and people who buy it are being cheated.
2. Some important factor in our experiment was overlooked.

Consider the second possibility. What was different in the experimental procedure from conditions in real gardens? One obvious difference was the soil—commercial potting mix rather than ordinary garden soil from the ground. What if the potting mix contained added fertilizer? If so, then the control plants might have had enough nutrients to grow as fast as the plants grown with added fertilizer! In that case, you would modify the hypothesis to this statement:

▾ FIGURE 8.21
Growth of corn
plants in garden
soil

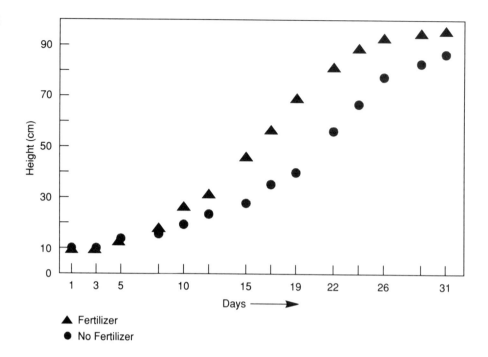

When grown in common garden soil, corn plants treated with fertilizer will grow taller than nontreated corn plants during the same length of time.

A new experiment based on the modified hypothesis might result in a graph like that in Figure 8.21.

Write a report similar to the example report on the plant experiment that resulted in the graph shown in Figure 8.18.

▾ EXPERIMENTING ACTIVITY 2

Reaction Time

Reaction time is an interesting variable of human beings. A simple way to measure reaction time is as follows: The experimenter holds a meter stick lightly by thumb and forefinger near the large number end so that it hangs with the small numbers down. The subject (person being tested) holds his or her thumb and forefinger wide apart on either side of the zero, or end mark, without touching. The experimenter drops the meter stick without warning and the subject tries to catch it between thumb and finger as quickly as possible after it begins to fall. The experimenter should wait varying amounts of time so that the subject cannot anticipate the drop. The number gripped by the subject is a measure of reaction time.

Using reaction time as the responding variable, design and carry out an experiment with classmates or family members. Possible manipulated variables include age, time of day, gender, and amount of time after heavy exercise. Perhaps you can think of others.

DISCREPANT EVENTS

The value of the more advanced processes becomes apparent when science instruction is organized into units of study on the same topic, rather than individual, unrelated lessons. Units allow pupils to become more familiar with the objects and events of the topic through informal exploration. Once this background of familiarity has been established, interest in planning and carrying out experiments is possible.

Perhaps you have had this experience in high school or college: You and your lab partner are following the steps in a workbook procedure to collect data in order to answer a question you never asked. Because the question is not yours, you have little or no interest in the outcome and soon forget it. A skillful teacher gives the

▼ A discrepant event is a kind of motivational surprise.

learners time to get the necessary firsthand background so that questions begin to arise naturally. That skillful teacher can often select the kind of background experiences that stimulate the production of questions. One kind of experience that is especially good at stimulating questions is a discrepant event. A discrepant event is a kind of surprise that sometimes happens spontaneously but can also be "engineered" by the teacher. In order for surprise to occur, a pattern of expectation must be broken, which implies that such a pattern must first be established. Although spontaneous questions arising in the learner are highly desirable, such questions are not always easy to elicit, or even necessary for all situations. Questions can also be stimulated during class discussion, in such a way that they belong to the pupil just as surely as spontaneous questions do. How to lead such discussions is the subject of Chapter 9.

▼ SUMMARY

For purposes of presentation, the processes of science were divided into two categories, basic and advanced. In fact, there is no specific point at which to make such a division. The types of mental activity required by the processes form a complex stream that is more like a continuum than two discrete groups. Individual processes are also highly interrelated. Different writers have dealt with them in various ways. The main idea to get from a discussion of science processes is that they can serve as tools for the teacher in planning and carrying out science activities. To interpret the processes as individual packets of knowledge that must be transmitted to learners would be unfortunate. They are only aids to thinking about science instruction.

▼ DISCUSSION QUESTIONS

1. What elements should be included in an operational definition of each of the following?
   a. A good student
   b. A good course
   c. A good lesson
   d. A rich coffee
2. What, in your opinion, are the advantages and disadvantages of using computers to assist in graphing for children at the elementary-school level? What differences, if any, do you think are important between graphing software that draws graphs after the user types in the data, and the microcomputer-based laboratory (MBL) that automatically graphs experiments in real time?
3. Should a teacher who never intends to teach fifth or sixth grade be excused from learning about the advanced science processes? Defend your position.

▼ ACTIVITIES FOR THE READER

1. Design and carry out an experiment on the melting time of ice. Make a list of factors that might have an effect on melting time. Choose one as your manipulated variable.
2. How good are you at estimating 60 seconds? If you have a stopwatch, you can test yourself. If not, ask a friend to watch a sweep second hand and measure your estimate. What factors might be related to a person's skill at estimating time? How could you investigate these factors?
3. Different brands of paper towels make various claims and differ from each other in many ways. Make a list of claims you have heard (or can imagine). Can you derive an experimental question or hypothesis from each of these claims? Which of them would be the easiest to test? The hardest?
4. Make a list of advertising claims you have collected from television or other sources. Discuss in class the possibility of operationally defining these claims as well as testing them.
5. Stereotypes and folklore often have "a grain of truth" to them. Three such statements are given below. Can you think of others? Choose one of these statements below (or one of your own) and design an experiment to test it.
   a. Californians are more "laid back" than other Americans.
   b. Southerners are more courteous than other Americans.
   c. Northerners talk faster than southerners.

▼ REFERENCES

Baratta-Lorton, M. (1976). *Mathematics their way.* Menlo Park, CA: Addison-Wesley.

Hoffman, M. S. (Ed.). (1990). *The new world almanac and book of facts.* New York: Pharos Books.

Mokros, J. R. and Tinker, R. F. (1987). The impact of microcomputer-based labs on children's ability to interpret graphs. *Journal of Research in Science Teaching, 24*(4), 369–383.

APPLICATIONS AND TECHNIQUES FOR GUIDED DISCOVERY

CHAPTER OUTLINE

▼
_____

The essence of guided discovery is captured in this question: What can children learn in and through their own actions on objects and through their own reasoning about those actions? Because primary-grade children are limited in their reasoning ability, the emphasis for them should be the shared experience with objects and talking about those shared experiences. As reasoning ability increases in the middle and upper elementary grades, critical thinking and analysis of the shared experience is added. Although even primary children can be asked to infer simple relationships and think about similarities and differences, older children can and should be asked to do a great deal more reasoning. Keeping this important overview in mind, consider the shift in roles that takes place at Autonomy Level II (see Chapter 4 for a discussion of autonomy levels).

In moving from Autonomy Level I to Autonomy Level II, shifts in both the role of the teacher and the role of the pupil will cause somewhat different points of emphasis in teaching techniques and procedures. Figure 9.1 compares the roles at the two levels. In the discussion of the various topics in this chapter, these similarities and difficulties in roles of teachers and pupils according to autonomy level will be spelled out in more detail.

The term *guided discovery* may seem to suggest that there is also "unguided discovery." Indeed, unguided, open, or free discovery is a viable teaching method that has merit in its proper context. Several variations of discovery learning in which pupils operate at a relatively high level of autonomy are described in Chapters 10 and 11. The term *inquiry approach* or *inquiry science* can be thought of as synonymous with discovery, either guided or open. Other hands-on, constructivist-based science programs or methods, such as the "learning cycle" (Renner and Marek, 1988) developed originally in the Science Curriculum Improvement Project, may differ in details but are essentially the same as what is called guided discovery in this book.

Beginning to learn alternative ways of teaching can be confusing if you have been thinking that there is a best way to do things. Having learned about teaching in a direct-instruction mode, you are now being asked to do certain teaching jobs in a quite different manner. The truth is, there is no "one right way" to teach. Experienced teachers can offer some suggestions and help you learn to be more critical in your thinking about the best methods for particular goals in certain situations. You must decide for yourself after experimenting with teaching methods. But remember that scientists do not form a conclusion on the basis of just one trial. Rowe (1978) comments that such an experimental viewpoint helps teachers to feel less disturbed when something does not work out as planned. Instead of self-blame, you can chalk it up to experience and think about what can be done next time.

Piaget's knowledge types can serve as a natural guide in the selection of appropriate teaching methods. Is the lesson objective social-arbitrary knowledge? Then use direct instruction. Is the objective physical knowledge? Then use hands-on experience with real objects. Is the objective logical knowledge? Then use a special kind of discussion following hands-on experience. In Chapter 7, guided discovery was in-

▼ FIGURE 9.1

Teacher and Pupil Roles at Autonomy Levels I and II

AUTONOMY LEVEL I	AUTONOMY LEVEL II
Teacher's Role	Teacher's Role
1. Set and enforce behavior standards and sanctions.	1. Same as Level I, but increase responsibility for pupils monitoring own behavior.
2. Speak clearly and as briefly as possible.	2. Same as Level I.
3. Listen carefully and check for understanding.	3. Same as Level I.
4. Decide beforehand on time allocation for parts of the lesson.	4. Think about time allocation, but prepare for greater flexibility.
5. Plan carefully for smooth, efficient distribution and pick-up of materials, involving children when possible.	5. Similar to Level I, but greater emphasis is placed on involving pupils in greater responsibility.
6. Provide direct information by telling, showing, or other means.	6. Direct information is used for giving directions for procedures only.
7. Provide hands-on experiences whenever possible during independent practice.	7. Provide hands-on experience routinely during data processing part of lesson.
	8. Facilitate discovery learning by indirect means.
Pupil's Role	Pupil's Role
1. Follow standards at all times during a lesson.	1. Same as Level I, but also begin to judge appropriateness of own behavior in situations not covered by standards.
2. Pay attention when others are speaking or demonstrating.	2. Same as Level I.
3. Follow directions.	3. Same as Level I.
4. Ask for help if you don't understand.	4. Same as Level I.
5. Answer questions when called upon.	5. Same as Level I, but begin to initiate more and generally take greater responsibility for discussions.
	6. Be helpful and courteous toward other pupils.
	7. Cooperate in group work and class discussions to develop ideas and interest.

troduced using relatively simple example lessons. The main topics of this chapter are the management skills necessary to operate hands-on activities and the verbal skills needed to facilitate growth of logical knowledge through discussion in more complex settings.

MANAGEMENT OF BEHAVIOR AND MATERIALS

The shift in roles at Autonomy Level II means that pupils are expected to start learning to manage their own behavior and materials. Since the behaviors are new, the pupils must be taught how to do them. Ironically, much of this kind of teaching is direct. Teaching children how to manage for themselves is very much like the steps in a direct-instruction lesson (though the time frame is much longer). The teacher gives motivation and then presents a procedure directly. The pupils practice, first with considerable guidance and later with less. Periodically, the teacher may call a class discussion to involve everyone in evaluating progress. The difference between Autonomy Levels I and II in this management learning process is that pupils are given more freedom at Level II and are expected to take greater responsibility for themselves. Now consider several specific points on teaching and learning self-management.

▾ Working with materials is a privilege for pupils who are learning to control their behavior.

NOISE

Noise is not bad unless it is excessive. Some teachers are uncomfortable with any level of noise, either because they feel they are expected to maintain a quiet room or because they believe noise will lead to serious disorder. If pupils are to be allowed to work in groups, there will obviously be more noise than if they are all reading silently. The amount of noise that is tolerable varies from teacher to teacher. When teachers have the opportunity to visit another classroom, they often comment that it is noisier or quieter than they are used to. This shows that experienced teachers are acutely aware of noise and of their own tolerance levels. While there is no specific decibel reading at which things always come unglued, too much noise can have a contagious effect that leads to disruptive behavior. In the past, many principals expected silence, but now—with newer methods such as cooperative learning gaining acceptance—most principals do not insist on totally noiseless classrooms. With experience, you will find a noise level that feels OK to you. The thing to listen for is an increase in the accustomed level.

USING PSYCHOLOGY INSTEAD OF COERCION

Children like to do hands-on science activities, and they usually like to work together. You can use this affinity to keep order. Explain that working freely with the materials is a privilege for those who can control their own behavior, and that if they forget, they will have to be separated from the work temporarily. (You may wish to review the Caution Points section of Chapter 7 on this subject.) Because you need to tailor special standards each time the type of activity or materials warrants, you will need to remind the pupils of the standards occasionally—perhaps each day. What to include in the standards is up to you, but they should be specific and few. Some teachers like to include "Stay in your seat unless you are a monitor." Even if trips to the drinking fountain or pencil sharpener are allowed during other subject activities, you may want to try restricting them during science group work. Allowing both talking and walking around at the same time may be too much novelty to handle. If one table discovers something especially exciting, for example, their "ooh's" and "ah's" may cause all the rest of the class members to leave their own work and crowd around that table.

A SIGNAL

You will need some kind of nonverbal signal to regain attention after group work begins. This could be a sound, reserved especially for this purpose, that can be detected over the hum of busy group workers, such as a chime or bell. Some teachers flip the light switch off and on. Some just flip the lights off and leave them off until they get attention. Other schemes include rhythmic clapping (to which pupils join in) and simply raising a hand. Whatever signal you choose, talk it over with the pupils before using it—do not just expect them to know what it means automatically. Also, the signal may have been used for something different before you came. A student teacher once tried sounding a chime to get attention, and all the children stood up and sang the Star Spangled Banner!

Another consideration for an attention signal is to use it sparingly. Consider a single science activity. After pupils begin group work, you will probably need your signal at least once, when it is time to stop working and begin cleaning up. In addition, you may need to use the signal to caution the class if you feel the noise level is increasing toward the "danger point." If such warnings happen more than once or twice, you should consider stopping the activity to review standards. A third use for the signal is when you find it necessary to give additional directions for the activity. Clearly, this last use is undesirable. The activity will go more smoothly if interruptions of this type, or of any type, are minimized. Still, interruptions will be necessary occasionally for some unanticipated problem, so having a pre-established signal is important. Remember to plan carefully to minimize the need for using the signal. If used too often, as with any frequent stimulus, it will lose its effect.

DISTRIBUTION AND CLEAN-UP

Plan carefully for quick distribution of materials. A waiting child is not only wasting time, but also getting restless and perhaps into trouble. On the first day of a new unit, some teachers like to set up all the tables while the pupils are out of the room, such as at lunch or recess. The problem of giving directions with materials already distributed can be handled by giving directions outside before the children come in, or in a special discussion area of the room. One teacher put out materials inside nontransparent containers. Children were asked to come in, to be seated quietly for directions, and to keep hands off the containers until given permission. After the unit is underway, however, a teacher should shift the setting-up and cleaning-up work to the pupils. They need to practice responsibility, and you need time to prepare your thoughts before beginning the lesson. A monitor system can be worked out, perhaps on a rotating basis—table captain of the week, for example. If necessary, special incentives such as extrinsic rewards can be used for groups showing responsibility in getting set up at the beginning and cleaned up at the end. The knowledge type involved here is arbitrary knowledge, a fairly low level of cognition, for which such rewards are appropriate.

DEALING WITH MESSES

Some teachers are reluctant about hands-on science because it is potentially messy. While careful planning and good directions will minimize messes, they can never be completely eliminated. So a child spills something—that is not the end of the world! The payoff from hands-on science is well worth an occasional mess. It is best to plan for the worst, though. Cover the tables with newspapers or towels, and have sponges, mops, and buckets handy just in case. If there is a potential for spilled liquids on the floor, restricting pupil movement around the room may be desirable to prevent slipping and possible injury.

INVOLVING THE PUPILS AT HOME

Sending simple materials home with children has the potential for getting parents and others at the pupil's home involved with your science program. Although such involvement sounds good, there are some possible drawbacks to consider. Your pupil may not have control over what happens to the material once outside the classroom. Because materials may be lost or damaged, use caution in what you send home. For the same reason, if the material is sent home for the child to use in a homework assignment, do not penalize the child if the work is not done and do not depend on the work's completion as a prerequisite for a subsequent activity. Some teachers like to ask pupils to bring things from home. For example, if each child brings a working flashlight, you have most of the expensive materials for teaching electricity activities. Also on the plus side, you may have interested the parents in what is happening in their child's science program. This means the child will get to talk about science at home. On the minus side, some children will not be able to get a flashlight. Rather than penalize or call attention to those children, just have some extra flashlights on hand. Any time you ask for such materials, it is good policy to send a note to the parents or guardians. Similarly, certain kinds of materials sent home should be preceded by request for "permission slips" to parents. Among these are any living things that require care or that might cause consternation of various sorts.

VERBAL TECHNIQUES FOR GUIDED DISCOVERY

In teaching at Autonomy Level I, direct telling and showing is the norm, both in procedural matters (giving directions) and for the substance of the lesson. At Autonomy Level II, the teacher's role becomes more differentiated. When giving directions, the teacher provides direct information by telling in much the same way as at the lower level. In guided discovery (in contrast to "free" or "open" discovery), pupils are usually not expected to devise their own procedures. When facilitating data collecting and when leading class discussions, however, new and indirect teaching methods are called for. The need for flexibility on the teacher's part is crucial when teaching by guided discovery. The "guided" part is what the teacher does to provide a focus and to limit serious frustration by keeping pupils from getting too far off the track. The "discovery" part is what the pupil does to notice things, to figure things out, and to make connections with past experience and other pupils' viewpoints.

GIVING DIRECTIONS

The process of giving directions is similar in guided discovery to the way it was in direct instruction. Since the role of the pupil involves taking greater responsibility at this level, however, the teacher places more emphasis on avoiding the need for repeating directions later. The main points now become brevity, clarity, and completeness. It is important to try to give directions for the entire data-collecting part of the lesson, in addition to reminders about behavior standards and special directions for distribution and clean-up of materials. Once data collection is underway, you will want to avoid interrupting the work with corrections or additions to the directions. Because giving complete directions must be planned more carefully, you may wish to review the detailed guidelines and suggestions for giving directions presented in Chapters 3 and 5.

FACILITATING DATA COLLECTION

It might be useful at this point to distinguish between the two main voices of the teacher. The teacher uses a *big voice* to address the whole class. When used effectively, pupils know they are all supposed to stop whatever else they may have been doing and listen. The teacher uses a *small voice* when speaking to one child or a small group. Pupils should know that they do not have to listen to the small voice unless it is addressed specifically to them. During data collecting, the pupil's role is to work with the materials, following the directions given earlier; the teachers role is to refrain from using the big voice and to use the small voice with restraint. In other words, during data collecting, the teacher is supposed to keep quiet and let the children work. Sometimes teachers get used to being the center of attention and in immediate direct control of everything. Learning to keep quiet and out of the limelight is one of the hardest things in learning to teach by guided discovery.

Why should the teacher keep quiet at this time? The pupils are supposed to be working with the materials—observing, recording, discussing with their partners. When a teacher uses the big voice, pupils are placed in conflict. They know they are supposed to be working, but they also know that they are supposed to stop and listen to the big voice. For a teacher to compete with a hands-on activity for the pupils' attention makes no sense. Because the materials are so compellingly interesting, they usually win. Not only do the children have trouble shifting attention in this situation, but also the authority of the big voice is eroded. The way to avoid—or at least minimize—the need for big-voice interruption during data collecting is to give brief, clear, complete directions in the first place.

In addition to keeping quiet, the teacher's role during collection of data involves noticing how pupils are doing. If a child is having trouble with equipment or has forgotten the directions, a small voice is called for. If it is possible, an indirect suggestion that leads the pupils to figure out the problem for him- or herself is best: "What does the directions chart say to do next?" "What would happen if you fastened this connector here?" "Do you remember what we did about this problem yesterday?" Occasionally you will find that a problem stems from faulty equipment or some other difficulty beyond the child's ability to work out on her or his own. Simply replace or fix the problem when possible, or arrange for the pupil to work with another team. Sometimes you may find one or more children misusing or playing with the materials in nonproductive ways. If proximity control or other mild management techniques do not work, remind the children involved (with the small voice) of the behavior standards and the possibility of being separated from the materials.

The teacher's main job during data collecting is to monitor how things are going as well as to watch how the children are using the materials. Watching pupils work with materials is like looking through a magic window into the workings of their minds. They act out their thinking in concrete, observable ways. One way to get fully involved with a group's thinking is to sit or bend down with them at eye level and then simply watch and listen without speaking. Suppose they are trying to make modelling clay float. You may see a child breaking the clay into smaller and smaller pieces before placing it in the water. Can you infer what this child's ideas about floating and sinking are? You may ask questions or make indirect suggestions to such a child (in a small voice), but avoid at all costs the temptations to "correct" the misconception. The feedback coming directly from the sinking slivers of clay is much more effective than anything the teacher could say, and is emotionally neutral besides. A child will revise his or her thinking about floating when that child is cognitively ready to do so.

In a task such as "Can you make the bulb light?" in a lesson on electric circuits, an intervention is necessary in the case of pupils who do not "get it" after a reasonable time. You might suggest that such pupils look around for ideas. An even more effective technique is to ask some pupils to draw diagrams on the board of circuits that "do work" and diagrams that "don't work." That way, everyone can be involved, and interesting arrangements that do not light the bulb are recognized. There should always be an open atmosphere of thinking and sharing ideas during guided discovery, never one of testing and "not cheating."

Another useful intervention is when you become aware that a child or group is drawing an incorrect conclusion from incomplete data. It is characteristic of children to jump to conclusions without looking at all the information available. In such a situation, you can ask a question to set up some conflict or sense of discrepancy, so that a natural need to reexamine the conclusion arises. For example, in an activity from a unit on electric circuits (such as the unit described in Chapter 13), a child might conclude that a certain diagram indicates a circuit will light a bulb because all the "special places" on the bulb and the battery are touching something. If the diagram shows a short circuit, the pupil's working hypothesis would be inadequate to make an accurate prediction. In such a case, you might ask the child to show you with the materials. In other cases, you might ask, "What would happen if I do this?" while indicating with the materials. Whenever possible, let the materials debunk faulty hypotheses or predictions. When that proves impossible, it is better to just let the matter pass uncorrected. Telling a child that a conclusion is wrong sets up emotional conflict between the authority of the child's teacher (social-arbitrary knowledge) and the child's own budding powers of reasoning (logical knowledge). The value of arranging for the pupil to find out for him- or herself is defeated and the child's trust of the teacher is probably damaged as well. If it is important for the pupil to get the right conclusion at that moment, then you will need to find a way for the materials to convince that pupil.

One final kind of intervention should be noted. Although the situation is rare, you may sometimes find a pupil who is shy or seems uninterested in working with the materials. Often, placement in the right group is helpful in such cases, but occasionally you may want to sit with this child yourself and, in your best nonthreatening manner, try to kindle interest: "I wonder what would happen if I connect the wire here?" "Have you tried this one yourself?" Feigning puzzlement over something you know the child can figure out is often effective: "I could never get this circuit— Number 7—to work. Juan said he couldn't get it either, but Emily did!"

There is no magic formula for deciding when to intervene during data collection and when not to. Facilitating guided discovery involves many judgments on whether and when to intervene to prevent excessive frustration and excessive boredom. (A little of each is usual.) Many of the potential needs for teacher intervention will be reduced by interactions with the other children in the group. The main guiding principle is that you cannot make a discovery for a child—the child must discover on his or her own. You can only facilitate, or arrange the environment so that the probability of success is increased. Most of the time, especially until you feel more at home with this new teaching method, the most effective intervention is none at all.

LEADING DISCUSSIONS FOR DATA PROCESSING

A good class discussion in a discovery (or inquiry) lesson involves many advanced teaching skills. No teacher is a perfect discussion leader, but everyone can improve by careful planning, a great deal of experience, and reflection. Because an effective discussion involves real thinking, the teacher must plan for flexibility.

The good data-processing discussion usually involves:

- A balanced mix of recall and higher-order teacher questions.
- A restriction of teacher judgments, including criticism and praise.
- An involvement of all pupils in speaking, listening, and responding, to other pupils as well as to the teacher.
- A use of "thinking time" to formulate responses, to complete responses, and to initiate reactions to responses of others.

RESEARCH ON QUESTIONING

Rowe (1978) found that teachers tend to ask a barrage of questions—some teachers as frequently as 10 questions per minute. Obviously, only the briefest and most superficial recall responses are possible in such rapid-fire exchanges. The pressure on pupils mounts during such a discussion. Recall that the guided-discovery method includes providing a safe emotional atmosphere for pupils' learning to think and encouraging thoughtful and mutually respectful exchanges among pupils and teacher. Clearly, guided discovery is incompatible with a barrage of low-level questions, which Rowe labels an "inquisition."

Raising the level of questions to call for higher-order thinking is often a good antidote to an excess of recall questions. Including such "thinking" questions is important, though research indicates that it is possible to have too much of a good thing. Achievement and balance of student responses is highest when the teacher uses a fairly even mix of recall and higher-order questions (Tisher, 1971; Riley, 1986).

Several systems of classifying questions have been developed, the best known of which is called Bloom's taxonomy (Bloom and Krathwohl, 1956). The higher the number of the category, the higher the level of thinking is considered:

1. *Memory*. Recalling or recognizing information.
2. *Translation*. Changing information into another language or symbol system.
3. *Interpretation*. Finding relationships.
4. *Application*. Solving realistic problems by identifying and applying rules.
5. *Analysis*. Solving problems that require conscious knowledge of the parts and processes of thinking.
6. *Synthesis*. Solving problems that require original, creative thinking.
7. *Evaluation*. Making value judgments as to good/bad or right/wrong on the basis of a designated standard.

Many teachers have found these categories useful in planning questions to bring out a variety of thinking types. The research is unclear on the value of using all the categories, only that there should be a mix of questions demanding high-level and low-level thinking. Categories 1 and 2 are generally considered to be low level, and categories 3 through 7 to be high level. It is probably not worthwhile for you to worry about making fine distinctions between the categories; simply use the system if it is helpful in generating questions that call for a variety of levels and categories, or find another system if it is not.

Good and Brophy (1987) describe five characteristics of good questions, based on work by Groisser (1964). Good questions are clear, purposeful, brief, natural and adapted to the learners' level, and thought-provoking. Clear questions are usually brief and long questions are hard to understand. But not all brief questions are clear. "How about the habitat?" is vague and may be misleading. "What alternative paradigm might be applied?" contains words that might be unknown to children. Questions should have vocabulary and word order that are natural to the children. Some beginning teachers plan a discussion by simply thinking up every question possible that has anything to do with the subject. A much more effective practice is to plan a logical sequence of questions, all of which are pertinent to the gradual development of the lesson objectives.

WAIT TIME

Discussions that are more than rote drill require some silent time for thinking, both by pupils and by the teacher. Rowe's research in this area has identified two kinds of wait time (see Figure 9.2). *Wait time 1* is the time after a teacher asks a question and before another word is spoken, either by the pupil responding or by the teacher calling on another pupil or speaking for some other reason. *Wait time 2* is the time after a pupil speaks before another word is spoken, either by the pupil continuing or by the teacher speaking. The average wait time of teachers not aware that this is a factor in learning is less than 1 second. Many teachers—especially those who engage in the barrage of rapid-fire questions—even interrupt responding pupils to praise inappropriately or to call on another child. When teachers learn to extend their wait time to 3 to 5 seconds, a number of desirable effects happen:

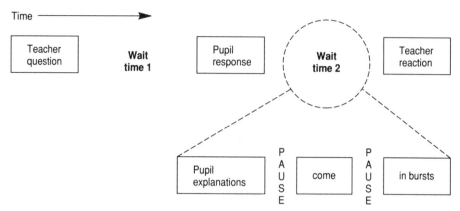

Source: Adapted from *Teaching Science as Continuous Inquiry: A Basic (2nd ed.)* by M. B. Rowe, 1978, New York: McGraw-Hill. Printed with permission of the author.

- Average length of pupil responses is longer.
- Pupils initiate more responses.
- There are fewer failures to respond.
- The quality of response is greater.
- Teachers become more flexible in their questions and reactions to pupil responses.
- Teacher expectations for previously "quiet" pupils increase.

PRAISE

Early in their preparation, teachers usually learn the undesirability of criticism and negative reactions to pupil responses. This is an easy lesson because no teacher likes to be negative and because many teachers are afraid that criticism will cause pupils to dislike them. Yet to the novice teacher, praise sometimes seems the only alternative to negativity; and praise may be used too much, in the wrong way, or inappropriately.

Praise is effective when it is genuine, appropriate, not overly dramatic, and directed to specific tasks or skills (Good & Brophy, 1987). Several research studies have reported that praise is often given for incorrect answers, especially when directed to low achievers (Natriello & Dornbusch, 1984; Anderson, Evertson, & Brophy, 1979; Brookover et al., 1978). How can this happen? Teachers often use global praise—vaguely worded, random phrases that cannot readily be identified as praise of pupil, effort, or solution. When asked about specific instances of inappropriate praise, teachers report that they were attempting to encourage effort.

Even when used for correct answers, praise often has certain undesirable effects. Praise of the child himself ("Good boy!") can make him or other children feel insecure ("What if I'm wrong next time? Does that make me a bad boy?"). Praise for effort or correct response can make other children reluctant to participate for fear that their response will seem poor by comparison. Praise definitely has a terminating effect on thinking. (She liked that answer a lot! No need to think about that any more.)

Pupils in a classroom where a great deal of praise is used are discouraged from learning to think for themselves. The probability of developing interest in the subject of discussion for intrinsic reasons is therefore reduced, and the primary payoff for the pupils becomes more praise. Like an addiction, praise tends to prevent normal development towards independent thinking. Most beginning teachers would stand to benefit from reexamining the effects of praise and enlarging their repertoire of discussion techniques to include some alternatives.

Rowe (1974) has also done extensive research on the effects of praise. She concluded that overt verbal praise is effective in changing social behavior as well as in drill activities for basic facts. But for establishing an inquiry atmosphere and encouraging higher-order, independent thinking, praise is actually counterproductive! In classrooms where praise was frequent, children showed lower confidence, as evidenced by inflected responses, and checking the teacher's face. When verbal rewards were high, pupils' responses tended to be short and their explanations incomplete. Additionally, pupils in high-reward settings showed more hand waving ("call-on-me!" syndrome) and less listening to other pupils' ideas. Clearly, discussions in high-reward classrooms are more likely to resemble a game of competition for the teacher's attention than an interesting conversation. In contrast, when the frequency of overt verbal praise is decreased, these negative effects tend to diminish or disappear.

If you wish to learn more about how and when to use praise effectively, study Chapter 5 in Haim Ginott's *Teacher and Child* (1972), Chapter 6 in Good and Brophy's *Looking in Classrooms* (1987), and Chapter 10 in Rowe's *Teaching Science as Continuous Inquiry* (1978). If you wish to experience what a science discussion with little or no praise is like, arrange to view Labinowicz's *Teaching by Listening* videotapes (1985b).

PLANNING A DISCUSSION

Planning is time well spent for the inexperienced teacher, or for any teacher trying a new method. Because the experience necessary to think on your feet is limited, planning can go a long way towards preventing problems and reaching the lesson objectives. Although flexible questions and responses are important, you can compose or collect some good ones ahead of time to choose from as needed. This guideline may be helpful: your job is not to pass judgment, but to find out about the children's thinking.

As you plan a discussion, consider that you will first want to ask pupils to report and compare their observations:

- What did you notice about the detailed structure of your mealworm?
- How many segments did the mealworms have? Was this the same for everyone?
- Should we count the head as a segment? The tail?
- Which characteristics do you think would be the same for all mealworms, and which might be different?

Later in the discussion, you will want to ask for speculation on relationships or generalizations based on the observations:

- Did you notice any patterns in the isopods' behavior?
- Which variables seemed to make a difference in the swinging of the pendulum?
- Did this experiment remind you of anything that people do on the playground?
- Can you make a general rule to explain that?
- Do you have an idea of what might have happened in this track picture?
- What are some possible explanations for the Cartesian diver?

Planning questions is only one part of planning a discussion. You will also want to think about your reactions to possible pupil responses. During reporting of data, very little reaction from you is needed or desirable. Simply accept the responses without judging—instant judgment is not required. Remember the knowledge types of Piaget. Observations are physical knowledge. The best feedback for questions of physical knowledge comes from the objects. If there is a discrepancy between observations of different children, the children will often raise a question themselves. If not, you could suggest that they check again to see if their observations can be duplicated. During initial reporting, you may wish to jot down the observations on the board, especially if you plan to refer to them later for comparison or analysis. This is a way of accepting without judgment. Another way is simply to acknowledge hearing by smiling, nodding, or making noncommittal remarks such as "hmm" or "I see." In the absence of the accustomed judgment—"right," "good," "wrong"—energetic and obvious listening is essential to let the pupils know that you are with them.

When children share their explanations, it is useful to probe for further thinking, regardless of whether the children are right or wrong. Remember, in discovery or inquiry science, thinking is at least as important as result. By asking for more ideas, you will not only get additional ideas already in place and ready to be reported, but you will also stimulate additional thinking. Sometimes in the process of explaining, the child will decide the idea needs more work. Sometimes probing by the teacher stimulates improved description that communicates the idea more fully or more clearly to other pupils. By probing for more, you let your pupils know that you value their ideas and their thinking.

Children's language is often imprecise; by asking for clarification, you help them develop more careful use of language as well as sharper thinking. Listen for "magic words" that seem to say more than they do: *gravity, force, friction, density, photosynthesis, oxygen,* and so on. Another common situation occurs when children report inferences or other speculations as if they were observations. When that happens, ask for observations with questions such as:

- How do you know?
- Did you notice something that supports your idea?
- That's an interesting inference. What observations did you base it on?
- What do you mean by friction?
- Can you say that another way?
- Please explain for everyone what that word means.
- Is that anything like the term used earlier?
- OK, that's your theory. Let's see if there are others.

Encourage pupils to listen and respond to one another. Avoid mimicry (repeating pupil responses). Instead, ask a child to repeat so that everyone can hear, or ask another child to paraphrase. When you mimic, you send two undesirable messages: (1) it is unnecessary to listen to other children because the teacher will repeat it, and (2) a child's comment counts for nothing until it has been "authorized" by coming out of the teacher's mouth. Ask questions such as:

- What do you think of Kab's idea? Who would like to agree or disagree and say why?
- Can you rephrase Jennifer's idea?
- How does Jeremy's idea relate to yours?
- Tyrone, you also mentioned decomposition. Would you like to react to Felipe's idea?

Sometimes pupils get stuck in a blind alley with untestable explanations. Try to redirect them into a more interesting line of thinking by indirect suggestions:

- Are other interpretations possible?
- Are there any other ways to think about this?
- Are there any other clues or observations that we haven't thought about?
- What other factors could be involved?
- What would happen if we. . . .
- And if that were changed, what would happen then?

Beginning teachers sometimes express discomfort in handling incorrect responses. Remember Piaget's knowledge types. Only errors in arbitrary knowledge need correcting by the teacher or some other authority, such as a dictionary. Physical knowledge (observations) is best "corrected" by further observation. Logical knowledge must be constructed in each learner's head; correcting logical knowledge only undermines the child's confidence in his or her thinking and makes the child dependent on the teacher. As seen in the various responses to the Piaget tasks, children's logical knowledge grows internally and at its own rate. Teachers must respect children's prelogical responses—such as "One field has less area because the barns are spread out"—as a temporary stopover on the long journey of mental development.

WORKING ON INTERACTIVE SKILLS

As important as planning is, the time comes when it is necessary to teach and see what happens next. Nobody is perfect, but by getting feedback on your teaching behavior, you can decide later what the effects of your actions were and consider whether anything needs changing. How can you get feedback on your teaching behavior? If you are fairly new to teaching, you may have a supervisor or mentor who watches your lessons and provides information. If you are lucky, that person gives you observations rather than judgments and solutions: "This is what you did" rather than "You are talking too much." You need respect during your professional development, just as children need respect during their cognitive and emotional development. You will not always do the best thing, but you need to learn to recognize your more-effective and less-effective behaviors, and you need to learn how to optimize effective behaviors on your own. A good supervisor or mentor helps you learn to be self-teaching.

Many teachers become so centered on what pupils are doing that they forget to notice what they themselves are doing. If you are unhappy with the way the children are acting during discussions (or any other time), examine what you could do to make a difference. It is not easy to notice details of your own behavior during the complexities of an ongoing lesson. One way to get more information is with a tape recorder. This is a simple, unobtrusive way to record questions, responses, and other verbal behaviors. Although videotape recorders also have their merits, they are harder to arrange, influence everyone's behavior to some extent, and take longer to become emotionally neutral to. It would take several experiences of viewing of yourself teaching on videotape before you could concentrate on pertinent behaviors. Generally, teachers are transfixed with their own appearance and style and are not even thinking about teaching behaviors during the first two or three tapes. With audiotapes, the shock wears off much quicker, allowing the teacher to concentrate on verbal behaviors. For leading discussions, very few nonverbal behaviors are important, so audiotapes are easier, more efficient, and record almost as much useful information.

There are many types of verbal behavior you can analyze from tape recordings, though you will probably want to select just one or two at a time for consideration. The activities at the end of this chapter will give you some specific ideas for analyzing taped lessons. A sampling of some verbal behaviors you can listen for on a tape, or ask an observer to note down, include:

- Wait time
- Length of pupil responses
- Quality of pupil responses
- Teacher questions, low-level and high-level
- Teacher reaction to pupil response
- Pupil-pupil interaction/ Pupil-initiated talk
- Failures to respond
- Inflected responses
- Mimicry
- Rhetorical questions, other coercive teacher talk
- "Yes, but. . . ."
- The "call-on-me!" syndrome (wild hand waving and "oo," "aah")

Some of these behaviors have not been mentioned here before, but all will be examined in this chapter.

A Contrast of Approaches

If you could observe classrooms in which an inquiry-style discussion was in progress and contrast what you see and hear with observations from a more typical "inquisition" classroom, you would notice many differences. In the typical classroom, the teacher would talk quite a bit, sometimes for several minutes at a time. Teacher questions would usually be at a recall level, paced for rapid exchange with a great deal of nonspecific praise and mimicry of pupil responses. Sometimes the teacher would ask a rhetorical question, an assertion disguised as a question: "Most of the air is nitrogen, isn't it?" Almost no one would have the nerve to say no, whether agreeing or not. A rhetorical question does not ask for thinking—it demands compliance or agreement. The pupils would only speak to answer questions. Their responses would be short, usually a single word. The responses would often be inflected with a rising tone at the end, as if to say, "Is that what you want?" You might notice that only certain pupils raised their hands regularly, and usually they were the ones called on to answer. Others might not respond at all, or sometimes respond, "I don't know." Another curious thing that often happens in such a classroom is that when a question is asked, some or all of the pupils wildly wave their arms and make "oo" and "aah" sounds.

In the inquiry classroom, pupils would do much more of the talking, and the teacher much less. Pupils would sometimes speak directly to each other, to ask and answer questions, to agree and disagree. You would notice that the pupils would somehow seem much more confident in their responses and that their comments were longer and involved more speculation. The teacher would show interest in pupil comments and would often probe for more information or clarity, or simply smile or nod without judging. The class discussion would seem more like a conversation among equals than what you might expect in an elementary classroom, and altogether a more pleasant and interesting atmosphere than the other one.

ESTABLISHING AN INQUIRY ATMOSPHERE

The pleasant, mutually respectful, stimulating atmosphere of the inquiry discussion requires the establishment of an atmosphere that is psychologically safe for speculation as well as the sharing of thinking that is not "finished" yet. This open climate does not simply happen. It is not enough for a teacher to know how to avoid behaviors that reduce trust and how to use behaviors that favor inquiry. There must also be cooperation from the pupils. Because children are usually accustomed to classrooms with fast exchanges, they tend to respond to questions immediately, with short, superficial answers. In other words, wait time 1, the pause following the teacher's question, depends on the pupil to a large degree: if the pupil answers prematurely, wait time is reduced. In the kind of discussion children are used to, a quick, short response is all the pupil is given time for. If you want inquiry to succeed in your classroom, the pupils must be taught (directly) the procedure of the new discussion method.

Labinowicz has described a way to teach children to function in a discussion in which thinking is valued more than correct answers. Chapter 9 of his book *Learning from Children* (1985a), from which many of the following ideas are taken, is highly recommended for further reading. Before beginning an inquiry discussion, Labinowicz recommends informing the children of the reason for wait time through these sorts of comments: Waiting time is thinking time. I will ask a question and then I will wait for a while before I call on someone. I will not always call on a person with a raised hand. I am interested in how people think. It is important not to call out and not to wave hands, so that everyone has time to think. Different people will have different ideas. This is good. You will be learning from each other.

In later discussions, the children will need to be reminded of the wait-time procedures. The teacher can explain that when someone forgets and calls out an answer,

▼ FIGURE 9.3
The learning-to-discuss cycle

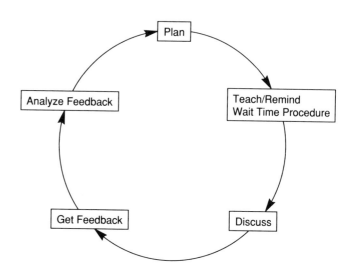

▼ FIGURE 9.3
The learning-to-discuss cycle

the person who is still thinking about it will stop thinking. And the idea that was interrupted could have been very interesting to everyone. Additional reminders will be needed for a while until waiting and respecting the views of others become habituated. The teacher can encourage pupils to tell whether they agree or disagree with another pupil's comment and to give their reasons. Hand signals can also be established to remind the impulsive or over-eager child to wait quietly while thinking is going on.

THE LEARNING-TO-DISCUSS CYCLE

Neither pupils nor teachers learn to function in an inquiry discussion overnight. It takes planning, practice, feedback, and time. Don't be discouraged if you are not perfect right away. The payoff for good inquiry—trust, respect for diverse thinking, taking responsibility for one's own learning—is worth the effort. A frame of mind that helps all the details fall into place is to adopt a diagnostic outlook. If you develop a great interest in how each pupil is thinking and value the development of independent reason and responsibility, it will seem natural to listen rather than to tell, and to probe rather than to praise. To continue growing in the complex skills of leading inquiry discussion, the cycle of teaching and learning shown in Figure 9.3 is recommended.

▼ *Mr. Newman:*   I enjoyed watching you lead that discussion, but when I think about doing it myself, I get really nervous. As new at this as I am, I'm afraid I would lose control of the children.

    Ms. Oldhand: I went through the same misgivings when I first heard of the wait-time idea. I was uncomfortable with the silence and constantly had the impulse to speed up the questions to keep control.

    Mr. Newman: Seems reasonable. How did you overcome it?

Ms. Oldhand:	I was taking a graduate methods course, and the professor made us analyze tape recordings of our teaching. I found out that I had better control when I was using wait time than when I didn't. I guess the children lost interest in the topic during the fast-paced lessons.
Mr. Newman:	I'll try to keep that in mind when I try my batteries-and-bulbs discussion tomorrow. I know I have a head start because you have already taught the children how to behave during a discussion. But I was wondering how you coped with those who blurted out answers before you called on anyone.
Ms. Oldhand:	I had a long talk with them the first time we tried it, and then shorter talks for many of the following discussions. When someone answered prematurely, I just ignored it. Sometimes I used this "shush" signal [*finger to lips*]. Gradually, they got better. The secret is consistency. If you accept a premature answer after reminding them to wait, it's just like erasing your reminder from their minds.
Mr. Newman:	I noticed that they didn't raise their arms to get called on, but just a finger.
Ms. Oldhand:	Yes, we figured out that less arm waving worked better and didn't distract others who were still thinking. Somehow, restricting large muscle motions also seems to keep everyone calmer and on track.

LANGUAGE DEVELOPMENT

Language development should be an integral part of all science instruction. Communicating, one of the basic science processes, involves both oral and written language. The traditional language-arts curriculum puts a great deal of emphasis on the receiving skills of reading and listening. The sending skill of writing also receives emphasis, but the other sending skill, speaking, is quite underemphasized in most classrooms. Science serves as a good forum in which to learn to express thoughts orally, and science is almost unique in providing an interesting common experience around which to practice and exercise all the communicating skills. Cazden (1979) has made a strong case for teaching science to limited-English-proficient (LEP) pupils directly in English because the elements of good science instruction, direct experience and discussion, are the same elements used in many ESL and bilingual education programs. Language arts curriculum is increasingly based on literature, including fiction and poetry. Shared science experiences provide not only a focus of interest around which to develop language but also a different genre, one that involves quantitative thinking, that concerns a verifiable reality, and that grows out of an interaction between that reality and the mental constructions of the child. The affective and moral aspects of learning to disagree amicably are important but rarely dealt with in elementary classrooms.

Class discussions involving description provide a ripe opportunity for language development. Children need help learning to describe. They need regular lessons in which lists of adjectives and adjectival phrases are generated and critically analyzed for appropriateness. Sometimes it seems that the only adjectives known to elementary children are "weird," "yucky," "far out," "rad," "cool," "totally awesome" and similar vogue words. These expressions describe emotional effects on the speaker rather than observable attributes of objects and systems. Get out those school dictionaries and your thesaurus for a communication process lesson. Start with some everyday adjectives, provided by you if they cannot generate any. Generate synonyms, antonyms, and homonyms. Use them in paragraphs. Put a list of new adjectives on the board for use in journal entries. Do not be reluctant to use some of the techniques from language-arts methods during science class. After all, language development needs a context, and science needs communication skills.

A regular instruction feature of some other subjects is the learning of vocabulary at the beginning of a lesson. This practice deserves some scrutiny as it applies to science. Why should vocabulary be given at the beginning of a lesson, complete with definitions and examples? The obvious reason is that there follows some reading matter or audiovisual presentation which uses the vocabulary. Now think about a guided-discovery lesson. The learning takes place from experience and from talking and thinking, not from reading or listening. Only when learning input is delivered through language does initial vocabulary learning become important. Even then, when the input is controlled by the teacher, important words could be learned on a flexible schedule, at the time they appear in the context of the lesson. The practice of separating word study from a meaningful context is unreasonable in most cases.

Pupils need help learning adjectives and other descriptive language, and they also need help with nouns to name objects and events under study. What they do not need is something that can be called "magic words," words used to answer questions or to "explain" when no explanation is provided and no understanding is present. Among the most notorious are *gravity*, *friction*, *photosynthesis*, *density*, and *oxygen*. How many general questions about science do you think you can ask (to people of any age) without hearing any of these words in the response? Very few. Try asking, "What exactly do you mean by *gravity*?" Does the speaker have anything more profound than "earth pull" in mind? Most unlikely. So everyone uses words occasionally to give the appearance of knowing it all. Perhaps such a misuse of words is not so terrible in a social situation among friends. But in a learning situation—especially in science, which involves learning to think about the world—there is something dishonest about clouding the air instead of communicating as clearly as possible. What is especially insidious about the practice is that the person using the magic words fools him- or herself as often as the listener is fooled.

Teachers of science need to be vigilant in the honest use of language among themselves and to probe for understanding when hearing jargon used by pupils. The actual meaning of most magic words is often too abstract for elementary pupils, and thus need not be taught at all. Teach the names of the objects and help pupils learn a rich descriptive vocabulary that can be used flexibly as the situation warrants. Explanations can often be framed in ordinary language without giving the impression of greater erudition than actually exists.

▼ SUMMARY

Because pupils must function more independently in guided discovery than in direct instruction, special, indirect teaching techniques are needed. Among the techniques described in this chapter were management of materials and behavior in a guided-discovery context. In order to function and think more critically and more independently, the child must learn to become more responsible. In order to facilitate growth in responsibility, the teacher must carefully plan management situations of limited complexity in which pupils can practice being responsible with a high probability of success. There must always be a possibility of failure, however, or else there is no value to the practicing done by the child.

A second major topic of this chapter has been verbal techniques as they differ from those used in direct instruction. Teaching by guided discovery requires a very different way of looking at teaching. One must realize that pupils can only learn social-arbitrary knowledge from the teacher's spoken word. In order for pupils to learn other, higher-order kinds of knowledge, the teacher must provide an appropriate situation and then allow the learners to do their own learning. For physical knowledge, the teacher provides objects and allows pupils to interact with those objects, essentially without interference. For logical knowledge, the teacher asks thought-provoking questions and then listens very carefully to the responses, often probing for additional thinking on the same idea before leaving it. Social-interactive knowledge as well as logical knowledge develops in an atmosphere of respectful give and take as ideas are compared and tested during group discussions. As for allotment of time, the discovery teacher seems to spend most of a lesson watching and listening. By thinking primarily about the children's learning and thinking processes, the teacher allows the pupils to concentrate on the topic of study.

▼ DISCUSSION QUESTIONS

1. What role does direct instruction have in fostering increased autonomy? Is this a contradiction of terms?
2. Some teachers manage to regain attention without a special signal, just by a loud "attention, please" or words to that effect. Discuss the pros and cons of this approach and of various signals.
3. With some children, especially the very young, it may be much easier for the teacher to do the setting up and cleaning up of materials. How important is it for children to do these tasks?

4. While circulating during the data-collection part of a lesson, a student teacher loudly announced "tips" and additional directions several times. When asked about this later, she said, "It was good advice. I figured that others could benefit from hearing it as well as the child I was talking to." React to this situation.

5. In an earlier chapter on direct instruction, you read that during guided practice a pupil should be corrected immediately in case of an error. Why is it different when a pupil demonstrates an erroneous concept during guided discovery?

6. React to this remark: "Teachers like to praise. Children like to be praised. What is the point of reducing or avoiding praise?"

7. Teachers need to let pupils know that they are listening to what the pupils say. What are some alternatives to praise and mimicry? What is different about their effects?

8. How would you begin to teach a new class to function well in a guided-discovery discussion?

9. Do all the following questions need the same amount of wait time? Explain. If you think not, which questions require more, and which less wait time?
   a. How many legs did you find on your mealworm?
   b. Do you think that all mealworms have the same number of legs?
   c. Have you noticed any patterns in what they do?
   d. Would any of these behaviors help a mealworm to survive?

10. What does it mean to disagree amicably and why is this important in science and life generally?

11. What are some examples of energetic and obvious listening a teacher can use in the absence of verbal sanctions?

▾ ACTIVITIES FOR THE READER

A practice cycle of the type in this activity was developed by Linda DeTure and used in an unpublished teacher education videotape called *Teaching by Listening* by Ed Labinowicz (1985b). DeTure reports that almost all teachers were able to achieve an average wait time of 3 seconds or more after only two practice cycles. For this activity:

1. Select about 10 children.
2. Audiotape a discussion of about 10 minutes length.
3. Chose a 5–7 minute portion to transcribe verbatim.
4. Record teacher talk and pupil talk on separate lines with space between.
5. In blank lines, note wait time as type 1 or type 2.
6. Time the wait time to the nearest second using a stop watch. If there is no wait time, record zero.
7. Calculate averages for wait time 1 and wait time 2 separately.

Tapes and written transcripts should be saved for several reasons:

- It is excellent reinforcement to listen to a "good" tape later.
- Others can benefit from hearing your tape.
- Transcripts or tapes can also be analyzed for verbal behaviors other than wait time.

▼ REFERENCES

Anderson, L., Evertson, C., & Brophy, J. (1979). An experimental study of effective teaching in first-grade reading groups. *Elementary School Journal, 79*, 193–223.

Bloom, Benjamin B. & Krathwohl, David R. (Eds.). (1967). *Taxonomy of educational objectives: Handbook I. Cognitive domain.* New York: David McKay.

Brookover, W., Schweitzer, J., Schneider, J., Beady, C., Flood, P., & Wisenbaker, J. (1978). Elementary school social climate and school achievement. *American Educational Research Journal, 15*, 301–318.

Cazden, C. (1979). Curriculum language contexts for bilingual education. In *Language development in a bilingual setting* (pp. 129–138). Los Angeles: National Dissemination and Assessment Center.

DeTure, L. and Miller, A. (1984). The effects of a written protocol model on teacher acquisition of extended wait-time. Paper presented at the annual meeting of the National Association for Research in Science Teaching. New Orleans.

Ginott, H. (1972). *Teacher and child: A book for parents and teachers.* New York: Avon.

Good, T., & Brophy, J. (1987). *Looking in Classrooms* (4th ed.). New York: Harper & Row.

Groisser, P. (1964). *How to use the fine art of questioning.* New York: Teachers' Practical Press.

Labinowicz, E. (1985a). *Learning from children: New beginnings for teaching numerical thinking.* Menlo Park, CA: Addison-Wesley.

Labinowicz, E. (1985b). *Teaching by listening: The time dimension.* A series of video-tape programs developed in cooperation with the Instructional Media Center, California State University, Northridge.

Natriello, G., & Dornbusch, S. (1984). *Teacher evaluative standards and student effort.* New York: Longman.

Renner, J., & Marek, E. (1988). *The learning cycle and elementary school science teaching.* Portsmouth, NH: Heinemann.

Riley, J. P. (1986). The effects of teachers' wait-time and knowledge comprehension questioning on science achievement. *Journal of Research in Science Teaching, 23*(4), 335–342.

Rowe, M. (1974). Relation of wait-time and rewards to the development of language, logic, and fate control: Part II—Rewards. *Journal of Research in Science Teaching, 11*(4), 291–308.

Rowe, M. (1978). *Teaching science as continuous inquiry: A basic* (2nd ed.). New York: McGraw-Hill.

Tisher, Richard P. (1971). Verbal interactions in science classes. *Journal of Research in Science Teaching, 8*(1), 1–8.

GROUP INVESTIGATIONS

▼ A BEGINNING TEACHER LEARNS ABOUT GROUP INVESTIGATIONS

Ms. Sanchez, a beginning teacher, has observed her mentor, Ms. Oldhand, several times during the year. One day she visited Ms. O.'s class and was surprised to see that the children, who had been in their seats carrying out directions on her first visit, were now spread out all over the room—some on the floor, some standing together in a corner, some talking excitedly in groups around their desks. The classroom was not quiet, but it wasn't really noisy either. It reminded her of a beehive: there was a low buzz of children talking, but no one voice rose above the others.

Ms. Sanchez walked over to Ms. O. and remarked that this certainly looked different from the last time she had been in the class. "Oh, yes," Ms. O. said, "The way I teach depends upon the goals of the lesson. When you visited this class before, I was teaching the children a specific skill that they needed to know in order to do other things later on. They were learning to use the balance and they needed to practice until they had mastered the skill.

"Today the goals are different. I like to think that I am not actually *teaching* a lesson but giving them an opportunity to learn on their own. Today each group is working on its own, planning how to find out something that the children of the group want to know about trees. Children in each group have thought of a question about trees that interests them, and now they are planning how to collect data to help them answer their questions."

"This must be an easy way to teach," remarked Ms. Sanchez, "It looks as if the children are doing all the work."

Ms. O. laughed. "Well it may *look* easy," she replied, "but actually this kind of teaching is a real test of a teacher's skill. In the first place, the pupils have to be taught to conduct themselves appropriately and responsibly when they are working independently. Then an attitude of mutual respect and trust between pupils as well as between pupils and teacher has to be developed. The teacher has to plan very carefully and thoughtfully and then has to monitor the pupils' progress toward the goals of the day's work."

"I'd like to walk around and observe what the groups are doing to try to get a better idea of what's going on," said Ms. Sanchez.

BACKGROUND

This chapter describes a teaching style based on pupils working together in small groups to investigate different questions about the same topic. You have already examined examples in Chapters 7 and 9 of a teaching method in which pupils work in groups, but the style described in this chapter has some important differences. In guided discovery, all groups study the same questions; in *group investigations*, each of the groups investigates a different question or set of questions, though all are related to the same general topic.

▼ Little teacher time is needed for overt management of behavior when pupils are busy and interested in their tasks.

The next chapter also deals with children working in groups, but in that case the pupils work on independent and group projects rather than on group investigations. The line between an investigation and a project is not always clear, but you will understand why they have been separated after you study the two chapters.

The style of teaching called group investigations has its theoretical basis in the work of the thinkers discussed in Chapter 2. Piaget, Bruner, and Papert have stressed the importance of active participation and exploration in the construction of knowledge and meaning. Vygotsky stressed the importance of social interaction among peers in the process of learning. And Kohlberg's ideas of moral development can only be realized in a classroom atmosphere of respect and trust between teacher and pupils and among the pupils themselves. All of these ideas are put into practice in this teaching method.

Although you may never have experienced this way of teaching, it is by no means a new method. It was advocated in the United States by John Dewey in the early 1900s and has been used successfully in other countries through the years. Of the science teaching materials published in the United States, those produced by the

Elementary Science Study (ESS) in the 1960s are probably the most useful as sources of ideas for group investigations. The ESS booklets contain a wealth of ideas for investigations of topics of interest to children and adolescents. The activity on clay boats described in Chapter 2, which was taken from an ESS publication, gives the flavor of those materials. Some of those booklets are available from sources listed at the end of Chapter 6.

Group investigations are a part of elementary science education in many schools in both Great Britain and Japan. Since the early 1970s, teachers in Great Britain have had available the *Science 5–13* materials, a set of books produced by a government-sponsored team for children between the ages of 5 and 13. These materials help teachers help children learn science through firsthand experience. Each of the books in the series deals with a particular topic or subject area. Among the topics included are structures and forces, minibeasts, metals, working with wood, and science from toys. Each book contains suggestions and directions for a great number of investigations. Some of the titles in this series are included in a list of sources at the end of this chapter.

Japan is another country where group investigations are used as a method of teaching science in elementary schools. Its use there is particularly interesting in view of international comparison studies in which Japanese children have been found to have high levels of achievement in science. Charron, an American teacher who spent many hours in elementary science classrooms in Tokyo, reported that group investigations were used by all the teachers she observed as well as by all those who answered a questionnaire she distributed. As she described what she saw: "The small group activity portion of the lesson usually consisted of team members completing their investigative designs, obtaining teacher approval for the plan, getting materials and equipment, carrying out the investigation, and describing the procedure and results on work sheets or in science notebooks" (Charron, 1987).

Charron also observed that Japanese teachers had to devote little time to overt management of behavior, because pupils were busy and interested with their tasks. She made another important observation: teachers spent the period interacting with students and asking questions focused on pupils' ideas, predictions, findings, and conclusions rather than on facts and memorization of information.

Her findings should reassure teachers who hesitate to try independent investigations because of a concern that pupils will not attend to their work or that they will even become loud and unruly. This chapter will include a section on cooperative learning that will show you how to set up productive groups.

PRACTICAL CONSIDERATIONS

The method of group investigations is most often used in the upper elementary grades or middle grades, though children in the primary grades can learn to work in this way if the projects are not too ambitious and if guidance is provided. Younger children often become tired and frustrated on long projects, but fifth, sixth, and seventh graders who have learned the advanced science skills will thrive in a class in which they work in this way.

In this chapter, it is assumed that you have been with your pupils long enough to have worked out basic rules of classroom behavior and that the pupils understand what is expected of them. Some important things for pupils to remember (or be reminded of) are to:

- Interact courteously with one another.
- Stay on task without constant reminders from the teacher.
- Use simple equipment correctly.
- Persist in a task until a "stopping point" is reached.

This teaching method makes high demands on both teacher and pupils. No one method can be successfully used for all instruction. The chapters in this book have been arranged so that each new level allows new instructional methods but does not rule out the use of methods previously described. The decisions about whether to use group investigations depends on the goals of instruction, the teachers' experience in guiding instruction, and the pupils' ability to assume responsibility for their own behavior and learning.

If you would review Table 4.1 on Autonomy Levels in Chapter 4, you may gain a better understanding of the differences between this teaching method and the other two methods, by comparing the goals, the pupil's role, and the teacher's role across the three levels.

CHOOSING A TOPIC

Topics suitable for this style of teaching are those that can be studied through first-hand exploration of objects and materials that are readily available. The region where you teach and the time of year may be important factors. For example, you probably would not choose to teach a unit on trees if your school were on the edge of the desert or if you were planning to teach the unit during January in North Dakota. In both of those cases, you would have to depend mostly on books and films rather than on the pupils' use of materials available in their own environment. But you could have a unit on plastics and metals, for example, at any time or place that enough materials could be assembled.

An important consideration in choosing the topic is the potential of the topic for further learning. Careful thought should be given to choosing a topic that is broad enough and important enough to form the foundation for your pupils' further learning later on. Such further learning is the idea behind Bruner's spiral curriculum mentioned in Chapter 2.

Remember that most of these children still think predominantly in the concrete mode; that is, their thinking is still based on their own experiences with objects and events. Investigations should always ,be based on children's own experiences, although that does not mean that they can never use books or other sources of information to answer questions their own investigations have raised. When the needed knowledge is arbitrary knowledge, such as the names of different kinds of trees, then the use of books or other sources of information will be necessary. Such information will be more meaningful for children who have already had firsthand experience.

Questions to ask yourself when choosing a topic include:

- Is the topic broad enough to allow for many kinds of investigations at different levels of ability?
- Are materials available in this locality at this time of year?
- Are the materials safe for children to gather and handle?
- Can children find out interesting things through activities they can do on their own?
- Will there be opportunities to use a variety of science processes in their investigations?

GROUPING FOR INSTRUCTION: COOPERATIVE LEARNING

If you have decided to use group investigations and have chosen a topic, you will then consider how to organize the pupils to ensure a successful learning experience. Since the children will be working on their own much of the time and will have a great deal of responsibility to monitor their own behavior and their progress toward task completion, it is important that the groups work cooperatively. Cooperative Learning, introduced in Chapter 7, will be described here in more detail because it is an essential component of this method of instruction.

SETTING UP GROUPS

As explained in Chapter 7, groups of four or five pupils seem to work best. The groups should be as heterogeneous as possible, which means a mix of male and female, students with special problems, low ability and high ability, and the various racial and ethnic groups in your class. Research on the effects of using cooperative learning has shown that this strategy is effective in promoting better working relationships in the classroom between boys and girls, handicapped and nonhandicapped children, and minority and nonminority children (Slavin, 1980).

The first thing to do in setting up groups is to make a list of your pupils, ranking them from high to low ability. Use whatever information you have in ranking your pupils, and do not spend time worrying about fine distinctions; approximations are all you need. Next, divide this list into four sublists of equal or nearly equal size—the top fourth, the second fourth, and so on. These sublists are called quartiles. Now choose one from each sublist (quartile) to form learning groups of four pupils each. As you choose from the sublists to form the groups, balance the groups as well as you can by sex, race, and other individual characteristics.

To see how this works out in practice, consider a sample class of 12 pupils. Ranking them in ability from 1 to 12, you will have a list like the one shown in the first column of Table 10.1. After you have made that list, go back and divide it into quartiles, as shown in the second column of Table 10.1. You will have as many groups as there are names in each quartile; in this case, you will have three groups.

Now, distribute the names in quartile 1 among the three groups, like this:

Group I—Judy   Group II—Bill   Group III—Joseph

Now distribute the names in quartile 2 among the three groups, trying to balance the groups by ethnicity and sex as well as you can. For example, you could make a group based on ability alone that would be composed of Judy, Takeisha, Dolores and Rita, but that would not be a good combination because it would contain only girls. A better distribution is this:

Group I—Luis

Group II—Marta

Group III—Takeisha

Continue the process of group formation by distributing the names in quartiles 3 and 4 among the groups. Finally, you will have three groups similar to those shown in the last column of Table 10.1. These will be heterogeneous groups because of the way you put them together.

The same groups should not stay together for longer than about six weeks. If you continue to use groups for guided discovery, group investigations, or other kinds of lessons, the memberships of the groups should be changed by repeating the process described.

Johnson and Johnson (1987) is a good source for those who want to know more about cooperative learning; this chapter provides only enough information to get you started.

▼ TABLE 10.1
Formation of cooperative-learning groups

RANKING	QUARTILES	GROUPS
1. Judy	1. Judy	Group I
2. Bill	Bill	Judy, Luis, Liam, Sam
3. Joseph	Joseph	
4. Luis	2. Luis	Group II
5. Marta	Marta	Bill, Marta, Dolores, Amos
6. Takeisha	Takeisha	
7. Dolores	3. Dolores	Group III
8. Nabeel	Nabeel	Joseph, Takeisha, Nabeel, Rita
9. Liam	Liam	
10. Amos	4. Amos	
11. Rita	Rita	
12. Sam	Sam	

TEACHING COOPERATIVE-GROUP SKILLS

Groups have two basic objectives—to complete a task and to maintain good working relationships among the members. To complete a task successfully group members must obtain, organize, exchange, and use information. Members have to contribute, ask for help when needed, accept help when offered, and keep the objective of task completion in mind.

In order for the group to function well, members must encourage each other to participate actively and must learn to manage differences of opinion, ideas, and interpretations in a constructive way. Such differences are often what cause people to reassess their assumptions and give up misconceptions or deepen their understanding of important concepts. Part of your responsibility as a teacher will be to help your pupils develop these skills as they work together in groups. The groundwork has to be done before you start the unit. Here are some steps you can take:

- Explain that pupils will be working in cooperative-learning groups. These groups will not be exactly like groups they have worked in before (unless they have already experienced cooperative-learning groups).

▼ In cooperative groups, children learn to work smoothly with peers of other abilities, gender, and ethnicities.

- Explain that they will be assigned to groups and will be expected to work productively with everyone in the group.
- Ask for their ideas about the behaviors that will be needed for groups to be successful. Suggestions may include acceptance of other's ideas, sharing materials, showing trust for each other, trying to communicate clearly, listening to each other, and trying to see another's viewpoint. Take time to discuss each of these ideas.

Make it clear that you expect each child to work within the assigned group and that you will be available to help them work through any problems that arise. You cannot expect the groups to function flawlessly, but group skills are needed everywhere in life and can be developed through patience and firmness. You will probably find that you have to call the class together from time to time to review the basic principles of cooperative learning as well as to remind them of some of the things they may have forgotten.

DEVELOPING A PLAN FOR A GROUP INVESTIGATION

Previous chapters have described lesson plans designed to be used for one class period. Daily planning is always necessary, but day-by-day planning is not adequate for the instructional method described here. In order to accomplish the desired goals, a group investigation must be planned as a unit, a series of integrated lessons taking place over a longer period of time. As you learn to use teaching methods that give more freedom and responsibility to children, you will see the advantages of unit planning. A more general description of unit planning is given in Chapter 13. The next section is a description of Ms. Oldhand's process of planning and implementing a group investigation, a specific kind of unit.

Most of the parts of this plan are ones with which you are now familiar. The main difference is that in developing lesson plans the teacher does the planning but in developing a plan for a group investigation pupils are also involved in planning. Because this is a plan for a series of lessons over a period of two weeks rather than a single lesson, it may seem complicated, but an examination of Ms. O.'s unit plan shows that the parts of a lesson plan with which you are already familiar can be adapted to a unit plan. Table 10.2 shows an outline of Ms. O.'s unit plan for a group investigation on trees.

Now return to Ms. O.'s class to observe the details of the planning and implementation of this unit over a period of about two weeks. Notice that the parts of the plan are not compressed into one day's lesson but are spread out over the entire series of lessons and activities.

▼ GROUP INVESTIGATIONS IN MS. OLDHAND'S CLASS

Ms. Oldhand began her sixth-grade unit by announcing the topic to the class.

▾ TABLE 10.2
A unit plan for a group investigation

UNIT PART	TEACHER ACTIVITY	PUPIL ACTIVITY
1. Goals	Determine expected out-comes	
2. Motivation	Build interest and enthusiasm	
3. Planning Activities	Work with pupils to identify questions and activities	Identify questions and plan how to answer them
4. Materials	Check pupil lists and help in securing materials	Develop lists of materials needed
5. Group Activities	Monitor pupils' work	Carry out planned activities
6. Closure	Work with groups to "pull it all together"	Present results to classmates
7. Appraisal and Feedback	Determine whether goals have been met and inform individuals, groups, and parents	Receive feedback
8. Reflection	Assess overall success and feasibility of unit	

UNIT PLAN 10.1

GRADE LEVEL: 6

TOPIC: Trees

These lessons take place over a time period of about two weeks. The parts of the plan are not compressed into one day's lesson but are spread out over the entire series of lessons and activities. Before she began the unit, Ms. O. thought carefully about the unit's goals.

GOALS

COGNITIVE GOALS

- *To gain knowledge of trees.* Children will be expected to learn many things about trees that they did not know before, but what they learn and how much they learn will depend on their own interests and activities. This kind of goal is very different from the goals of a lesson, in which pupils are expected to have acquired specific knowledge that has been determined by the teacher ahead of time. When you think about it, there is very little essential knowledge about trees that every sixth grader needs to know. It is more important at this age for children to become interested in trees—or whatever topic the teacher selects for a unit—and to develop the motivation, the confidence, and the skill to find answers on their own to questions that interest them.

- *To acquire skill in use of science processes.* Most of the group investigations will require children to use these processes: (1) making, recording, and organizing observations; (2) recognizing patterns and relationships; (3) making inferences or drawing conclusions; and (4) representing and reporting results. In some cases pupils will also carry out experiments to test their inferences and may seek information from other sources.

Affective Goals

- *To build self-reliance and self-confidence in their own ability to think.* Children learn to believe that their ideas are valuable when adults value those ideas. Self-confidence grows when a child is encouraged to plan and carry out a task through using his or her own ideas and initiative. When, on the other hand, science is taught as facts, formulas, and theories to be memorized or "experiments" performed by carefully following directions, pupils need to make no decisions nor even think about what they are doing. In contrast, a teacher who uses group investigations assumes that pupils have their own ideas and interests and that these will be motivating and sustaining.
- *To increase awareness of and interest in the subject of study.* Children learn to look at things more closely, to understand them better, and to value them more highly. Think about something you have studied or observed in detail— whether football or birds or automobiles—and you will realize that you have a greater appreciation for that subject than someone who knows little about it.

Social Goals

- *To learn to work cooperatively with others.* This social skill is probably as important as any single skill a child can learn in school. This style of teaching gives children the opportunity to develop and practice the skills of cooperative group work under adult guidance.

Psychomotor Goals

- *To practice care in handling materials.* Many things of interest to children are fragile and must be handled with care. This is particularly true of things that are alive or come from living materials. Flowers, insects, moss, and small plants are examples. Telling children to be careful is not as helpful as showing them how to exercise care and patience and recognizing that there are large differences in children's physical coordination. Note well: *The use of dangerous materials or equipment should not be allowed. The close supervision needed to handle even minimally dangerous materials is not advisable in this method of teaching.*
- *To acquire skill in handling equipment.* While every effort should be made to provide children with sturdy equipment, there will be some items that require care and skill in handling. As in the handling of materials, pupils cannot be expected to know how to handle equipment without instruction. Even when reasonable care is exercised, there will inevitably be some breakage along the way.

- *To learn to work in proximity to others.* Everyone has seen children who cannot move around a room without bumping into other people, stepping on someone's materials, and knocking something over. These children will need help and patient guidance in developing spatial awareness and in learning how to exercise more control over their bodies.

MOTIVATION

Before the pupils began the work projects that Ms. Sanchez saw when she entered the classroom, they had already spent several class periods on the unit about trees. A day or two before Ms. Oldhand started the unit, she had arranged on the bulletin board several newspaper articles to stimulate pupils' interest and thinking. One article described the damage caused to trees in their state by acid

▼ FIGURE 10.1
Samples of branches with leaves

rain. Another article described the destruction of the rain forest in the Amazon valley, showing large logs floating down the river. And a third article was about a group of local people who were trying to save a large, old tree from being cut down to make way for a shopping mall.

On the day she began the unit, Ms. O. brought in branches with leaves from five or six different kinds of trees. Ms. O. had selected them to show contrasts in leaf size, shape, color and type as well as contrasts in color and texture of tree bark. Some of the leaves Ms. O. brought in are illustrated in Figure 10.1. She assigned pupils to groups, gave a branch and a short list of questions to each group, and allowed a few minutes for groups to decide on answers before she called on each group in turn.

The questions were simple enough that Ms. Oldhand thought at least one person in each group would be able to answer. Her questions included: What is the name of the tree that this branch came from? Where does it grow? What color do the leaves turn in the fall? Do they fall off in the winter? After each group had been given a turn to answer its questions, she called attention to the articles on the bulletin board. Then she called on a few volunteers to tell why they think trees were important or to tell about their experiences with trees. Ms. O. allowed a few minutes for the children to talk and then brought the lesson to a close.

PLANNING ACTIVITIES

On the following day Ms. O. moved into the next phase of the plan by asking the pupils to think of some things they would like to find out about trees. As the children thought of questions, they raised their hands. Calling on one pupil at a time, she wrote the questions on a transparency on the overhead projector. When she had written six questions, she asked the children who had not spoken to write their questions on pieces of paper and to save them for later. The questions she wrote on the transparency were these:

1. What kinds of trees grow in our town?
2. What kinds of fruits grow on trees? Do all trees have fruits? What is inside?
3. What happens when a tree dies?
4. What is the difference between an evergreen tree and a tree that loses leaves?
5. What is a tree like on the inside?
6. How is wood from one kind of tree different from wood from another kind of tree?

By then it was time to move on to another subject, so the questions were saved for the next day's lesson.

When Ms. O. returned to her questions the next day, she said, "Now we will decide how we might find the answers to these questions. What data would we need? How could we collect it? Let's start with the first question and see what we can do with it." After 15 minutes of skillful questioning and a few suggestions from Ms. O., this is what the children read on the overhead projector:

1. What kinds of trees grow in our town?

<u>How will we answer this question?</u>

a. Look around the area where we
   live and identify all the
   different kinds of trees.

b. Find out the names of the trees.

1. What happens when a tree dies?

<u>How will we answer this question?</u>

a. Bring a rotting log to school
   and find out all we can about it.

At this point Ms. O. said, "Now that you have seen how we tackle these questions, it's time for you to do some of this on your own." She assigned children to groups of four or five and wrote these instructions on the board:

1. Decide on a question for your group.
   It may be one of the questions already identified or it may be
   another question that your group likes.

2. Record the question.

3. Decide what you need to know or do in order to answer the question.

4. Write this down.

5. What materials or resources will you need?
   Which can you get yourselves and which will require some help?

After writing these directions on the board Ms. Oldhand said, "I will come around to each group and hear your plans and answer questions. I am really looking forward to hearing all your ideas because I know they will be good ones. At the end of the period I will collect your plans." By the end of the class period, each group had a plan. The following is what each of the groups wrote.

Group One

Our question is: What kinds of trees grow in our town?

We will each take an area close to our homes and make a survey. First we will look for as many different kinds of trees as we can find. Each person will bring in a few leaves from each different kind of tree. If we can't reach the leaves, we will draw a picture. We will bring those all in to class and see which are the same and which are different. Then we will have samples of all the different trees that we found.

We will identify the leaves by looking them up in a book from the library.

If we have time we will go back and look at the shapes of the trees and try to draw them, because the shape of the tree may tell what kind of tree it is.

Group Two

Our question is: What happens when a tree dies?

We will bring two pieces of wood into class. One will be a log that is freshly cut and the other will be an old rotting log. We can find a fresh piece of wood from someone who has bought wood for their fireplace. For the rotting log someone will have to find one in the woods or get one from someone who sells firewood and has an old piece lying around. A parent may have to help on this.

We will compare the bark and the inside of the logs.

At this point Ms. O. came over to the group and heard their plans. She asked whether they thought anything might be living in the old log. With this suggestion they added to their plans:

We will put the log down on a big piece of white paper and watch to see whether anything crawls out. If it does, we will save it. Then we will dig into the log to look for insect eggs, cocoons, and other signs of life.

We will need something to gently dig into the rotten log, a big piece of paper, and a container for insects (if we find any).

Group Three:

Our question is: What kinds of fruits grow on trees? Do all trees have fruits? What is inside?

We will collect nuts and other kinds of things that grow on trees in the neighborhood. First, we will make a chart to compare them for size, shape, color, and so on. Then, we will find out what is inside the nuts and fruits and seeds and compare them.

Group Four

Our question is: Do all trees float in water after they have been cut down?

We will get samples of wood from different trees and see whether they all float.

When Ms. O. came over to this group she suggested that they could expand their question. She thought that the group needed to dig deeper into the subject of floating than just determining that wood floats—which most of them knew already. They could ask whether all kinds of wood float the same way. Do some kinds of wood sink farther into the water than others? What else happens when wood is put in water? How could you make an experiment that would be a fair test of this? Her questions prompted them to expand their investigation.

We will get blocks of the same size of different kinds of wood, put them in water, and mark the level of the water on each one. Then we will compare them. Next we will weigh them, put them in water, leave them there for three days, and then weigh each block to see if it changed weight. We will see if woods from different trees absorb different amounts of water.

GROUP FIVE

Our question is: How are evergreen trees different from leafy trees?
We will get branches from evergreen trees and from broad-leafed trees and compare them. Some of the things we will observe and record are:

Bark

Shape of leaves or needles

How leaves or needles are attached

Smell

The kind of seeds on the tree or lying on the ground under the tree

Shape of the tree (we will have to go after school, observe the trees, and draw them if we can

Anything else that comes to our attention

GROUP SIX

Our question is: What is on the inside of a tree?
We will get four different logs, if we can. Each person will observe and draw the cut surface of a log and then cut away the bark and observe what is underneath. We will also count the rings, because that tells how old a tree is.

At the end of the period Ms. O. collected the papers so that she could read them over and see whether she needed to make any further suggestions. She told the children that they would have several days to collect their materials in order to be ready to begin their investigations on Monday. This would give them a reasonable amount of time to enlist the help of their parents and find all the materials that they would need.

MATERIALS

Ms. O. looked over the papers the pupils had handed in and noticed that there were very few things that she would have to provide for the investigations. She was pleased to see that the children were planning to find most of the things themselves. She made a note of the materials that she would have to assemble and planned to have most of them ready by Monday.

GROUP ACTIVITIES

On Monday the groups went to work, collecting data, making observations and carrying out the tasks that they had assigned themselves. Each pupil kept a notebook to record what was done each day. Sometimes pupils recorded their observations by drawing a picture or making a chart.

Although the children were interested and busy, Ms. Oldhand did not relax. She moved about from one group to another, asking questions, answering questions, and keeping an eye on everything that was happening in the room. She was particularly watchful to see whether the children were using science processes appropriately. For example, she noticed whether children took variables into account when they made comparisons so that a test of an idea was a fair test. As she moved around from group to group, she asked these questions:

- "Group 1, how can you find out which kind of tree is more abundant? Would you have to count all the trees in town? When you have thought of a way it might be done, let me know your idea so we can discuss it."
- "Group 3, have you decided on categories for size, shape, and color? How will you agree on what category a seed belongs in?"

Ms. O. also checked frequently to see that all children were keeping up their notebooks and required them to turn in their notebooks each Friday, so that she could take a look during the weekend. Sometimes a question from her helped children think again about how best to make an observation or test an idea.

During this time Ms. O. was keeping in mind the objectives of group investigations. She had made a notebook that contained the class list, with spaces beside each child's name for recording a bit of information each day. This was not the formal grade book that every teacher must keep, but her own way of appraising and recording performance. As she moved about the room she noted whether each child was on task and contributing to the group. At the end of the period, she put +, − or √ by each pupil's name (see Figure 10.2). She used the + to indicate extra effort, the − to indicate too much time off task, and the √ to show what she considered appropriate effort and behavior. She had a line in her book for each pupil. At the end of the group investigations, Ms. Oldhand used this as part of the appraisal. This also helped her give feedback to parents about their children's participation and effort in science.

Ms. Oldhand was also interested in the science processes that the children were using. In the same notebook that contained the children's names, she had other pages for recording the use of science processes. This page listed the groups, rather than individual children, and had spaces for each of the processes listed above as objectives in the unit plan. She had a separate space for each group. As Ms. Oldhand moved about the room, she watched for indications that groups were making observations, gathering data, and using other science processes. She made little checks in her notebook to record her own observations. The record for group 1 is shown in Figure 10.3. Note that she kept a record like this for each group.

Daily Record of Effort

Name	Day 1	2	3	4	5	6	7	8	9	10
Adams	✓	✓	+	+	✓	✓	✓	+	✓	+
Berkonsky	−	−	✓	✓	✓	−	✓	✓	✓	−
Chavez	+	+	✓	✓	✓	+	+	✓	+	+
D'Amato	✓	✓	✓	✓	+	+	✓	✓	−	−
Edmister										
Fussell										
Goldsmith										

▼ FIGURE 10.2
A page from Ms. O.'s notebook

Notice that Ms. Oldhand was actually using the science processes that she was teaching her pupils. She had made *observations* of pupil behavior, *gathered data* about their activities, *recorded data*, and she would eventually *draw inferences*. She was modeling for her pupils the behaviors and thinking processes that she was teaching. When she had an opportunity, she pointed this out to them to show that what they were learning in science class has many useful applications.

The pupils and teacher continued to work in this way for the remainder of the week. When a group became satisfied with the answers to their questions, they began to plan how they would present their results to the class by means of charts, graphs, and illustrations.

Daily Process Record

Group 1

Day	Observe	Organize	Record	Infer	Experiment
1	✓✓✓	✓	✓✓✓	—	—
2	✓✓✓	✓	✓✓✓✓	—	—
3	✓✓✓	✓✓	✓✓✓	—	—
4	✓✓	✓✓✓✓	✓✓	✓	—
5	✓✓✓	—	✓✓✓	—	✓✓✓
6	—	✓✓✓	✓✓	✓✓✓	—

▼ FIGURE 10.3
Ms. O.'s record for group 1

CLOSURE

Ms. Oldhand reminded the class on Wednesday that they would have to bring their investigations to a close in time to present their results to the class on Monday. There was a great scurrying about to finish up. Some groups planned to meet on Saturday to complete their displays. On the following Monday each group was given time to explain what they had done, and each group displayed their results for the class. Two of the presentations are described.

GROUP ONE

This group displayed a poster with labeled drawings of the trees they found. Under each drawing of a tree, there was a drawing of the corresponding leaf. Figure 10.4 shows some of the drawings they made to use on their poster. They had also made a map of the town, with their neighborhoods outlined and indications of the kinds of trees found in each area. Finally, they had made a bar graph to show and compare the number of trees of each kind. The group explained their posters and graphs and answered questions.

GROUP TWO

This group had found some interesting signs of insect life in their dead log. They drew pictures of what they had found and identified as many things as they could. They also had found moss and lichen, which they put into plastic bags and displayed on a poster. Another item of interest was some of the dead and rotted wood, also in a plastic bag, displayed beside a small piece of wood from a tree that had just been cut. This group, like the previous one, explained what they had found and answered questions.

Oak   Maple   Alder

▼ FIGURE 10.4
Drawings for poster on local tree population

APPRAISAL AND FEEDBACK

Now it was time for the teacher to decide whether the objectives of the lesson had been met. Since Ms. O. kept the objectives in mind all along, she had several things that could help her make an appraisal.

The reports that the children gave were one indication of whether the cognitive goals had been met. Did the children learn anything about trees in their groups? And did they present what they learned in such a way that other children learned something, too? Because this style of teaching allows children to make many decisions about their own learning and because there was no predetermined information that all children were required to learn, Ms. O. did not give a multiple choice or fill-in-the-blanks test. Instead, she asked pupils to write answers in their own words to two questions.

"I'm going to give you two questions," she said, "and I want you to close your eyes and *think* about what you have been doing for the past three weeks. After you have thought about it, write the answers as clearly as you can. It is important to express your thoughts clearly. I want everyone's *best* answers." Her questions were:

1. List three important things about trees that you learned by working in your group.
2. List two things you learned about trees from other people's reports.

Ms. O. did not expect everyone to have learned the same things. She wanted to know what the children would take with them for the future, not what they had memorized and would forget quickly.

The answers to her questions gave Ms. O. some data about what the children had learned. Did they consider trivial facts to be most important or did they learn something that they would take with them as the basis for further learning? Did the groups present their reports in such a way that other children understood what they had done?

Ms. Oldhand also had her record of the children's use of science processes to help her decide whether that objective had been met. And she had her record of daily performance to help her make judgments about an individual child's progress in becoming an autonomous learner. She would also use this information when she talked to parents about individual children.

Ms. O. gave feedback to each group in the form of written comments, indicating the objectives that had been met and suggesting areas that remained to be worked on. She emphasized the positive outcomes, because her pupils were still learning to work in this way and she did not wish to discourage them. Besides, she always takes responsibility herself for much of what occurs in her classroom—if a group did not accomplish an objective, then she had not done her part in motivating and monitoring the pupils' work.

REFLECTION

Now it was time for Ms. O. to reflect on the unit. She had to use her intuition and common sense to decide whether the topic and the activities captured and maintained children's interest. She asked herself some other questions. Did she allow enough time? Too much time? What would she do differently? Would she select this topic again? Ms. O. reflected on these questions and then wrote her own appraisal in her journal for her own future use.

GROUP INVESTIGATION OF INSECTS AND "BUGS"

This plan will not be explained in the same detail as the previous example, but the investigations would be carried out in the same general way. The teacher chooses a topic, the children think of questions, the teacher helps them organize their thoughts and ideas, and they then carry out group investigations and record and present their results. Appraisal and feedback follow as in the unit on trees.

▼ UNIT PLAN 10.2

GRADE LEVEL: 4–6

TOPIC: Insects and "Bugs"

MATERIALS

- jars with lids
- butterfly nets
- cages
- magnifiers

GOALS

COGNITIVE GOALS

- To gain knowledge of the topic.
- To acquire skill in use of science processes.

AFFECTIVE GOALS

- To build self-reliance and self-confidence.
- To increase awareness and interest in the subject.

SOCIAL GOALS

- To learn to work cooperatively with others.

PSYCHOMOTOR GOALS

- To practice care in handling materials.
- To acquire skill in handling equipment.
- To learn to work in proximity to others.

MOTIVATION

Plan ahead to have some kind of interesting insect to bring into the classroom in a cage or terrarium. Starting with questions and observations about this example, arouse the children's interest in learning more about other insects and small creatures, such as isopods and spiders. If possible, plan a field trip for children to collect a variety of insects and other creatures that they will bring back into the classroom to study.

PLANNING

Planning for the field trip should include instructions in safety, discussion of some things to observe about insects in the field, discussion of how to capture the creatures that will be brought back, and development of questions pupils wish to ask about the creatures once back in the classroom. Children can begin keeping their logs by writing down some questions they have.

GROUP ACTIVITIES

In this group investigation, each group will first focus on the insect(s) or other creature(s) they find and observe in the field and then focus on those collected and brought back. Different groups may be asking the same questions, but they will have different answers because their insects will be different.

Children may need some suggestions at first for places to look for insects, slugs, spiders, and other interesting invertebrates. This depends to some extent on the time of year. As long as the weather is warm, insects can always be found in grass or weeds, and interesting creatures live under stones and logs. In the fall, insects will be found in fallen and rotting fruit, spiders will be found in webs in corners around buildings, and galls will appear on trees after leaves have fallen. In the spring, there are pupae in the soil under trees; then caterpillars can be found on leaves; later, butterflies can be found around flowers and moths can be found resting on trees.

On the field trip each pupil will take a small notebook so that observations can be recorded, including:

- *Size and appearance:* What color is it? How big is it? What special features does it have?
- *Habitat:* Where was it found? Was the place dry or wet? Light or dark? How many were in one place?
- *Behavior:* What was it doing? How does it move? Did it react if you touched it?

The easiest way to observe bugs at close range is to keep them indoors in jars or petri dishes for a day or less. Most species will tolerate short periods away from food and normal surroundings. Short-term captives can be observed for general behavior, such as locomotion and grooming. With the help of a magnifying glass, structural features can be observed. Each child should try to draw his or her special bug. If the diet is known and can be provided, feeding behavior can be observed.

If the proper conditions are maintained, bugs can be kept for longer periods in the classroom, allowing children to observe changes and carry out experiments. Some events to watch for are egg laying and hatching, eating, molting, mating, and life-cycle stages. Pupils can find out what foods are preferred, what effect changes in light or temperature have, and how the bugs react to various stimuli.

An important part of this project is the children's use of reference books to identify the creatures, as well as to check their own drawings and information against what they find in books.

CLOSURE AND APPRAISAL

Pupils should have an opportunity to display drawings, observations, and results of experiments. A special time for parents to visit might be arranged. As in the previous lesson plan, appraisal will be designed to let each child say what was learned and what else he or she would like to know.

EXTENSION TO OTHER SUBJECTS

Writers and artists as well as naturalists and scientists have found insects, spiders, and other "bugs" to be endlessly fascinating. One of the favorite children's books of all time is E.B. White's *Charlotte's Web*, a story about Charlotte (a spider) and a friendly pig. "Castles in Clay" is a nature film about the large and wonderful structures built by termites in Africa. Drawings and paintings in art class, poems and stories in language arts, counting and estimating in math, and studying the habits and ways of social insects in social studies are ways to extend this topic to other areas of the curriculum. One class of younger pupils who studied caterpillars and butterflies made up a dance that represented butterflies flying over a field. When knowledge is represented in more than one way it is more likely to be learned and remembered.

OTHER TOPICS FOR GROUP INVESTIGATIONS

SMALL CREATURES FOUND IN WATER

Ponds and streams produce as interesting an array of small creatures as fields and woods. A field trip to a pond can produce both insects found around the edge and other creatures found in the water. Many of the questions asked about insects and other invertebrates can be asked about these creatures.

THE ENVIRONMENT AROUND THE SCHOOL

This topic is interesting when the school is in a small town or rural area. What plants grow around the school? What insects, worms, slugs, spiders, and other creatures can be found? How tall are the trees nearby? What kinds of trash and refuse can be found?

One popular activity is for each group to choose a square meter (which the group measures and marks) and then to count and label all the plants, insects, and other living things found in the square. Groups compare their findings, and the class discusses possible reasons for differences. What plants grow in sun and what plants grow in shade? Where are insects likely to be found? What difference does dampness make?

SIMPLE MACHINES

Each group chooses one kind of machine to observe and explore. Building models and demonstrating the uses of each kind of machine leads to learning experiences of more variety and depth than might be accomplished through other teaching methods. Since this is a topic that is a requirement in some state syllabi, sufficient time should be allowed at the end of the unit for each group to report and, in effect, teach the other pupils about its machine(s).

EXTENSION TO OTHER SUBJECTS

This topic lends itself to integration into a history or social studies unit. Simple machines were the only tools available to the ancient Egyptians who built the Pyramids,

▼ Group investigations foster independent thinking.

the Greeks and Romans who built Athens and Rome, and the medieval architects and artisans who built the cathedrals of Europe. There has been much speculation about how the ancient Britons moved the huge stones to Stonehenge and set them in place. Many books on these topics are available for upper-elementary age children.

FLOWERING PLANTS

In some parts of the country flowers are in bloom for several months during the school year, making this a suitable topic for a group investigation. Pupils can identify flowers on a field trip and examine specimens in the classroom using hand lenses or the naked eye. The plants from which the flowers came should also be observed and described. Where does the plant grow? Is it in sun or shade? What parts of the flower can you identify? What is its name? Does it grow wild or have to be cultivated?

▼ SUMMARY

Group investigations is an instructional method that allows pupils freedom to choose what they will study about a topic that has been chosen by the teacher. Small groups of pupils, whose interest is aroused by the teacher, design investigations to answer questions that are of interest to them. The teacher is available to help in defining and refining questions as well as to help in planning. The teacher monitors pupils' progress toward finding answers to their questions, and makes suggestions for further questions, plans for ways to bring closure to the unit, appraises pupil outcomes, and reflects on the overall outcomes of the unit.

This method fosters independent thinking and learning when it is planned around a topic that can be studied by children through firsthand experiences and when the teacher has structured the classroom so that pupils understand the expectations and limits. The teacher's role is to provide an environment that encourages independent learning and responsible action. The teacher helps the children think about and understand the meaning of their experiences.

▼ DISCUSSION QUESTIONS

1. Choose a grade level and list three problems you foresee in using the method of group investigation with that age group. What might you do to prevent each of the problems?
2. Describe in your own words the activities probably carried out by Group Three, as represented in Figure 10.3.
3. In what ways is evaluation of pupil outcomes different in Autonomy Level III from evaluation in Autonomy Levels I and II?

▼ ACTIVITIES FOR THE READER

1. Choose a grade level and outline a plan for a group investigation. Select a topic, list objectives, and describe motivational activities for five possible group investigations, and then describe your method of appraisal.
2. As a class project, divide yourselves into groups of five. Each group should choose a grade or several grades, depending on the number in your class. Each group then should develop an annotated list of books and articles that could be used at the chosen grade level(s) as sources of ideas for investigations. Share these lists by distributing copies to all class members.
3. Working with a group of four or five students from your methods class, plan, carry out, record, and display the results of an investigation that would be suitable for a grade of your choice. Report to the class what you learned that will be valuable to you as a teacher.
4. Make a list of five topics that are suitable for group investigations. Using the criteria in this chapter, explain why each topic is suitable.

▼ REFERENCES

Charron, E. (1987). *Teacher behavior in Japanese elementary science classrooms.* Paper presented at the annual meeting of the National Association for Research in Science Teaching. Washington, DC.

Johnson, D.W. & Johnson, R.T. (1987). *Learning together and alone: Cooperative, competitive and individualistic learning.* (2nd Ed.). Englewood Cliffs, NJ: Prentice Hall.

Slavin, R. (1980). Cooperative learning. *Review of Educational Research, 50,* 315–342.

Schools Council Publications. (1972). With objectives in mind. *Guide to Science 5–13.* London: MacDonald Educational.

▼ SOURCES OF IDEAS AND MATERIALS

Brockman, C. (1986). *Trees of North America: A guide to field identification.* New York: Golden Press. *A comprehensive guide with clear descriptions and colored illustrations of leaves, barks and tree shapes.*

MacDonald Educational. *Science 5–13.* London: MacDonald Educational. (49–50 Poland Street, London, England, W1). *The following titles contain a wealth of information and ideas for group investigations.*

Using the environment 1: Early explorations

Using the environment 2: Investigations

Science from toys

Trees

Minibeasts

Structures and forces

Working with wood

National Science Resources Center. (1988). *Science for children: Resources for teachers.* Washington, DC: National Academy Press. *A comprehensive annotated list of available materials in all areas of the elementary science curriculum.*

Roth, C. E., Cervoni, C., Wellnitz, T., & Arms, E. (1988). *Schoolground science activities for elementary and middle schools.* Lincoln, MA: Massachusetts Audubon Society (South Great Road, Lincoln, MA 01733). *A collection of ideas for projects that can be done on the schoolgrounds by children from kindergarten through ninth grade.*

Smith, R. (1980). *Ecology and field biology.* Boston: Harper & Row.

U. S. Department of Agriculture Forest Service. (1970). *Forest insects and diseases.* Washington, DC: Superintendent of Documents. *(free)*

U. S. Department of the Interior/Geological Survey. (1987). *Tree rings: Timekeepers of the past.* Washington, DC: Superintendent of Documents. *(free)*

Young Entomologists' Society. *Insect Identification Guide.* Lansing, MI: Young Entomologists' Society (1915 Peggy Place, Lansing, MI 48910). *Detailed information to help teachers and students learn to identify insects.*

Young Naturalist. *Nature education kits.* Newton, KS: Young Naturalist (614 East 5th Street, Newton, KS 67114). *These include natural specimens, directions for hands-on activities, and a teacher's guide. The following kits are available:*

"What leaf is it?" (Grades 1–12)

"What seed is it?" (Grades 1–12)

"What crop is it?" (Grades 1–12)

"Leaf and seed matching game" (Grades pre-K–3)

INDIVIDUAL AND CLASS PROJECTS

▼ Ms. Sanchez approaches Ms. Oldhand after school.

Ms. Sanchez:	I've come to you for some advice. The principal has announced that our school is going to participate in a science fair. I know that your pupils win prizes every year so you must have some secrets of success. Will you share them with me?
Ms. Oldhand:	Well, I don't really have any secrets, but I will be glad to tell you how I help my pupils plan their projects and manage their time. I guess the most important thing is encouraging the children and helping them improve their ideas—but after that it's just planning ahead and staying on schedule all the way to the end.
Ms. Sanchez:	I remember starting a project when I was in the fifth grade, but I ran out of time and didn't feel very good about the final result.
Ms. Oldhand:	Independent projects require a lot of planning and monitoring. Otherwise time can slip by, pupils lose interest, and the final days bring a frantic flurry of activity that leaves everyone—especially parents—exhausted and disappointed. Come by my room tomorrow, and I'll help you make a schedule and give you some ideas of the way I plan.
Ms. Sanchez:	Will you regret it if you help me and then some of my pupils win?
Ms. Oldhand:	Of course not! To tell you the truth, I don't really like the competition. The important thing is for all the boys and girls to enjoy doing their projects and have a sense of accomplishment when it's over. As far as I'm concerned all of those who make a real effort are winners.
Ms. Sanchez:	I'll see you tomorrow.

INDIVIDUAL PROJECTS

The last chapter described projects that take place over several weeks, with classwork supplemented by out-of-class activities that might be thought of as a kind of homework. This section also describes activities and projects that take place over a number of weeks, but these projects are different from those in the last chapter. Although these projects may be discussed and planned in class, the students do most of the detailed planning and work outside of class. Projects for science fairs, for a parents' night, or for the culmination of a unit fall into this category. Although most of the actual work is done outside of class, children need guidance and encouragement as well as monitoring when engaged in these activities. The purpose of this chapter is to help you develop the skills and understanding needed to assist pupils in selecting, planning and completing projects and then to guide pupils toward successful completion of the projects they have chosen.

Think back a moment to the group investigations described in Chapter 10. Those investigations take place mostly in the classroom and within a series of class periods. They begin and end at specified times, and they use all the class time allotted to science while they are going on. Another characteristic is that all the children in a class are investigating aspects of the same topic. Individual projects, in contrast, usually stretch out for several weeks and take place while other science topics are being taught in regular class time. Children may work alone, in pairs, or groups, though teachers should probably encourage children to work in pairs or groups more often than alone. Children who prefer to work alone have opportunities to do this outside of school, but for many children school is the only place where they have the opportunity to work productively with other children.

A recent study on out-of-school science activities of third and fourth graders found that many children were carrying on little projects of their own without the help or even the knowledge of parents or teachers (Charron 1990). For instance one fourth-grade girl said, "Sometimes I do stuff, but I don't really know that I'm doing science then. Sometimes I'll just follow an animal around and see what it does—like a worm" (p. 10). The wide variety of science activities of the children in this study make plain that children are interested in science and that they have ideas that they would like to try. Individual projects give them that opportunity and also stimulate other children to think of things that they might like to do.

The overall goals of independent projects are similar to those of group investigations. The cognitive, affective, social, and psychomotor goals are the same as those listed in the last chapter. The major difference between projects and group investigations is not in the goals but in the degree of independence and responsibility expected of the pupils. When pupils are doing much of the work outside of class—as they are in the projects described in this chapter—they cannot be monitored in the same way that they can when in the classroom under the watchful eye of the teacher. They are on their own more, and this independence requires them to be more autonomous and responsible.

As in group investigations, the particular knowledge to be gained by each pupil is not specified in advance by the teacher but is left up to the interests of the individual pupils. By allowing pupils to choose a project that interests them, the teacher is demonstrating that the pupils' ideas and interests are important and worthy of consideration. When pupils see that the teacher values their ideas and believes that they can learn on their own, they begin to believe it themselves. This is one of the most important goals of science teaching—for children to believe that they can learn on their own; that is, that they can become autonomous learners. By working on projects of real interest to them, children are stimulated to make the mental connections that result in new knowledge and understanding; that is, they construct their own knowledge.

Successful independent projects require an overall plan that takes teacher and pupils through from the first day to the last. It is not accidental that some teachers' pupils produce interesting and successful projects year after year; this is usually the result of careful planning, encouragement, and monitoring on the part of those teachers.

Before embarking on independent projects, you will have to give serious thought to what is required for the successful completion of projects. The following are some questions to ask yourself before you decide to go ahead. You should proceed only if you can honestly answer yes to these questions:

- Have the children developed the necessary skills and attitudes to plan and carry through?
- Are the outcomes likely to be worth the necessary time and effort, or could the same objectives be met as well in other ways?
- Are you willing to spend the extra time required?

SCIENCE FAIRS

This section describes a plan for independent projects for a science fair. Not everyone agrees that science fairs are appropriate for elementary children, but they are popular with parents and administrators. In addition, participation can be a positive experience for many pupils. If you plan for your class to participate in a science fair, you have the responsibility to make it a learning experience for all of your pupils. Here are some guidelines that may help you achieve that goal:

- Emphasize the learning experience rather than the competition.
- Do not use participation in the fair as a basis for the course grade.
- Let the activities supplement rather than replace the regular science classes.
- Insist that the children do the work themselves.

Children younger than fourth graders do not usually participate in science fairs because of the difficulty young children have in sustaining interest and motivation over a period of time that is long enough to complete their projects. For younger children, shorter-term projects without competition are more appropriate. In the project plan that follows, the assumption is that all pupils will participate in the fair. There are arguments both for and against having everyone participate. The argument against having all pupils participate holds that children who are not interested in science are forced to undertake a project they have no real interest in. The argument for total participation holds that children who are not initially interested in science may develop that interest if allowed to choose a topic on their own. And since the objectives of the projects are broader than learning about a specific science topic, those who do not participate will lose important learning opportunities. Different viewpoints on participation and other aspects of fairs (along with many suggestions and ideas for projects) are presented in a useful booklet published by the National Science Teachers Association (in the references list at the end of this chapter).

Most projects for science fairs can be divided into three categories: (1) collections, (2) demonstrations, and (3) experiments. All three can be planned to include the use of science processes and should be expected to produce an increase in knowledge and understanding. These categories are described later in this chapter with suggestions of some things to keep in mind for each type of project.

As you study the following plan for projects for a science fair notice how the parts of a lesson plan that are now familiar to you have been adapted for this purpose. You will see that the plan includes Objectives, Motivation, Materials, Learning Activities, Closure, Appraisal, and Feedback.

INDEPENDENT PROJECTS PLAN 11.1

GRADE LEVEL: 5

TOPIC: Projects for a Science Fair

OBJECTIVES

The learner will participate in :

1. Planning a project
2. Carrying out a project
3. Communicating the results

MATERIALS

These will depend on the projects and will be gathered as needed.

SCHEDULE OF ACTIVITIES

This schedule is for a five-week period preceeding the science fair, which takes place on a Saturday. Other science lessons continue in the classroom during this five-week period, but time is set aside every Monday, Wednesday, and Friday for planning and discussing the pupils' projects.

FIRST WEEK

Objectives—By the end of the week pupils will have :

- Decided whom they will work with
- Selected a project

MONDAY (1)

Motivation: "You have done so well in all your science work this year that I think you are ready to take part in the science fair that will be held right in this school five weeks from last Saturday. Has anyone in this class ever been to a science fair?" The teacher explains that there will be three categories—experiments, collections, and models—and gives a short description of each category:

- *Experiments*. Each experiment starts with a question that can be answered by collecting data and putting the information together in a meaningful way. The questions chosen have to be answerable by the pupils themselves from the data that they collect. To do this successfully, it is best for pupils to plan to control as many factors as possible and then vary only one thing (or one thing at a time) and measure the result. One way to help pupils plan their experiments is to give them a checklist to be filled in before the experiment is approved. An example of an experiments checklist is shown in Figure 11.1a.

• *Collections.* Almost any natural materials that can be found locally and in some variety are suitable, including shells, leaves, rocks or minerals, nuts and acorns, insects, and flowers. Finding, identifying, classifying, and arranging

▼ FIGURE 11.1a
Example of a
checklist for
experiments

Birds' Feeding Habits

The question we want to answer:

Will more birds come to a feeder hanging from a tree or to a feeder placed on the ground?

What we will do:

Get two similar bird feeders. Place one feeder on a wire and hang it from a tree limb and place the other on the ground. Observe both feeders for one hour each morning and evening and count the number of birds that come to each feeder.

The variable we will change:

Placement of the bird feeders.

The variables we will keep constant (unchanged):

1) Bird feeders are the same type
2) Time of observation
3) Length of time of observation
4) Kind of bird food

The variable we will measure:

How many birds will come to each feeder

How we will measure it:

Counting the number of birds

How we will report our results:

A bargraph that shows the number of birds that came to each feeder. We will also show how many came in the morning and how many came in the evening. (We may be able to keep a record of the number of each kind of bird, such as sparrows, blue jays, etc, but if there are too many kinds we will not be able to do this.)

for display are important processes for children at this age. Observations may also fall into this category, such as a record of sighting of birds or observations of the night sky over several weeks. Such observations would be interesting to some children and would provide data for conclusions about patterns. An example of a collections checklist is shown in Figure 11.1b.

- *Models.* Some teachers have justifiably criticized the use of models, because so many of the same models have appeared over and over at science fairs. An example of this is a volcano model: a plaster cone with a center filled with a chemical that burns and gives off smoke and sparks. (This can be dangerous and should not be allowed.) The models that are most interesting and teach the most are those that demonstrate a scientific principle or show a cause-and-effect relationship. These models are ones children design and make themselves to illustrate a principle or to show how something works. Simple models with working parts can be fun to build—but they must be kept simple. If complicated pieces of apparatus are attempted, the children will become frustrated and either abandon the project or get their parents to step in. Anything that incorporates gears, pulleys, switches, or similar mechanisms is interesting and motivating. The construction of an object or a model that illustrates a principle or relationship requires knowledge of the principle

▼ FIGURE 11.1b
Example of a checklist for collections

Microorganisms in a pond

What we will collect:
Samples of water from different places in a pond; then we will look at tiny drops under a microscope.

Where we will find them:
In a pond near one of our homes

How we will identify them
Using books in the school library (we have found the books we need)

How we will classify them
We will decide after they are collected

How we will display them
For each organism we will display a drawing, give the name, tell where it was found, and any other interesting information.

▼ FIGURE 11.1c
Example of a
checklist for
models

Building a Periscope

What we will build

A periscope

Draw the model

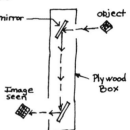

What it will show or demonstrate

Light is reflected from a mirror at the same angle as it struck the mirror. Two mirrors can be placed so that light, which travels in a straight line, will reflect off of one onto the other and then off of the second mirror to allow a person to see around a corner.

How we will display the project

Set up a screen so that people can use the periscope to see over the screen.

or relationship and, in addition, psychomotor skills and imagination. An example of a models checklist is shown in Figure 11.1c.

After a 10-to-15-minute discussion in which pupils are asked for ideas and the teacher mentions some possible projects, the teacher asks them to think about some things they might like to do and be prepared to talk about them on Wednesday.

WEDNESDAY (1)

Discussion: Discussion continues, with teacher asking for ideas, reacting to suggestions and guiding discussion toward projects that are suitable and appropriate for the children in the class. *Projects should be simple.*

Assignment: On Friday each group, pair, or individual will turn in a paper giving a brief, general idea of what they want to do. Questions about this are answered. Any who have not been able to think of a project that they really want to do can talk to the teacher, who is prepared to make suggestions as well as to help those who are ready to come to some closure.

FRIDAY (1)

Pupils turn in papers. Only a few minutes are spent collecting papers and answering questions.

SECOND WEEK

Objectives—By end of week each pupil or group will have:
- Developed a plan for project
- Made a list of materials and identified sources

MONDAY (2)

The teacher approves and returns the plans or works with pupils to improve plans if necessary. He or she has prepared a checklist for each category of project: experiment, collection, or model. Examples of a checklist from each category are shown in Figure 11.1a, Figure 11.1b, and Figure 11.1c. The teacher hands these out and explains how they should be used. Pupils respond to the items in the checklist with specifics about their projects. They will hand in their responses on Friday. They will also hand in a list of materials needed and how they may be obtained. (A strict limit should be placed on cost of materials. Pupils who need help in obtaining materials are advised to speak to the teacher. The teacher may need help from the PTA, a Mothers Club, or some other source for children who need assistance.)

WEDNESDAY (2)

Question and Answer Period: Teacher asks and answers questions but spends only a few minutes discussing any problems pupils are having.

▼ Fascinating creatures live in a drop of pond water.

Friday (2)

Turn in Notebooks: A few minutes are spent collecting notebooks.

Third Week

Objectives—By the end of the week the pupils will have:
• Completed their models, experiments, or collections

Note well: This phase may take two weeks instead of one week. The teacher will revise the schedules if necessary.

Monday (3)

Discussion: Teacher returns notebooks with comments and suggestions and then gives opportunities for pupils to spend a few minutes talking about their plans, including what materials are needed. Now the pupils go to work in earnest on their projects.

Wednesday (3)

Monitoring: The teacher takes a few minutes during the day to check on progress and answer questions.

Friday (3)

Monitoring: Teacher continues to check to see that all pupils are working and keeping records. Teacher announces that notebooks are to be brought in next Monday.

Fourth Week

Objectives—By the end of the week the pupils will have:
• Turned in their notebooks and given quick, informal oral reports
• Learned methods of reporting results
• Produced a plan for reporting results

Monday (4)

Monitoring and Informal Reporting: Pupils turn in their notebooks and give quick, informal reports about their projects.

Wednesday (4)

Direct-Instruction Lesson on Ways to Report Results: For this lesson, refer back to Chapter 5. This will be a one-period lesson with a lesson plan that includes objectives, guided practice, and all the other parts of a direct-instruction lesson. Ways to report results include bar graphs, line graphs, drawings, and written accounts.

Assignment for Friday: Bring in a plan for reporting your results.

Friday (4)

Discussion of Ways to Report Results: This is a continuation of Wednesday's lesson but allows for pupils' input through questions and answers related to the assignment. Pupils can make changes in their plans if they decide to do so. Plans are handed in to be reviewed by the teacher over the weekend. (The teacher should set aside time over the weekend for this.) Pupils will collect materials that they anticipate needing.

FIFTH WEEK

Objectives—By the end of the week the pupils will have:
- Completed a poster or other means of presenting results
- Practiced explaining project to classmates

MONDAY (5)

Reporting Plans Returned to Pupils: All plans for reporting should be approved by this time. The teacher will need to make constructive suggestions for those that need strengthening so that pupils can begin their charts, posters, etc. immediately. Class time will be allowed for working on Project Reports.

WEDNESDAY (5)

Continuation of Work on Reports

FRIDAY (5)

Final Touches on Reports: Pupils will form in groups of four and take turns explaining their projects to each other.

APPRAISAL AND FEEDBACK

Informal methods of appraisal, similar to those suggested for group investigations, are appropriate for projects. Questions that could be asked include:
- What scientific process or principle was demonstrated in your project?
- How was that process or principle demonstrated in your project?
- What was the most important thing you learned from your project?
- What would you do differently if you could do it again?

The teacher will give feedback to each child, the method depending on the kind of project. When independent projects are undertaken for a science fair (as in the example plan), the winners will have feedback from the judges and all other participants will receive a certificate. The teacher will praise all of those who participated and perhaps point out to the class some aspects of the winning entries that were particularly good.

All pupils who completed their projects should receive positive feedback and encouragement. This kind of teaching is developmental and requires sensitivity, patience, and persistence on the part of the teacher.

At the end of this chapter you will find a list of sources that may be useful if you plan to have your pupils participate in a science fair. Remember that projects of this kind do not have to be used as entries in a science fair. Shorter, simpler projects can be prepared for parents' nights, for a school fair, or to display one at a time on a Science Table. Requirements for planning and monitoring are the same, though simpler projects take less time. For example, one teacher assigned pairs of pupils to prepare projects for display in class throughout the year. The teacher did the first one, and then twice each month thereafter a pair of pupils installed a new display or experiment. The children kept their projects a surprise until the day the project was "unveiled" and explained to the class.

CLASS PROJECTS

The projects discussed in this section to some extent defy categorization. These are projects that teachers over the years have found to promote development and learning in ways that more structured lessons and units may not. In general these projects have broader and less well-defined goals than the projects described previously. Although cognitive objectives may be met, in many cases these projects are more effective in meeting affective, social, and (in some cases) psycho-motor objectives.

These projects the class carries out as a group. They are similar to group investigations and individual projects, but they fall into a separate category because the children are working on a joint class project. In most cases individuals or groups collect data or carry out other activities that will be assembled and displayed in some way when the observations have been completed.

These projects encompass activities that all children can participate in—the less academically able and the handicapped as well as children who simply have difficulty "fitting in." Everyone can make a contribution. When children plant a garden and tend their plants, they will learn some things that you can identify ahead of time as instructional objectives, but they will also gain other important things from the experience that are intangible and would not be in your list of objectives.

These projects have a science focus, but other areas of the curriculum can be integrated easily and naturally. In almost all projects there are things that need to be measured and then graphed, providing an opportunity to use the skills that have been learned in mathematics. There is a need for keeping written records and opportunities for descriptive and imaginative writing. Drawing should not be neglected as a means of representation of observations, and geography can be a natural extension of many projects. Once you start to think about the interconnections of all areas of the curriculum, you will have many more ideas than you can find time to use.

Several projects are described briefly. Some are very low-key and easy to carry out; others require more planning and more time. The purpose of describing these projects is to give you some examples of simple learning experiences that children enjoy, as well as to stimulate you to think of similar projects for your classes. There are many, many projects—large and small—that will add to the interest of your science teaching. Actually, these are the kinds of things that children remember most about their science classes, so it is important to include them if you can.

▼ For many children, school is the only place where they have the opportunity to work productively with other children.

A GARDEN

If you are fortunate enough to teach in a school that has a suitable climate and space for a garden, as well as a principal who understands—or can be convinced—that a garden can provide an important learning experience for children, then by all means take advantage of the opportunity. If you have never had experience with growing things outdoors, try to enlist the help of a parent, a friend, or another teacher. It would be helpful if you received advice from someone who has grown plants in the area and knows what will grow easily, what time to plant, what insects to watch for, and similar information. Materials needed include: seeds, small rakes and hoes, string, fertilizer, small stakes.

PREPARATION

You will have to arrange to have the garden plot plowed or "cultivated" as early as possible in the spring, and you should decide on a few vegetables and a few flowers from which children can choose. For example, in many parts of the United States lettuce, radishes, green onions, and peas grow easily and mature quickly; zinnias and marigolds are flowers that germinate quickly and bloom early. All of these are good choices.

An economical way to provide seeds is to allow each pair of children to choose several plants they wish to grow and "take orders" for seeds. You can buy the seeds in bulk rather than in tiny packages and then place seeds in inexpensive envelopes to fill the "orders."

A space 6 ft by 6 ft is ample for each pair of children. After the garden is divided into individual plots and the plots have been assigned, plan to spend one or two days a week outdoors, first working the soil and then adding fertilizer, setting strings out to mark the rows, planting, weeding, and, finally, harvesting. One way to keep motivation and interest high is to select each week the straightest rows or the plot with the fewest weeds, posting the name or giving a certificate to the week's winner.

An alternative to individual garden plots is a garden that is planned and planted cooperatively by the whole class. For a garden of this kind, the first step is the development of a plan—what to plant, where to plant it, and how to divide up responsibility for all the required tasks. The children can do much of this themselves, but you will have to help all along the way and be ready to step in when needed to keep the project going in the right direction. The National Garden Association has a comprehensive guide that will help you make this a lively learning experience (Ocone & Pranis, 1990).

WEATHER CHART

Observations of changes in weather can be the topic for a class project at a wide range of grade levels. Younger children can make simple observations and keep very simple records, using symbols that are easily understood. Older children may make their own measuring instruments for a weather station, with groups taking responsibility for different aspects of recording and reporting weather changes. You may make this a major project or keep it simple, at any grade level, using it as an addition to the science activities going on every day in class.

In keeping such a class project simple, the basic idea is to keep a daily record of the weather over a period of four to six weeks and to use the weather data to look for trends and patterns. The project begins by asking for volunteers to make a large weather chart, which is then placed on the wall. All pupils sign up for the days they will collect weather data; at the same time each day, two pupils collect data and put it on the chart. For a simple weather chart, the data that might be gathered are: temperature, sunshine, rainfall in 24 hours, type of clouds, and wind force.

For collecting *temperature* data, a centigrade thermometer should be located in an area that is protected from direct sun and is at a height that is comfortable for all the pupils to read. The *amount of sunshine* can be indicated simply by "sunny, light clouds, heavy clouds, rain" or some similar system. *Rainfall* can be measured by placing a Mason jar or a similar container in a protected place that is open to the sky and measuring with a metric ruler. You need not worry that this is not a really accurate

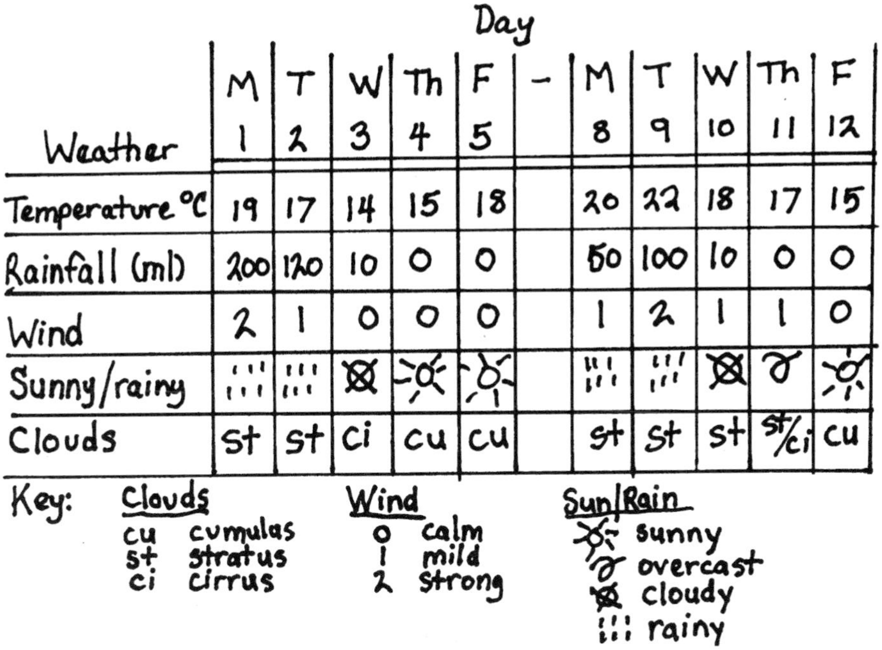

▼ FIGURE 11.2
A weather chart
made by a fourth-
grade class

Day											
Weather	M 1	T 2	W 3	Th 4	F 5	–	M 8	T 9	W 10	Th 11	F 12
Temperature °C	19	17	14	15	18		20	22	18	17	15
Rainfall (ml)	200	120	10	0	0		50	100	10	0	0
Wind	2	1	0	0	0		1	2	1	1	0
Sunny/rainy	⁝	⁝	⊠	☼	☼		⁝	⁝	⊠	⊘	☼
Clouds	st	st	ci	cu	cu		st	st	st	st/ci	cu

Key: Clouds   Wind   Sun/Rain
       cu cumulas   o calm   ☼ sunny
       st stratus   1 mild   ⊘ overcast
       ci cirrus   2 strong   ⊠ cloudy
                                          ⁝ rainy

measure; if children are interested they will start checking their measurements with
those published in the daily newspaper.

   Clouds can be identified by reference to a book, or you can have a direct-instruction lesson on cloud forms. Here again, accuracy is not a major concern; let the children decide among themselves what to record. *Wind force* can be indicated simply as
"calm, mild, strong, very strong" and left up to the children to determine. If you
wished to go into this in more detail, a weather vane could be used for wind direction
and a scale could be devised for force, but that is not necessary for this simple activity. Figure 11.2 is an example of a weather chart made by one fourth-grade class.

   After several weeks the class will have enough data to search for relationships between temperature and rainfall, between wind and clouds, and perhaps others. They
can calculate average temperature, average rainfall, and days of sunshine and then
graph the data obtained. Figure 11.3 and 11.4 are examples of graphs that pupils produced, using 1-cm graph paper. Such graphs can be used as the basis for class discussion of changes in weather and of various relationships.

SQUARE METER OF EARTH (GRADES 3–6)

The purpose of this project is to develop understanding of the concept of *ecosystem*.
The project requires an open area adjacent to or close by your school. It is more interesting if the spot selected has some variety in the amount of sunshine received or
in the moisture content of the soil, but any spot will do.

Each pair of pupils measures off a square meter of earth, labels it with their names, and investigates this area intensively. They learn as much as possible about the plants growing there, the insects and other creatures there (or tracks or droppings), the soil itself, the rocks, the number of hours of sunshine the plot receives in one day, and any other characteristic that the pupils may think of. You may discuss these possibilities and suggest some things to look for, ways to measure, what they may collect, and some general ideas; but the details of deciding what to observe, measure, or collect is left up to each pair of pupils to plan cooperatively.

In deciding how long to continue the observations and collection of data, you will have to be guided, as always, by the age and skill of your pupils. The data will then be compared and combined, perhaps in a map of the area with predominant plants and insects superimposed on the map. If there is enough variety in the plots, pupils can

▼ FIGURE 11.3
A pupil-produced
temperature graph

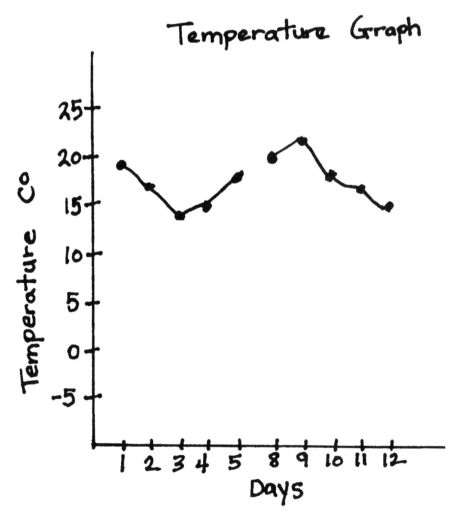

▾ FIGURE 11.4
A pupil-produced
rainfall graph

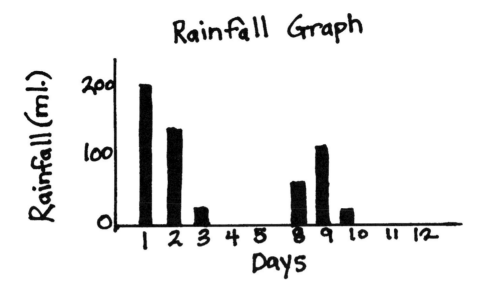

note the relationship between amount of sunshine or moisture in the plots and the organisms found. It is important to pull the data together in some way to broaden and reinforce the pupils' understanding of the tiny ecosystem that they have studied.

MOON WATCHING (GRADES 1–6)

This project requires the cooperation of parents, since it takes place outside of school. The idea is simple. For about five weeks children observe and record the appearance and location of the moon every evening at the same time and observe the moon rising when they can. Of course, the moon rises at different times during the lunar cycle, and whether they will be able to see the moon rise depends on both the time of moon rising and their own bedtimes. They bring their data to school, put their observations together, and discuss what they have observed. After the first cycle is over, they will see that their initial observations are being repeated. At this point, they make predictions that they then test by observation. This is enough for the younger children. Older pupils will be ready to study the relationship between the earth and the moon, including phases of the moon, eclipses, and other phenomena.

TEACHING AT AUTONOMY LEVEL III

In this chapter and the preceeding one, you have studied examples of teaching at Autonomy Level III and have seen that the teacher's role and many of the responsibilities are different from those needed for direct-instruction or guided-discovery lessons. At Autonomy Level III the pupils assume responsibility for some of the things that the teacher did at Autonomy Level I or II, but it is still up to the teacher—up to you—to see that standards are understood and that you enforce them resolutely and fairly when necessary.

TEACHER'S ROLE

Beginning teachers often worry that this kind of teaching will lead to children's spending too much time off-task. This may happen, but there are some actions you can take to prevent this or to deal with it if the problem arises.

1. Provide an environment that encourages children to work on problems that interest them. Their natural enthusiasm for their projects will keep them interested and busy.
2. Let pupils know that, once projects are chosen, they are expected to remain on task.
3. Remind pupils of behavior standards and sanctions that have already been set for your class, and discuss with the class why behavior standards are needed.
4. Guide pupils to see that additional standards are needed for working with materials and for working in groups, including an acceptable noise level.
5. Apply sanctions fairly and consistently, just as you would in any kind of teaching situation. This applies to deadlines for submitting plans for independent projects, for example, as well as to off-task behavior during classroom activities.
6. Move about and interact with groups as they work. Be alert for groups who are off-task or those having difficulty with the work.
7. Lead class discussions that allow interaction between students, the expression of different ideas, and explanations of different solutions to problems. Encourage open-ended discussions.
8. Set deadlines and time limits to manage pupils' use of time. Although most of your pupils can learn, with guidance, to control their own behavior most of the time, many of them will have more difficulty in learning to manage their time.

These teaching methods are possible only if your pupils are ready to assume responsibility for their own behavior. That is unlikely to be the case in the beginning of the year; it is more likely that you will have to work patiently and thoughtfully to help your pupils develop these skills. If you have started out by setting and enforcing standards as explained in Chapter 5—gradually allowing pupils to take more responsibility and gently guiding them toward acceptable behavior as explained in Chapter 8—they will respond by becoming more responsible for their own behavior and will help each other to maintain standards. Then they will be able to work independently, though they will always need monitoring and reminding. Ultimately, it is always up to the teacher—up to you—to see that acceptable standards of behavior are maintained.

Another aspect of classroom management that you will have to monitor is the noise level. It is normal for children to get carried away with what they are doing and to let their voices rise. You cannot have—and should not wish to have—a silent classroom or one in which children are talking in whispers; some noise is expected and is a healthy sign of interested children at work. But there will be times when the class-

▼ Children's natural enthusiasm for their projects will keep them interested and busy.

room noise level exceeds acceptable limits, and you will have to give a signal that is understood by everyone to mean "quiet down." The signal for lowering the noise level is up to you; just make sure that it is understood and that it does not have to be enforced too often. Remember that some noise is inevitable, expected, and accepted.

Be open to pupils' suggestions for changes in standards for behavior and materials management. After you have been teaching for some months, you should know your pupils and they should know you. If they have a reasonable suggestion for a change, you might agree to try it for a set period of time—two weeks, for example—and then evaluate the effects of the change. Whether you decide to make the change permanent is not as important as your pupils seeing that you take their ideas seriously and that they can have some control over the conditions of their life in the classroom.

PUPILS' ROLE

Pupils can be reminded that it is their responsibility to:

1. Monitor and control their own behavior.
2. Remind partners or members of their groups to maintain behavior standards.
3. Pay attention when the teacher or other pupils are speaking.

4. Move about the room quietly and carefully so as not to disturb others.
5. Ask for help when needed.
6. Help each other as much as possible.
7. Participate thoughtfully in class discussions.

MANAGEMENT OF MATERIALS

Children will be working with many different kinds of materials and will probably be carrying out some activities that you have not experienced. Remember from the chapter on guided discovery, you should try out everything beforehand. That is not possible in this kind of teaching, but here are some general guidelines:

- Be sure that no dangerous materials are included when you check pupils' project plans.
- Enforce guidelines for management of materials.
- See that children obtain materials that they need. In some cases, children will obtain materials on their own or with help from parents; in other cases, you will have to help.

MANAGEMENT OF TIME

One aspect of management that becomes important in this kind of teaching is the management of time in the classroom and the scheduling of deadlines for submitting work completed outside of class. When all pupils are doing the same thing in class, as in a direct-instruction lesson, they are led by the teacher from step to step, told when to hand in papers, and so on. In contrast, when they are doing many different activities and some of the work is done outside of class, the management of time and the monitoring of their work becomes a very important part of your responsibility. Be firm in setting deadlines, as explained in the example unit plans. Remember to remind them when the end of the class period is approaching, and be firm in insisting that they put away materials and clean up in good time.

▾ SUMMARY

In this chapter you have seen how to plan and carry out units of instruction in which the pupils learn about some part of their environment by conducting group investigations and independent projects. Both of these require a high level of independence on the part of the pupils and a high level of planning and group-management skills on the part of the teacher.

Group investigations are planned around a topic that can be studied by children through firsthand experiences. Small groups of pupils, whose interest is aroused by the teacher, design investigations to answer questions that are of interest to them.

The teacher is available to help in defining and refining questions and in planning. He or she monitors pupils' progress toward finding answers to their questions and makes suggestions for further questions, plans for ways to bring closure to the unit, appraises pupil outcomes, and reflects on the overall outcomes of the unit.

Independent projects are similar to group investigations in that pupil independence is required and the role of the teacher is the same. Major differences are that much of the work of the projects is done outside of class and that the projects may or may not be focused on answering specific questions. Projects can include construction of models, forming collections, and other science-related activities that are of interest to children.

Remember this well: your pupils will not be able to have any of these interesting learning experiences until you have guided and helped them become responsible and independent learners who can cooperate with classmates and stay on task.

▼ DISCUSSION QUESTIONS

1. What problems do you foresee in using this method? What might you do to prevent some of the problems?
2. What are some pros and cons of science fairs? Do you think that all pupils in a class should be required to participate? Why or why not?
3. Do you think that the amount of monitoring suggested in this chapter is appropriate? On what have you based your answer?
4. How can you "cover" all the topics in the school curriculum using these methods?
5. Compare the list of the teacher's responsibilities for group investigations and independent and group projects with the list given for the teacher's responsibilities for guided discovery and direct instruction.

▼ ACTIVITIES FOR THE READER

1. Describe two appropriate independent projects for each of the three categories (experiments, collections, models).
2. Develop a set of criteria and procedures for judging an elementary science fair for grades four and five.
3. Develop a detailed plan for a class project, using one of those suggested here or one of your own selection.
4. Develop a list of books and articles that could be used by fourth to sixth graders as sources of ideas for individual projects.
5. Write a lesson plan for a direct-instruction lesson on reporting results (refer back to Chapter 4 for guidelines of a direct-instruction lesson plan).
6. Make a list of four topics that are suitable for class projects. Using the criteria in this chapter, explain why each topic is suitable.

▼ REFERENCES

Charron, E. (1990). *Science activities children choose outside the school*. Paper presented at the Annual Meeting of the National Association for Research in Science Teaching, Atlanta, GA.

Howe, A. (1987). Collecting as a science activity. *Science Activities, 24*(3), 17–19.

▼ SOURCES OF IDEAS AND MATERIALS

Cornell, J. B. (1979). *Sharing nature with Children*. Nevada City, NV: Dawn.

Daab, M. (1990). *Science fair workshop*. Carthage, IL: Fearon Teacher Aids. A step-by-step guide with pages that may be copied for individual or class use.

Grice, N. *Touch the Stars*. Boston, MA: Museum of Science. Forty-four page astronomy textbook printed in Braille with 11 tactile illustrations of stars, solar system, galaxies, and constellations.

Lehr, Burnett, & Zim. (1987). *Weather: A guide to phenomena and forecasts*. New York: Golden Books.

Macaulay, D. (1988). *The way things work*. Boston: Houghton Mifflin. Explains the inner workings and principles behind all the things you use every day but don't usually think about. Many illustrations.

Mogil, H. M. (1989). *Weather study under a newspaper umbrella. How the weather works*. Educational Weather Service. Using the newspaper to study ordinary and severe weather, geography, energy, geology, astronomy, and other interrelated topics. Includes forms to be used for observation of clouds, moon watching, and other record keeping. Grades K–12.

National Science Teachers Association. (1978). *Safety in the elementary classroom*. Washington, DC: NSTA.

National Science Teachers Association. (1985). *Science fairs and projects: Grades K–8*. (2nd ed.). Washington, DC: NSTA (1742 Connecticut Avenue N.W., Washington, DC 20009). A collection of articles including a range of opinions on fairs, guides for teachers planning fairs, and many ideas for projects.

Ocone, L., & Pranis, E. (1990). *Guide to kid's gardening*. Burlington, VT: National Gardening Association. A guide for starting and maintaining a youth garden in your school and neighborhood, including experiments, activities, and projects for grades K–12.

INTEGRATING SCIENCE WITH OTHER SUBJECTS

▼ Mr. Newman was nearing the end of his student teaching assignment and had just finished teaching a fifth-grade science lesson. He found that he was not able to finish what he had planned for the day, though the lesson had gone longer than scheduled. At the next opportunity, he talked about the lesson with Ms. Oldhand.

Mr. Newman: The children really enjoyed their science lesson today and I think they learned a lot, but I feel very frustrated because there is never enough time for the children to do all that I want them to do.

Ms. Oldhand: That's a problem that we all have and one that I'm afraid you will always have to live with. The school day is never long enough for all the things that need to be done.

Mr. Newman: Well, you always seem to be able to get a lot more done in science than I can manage to do. When you teach the children move along through the curriculum in math and language arts as fast as all the other classes, and you still have time for special science projects that I can't seem to find time for.

Ms. Oldhand [laughing]: I can assure you that I sometimes feel frustrated, too, but teachers learn to become more efficient as they gain more experience. I certainly don't have any secrets that I'm keeping from you, but I think the one thing that has helped me the most is learning to integrate science with other subjects.

Mr. Newman: What does that mean?

Ms. Oldhand: That means working out ways for the children to reach the objectives in science at the same time that they are reaching the objectives in other subjects. There are many obvious ways to do this, such us using science books in reading and using examples from science when you make up word problems in arithmetic. A less obvious way to do this is to use the various science processes in other areas of the curriculum. After all, the processes of observing, measuring, communicating, and hypothesizing are not confined to science. Those skills are needed in all areas of the curriculum, as well as in everyday life. To me, this kind of integration really promotes higher-order thinking across the curriculum. Actually, science is such an important and pervasive part of our lives that I find it just works its way into the curriculum all the time.

RATIONALE FOR INTEGRATION

In previous chapters, we have suggested many ideas for extending science lessons or units into other areas of the curriculum. In this chapter we go a step further and demonstrate ways to develop integrated lessons and units in order to expand and deepen children's subject-matter understanding and skill development. To *integrate* means to combine things in such a way that together they form a unified whole; the aim when integrating subjects is to interweave them so that children's understanding embraces both subjects as if they were one.

Integration of subjects may be easier for a teacher in a self-contained classroom than for one who teaches science as a special subject. In the latter case, the science teacher needs to work with classroom teachers to plan units and coordinate the integrated lessons taught by the science teacher with those taught by the other teachers. What makes the effort worthwhile is that "students' understanding within the subject matters can become deeper, their understanding of the relationships among the subjects can become sharper and their thinking can become more insightful and systematic, in school and out" (Jacobs, 1989).

There are both practical and theoretical reasons for integrating science with other subjects. Four good reasons for integration are:

- *Time pressure.* As Ms. Oldhand explained, a teacher has difficulty finding the time to do everything that needs to be done in elementary school, and science is sometimes the subject that gets neglected. By integrating science with other

▼ Research has shown that keeping written records helps children understand and remember their experiences in science.

subjects when appropriate, the teacher can accomplish the objectives of the science lesson along with the objectives of one or more other subjects. Later in this chapter you will see some examples that will help explain how this can be done.

- *Fragmentation of the curriculum.* A rigid schedule—30 or 40 minutes for reading, followed by 30 minutes for math, followed by a lesson in writing, and so on through the day—does not help children see the connections between subjects and the purpose of learning the skills that they are taught. This can lead to what has been called *inert knowledge,* knowledge that can be delivered upon request but that is not used spontaneously in solving real problems. For example, a pupil might be able to work exercises in addition and subtraction during arithmetic class but not be able to figure out differences in mileage between two points on a map during social-studies class. In contrast, integration of subjects requires that children use their skills and knowledge in multiple contexts.
- *Pressure for the 3 Rs.* Some parents and others believe that teachers should spend most of their time on reading, writing, and arithmetic. Teachers who feel they are required to emphasize these subjects at the expense of all others can kill two birds with one stone by using science activities and concepts as the basis for work in other subjects.
- *The explosion of knowledge.* There is so much to be learned in science that no one can hope to teach everything children need to know. It is more useful if teachers can help them learn how to learn on their own. When subjects are integrated at the concept and process levels, children begin to understand how knowledge in one area is connected with knowledge in another area. This understanding will be helpful when they start to learn something new, because they will know that new knowledge can be tied into knowledge they already have.

CRITERIA FOR INTEGRATING SCIENCE

Although there are good reasons for integrating science with other subjects, that does not mean all lessons should be integrated. Before you decide to teach an integrated lesson or unit you should ask yourself these questions:

- Does the lesson meet important goals or objectives in both science and the other subject(s)? It serves no useful purpose to include unimportant facts or something far outside of the science curriculum just to have an integrated lesson.
- Does the integrated lesson or unit do a better job than could be done in single-subject lessons? Does it lead to more understanding or a higher level of performance of a skill? If not, why are you doing it?

Whether you are in a self-contained classroom or working as a special science teacher, planning and gathering materials for any lesson takes time and energy. It probably takes more time to plan integrated lessons than single-subject lessons. When you need to coordinate your work with that of other teachers, as you will if you are a special science teacher, even more time and energy are needed for planning. That is why you must ask yourself those questions and try to give honest answers. Unless you can answer "yes" to those questions, it may be best to teach a single-subject lesson.

TYPES OF INTEGRATED LESSONS AND UNITS

Curriculum integration includes not just the interweaving of subjects, such as science and social studies, but also the interweaving of skills and processes that may be taught more effectively in relation to one another than separately. Three ways to integrate subjects or skills are first described and then illustrated by examples later in the chapter.

TOPIC-ORIENTED INTEGRATION

This is probably the simplest way to integrate science with other subjects. Children explore a topic in science and look at the same topic in another area of the curriculum. For example, you could have a unit on rivers in which content from earth science, geography, and literature are combined. To meet science objectives, children would study how rivers are formed, how they change over time, and what the characteristics of flowing water are. To meet social-studies objectives, they would learn something about the major rivers of the world, where they are located, and how they have affected the development of civilization. In literature they might read *Huckleberry Finn* or other books in which a river plays a major role.

In a unit of this kind, the pupils are not aware that one part of the unit is science and another part is social studies or literature. You, as the teacher, have planned the unit to integrate these subjects and meet the various learning objectives, but in the minds of the pupils, all the parts should come together to make the topic more interesting and meaningful.

CONCEPT-ORIENTED INTEGRATION

Many important concepts in science have counterparts or similar concepts in other subject areas. An example is the concept of *network* or *web*. In science this is an important ecological concept, used particularly in teaching about the interdependence between one life form and others. This is also an important concept in social studies, where children learn that peoples are interdependent and that they themselves live in a network. Such integration helps children acquire higher-order concepts that are applicable and important in more than one, and often in many, contexts.

The value of both topic-oriented and concept-oriented integration is that children may deepen their understanding of topics and concepts by seeing things from many points of view, making comparisons, and seeing connections.

SKILLS-CONTENT INTEGRATION

Important learning skills can be enhanced and made more meaningful when they are taught and used in several subjects. Skills to be integrated include both symbolic skills and thinking skills or processes.

Symbolic skills include arithmetic, writing, drawing, graphing, and mapping. When children watch a butterfly emerge from its cocoon and then write about it, the writing has immediacy and meaning. Mathematics and science are often integrated at all levels because so much of science depends on the use of mathematics as a tool. Writing should be a part of any science program, and drawing should not be neglected as a way to represent knowledge.

Thinking skills or processes include observing, classifying, inferring, hypothesizing, and various higher-order thinking skills, many of which have been discussed earlier in this book. Once you begin to think about using these processes in teaching other subjects, you will see many opportunities to reinforce their use. In a reading lesson even with the youngest children, you can read a few lines of a story and then ask, "What do you think will happen next?" and "Why do you think that?" When you ask those questions, you are asking children to form hypotheses based on evidence in the story, a process quite similar to forming simple hypotheses in science.

Classification is a basic and important process that can be used in all subjects—reading, writing, mathematics, social studies, art, music. As children see that they can classify in all subjects, they will begin to consider this a tool for understanding and a useful way to think about the things they encounter in their daily lives.

In planning lessons for this kind of integration, your chain of reasoning may be something like this:

1. What are the content objectives of the lesson?
2. What activities will the pupils be carrying out?
3. What skills will they need to meet the lesson objectives?

Or you might follow this line of reasoning:

1. What skill will the pupils learn?
2. In what area of the curriculum is that skill needed?
3. What activities will use the skill to meet content objectives?

In either case the skill is taught and practiced as a tool to aid learning.

Since you have now had many examples and a lot of practice in developing lesson plans and designing units, all the details in the following examples will not need to be spelled out. You should now be capable of using those outlines to write complete lesson plans that incorporate all the elements described and discussed in previous chapters.

SCIENCE AND SOCIAL STUDIES

Once you start to think "integratively" you will find many opportunities to integrate science and social studies because many concepts and processes used in science are also used in social studies. Both science and social studies are complex subjects that include many areas of knowledge within each one. Science includes biology, chemistry, physics, geology, meteorology, and other branches, each of which has its own history, methods, and traditions. Social studies includes geography, history, economics, and other subjects, each of which also has its own history, methods, and traditions.

In earlier chapters you have been introduced to lessons that provide experiences designed to help children learn science processes, including observing, classifying, measuring, predicting, and inferring. Many of these and other processes are also applicable to social studies. Classifying, for example, is as useful to the historian and the geographer as to the biologist, the chemist, or the physicist. Classification is a thinking process that can be, and should be, used in many contexts and with many kinds of objects, characteristics, and ideas.

There is another practical reason for integrating science and social studies. Because the elementary school curriculum is now focused so heavily on skills development, very little time may be allotted to either science or social studies. In order to fit these important subjects into the curriculum, many teachers schedule their class time so that science and social studies are taught at the same time on different days. That is, social studies is taught at 1:30 on Mondays, Wednesdays, and Fridays, and science is taught at 1:30 on Tuesdays and Thursdays. It is easy to see the advantages of integrating these two subjects if you have that kind of schedule. Instead of teaching social studies two or three days each week and science the other days, the integrated unit is taught every day.

The unit described in the next section is not only an example of an integrated unit but also an application of Bruner's ideas about what kinds of things to teach in science, social studies, and other subjects. As you read in Chapter 2, Bruner advocates the teaching of important and powerful ideas in simple ways that children can understand and relate to. He believes that the curriculum should then return to those ideas in later years at a deeper level. Relativity is an example of a concept that will be understood at a deeper level later in a child's life, but here it is treated in a way that elementary children can understand.

▼ UNIT PLAN 12.1

GRADE LEVEL: 5–6

TOPIC: Relativity

GOALS

This unit starts with a series of science lessons followed by a series of social studies lessons. The science lessons introduce the concept of relativity, a higher-order concept that is applicable both within and outside of science. The social-studies lessons complement and extend the insights gained in the science lessons. The activities of the two parts of the unit are designed to provide experiences that will enable children to move beyond their natural egocentric viewpoint and take other perspectives as they view the world and themselves. The word *relative* will take on new meaning for them.

MATERIALS

- Spacey (a cardboard figure, patterned after the illustration in Figure 12.1)
- graph paper
- large photographs of street scenes, landscapes, etc.
- appropriate stories or books

OVERVIEW OF UNIT'S SCIENCE ACTIVITIES

These activities are derived from ideas incorporated in *Relative Position and Motion*, a unit originally developed by the Science Curriculum Improvement Study (Berger, Karplus, Montgomery, Randle & Thies, 1972). The basic concept is that position and motion of objects can only be perceived, described and recognized with reference to other nearby objects. These other objects form the *frame of reference*, which is used to define the position of the original object.

Activities for this unit are outlined as Lesson 1, Lesson 2, and so on, but you should not assume that a lesson can be finished in one class period. That will depend on the detailed plans developed by each individual teacher.

LESSON 1

Begin with questions and games involving the location of objects in the classroom. Ask such questions as these:

- The window is to my left. Juan, is it also on your left? If the window is on my left and on your right, is it *really* right or left?
- The desk is in front of me. Tina, is it in front of you, too? How can the desk be between you and me and still be in front of us both?

▼ FIGURE 12.1
Spacey

- Suppose you were a fly crawling on the ceiling. Would the ceiling be under you or over you?

Finally, introduce the term *point of reference*. The position of an object depends on the point of reference. You may call on children to stand in designated places and ask questions about locations of objects, using themselves as points of reference. In this way children learn to use reference points in describing the location of objects. A certain chair will be "to my right" or "behind Jane's desk."

LESSON 2

In this lesson you will introduce Spacey, a cardboard figure who defines the position of everything in reference to himself (see Figure 12.1). Spacey does not say, for example, that he is standing on the table; he says that the table is under his feet. He sees the whole world from one point of view.

In this lesson you will involve children in describing positions of objects relative to Spacey, who is first placed on a table. The children are asked to describe objects as if they were Spacey. They say "the window is to my left" or "the table is above my head." More complicated descriptions are then required, such as "to my left and higher than my head" or "behind me and to my left."

LESSON 3

When the children return from lunch or arrive in the morning, Spacey will be turned upside down and hung from the ceiling; now the objects in the room are "over my head" and the ceiling is "under my feet."

LESSON 4

Introduce the concept of frame of reference. Children identify the position of objects by reference to landmarks. For this lesson you will need photographs—preferably large ones—of familiar scenes. Children may bring pictures to share and they may be placed on the bulletin board. The photographs are used as the basis for identifying relative positions of buildings, automobiles, trees, and other objects, as well as the direction from which each photograph was taken.

If your pupils have had practice in making graphs, this section of the unit may be extended to include drawing graphs whose coordinates are labeled with reference to a zero point.

OVERVIEW OF UNIT'S SOCIAL-STUDIES ACTIVITIES

In the social world, as in the physical world, each person's perceptions are structured by a reference frame. The way one person relates to another person and is perceived by the other person depends on where they are in relation to each other. For example, a child may have a close relationship with an aunt or an uncle but the relationship is not the same as a relationship with a cousin.

The first objective of these activities is to increase children's awareness of and sensitivity to other individuals who occupy roles unlike their own within their own reference group. The second goal is to help children learn to see things from another person's point of view and to be able to withhold judgment until other perspectives have been considered. The third and larger goal is to help children understand how membership in a group may determine their point of view and how the group appears to those on the outside.

LESSON 1

Introduce this part of the unit by saying that the class has studied relativity in the physical world; now they will think about relativity among people. Read a story about an extended family. Many books are suitable for this purpose; choose one that you think the children will like. The story should have many family members who can be identified by name; add family members and a few neighbors if more are needed. Ask questions as you go along and at the end.

Assign roles from the story to children, and give each a large name tag. Now you will play a game of introductions in which you assume the role of the mother, called here Ms. Chin. You and the children will role play a series of introductions roughly like this:

Ms. Chin:	Mr. Green, I want you to meet my son Jack.
Mr. Green and Jack:	How do you do?
Ms. Chin:	Susie, introduce Jack to Mr. Brown and say how he is related to you.
Susie:	Mr. Brown, I'd like you to meet my brother Jack.
Ms. Chin [*to the class*]:	Is Jack a brother? I thought he was a son.
Class:	He is both.
Ms. Chin:	How can that be?
Class:	It depends.
Ms. Chin:	Depends on what?

[Continue with the introductions—grandmother, classmate, uncle, cousin, etc.]

You, the teacher, then say, "This is getting confusing. Tomorrow we will make a chart to organize these relationships."

LESSON 2

Remind the children of the story and ask individual pupils to recall the relationships. Write names on the board. Draw a chart on the board and ask the class to tell you what to put in the cells. For example, ask, "What is Jack's relation to Susie?" Or, you could ask, "Susie would say that Jack is her [blank]?" Continue in this way until the chart is filled in. (This chart must be based on the particular story you have used in introducing this lesson.) Figure 12.2 shows a chart of an extended family.

Ask the children for a word that describes all of these people (*relatives* or *relations*). Then ask them to recall Spacey and compare the meaning of *relative* in the two contexts.

The assignment for the following day is for each child to choose four family members or friends and make a chart similar to this one. Children may bring in

▼ FIGURE 12.2
Chart of an extended family—"relativity" among people

RELATIVES	JACK	SUSIE	MS. CHIN	MR. CHIN	MRS. PARKER	MR. PARKER	TOM PARKER
Jack	self	brother	son	son	nephew	nephew	cousin
Susie	sister	self	daughter	daughter	niece	niece	cousin
Ms. Chin	mother	mother	self	wife	sister	sister-in-law	aunt
Mr. Chin	father	father	husband	self	sister-in-law	broth.-in-law	uncle
Mrs. Parker	aunt	aunt	sister	sister-in-law	self	wife	mother
Mr. Parker	uncle	uncle	broth.-in-law	broth.-in-law	husband	self	father
Tom Parker	cousin	cousin	nephew	nephew	son	son	self

pictures of occasions, such as holidays, birthdays, or reunions, when the family is gathered together.

(Warning: Make no assumptions about living arrangements of the families of your pupils. Accept as normal any arrangements that the pupils put in their charts. If a child says he or she has no family, say that sometimes other people are the same as family. A good friend may be the same as a brother and the mother's friend may be like an aunt. If you find that you have homeless children in your class, you may not be able to do this as written but have to modify it to suit the situation as well as you can. You must be sensitive on this issue.)

When the charts are brought in, you can discuss them and let those who want to share with others do so. The pupils will paste their charts in their notebooks.

LESSON 3

Introduce the idea of different points of view in a conflict. The children will role play the resolution of a conflict that they might encounter. The objective is to see other people's points of view, or *reference points*. There are several ways this can be done. You can read a story that involves conflict, stop at a crucial point, and have the children act out what the characters would do. This can be accomplished by your choosing a few children to demonstrate or—if they are used to working in cooperative groups—you can have the pupils move into groups and let each group act out the rest of the story. Each child assumes a role and explains the conflict from the point of view of the role assumed. Remind them of Spacey.

Another way to do this would be to use an incident that is familiar to the children and have them take roles to act out the incident, showing how each participant has a point of view. However you do it, the point is to get children to see that a situation looks different to the different people involved in it and that they should try to see a situation from other people's points of view as well as their own.

One way to end the unit is to read a story about a child who was excluded from a group. Ask questions about how it feels to be on the outside rather than the inside of a group. It is better to leave children thinking than to have a neat wrap-up.

▼ UNIT PLAN 12.2

GRADE LEVELS: 4–8

TOPIC: Acid Rain

MATERIALS

- acids and bases
- indicator papers (pH paper and others)
- radish or bean seeds
- potting materials
- prepared inventory sheets
- reading materials

GOALS

Children will learn what is meant by the term *acid rain*, how acid rain affects living organisms, what causes it, how we contribute to it, and some possible future consequences of current behavior and policies.

OVERVIEW OF ACTIVITIES

Many of these activities are described in detail in *Acid Rain: Science Projects* (Hessler & Stubbs, 1987), available from The Acid Rain Foundation. This unit integrates science, social studies, math, language arts, and art, but it emphasizes the integration of science and social studies.

LESSON 1

Acids and bases including vinegar, baking soda, antacid tablet, lemon juice, and other materials are tested with pH paper and classified as to pH above or below neutral. (It is not necessary for pupils to know the definition of pH, only that it is a way of testing whether something is an acid, a base, or neutral.) Explain that they will be collecting rain samples to test for acid rain, and begin preparations for testing on the next rainy day. (Be prepared to deal with the possibility that the rain in your area is not, in fact, acidic.)

LESSON 2

Seedling response to acid rain is tested. This is a pupil experiment to be conducted as a controlled experiment. Radish or bean seeds are planted (two to a pot) and watered with water of varying acidity (pH from 3 to 6). Three weeks after the seeds are planted pupils measure and record height, number of leaves, and leaf midrib length. (Other activities that would be suitable are to find the effect of acidic water on leaves and on the tiny organisms found in pond water.) Their measurements should be carefully recorded and used to make simple bar graphs.

LESSON 3

Introduce the idea of acid rain and some information about its effect on trees. What is the evidence that acid rain has caused trees to die? This will lead them to search for sources of information. Your next questions should seek to relate the

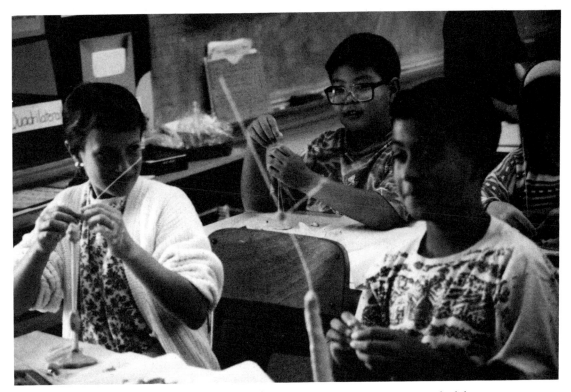

▼ Science units involving quick changes such as properties of liquids are easier to schedule than units with slow changes such as growing seeds.

results of acid rain to social questions. How would it feel to live near a forest where the trees are dying? This could be an opportunity for creative writing or role playing.

LESSON 4

Where does acid rain come from? Ask questions about sources of air pollution. Questions and discussion follow about the meaning and origin of fossil fuels, what happens when they burn, and how they provide usable energy. (Children of this age all know something about dinosaurs and other prehistoric animals.) Pupils are assigned to collect pictures of sources of air pollution from magazines, newspapers, and other publications to bring to class. You or a committee will make these into a collage and add pictures as more come in.

LESSON 5

Sources of energy in the pupils' homes and in your city or town are addressed next. Begin by making a list on the board or overhead projector of machines and appliances pupils used before coming to school that day. They discuss where energy comes from. Does the electricity in your area come from water power, coal, or another source? Pupils take a worksheet home and, with the help of parents, list all energy users in and around their home and what they think the source of energy is. These form a basis of discussion on the following day.

Throughout these lessons don't neglect preparations for and actual collection of rain samples. When samples have been collected they will be tested to determine whether the samples are "acid rain."

LESSON 6

Wrap up the unit by forming groups to discuss "What if?" questions that you will assign: What if we did not have any more fossil fuels? Would that be good or bad? What if we continue to pollute the air as we are now doing? What if our country makes laws prohibiting air pollution and other countries do not? What effects will that have on the environment and our relations with other countries? What if people have to pay higher taxes and lose jobs in order to lower pollution? Each group writes out answers on big sheets of newsprint, and these are read and discussed by all.

OTHER IDEAS FOR UNITS: INTEGRATING SCIENCE AND SOCIAL STUDIES

WEATHER: CAUSES AND AFFECTS (UPPER ELEMENTARY)

Weather is included in almost all lists of topics to be taught in science in the elementary school. A brief outline of such a unit was given in Chapter 11. This may be extended and enhanced by getting information from a newspaper, over a period of days or weeks, about weather in other parts of the United States and the world. This can lead into an exploration—through books, films, and other media—of how animals and people protect themselves in extreme climates, such as the Arctic, the Sahara, and the Amazon rain forest. Field trips to a local park will add interest and knowledge, particularly if you can arrange several trips to the same spot at different times of year.

ANIMAL HABITATS AND PEOPLE'S HOMES

This is related to the previous idea but is not really the same. Animal habitats are included as a science topic in many sixth-grade curricula. This can be extended to a study of the houses people build and live in throughout the world—a topic that is also often included in social studies curricula. Provide materials and experiences that will lead the children to understand that both animals and people use the materials at hand and adapt them to their own needs.

ROCKS OF THE EARTH AND STONES FOR BUILDING (PRIMARY OR UPPER ELEMENTARY)

An earth science unit on rocks and minerals can be integrated with an exploration of the stones used in buildings, monuments, tombstones, walls, and other constructions in your town or city. Science objectives will include learning how rocks are formed, identifying different rocks and minerals, and finding out what forms are present in the local area. This will lead into identifying the stones used for various structures and finding out where they came from, why different stones are used for different purposes, how they are quarried, and how they have figured in the town's history.

In order to make a unit of this kind successful, you will need to make certain beforehand that adequate sources of information are available. Work with your school librarian to ensure that there are resources available for the children to use. It will be frustrating and unproductive to have children searching for information that is not available in any form or in any place to which they have access.

SIMPLE MACHINES IN THE ANCIENT WORLD

In Chapter 10 you saw that simple machines are a suitable topic for a group investigation and that this topic could be extended to include learning about the building of the Pyramids, cathedrals, or other structures of the ancient and medieval world. Whether this is carried out as a group investigation or guided discovery, it is essential to have a good supply of machines and tools. Strong hooks should be screwed into the ceiling so that pulleys can be attached and used for hands-on activities, including measuring the force needed to lift loads by various combinations of pulleys. Levers of several kinds should be available, as well as bricks or rocks to lift. Children will first learn about these machines by using them to lift real weights and by measuring forces and masses. After they have had enough experience to achieve some understanding of how the machines work, they will study the building of the pyramids as an introduction to life in ancient Egypt and, by extension, the ancient world. Building a model of a pyramid or other structure can be an interesting and worthwhile class project if several areas of the curriculum are integrated so that the learning objectives are kept in mind.

SCIENCE AND READING

As one of the "three Rs," reading has always consumed a major portion of the school day in the primary grades and has received serious attention all the way through the elementary school. Learning to read is a major developmental task for young children and of great concern to teachers and parents. If you are a teacher in a self-contained classroom, a good deal of your time will be spent on teaching your pupils to read, from early stages of emergent literacy, through skill at decoding and comprehension, and finally to the ability to use reading as a means of learning other subjects and understanding the world. Classifying, inferring, and hypothesizing—processes needed in science—also have a place in reading. As children get past the earliest stages of learning to read and begin to read for comprehension, these processes become important in their progress.

Reading is probably the subject that causes the most concern to parents, school boards, and school administrators. There is an extensive body of research on reading education, much more than there is on science education, and debates about how to teach reading have gone on for generations. At present there is much discussion about the relative advantages of using basal readers as opposed to using other methods. (For a recent example of one such debate, see Stahl & Miller, 1989; McGee & Lomax, 1990; and Schickedanz, 1990.)

A discussion of the relative merits of various approaches to teaching reading is beyond the scope of this book, but two ways that science and reading may profitably be integrated are: (1) the use of science experiences as a basis for the experiential approach to teaching beginning and remedial reading, and (2) the use of books as supplements to classroom science experiences.

USING SCIENCE AS THE BASIS FOR READING

Use of basal readers remains the primary means of instruction in beginning reading, but *language-experience* and *whole-language* approaches are other methods now in use. These personalized, reality-based approaches encompass listening, speaking, reading, and writing, and children are encouraged and guided to use language in regard to a shared experience of the group. Both of these methods—similar in many respects—can use science experiences as the basis for narratives constructed by the children. In the older, language-experience method, children tell their experiences to the teacher, either individually or in a group, and the teacher writes what they say. In the whole-language approach, the children write their experiences themselves, spelling the words however they can. A science lesson on observing and classifying objects, for example, can form the basis for a language-experience or whole-language lesson.

The following example lesson is a simple activity that illustrates how a science experience can form the basis for a reading lesson. Almost any of the common topics of the kindergarten and first-grade curriculum—animals, parts of the body, the five senses, the seasons, shadows, magnets, floating and sinking, balancing—can be used as the basis for a language approach to reading.

▼ LESSON PLAN 12.1

GRADE LEVELS: K–1

TOPIC: Classifying Leaves

OBJECTIVES

By the end of these activities, the learner should be able to:

1. Observe and classify leaves
2. Represent their own experiences in writing and read what they have written or dictated.

ACTIVITIES

When the leaves have begun to turn in the fall the teacher brings a few leaves to class, shows them to the pupils, and asks questions to allow children to tell what they know about leaves, such as that some trees have leaves that change color in the fall and other trees stay green all year.

An alternative would be to do this late in the spring after leaves have appeared on local trees. In that case, the questions would be about leaves coming out in the spring.

After a brief discussion the children go for a nature walk on the school grounds or nearby where leaves can be found. All children should collect a few leaves to bring back. Back in the classroom the children examined the leaves for color, shape, and size, perhaps with small hand lenses. Then they classify the leaves by color, shape, or other characteristics. The next phase is for the teacher to draw out from the children a story about the walk (including what kinds of leaves they found) and write that story on the board or on large paper, following the usual procedure for a language-experience lesson.

OTHER IDEAS FOR LESSONS OR UNITS: INTEGRATING SCIENCE AND READING

HATCHING CHICKENS

Watching chickens hatch is always exciting to children. This activity is usually reserved for kindergarten and first grade, but all children find it absorbing and fascinating. Eggs that have already been incubated can be bought from a hatchery and kept in the room for the final two or three days before the first cracks appear in the shells. Children will watch the eggs and be allowed time to write their observations each day. The teacher leads discussions each day about what is happening, asking whether anyone has heard anything, noticed any differences, and so on.

EFFECT OF DIET

Another experience suitable for beginning readers and writers is observation of the effect of a poor diet on white mice. For this you will need two mice in separate cages, some advice about mouse nutrition, and a supply of food. (The National Dairy Council will supply information about good and poor diets.) After introducing the subject and explaining what each mouse will be fed—discussing how food affects our bodies and making whatever points seem appropriate—the experiment is begun. The mice are fed at the same time each day, a good diet for one and a poor diet for the other. Children record their observations and read them back, or the teacher records them on the board if this seems preferable.

After about a week, the children will be able to see definite differences in the appearance of the two mice. After this has been noted and discussed, the ill-fed mouse is given the same diet as the other mouse. After another seven days, this mouse will look very similar to the other one. At each stage, the children record their observations and read their own words.

READING ABOUT SCIENCE

A wonderful variety of books on every imaginable science subject is available for readers of all ages. These range from books written at the lowest vocabulary level to detailed, accurate treatments of subjects of interest to those upper-elementary children who by this time are excellent readers and have a special interest in science. In between these two extremes are many science books that have wide appeal. All pupils should be required to read and report on, either orally or in writing, books about science subjects, along with works of fiction, history, and other areas of interest.

It is useless to require pupils to produce book reports unless you are willing to put thought and time into how they will carry out the assignment. To make the assignment is easy, but to follow through can prove difficult. There are a number of steps that pupils will have to take and you will have to monitor their progress, including selecting a book (in this case, a book on a suitable science subject), having the book approved, reading the book and taking notes, submitting for approval an outline of the report, and getting the report in on time. In effect, the reports become independent projects, similar to those described in Chapter 11. You can determine whether writing a book report will be a growth-promoting process or a frustrating one for most of your pupils.

Books will also be needed for information on subjects studied in class, particularly in the case of group investigations and independent projects, such as for a science fair. School librarians are always ready to cooperate, within the constraints of their budgets, in securing books that children need for carrying out science assignments. You, the teacher, need to let them know ahead of time what your pupils will need for their science projects and assignments.

Although science must primarily be taught by means of an active, hands-on, experiential approach, that does not mean there is no place for books and reading. Reading can make experience more meaningful and provide vicarious experiences that cannot be had directly. The problem arises when reading becomes the primary means by which children learn science. *Reading should supplement experience, not take the place of it.*

SCIENCE AND WRITING

This is an area in which skill and content can be integrated so that each is enhanced by the other. Writing shapes experience and helps in understanding it. This is as true for experience of the natural world as it is for other kinds of experience. Thus, writing should be an integral part of science instruction from the earliest grades. Science can be used as a basis for writing about observations, thoughts, and feelings. Integrating science and writing is in keeping with the current interest in writing across the curriculum and the whole-language approach in elementary school, both of which reject the notion that writing can be separated from experience and from other ways of learning.

Keeping records and describing observations and experiments is an essential part of science and should be considered as a normal part of a science lesson. There is good evidence to show that keeping written records helps children understand and remember their experiences in science.

Precision, accuracy, and clarity of expression are important characteristics of science writing and should not be neglected in elementary school. Analysis and theorizing (or hypothesizing) may begin to be encouraged toward the end of elementary school, but children first have to learn to communicate what they have done and observed in a way that others can understand. This emphasis encourages children to think of writing as a means of explaining to someone else what they have seen and done and, in the process, to understand it better themselves.

Several years ago a pupil wrote this description of an accident: "I seen a reck at Main St. and Aurora Bldv. The blue car was dent and the white car was smushed." Although the pupil still had a lot to learn about grammar and spelling, these two sentences show that he was observant, since he remembered the street names and the color of the cars, and that he could give the reader a graphic picture of the scene in a few words. This is what you want to encourage pupils to do as they learn to communicate their experiences and thoughts to others. Grammar and spelling are important, too, but their purpose is to aid communication, not inhibit it.

KEEPING NOTEBOOKS

Beginning no later than fourth grade, pupils should keep a science notebook in which they record their activities in science class. At the beginning of the year, explain that each pupil needs to bring a small notebook and that the notebooks will be used only in science class and will be left at school.

The notebooks should be handed out or picked up by pupils at the beginning of science class and returned to a special place at the end of class. This is one of the things that you should monitor, or assign as a responsibility to one of the pupils, at the beginning and end of each science class period. The notebooks should be reviewed by you once a week and returned with appropriate comments to the children.

If you choose to grade the notebooks, you should grade them for completeness, organization, and evidence of thinking, but not for spelling or writing, since children's writing skills are in various stages of development. Whether you grade them or not, the notebooks should be checked to see that they are being kept up and that all important observations and information are included.

A page from a fifth-grade pupil's notebook is shown in Figure 12.3. Note that it is neat and carefully kept, though the child has corrected a few mistakes. Note also that this is a record of a rather simple experiment, but one that fifth graders can carry out and understand without much explanation or help from the teacher. That is, the experiment is at their level of ability and understanding. The writing that is necessary is also quite within the ability of most fifth graders.

In order to become autonomous learners, children have to be able to work on their own without constant adult guidance. For this to happen, they have to have sci-

Our experiment was to find ʃ which materials could push what ~~wait~~ weights. Here is our table:—

Weights	Pushing		
	B. Cotton	alloy	Copper
5 g	no	yes	yes
50 g	no	yes	yes
10 g	no	yes	yes
20 g	no	yes	yes
100 g	no	yes	no
200 g	no	no	no
1 Klo	no	no	no
5 klo	no	no	no

Concurlsion

By looking at the table it shows that the cotton could not push any of the weights, so that means it is terrible at pushing. The Alloy and Copper did quite well but by looking at the table it shows that alloy is the best pusher because on the log copper could not push it and alloy could.

▼ FIGURE 12.3
A fifth grader's notebook page

ence lessons based on activities, including writing, that they can manage mostly on their own. When science lessons become too abstract or too complicated—or the necessary record keeping and arriving at conclusions is too difficult—children are forced to rely on adults and cannot grow toward autonomy.

The lesson that follows is an example of a simple activity that helps pupils learn the importance of choosing words carefully in order to convey the intended meaning to others. The teacher does not have to correct the children's language; the consequences of using imprecise words are built into the activity. This activity has some of the characteristics of a game, and children usually enjoy it. If it is successful, you may want to use it with other objects at a later time. If you use it first with rocks, you can use it later with shells or leaves, for example.

▼ LESSON PLAN 12.2

GRADE LEVEL: 3–4

TOPIC: Describing and Identifying

GOAL

To write a description of an object that allows another person to distinguish that object from other similar objects.

MATERIALS

- a collection of rocks
- paper and pencils

Any interesting objects may be used, provided they are of the same category and that there are significant differences between the individual items.

Distribute rocks, giving one to each child if there are enough to go around; otherwise give one each pair of children. Ask the children to observe their rocks carefully and to think of some words that could be used to describe them. Walk around the room to encourage children to attend to task.

After a few minutes, go to the board and ask for raised hands from those who have thought of a word to describe their rocks. Call on a child and write the word on the board. Repeat until there are six to eight words on the board. If a child suggests *big* or *small* say, "Bigger than what?" or "Smaller than what?" You might suggest that they could use an egg for comparison and ask, "Is it bigger than an egg?". Continue until you have drawn out the idea that *big* and *small*, *light* and *dark*, and similar words are comparative.

Distribute half sheets of paper and tell children to observe their rocks carefully and to write a description of his or her rock, using any words that describe something about the rock. Direct them to write their names at the bottom of their papers and to fold the papers over when they are finished.

After they have had time to complete this task, they should bring their rocks up to the front of the room and place them together on a table or in a space marked out on the floor. At the same time they should place their folded papers with descriptions in a container (a basket or box).

When all rocks and descriptions have been placed as directed, take the container with the descriptions around the room and have each child take one and read it silently. Then have the children come up in small groups, each picking out the rock described on his or her paper. If a child cannot find the rock described on the paper, return the paper to the child who wrote the description for improvement. Once improved, the description is handed back to the other child.

When all rocks have been identified, spend a few minutes letting the children discuss what makes a good description and which words they found helpful or unhelpful. The activity may be repeated, or the lesson can end with a few words about situations in which an accurate description is very important.

OTHER WRITING

Many scientists have written poetically and expressively about the beauty of science and their feelings about it. Children should also be given opportunities to write about their experiences in whatever way they wish. In most schools, children are more often given opportunities for expressive writing than they are required to convey information accurately and clearly. Science experiences can provide the basis for the development of clarity and accuracy.

SCIENCE AND MATHEMATICS

Mathematics is often taught as algorithms to be learned and problems for which there is one and only one right answer that can be arrived at by only one "correct" method. Doing mathematics is identified with searching for the unique solution to a problem that is stated in a uniquely acceptable way. Since mathematics is usually first taught in mathematics class and then applied in science class, it is often assumed that a problem in science must first be mathematically formulated and then the answer can be obtained by some means of automatic processing. Applying mathematics in science has come to be identified with writing down equations for end-of-chapter problems.

If mathematics and science are to be integrated in the elementary classroom, a different approach is needed, one that teaches and uses mathematics within the context of classroom experiences in science. Mathematics may then be considered a useful and necessary means of representing observations that have been made and working out problems that have presented themselves. One writer who has argued forcefully for keeping the teaching of mathematics in the context of real problems has noted that students often look for the variables in a problem and try to fit them into what they hope are appropriate equations. "It is quickly understood by students," he writes, "that it is preferable to forget about the situational meaning of the variables, operations or rules. In fact, for most cases the mathematical tricks will do the job" (Janvier, 1990).

Children develop many mathematical ideas on their own from experiences they have or just by thinking about things, but they do not usually associate these ideas with the math they learn in school. A story will illustrate the point. A group of four first graders earned six dollars through a yard sale. After they had divided the money equally among themselves, they were asked how they did the arithmetic involved. "That's not arithmetic," they answered. "That's just common sense." Often, children who work in their parents' shops or market stalls can make accurate change for customers at an earlier age than most of their classmates can do the same calculations with paper and pencil.

In a previous section, you read that pupils keep notebooks in which to record their observations, experiences, experiments, and conclusions. These notebooks should also contain notations of the mathematics associated with the work done in science, including measurements, graphs, and the calculations necessary to understanding their observations.

It is hard to think of many science experiments, however simple, that do not use mathematics in some way. The idea of growth, for example, can be explored in many contexts, and the questions raised can be tackled using various representations, according to the age of the pupils: verbal descriptions, tables, bar graphs, growth curves and equations. Previous sections have included ideas describing changes in animals and for measuring differences in plant growth (the acid-rain experiment). A similar context for studying and representing growth is given in the example unit that follows.

▼ UNIT PLAN 12.3

GRADE LEVELS: 4–5

TOPIC: Change Over Time—Growing Plants

OBJECTIVES

By the end of these activities, the learner should be able to:

1. Observe, record, and represent plant growth
2. Consider how other things change over time

MATERIALS

- bean seeds
- potting soil
- containers
- clear plastic rulers

ACTIVITIES

On the first day ask questions about planting seeds and growing plants. Give children an opportunity to tell what they know about how to plant seeds. Build on these responses to explain how to plant bean seeds and maintain the plants. Distribute seeds, potting soil, and small containers. Children then plant seeds, label containers, and set them in a sunny window. The children should keep a record of all this in their notebooks, not forgetting to include the date of each observation.*

It is important for pupils to watch for the first sign of a leaf pushing through the soil and to record the date. From that point on, the plants should be watered on schedule and measured about twice a week. Measurements should include height of the plant, length and width of leaves, and an estimate of the total volume of the plant. (An estimate may be too difficult for many pupils; if that is the case, omit it.)

How the data are represented will depend on the age and ability of your pupils. The simplest thing to do is to draw a bar graph—there is a direct relationship between the height of the bars and the plant itself. The next step is to draw a graph of the amount of growth once or twice a week. This is found at a given time by subtracting the previous day's height from the current height (or width, if that is being measured) and gives an indication of the *rate of growth*, an important concept.

The unit is brought to closure when the plants become spindly and interest lags. Let the children take their plants home, and then display the graphs and charts in the classroom.

OTHER IDEAS FOR LESSONS OR UNITS

THE CHILDREN'S GROWTH THROUGHOUT THE YEAR

Another context for measuring and recording growth is the children's own bodies. This can be done throughout the year or, possibly, for half a year. Because rates of growth vary so widely, it is best to use averages in presenting results. (This presents an opportunity to practice calculating averages.) Growth and change is an important concept, one that pupils will return to again and again throughout their school years.

TIME LINE

A roll of paper used in calculating machines can be attached to the wall to illustrate the length of time that has passed since dinosaurs were alive or, in earth science, since the various eras of geologic time. Children will not automatically associate the length of the paper with time; you will have to help them understand this concept.

MATHEMATICS AS A SCIENCE

This section has focused on the use of mathematics as a way of representing and analyzing data collected during science activities. The reader should not be misled into

---

*If you have access to the new, fast growing plant now on the market, that would speed up the process of observing and measuring change.

thinking that these practical uses and representations of the physical world are all there is to mathematics. Mathematics is a science as well as a tool, and from the constructivist point of view an understanding of mathematics does not depend only on experiences in the "real" world but also, and importantly, on logical thinking.

In the primary grades mathematics and science merge in many ways, such as learning to identify shapes, understanding one-to-one correspondence, recognizing patterns in numbers as well as in objects, classifying numbers, and understanding concepts of area and volume. Learning activities associated with these processes and concepts are truly integrated, since mathematics and science are one at this level.

INTEGRATING SCIENCE WITH THE EXPRESSIVE ARTS

Music, art, and expressive movement are other subjects taught in elementary school that offer many opportunities for integrated lessons and units. Once you give up thinking about individual subjects and start thinking about ways to combine and integrate them, you will think of many ways to accomplish this. A bit of imagination and understanding of both science and the other subject are necessary, but you can find help among your colleagues and perhaps some of them will join with you.

VISUAL ARTS

There are many examples of trivial exercises planned in an effort to extend science lessons into other areas. In art, for example, teachers have been known to hand out "dittoed" sheets that are to be cut out and pasted together in some way to represent a small animal or plant. Other teachers give first-grade children outlines of dinosaurs or farm animals to be colored in. It only takes a moment to reflect that these activities do not meet the criteria provided at the beginning of this chapter and thus are appropriate for neither art nor science.

All styles of drawing and painting can be integrated with science lessons. Children can often represent more of what they know in a drawing than in writing and should be encouraged to include in their notebooks drawings of the animals, plants, and other things they have studied (Howe & Vasu, 1989). They can also be encouraged to express their feelings about other living things. You can imagine that the little girl who said she had followed and observed a worm might be happy to express her thoughts and feelings about the worm in some art form.

Natural structures of plants and animals are excellent "taking-off" points for a unit that integrates science and art. The natural structures and patterns found in plants, seashells, insect webs, and honeycombs are but a few of the many to be seen in natural objects. For older pupils, optics is a topic that can be the basis for a unit on light, color, and design.

MUSIC

There are many areas of overlap between physical science and music. A unit can begin with the physical properties of sound and move into the relationship of sound to musical instruments. Children can make a number of different simple instruments that will produce a few distinct notes. Lessons on recognizing patterns in sound will use science processes in another context that will serve to increase pupils' understanding of the process.

DRAMA AND DANCE

An earlier chapter referred to children's dancing to represent the flight of butterflies at the end of a unit on the life stages of insects. Other ways that children can use their bodies to represent the movements of animals include moving sideways like a crab, hopping like a kangaroo or rabbit, and walking like a bird, as well as too many others to list. These are not trivial activities but ways of taking another point of view, and as such they are important ways to increase understanding of the other creatures of the earth.

▼ SUMMARY

In this chapter you have seen examples of a variety of ways that science may be integrated with other subjects to increase understanding, make better use of time, and make school work more meaningful for children. Subjects may be integrated by topic, by concept, or by using a skill from one subject in learning activities from another area. In all cases it is important to identify objectives for both subjects and plan the lesson or unit so that objectives in both subjects are met.

There are many topics and concepts that social studies and science share. In this chapter you have seen two units used as examples of ways these two subjects may be integrated. The unit on relativity focused on relative position in the physical world as well as on social relations between people. The unit on acid rain focused on specific chemical reactions and on how people's lives are affected by the uncontrolled occurrence of these reactions.

The integration of science and language arts may include using writing as a means of representing science experiences and using science as the basis for reading and writing. Science processes can be thought of in a broader sense as thinking processes and were shown to be applicable in reading comprehension. Although firsthand experiences are the primary way for children to learn science, there are many experiences that are available only vicariously through reading. These can be memorable and valuable and should be a part of the science program in elementary school. Books of information are also required for a well-rounded science program.

Mathematics is an indispensable tool for representing and understanding science. Both geometry and arithmetic are so interwoven with science at this level that it is hard to separate them in a good science program. The focus in this chapter was on the uses of mathematics in collecting and analyzing data, but it is recognized that mathematics is concerned both with applications to real world problems and also with ideas based solely on reasoning.

Integration of science with other subjects is an opportunity and a challenge for you to make science more meaningful to children. The world did not divide itself up into distinct subject areas; these divisions have been made by human beings who have classified and categorized what they found in the world in order to make it more comprehensible. There are many simple, though important and even profound, ideas that cut across disciplines. In fact, most powerful ideas are not confined to one subject but cut across the range of human experience.

▼ DISCUSSION QUESTIONS

1. Consider the unit on relativity. Is this an example of topic-oriented integration, concept-oriented integration, or skill-content integration? Explain the reasons for your answer.
2. Now consider the unit on acid rain. Is this unit topic-oriented, concept-oriented, or skill-content integration? Explain your answer.
3. Many teachers hand out prepared sheets with blanks to be filled in rather than have pupils keep science notebooks. The reasons they give are that pupils cannot write well enough, it takes too much time, pupils lose the notebooks, and notebooks take too much time to grade. What arguments can you give to justify the use of notebooks?
4. Explain and discuss the meaning of this statement: "Reading should supplement experience, not take the place of it." Do you agree?
5. Discuss the pros and cons of self-contained classrooms as opposed to having content specialists in elementary schools.

▼ ACTIVITIES FOR THE READER

1. Outline a topic-oriented integrated unit.
2. Outline a concept-oriented integrated unit.
3. Outline a skill-content integrated unit.
4. Select suitable books to be used in the relativity unit and give your reasons for each selection.
5. Outline a lesson for first grade that integrates reading and science.
6. Make an annotated list of 30 science trade books. Select 5 for each grade level from first through sixth grade, giving the correct citations for each. Write a short paragraph describing each book.
7. Design a third-grade lesson integrating art and science or music and science.
8. Write a lesson integrating health and science.

▼ REFERENCES

Berger, C. Karplus, R., Montgomery, M., Randle, J., and Thier, H. (1972). *Relative position and motion.* Chicago: Rand McNally.

Britton, J. (1970). *Language and learning.* London: Penguin.

Durst, R. K., & Newell, G. E. (1989). The uses of function: James Britton's category system and research on writing. *Review of Educational Research, 59*(4), 375–394.

Hessler, E., & Stubbs, H. (1987). *Acid rain: science projects.* Raleigh, NC: The Acid Rain Foundation.

Howe, A., & Vasu, E. (1989). The role of language in children's formation and retention of mental images. *Journal of Research in Science Teaching, 26*(1), 15–24.

Jacobs, H. H. (Ed.). (1989). *Interdisciplinary curriculum: Design and implementation.* Washington, DC: Association for Supervision and Curriculum Development.

Janvier, C. (1990). Contextualization and mathematics for all. In T. J. Cooney & C. R. Hirsch (Eds.), *Teaching and learning mathematics in the 1990s.* (pp. 183–193). Reston, VA: National Council of Teachers of Mathematics.

McGee, L. M., & Lomax, R. G. (1990). On combining apples and oranges: A response to Stahl and Miller. *Review of Educational Research, 60,* 133–140.

Schickedanz, J. A. (1990). Critique of Stahl and Miller's study. *Review of Educational Research, 60,* 127–131.

Stahl, S., & Miller, P. (1989). Whole language and language experience approaches for beginning reading. *Review of Educational Research, 59,* 87–116.

▼ SOURCES OF IDEAS AND MATERIALS

The Acid Rain Foundation, Inc. (1410 Varsity Drive, Raleigh, NC 27606). Materials are available for teachers and pupils, including:

Acid Rain: Science Projects

The Air Around Us

Elementary Acid Rain Kit

Delta Education, Inc. (P.O. Box M, Nashua, NH 03061) now publishes materials originally produced by Science Curriculum Improvement Study (SCIS), including *Relative Position and Motion.*

Macaulay, D. (1981). *Cathedral.* Boston: Houghton-Mifflin.

Macaulay, D. (1981). *Pyramids.* Boston: Houghton-Mifflin. *Both of Macaulay's books are illustrated narratives of the building of those spectacular structures.*

All materials of the Elementary Science Study (ESS), Science Curriculum Improvement Study (SCIS), and Science—A Process Approach (S—APA) are now available on a compact disk–ROM: *Science Helper K–8,* Knowledge Project in Science. Sunnydale, CA: PC-SIG/IASC, CD-ROM Publishing Group.

LONG-TERM PLANNING AND EVALUATION

▾

A science program that leads to meaningful and long-lasting learning requires thoughtful, purposeful planning and evaluation that are tied to both short-term and long-term goals of instruction. A series of unconnected lessons, no matter how interesting or exciting, does not constitute a good science program. Effective instruction also requires careful attention to assessment and evaluation. An interest in what has come to be called *authentic assessment* has arisen because there is a feeling that much of the testing that takes place does not measure what teachers really want to measure. Tests are often designed to measure what is easy to measure rather than the more important, but difficult to measure, goals of instruction.

Previous chapters have included evaluation as a part of lesson or unit plans. This chapter presents a number of ways that you may evaluate your pupils' progress. Learning about these ways will expand your understanding of what evaluation is and stimulate you to think of other ways to carry out this necessary part of your total science program.

THE VALUE OF UNITS

Instructional units have many advantages over stand-alone lessons. The main advantage is that a unit facilitates in-depth learning in a particular area. By staying with the subject of the unit for a longer time, pupils have more opportunity to experience and reflect, and the teacher has more opportunity to integrate the unit topic with other subjects and life in general. These enhanced learning opportunities are more than enough justification for selecting instructional units rather than relying on one-day lessons. There is another advantage, however, that should appeal to busy teachers. Teaching instructional units is easier for the teacher and much more efficient of both instruction time and evaluation time. The additional time and effort required to plan a unit is more than compensated by time and effort saved later, during presentation and evaluation. Because of the continuity of materials and ideas, start-up time for individual lessons is reduced. The materials, once collected, require little additional teacher preparation time. When pupils are taught to manage materials, the teacher's preparation time is further reduced. Little time is needed to focus or motivate once the unit is initiated, because enthusiasm and interest not only carry over but also actually increase from lesson to lesson. Finally, evaluation is much easier and more comprehensive when the teacher has planned in advance to take a look at various areas of growth and to coordinate not only the cognitive but also the affective, psychomotor, and social domains as well.

DEVELOPING A UNIT

A number of steps are involved in developing a science unit. Although there may be some variation in your procedure, a common sequence involves:

1. Choosing a topic
2. Deciding on unit timing
3. Setting goals
4. Outlining a sequence of activities
5. Trying out the activities with actual materials
6. Writing the lesson plans
7. Planning for noncognitive goals
8. Providing continuity elements
9. Planning an ending
10. Developing means of evaluation

CHOOSING A TOPIC

This chapter—in fact, this whole book—advocates a science for children that depends on real experience with the actual objects and events as well as reflection upon those experiences. Secondary materials, such as books, films, and speakers, should be used secondarily, if at all. If a choice is open between two topics, the one lending itself more easily to direct experience should be selected. Topics that cannot be studied through direct experience, such as molecules, planets, or cell division, should be postponed as long as possible, preferably until junior or senior high school, when mental maturation makes the possibility of learning from abstract input more likely. When you think about selecting a science unit topic, always ask yourself, "What can my pupils learn by direct observation of real things, and what relationships and other ideas can they figure out based on those observations?"

Topics from the Elementary Science Study (ESS) make a good starting place for planning a science unit.* The topics were well researched and trial tested. They are interesting to children and can be presented through direct experience. But additional planning is needed when these topics are used by teachers inexperienced in presenting discovery-based science. Each teacher needs to develop well-structured lesson plans to facilitate learning with a minimum of problems. The titles of some teacher's guides in this ESS series include:

Light and Shadows

Sink or Float

Mystery Powders

Clay Boats

Starting from Seeds

Colored Solutions

Kitchen Physics

Growing Seeds

---

* Booklets on the topics were originally published in 1966 by Educational Services, Inc. (Education Development Center). Later revisions of selected booklets were published by McGraw-Hill and Delta Education. Full bibliographic information for each booklet is given in the references at the end of the chapter.

Butterflies

Eggs and Tadpoles

Changes

Tracks

Earthworms

Batteries and Bulbs

Microgardening

Behavior of Mealworms

Primary Balancing

Musical Instrument Recipe Book

Structures

Peas and Particles

Mapping

DECIDING ON UNIT TIMING

A major consideration in a unit of study is the time dimension. During a science unit, pupils can take a leisurely look at the topic and make "before and after" comparisons. Pupils are able to consider change, rather than just make static observations. All science involves change; the type and speed of the changes vary, however, and require some thought during the planning phase. Units about living things, such as plant growth or animal life cycles, usually involve slow changes. Children will be making a series of observations over a period of days or weeks before the changes are complete. Studies of physical or chemical topics usually involve rapid changes. In the Mystery Powders unit, pupils test common household powders (salt, sugar, baking soda, starch, etc.) with water, vinegar, iodine, and heat. The reactions occur immediately or within a few seconds. The child does something, and there is a quick result. Planning for Mystery Powders is different from planning for Growing Seeds. In Growing Seeds, for example, the child plants a seed (or sets up a germination test on one day) and the results of this action may not become apparent for several days, or even longer. Both kinds of change—rapid and slow—are interesting and important for children to experience. Each requires somewhat different planning considerations, however.

Rapid-change topics are easier to plan in that there is immediate feedback to pupils on a particular activity. Data collection and data processing for a particular activity can occur during the same class period. A teacher can make a list of activities and plan to have a discussion about each activity before beginning the next activity. With slow-change topics, several activities may need to be scheduled before the observations on the first activity are ready to be discussed. This means the teacher must plan something similar to a three-ring circus, with several lines of activity taking place more or less at the same time. While waiting for seeds to grow or plants to mature, other lessons can be scheduled that involve shorter time frames, such as dissecting soaked seeds, examining roots in germination jars (set up earlier), or observing colored liquids moving up celery stalks.

Children should have experience with science units involving both rapid and slow changes. Slow changes are especially useful for primary children as an aid to developing reversible thinking. When children keep daily records, especially in the form of pictures and simple graphs, they can look back over the records and mentally reconstruct the past events. By thinking about how a plant grew taller bit by bit and how it was at the beginning compared to the present, they practice thinking about a series of events both forward and backward in time. This valuable kind of thinking practice is often lacking in the curriculum.

In addition to scheduling needs and opportunities that depend on speed of the changes involved, some topics have other special considerations. Light and Shadow, for example, involves relationships among light sources, object position, and shadows. Some activities are done with artificial light, and some are done outdoors using sunlight. It is important to have several indoor activities well-planned and ready in advance in case bad weather or heavy cloud cover makes an outdoor activity impossible on the day for which it was planned.

Holidays and vacations offer their own opportunities and constraints on planning science units. Units about living things that need daily care should be scheduled so they are uninterrupted by vacation days. Ordinarily, a unit can be planned to end just before a vacation or begin just after one. If this is not possible, then a unit involving rapid changes will work best. Each lesson can provide a particular event without need to hold over the actual setup for further observation on another day. The resourceful teacher always looks for ways to turn adversity into opportunity, however, and scheduling gaps are no exception. Slow changes that do not require daily attention are naturals for holiday periods. How much water will evaporate from an aquarium tank in two weeks? Which materials decompose most, or least, when buried in a terrarium? How much do various crystals dissolve when placed and left in water without stirring?

A topic involving rapid changes will be used as an example in this chapter because it can be scheduled in a straightforward way. Thus it makes a good place to begin in learning to plan units. The unit, which covers simple electrical circuits, is called Batteries and Bulbs.

SETTING GOALS

In Chapter 4 the idea of goal statements in the various domains was introduced (see pp. 86–87). The example goals given were from the Batteries and Bulbs unit. They are reproduced here for your convenience:

1. Cognitive Content Goals

   a. Know the elements of a simple circuit and their arrangement.
   b. Diagram actual circuits using standard electrical symbols and construct actual circuits from provided diagrams.
   c. Know the effects of adding resistance to a circuit.

2. Cognitive Process Goals

a. Predict and verify arrangements of elements that will cause a bulb to light.
b. Predict and verify the relationship of electromagnet strength to number of turns in the coil.
c. Infer pathways inside a mystery circuit board based on observed effects.
d. Measure the brightness of a bulb with a simple meter.

3. Psychomotor Goal

a. Handle circuit elements and connectors with increasing skill.

4. Affective Goals

a. Show curiosity and persistence in working with materials and related problems.
b. Behave responsibly toward use and care of materials.

5. Social Goal

a. Show cooperation and courtesy in group work.

Although you may imagine that developing a set of goals would be the next task to tackle after choosing a topic for your unit, in fact most teachers think about the particular lessons or activities before setting down the goals. This is fine. You will need the goal statements to guide your development of evaluation devices, so it should come early in the development of the unit, but perhaps not too early—you may work back and forth between lesson ideas and goals. As long as there is a close relationship between goals and lessons, the exact sequence of writing them is not critical. Just because the development of goals is described first in this chapter does not mean that you must develop your goals completely before thinking about lessons.

OUTLINING A SEQUENCE OF ACTIVITIES

Batteries and Bulbs is a unit on simple electrical circuits. It involves use of flashlight batteries (D cells) and bulbs, as well as some additional simple materials. A few of the materials were developed especially for the unit, in order to be inexpensive and to allow easy visualization of key elements. For example, the bulb holder is cheaper and easier to understand than ceramic bulb sockets, which serve the same purpose electrically. Most of the materials, however, can be obtained locally at fairly small expense. There is no danger of electric shock with the low voltages involved. Teachers should warn pupils to avoid any experimentation with household current, however.

If you could scan through the ESS teacher's guide for Batteries and Bulbs, you would see many activities described. To present them all to your pupils would be fun but perhaps not practical for one reason or another. A more modest unit of about eight lessons, followed by projects, will be described here. Some lessons depend on others to establish prerequisite ideas, whereas other lessons may be interchanged in the sequence without causing problems. These eight lessons will constitute the unit:

▼ These children are engrossed in their experiment with batteries and bulbs.

1. *Beginning Circuits.* In this lesson, each pupil is given three objects—a piece of wire, a battery, and a bulb—and then asked to make the bulb light. After a few minutes, children begin to find ways to light the bulb. Some will copy others, and this is fine. They share ways that work and ways that do not work by drawing diagrams on the board. During the data-processing discussion, the teacher indirectly guides the pupils to identify the characteristics of a circuit.

2. *Holders and Added Elements in Circuits.* Pupils explore putting more than one battery, more than one bulb, and more than one wire into circuits. They become familiar with bulb holders and battery holders as tools to make circuit building easier.

3. *Bulbs and Their Innards.* Pupils examine bulbs with magnifiers and compare burned-out bulbs with functional ones. An optional activity is removing the glass from a bulb to see if and how the remaining parts function. The main objective of the lesson is to realize that there is a particular pathway inside the bulb that forces electricity to pass through the filament, which produces the light.

4. *Testing for Conductors.* Pupils make a circuit tester from a bulb and battery (each in its holder) and three wires. They use the tester to classify "junk" and other objects as conductors and nonconductors.

5. *Inferring Hidden Circuits.* Pupils use circuit testers to make observations on unseen circuits, and generate inferences about possible wiring. Finally, they verify the wiring by opening the circuit boards and then discuss reasons for inferences that were verified and those that were not. (This lesson was presented in Chapter 8.)

6. *The Secret Language.* Pupils learn to use standard electrical diagram elements in the place of realistic renditions of batteries and bulbs in their diagrams. This lesson is presented by the modified direct-instruction method described in Chapter 7. All the other lessons are primarily guided discovery, though some procedures in these lessons are presented directly.

7. *Brightness Meter and Nichrome Wire.* Pupils construct and use a simple light meter composed of 10 pages of white paper fastened together. The number of pages through which the light can be seen is the measure of brightness. The meters are then used to measure changes in light as increasing lengths of Nichrome wire (a poor conductor) are added to a circuit.

8. *Electromagnets.* Pupils explore electromagnets made from coils of insulated wire wrapped around soft iron cores (common nails) and placed in a circuit. Pupils decide how the number of turns of wire in a coil affects the number of paper clips that can be picked up.

Once the activities (such as these eight) are selected, they must be placed in a logical sequence. Beginning Circuits is a good starter because it develops the concept of a circuit, which is basic to all the other activities. Holders and Added Elements fits well as a second lesson because it uses the ideas and materials from the first lesson and develops from there. The Bulbs lesson could have been placed later in the unit, but not earlier, because it needs both the basic concept of circuit and also uses holders. Testing for Conductors is needed before Inferring for Hidden Circuits, because the idea of the circuit tester, which is used in Hidden Circuits, is developed in Testing for Conductors. The last two lessons could have been used in either order, but both depend on many of the concepts and techniques developed earlier. The Secret Language could have been placed anywhere near the middle of the unit. It depends on prior understanding of the circuit and on previous experience diagramming circuits with realistic drawing. You would want to place it before lessons in which standard diagrams were to be used.

TRYING OUT ACTIVITIES

An important—actually, crucial— step in unit planning is for you to try out the activities with the actual materials to be used in the classroom. A basic reason for this is to deepen your own understanding of the phenomena involved. Everyone tends to think just reading about something provides understanding. But actually doing usually makes some aspects much clearer. Other reasons are to make sure the materials behave in the way we expected and to watch for any unexpected difficulties the equipment may cause.

There are many horror stories of lesson failures caused by equipment malfunction. One student teacher tried out all the activities in the Batteries and Bulbs unit she planned to present in class. This helped her write good lesson plans, but was not enough. Shortly before beginning, she bought additional wire at a different hardware store. None of the pupils could light the bulb in the first lesson unless the cut cross section of the wire was placed in firm contact with the appropriate circuit element. She discovered later that she had inadvertently bought wire that was covered with a thin film of transparent plastic, so that electrical contact was impossible except at the cut surfaces of the wire.

Other teachers have bought what they thought was iodine to use in the Mystery Powders unit as a test for starch (iodine causes starch to turn purple). When the expected dark purple color did not develop with starch, the label was read more carefully. It turned out to be an *iodide* of some salt, that is, iodine that had already reacted with something else besides starch. It may have been fine as an antiseptic, but it no longer worked as a test for starch.

Many teachers have tried out the Mystery Powders activities at home in glass or ceramic containers, and then bought paper souffle cups or paper picnic cups for pupils to use in class. Sometimes they found that in class everything—all of the powders—gave a positive reaction for starch! A bit of research revealed that it was the paper that was turning purple in the presence of iodine. In fact, many paper products are made with starch added to give extra stiffness. Nobody can be held responsible for knowing all the facts about things that can cause a problem. What you can do is test the actual materials in the way the children will use them in order to be sure everything is as it seems.

You may be lucky enough to avoid spectacular problems, and still have problems with untested materials. Children sometimes find equipment awkward to hold or have other problems that adults may not have noticed. Always observe your pupils carefully when they are working with new materials, not only to monitor their learning but also to assess the adequacy of the materials for the purpose at hand. Minor problems noticed can be corrected before using the same or similar materials with the next class.

WRITING THE LESSON PLANS

This next step in unit planning should be second nature to you by now. Two lesson plans from the Batteries and Bulbs unit are presented here as examples, Beginning Circuits and The Secret Language.

▼ LESSON PLAN 13.1: Guided Discovery

GRADE LEVEL: 4–6

TOPIC: Beginning Circuits

PERFORMANCE OBJECTIVES

By the end of this lesson, the learner should be able to:

1. Demonstrate four arrangements that light the bulb, given a battery, a bulb, and a wire.
2. Identify the key points of contact on both the battery and bulb.

MATERIALS

For each pupil:
- 1 "D" battery
- 1 flashlight bulb
- 1 bare copper wire, about 25 cm long
- Prediction Sheet (Figure 13.1)

LEARNING ACTIVITIES

MOTIVATION

The materials are highly interesting. No special motivation is needed.

DATA COLLECTION

1. Distribute a battery, bulb, and wire to each pupil. Ask, "Can you make the bulb light?" Allow 10 to 15 minutes. Notice what pupils do but do not interfere with their discoveries. Do not give away information. Be friendly but noncommittal.
2. When a pupil gets the bulb to light, ask, "Can you find another way?" Keep them challenged but not overwhelmed. Don't give too many tasks at once. Other pupils will see how the first ones lit the bulb and then try their own variations.
3. Start diagrams on the board of arrangements that work and those that do not. Write headings above the two sections of board: "Works," and "Doesn't Work." Invite volunteers to add diagrams from their discoveries. When a student seems to need additional structure, hand out the Prediction Sheet. Eventually, give it to all, but don't rush them from productive explorations of their own. Speak only to individual pupils, only as needed, and only with the small voice. For example, "Does the wire *have* to wrap around the bulb?"
4. For clean-up, distribute shoe boxes, one to a table. Ask pupils to disconnect all their equipment, place it in the box, and label the box with their group name. Ask table monitors to put boxes in the storage area. Keep a set of materials out on the teacher's desk for demonstration.

DATA PROCESSING

1. Guided discussion. Ask, "What special places on the battery and bulb have to touch something?" Lead them indirectly to identify the two places on the battery and the two places on the bulb. Establish class names for these, such as "top and bottom of the battery," "side and bottom of the bulb."
2. If the four basic circuit arrangements that light the bulb have not all been drawn on the "Works" board, lead the class to figure it out. "The side of the bulb touches a wire in both of these diagrams. Could the side of the bulb touch something *other than* a wire? What about diagram C on the prediction sheet?"
3. Continue discussing the Prediction Sheet. If the picture is not clear, discuss various interpretations of what it could be. Demonstrate with real materials in some cases. For example, if a pupil suggests something that you know is wrong, ask that pupil to come up and show you. Also have some correct responses shown, so that demonstration is not always associated with wrong answers.

▼ FIGURE 13.1
Prediction Sheet

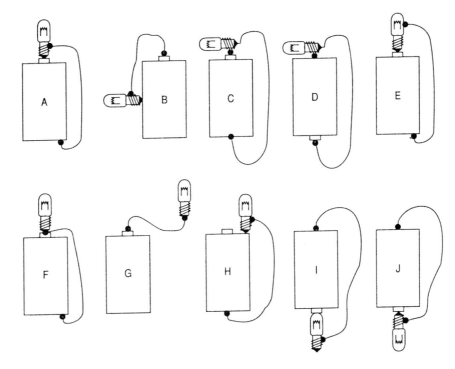

CLOSURE

Say, "This was the first activity of a new science unit. We will have lots more. Begin thinking about what else you would like to discover about electricity. For now, please pass in your prediction sheets and let's get ready for lunch."

APPRAISAL

Use informal observation during the lesson and the Prediction Sheet.

The Secret Language lesson involves teaching the standard diagramming system with a number of elements that would be recognized by engineers and electricians all over the world. At this point in the unit, the pupils would have been drawing more-or-less realistic pictures to represent their circuits. The introduction of the standard system will allow circuit diagrams that are easier to draw and easier to interpret clearly, as well as make possible communication with others beyond the classroom. The system is an example of social-arbitrary knowledge—it was made up by someone in the same way that the alphabet, the numerals, or the English language was made up or invented by people. It is not something that can be discovered. Arbitrary knowledge, as you have seen, is best presented by direct instruction. You may choose to teach the system in straightforward direct instruction, or you may prefer to use modified direct instruction that uses an inductive method to add interest, as this example lesson plan does.

▼ LESSON PLAN 13.2

Modified Direct Instruction

Grade Level: 4–6

Topic: The Secret Language

Performance Objectives

By the end of this lesson, the learner should be able to:

1. Name and identify actual objects represented by the elements of the standard diagram system.
2. Construct actual circuits using standard diagrams for plans.
3. Construct standard diagrams for either actual circuits observed or for realistic drawings of circuits.

Materials

For the teacher:

- overhead projector
- Transparency I (Figure 13.2)
- Transparency II (Figure 13.3)

For each pupil:

- 4 wires
- 2 bulbs and holders
- 2 batteries

Learning Activities

Motivation

Project Transparency I. Ask, "Would anyone care to guess what this might be?" Accept guesses without comment.

Presentation

Say to pupils, "Today's science lesson is about a secret language. First you have to interpret it—crack the code. Once you have it figured out, you will find that it is

▼ FIGURE 13.2
Transparency I

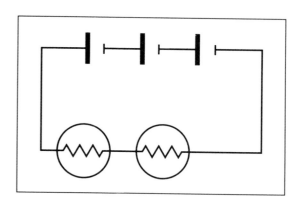

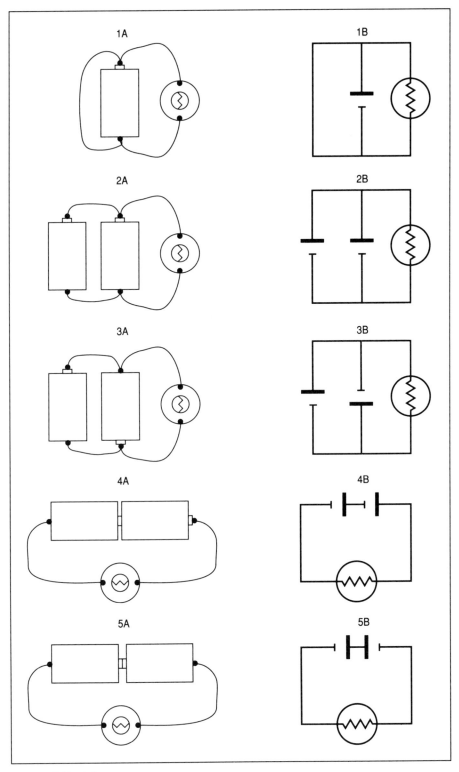

▼ FIGURE 13.3
Transparency II

very useful for communication. Take a look at these clues. The secret language diagram on the right has the same meaning as the drawing on the left." Show Transparency II, but uncover only the first pair of drawings. "Study this pair. They mean the same thing. When you think you understand the secret code, raise your hand." Take a few responses if any are offered. If there are disagreements, let them ride for the moment. Slowly continue to reveal additional pairs of diagrams on Transparency II. When all are revealed, hold a short discussion. Ask pupils to justify their responses. If disagreements among pupils are still evident, ask them to convince one another. Finally, clear up any misunderstandings that may still remain.

GUIDED PRACTICE

Ask five pupils to come to the board and each draw a circuit diagram in the realistic way they have been using. When they are finished, ask for five more pupils to come up and draw the corresponding secret-language diagram next to each. Discuss with class as a whole. Ask them to predict which bulbs will light. Correct any problems with the diagrams.

INDEPENDENT PRACTICE

Ask each pupil to draw a secret-language circuit diagram and exchange the drawing with a neighbor. Each pupil should then construct the actual circuit with batteries, bulbs, and wire and then draw a realistic diagram on the same page. Circulate and help any having trouble. Ask both pupils involved to sign their work on the papers.

CLOSURE

Collect papers. Hold short discussion. "Why do you suppose scientists and engineers use the secret language for electrical plans rather than draw pictures as we have been doing? Tomorrow, I will give you a circuit plan drawn in the secret language. You will need to remember how to do what we learned today. It will save you a lot of time and trouble."

APPRAISAL

Informal observation during the lesson and checking the papers.

PLANNING FOR NONCOGNITIVE GOALS

Lesson plans generally take care of planning for the cognitive goals. Psychomotor goals are fairly easy to plan for, once they have been stated. When the activities are interesting and the pupils persevere in working with the materials, it is only natural that they get to be more skillful. Your role as teacher is to notice who is having greater-than-average trouble, give special tips and mini-lessons on equipment handling, and (in some cases) find or redesign equipment that is less difficult for the pupils. If you notice a child who is unusually awkward with the materials but you cannot think of a better way, try asking the other pupils: "Who has found an especially good way to put Fahnstock clips on the rubber bands?" When using eye droppers with young children, you can demonstrate good technique for the whole class by using a meat baster (which looks exactly like a huge eye dropper).

Mini-lessons and special individual help can also be used to facilitate pupil growth in the affective and social goals. Unless something especially undesirable happens, you may not notice that certain pupils are falling behind in their affective and social development. The section on evaluation will present some simple-to-use methods for systematic record keeping in these areas.

Once you have decided a mini-lesson is desirable, you can insert it as an extra step in one of the lesson plans. Because growth in these domains is developmentally linked, performance objectives may not be useful. Long-term evaluation is important, however, and the ideas presented in the evaluation section should be applied in some form that makes sense for your situation.

PROVIDING CONTINUITY ELEMENTS

Journals are a wonderful way to integrate language skills and provide a thread of continuity that unites the individual lessons. Journals can serve as data books to collect the observation records and can be the place pupils write their interpretations, infer-

▼ The *structures* unit integrates science with art, mathematics, and social studies.

ences, and plans for further experiments. In short, the journal can be anything you decide for it to be. In all cases, it provides an on-going record of the pupil's actions and thoughts about the unit topic. A journal lets the child see how his or her thinking has grown, and it gives the child a real way to apply writing skills. When a pupil needs to remember what happened in a previous activity, the journal provides that information. When a child engages in real application of skills in a way that both makes sense and is useful, the child learns to value writing in a way that no amount of disembodied practice can provide.

You will probably have some structured record sheets duplicated to make record keeping easier for pupils in some activities. Consider whether these worksheets should be pasted into the journals or whether they should be bound into a booklet along with blank sheets. You may not want pupils to see some worksheets before needed. Sometimes the worksheets give away the discoveries the pupils are supposed to make, or perhaps cause other undesired effects. Regardless of whether and how you include structured record sheets, there should always be plenty of blank sheets for drawings and free description and other writing. If you have a computer and printer in your room, you could let pupils use a word-processing program, such as FrEdWriter to facilitate their writing and add a special element of motivation.*

Learning centers can be provided to allow individual work with related materials during times other than science period. Although the purpose of centers varies, most science centers coordinated with a unit of study provide additional practice with a skill or provide extended applications of particular lessons, such as projects. Centers may also provide opportunity for periodic observation of slow changes. In a unit on the behavior of mealworms, the main lessons usually involve working with the larval form of the species. When not in use, the larvae are kept in the refrigerator, which prevents them from pupating and emerging as beetles. A mealworm culture can be set up in a center to allow pupils to observe the insects progressing through their full life cycle. To make a culture, place a handful of mealworms (available from pet shops) in a half-gallon container partly filled with corn meal. Place a cut carrot or apple half on the surface to provide moisture. Cover to keep out light but allow air to enter. Dig up larvae and pupae as needed. Beetles come to the surface but are poor climbers and don't escape. In the Batteries and Bulbs unit, a learning center would allow additional exploration as well as planned construction of electrical projects.

PLANNING AN ENDING

One or more activities should be planned to help pupils see how the individual lessons fit together into a "big picture" and relate to other subjects as well as to life outside of school. You may choose to have a culminating activity that is developed into a regular lesson, or you may have other types of activities, including field trips, speakers, and simple show-and-tell discussions. When projects are involved, a small

---

* FrEdWriter, developed by Al Rogers and documented by June Wedesweiler Dodge, is "freeware," that is, intended to be given away. Hence the name: *Free to Ed*ucators. It may be obtained from Computer Using Educators (CUE) Softswap Project, P.O. Box 2087, Menlo Park, CA 94026. Many individual computer education coordinators or local computer organizations can also make you a copy.

science fair could be appropriate, especially if it coincides with an open house or another function for parents. Some teachers prefer not to have an end at all but to initiate open-ended projects at the end of the formal lessons.

An example of a culminating activity for Batteries and Bulbs might be as simple as a class discussion reviewing what was learned in the unit and relating the learnings to life outside school. The Nichrome wire acted as a variable resistor; real-world examples are light dimmers, the volume control on radios, and fan speed switches. Burning out a bulb can provide good background experience for discussing fuses and circuit breakers. Short circuits can easily be demonstrated with simple equipment, as well as their potential danger by allowing a battery short circuit to heat the wire. Electromagnetic cranes for scrap metal are usually familiar to children, through television if not real life.

Other possible culminations could involve a field trip to a power plant or other electrical facility, to a museum of science and industry, or to a scrap yard to see an electromagnetic crane in action. If you choose to extend the unit with open-ended projects, your task will be simplified by reference to *Batteries and Bulbs II* (ESS, 1971).

EVALUATION

What comes to your mind when you hear the word *evaluation*? There is a good probability that you thought of paper-and-pencil tests, and also a good probability that you feel rather ambivalent about evaluating pupil growth. You know it is important, but you are afraid it is going to cause tension and may be unfair to some pupils. The purpose of this section is to introduce some balanced and fair ways to evaluate pupil learning that you will be able to use with confidence and ease.

Methods of lesson appraisal have been discussed in previous chapters. The main intent in those discussions was to describe gathering information for use in judging the success of lessons. Many of the guided-discovery lessons used informal observation as a major component in the appraisal. Although you can get a general idea about the growth and ability of individual pupils through this kind of lesson appraisal, you need something more systematic on which to base report-card grades.

The difference between *informal* and *systematic* evaluation may be hazy in your mind. By *informal* in this context is meant a sort of careful looking around, with special questions when problems seem apparent. Thus informal observation is not casual, but it may not be equally discerning about the growth of each individual pupil and usually does not involve record keeping. Systematic evaluation may be observation of pupil behaviors in much the same way as in informal checking, but it is systematic because it involves entering a record for each pupil. By the end of a science unit, or by the end of a report-card period, you will need a system, neatly filled in with a number of data entries for each pupil. Having a good record system will not relieve you of having to make professional judgments about the grade, but it will provide the necessary information upon which to base a judgment and will also be there to back you up in case there are any questions from parents.

▼ It is easy to evaluate this pupil's understanding of simple circuits.

TYPES OF EVALUATION

In addition to paper-and-pencil tests, there are several different ways to evaluate learning in elementary science. The main consideration in planning evaluation is to match each unit goal to an evaluation method best suited to assess it. Several methods that have been widely used will be described, though they are not the only possibilities. Like many topics in education, nobody knows the very best way to evaluate in every situation. You may invent a method that will work even better! In every case, though, the selection and mix of these methods must be the final decision of you, for only you as the teacher can know and appreciate both your science unit goals and the individual pupils.

Journals can serve a function in evaluation. In addition to the instructional purposes described in the previous section, journals also provide the teacher with a great deal of useful evaluative information. General questions or headings that guide the pupil are often helpful. These include:

- What I did:
- What I found out:
- Ideas for next time:

The open-ended form of responses allows pupils to express themselves freely, and thus reveals more than you may have asked for directly. For example, misconceptions are sometimes apparent in children's responses: "I think the black stuff [in the aquarium] may be from the sand when they ground it up." Did you know that many children think naturally occurring sand is created by humans grinding up rocks? Length and style of a child's response can be indicators of interest and enthusiasm. You do not have to rely completely on reading between the lines, though. You can ask pupils to respond in their journals to specific questions and directives. Here are some examples:

1. Draw a picture of your mealworm and label the parts.
2. Did your mealworms seem to like one color more than others? What is your evidence?
3. Write a paragraph on:
   a. What you learned from today's discussion.
   b. What you liked or disliked most about today's activity and why.
   c. How your group is working out. Does everyone get along? Are you doing your part? What could be done to make things work more smoothly?
4. In what ways are you taking good care of the materials?
5. Write your suggestions for improving our clean-up system.

By reviewing the journals periodically, you will be able to collect much information. To serve as a basis for evaluation, the information you select should be summarized and recorded in some way. This could be in the form of a checklist or anecdotal record. Examples of such checklists for the first two questions are shown in Figures 13.4 and 13.5.

Behavior checklists can be used to make your observations of pupil behaviors during learning activities more systematic. Planning ahead which behaviors to notice and then listing them on a checksheet serves two functions: (1) to focus your observations and (2) to provide a convenient way to record them. The behaviors you choose to watch for will depend on your unit goals. Because goals are normally stated rather

▼ FIGURE 13.4
Journal summary
for Question 1

	A	B	Comments
Susan			
andy			
Jose			
Jared			
Kelly			

A. Drawing is realistic rather than fanciful.
B. Labels are complete and accurate.

▼ FIGURE 13.5
Journal summary for Question 2

	A	B	Comments
Susan			
Andy			
Jose			
Jared			
Kelly			

A. Shows understanding of the experiment.
B. States observations supporting Conclusion.

broadly, they are not good as checklist items by themselves. You will need to generate some *behavioral indicators* that could serve as evidence that the goal is being met. Although behavior checklists can be used in any of the goal domains, they are especially useful in the noncognitive domains, partly because these are more difficult to assess directly. For example, if one of your affective goals was for pupils to develop persistence, you might have a behavior checklist like the one in Figure 13.6.

▼ FIGURE 13.6
Behavior checklist for persistence

	A	B	C	D	Comments
Susan					
andy					
Jose					
Jared					
Kelly					

A: Continues after novelty wears off.
B: Completes task that others did not.
C: Records data spontaneously.
D: Repeats experiment despite apparent failure.

Checklists should be designed so that difficult judgment calls are not required. Rather than use a rating scale from 1 to 10, for example, simply use a check mark for satisfactory, a plus sign for especially noteworthy, or a minus sign for not observed. A checklist must be easy to use so that a record is feasible on each behavior for each child.

Products made by the pupil can be useful in evaluation. The circuits constructed (or more elaborate projects) give quick and reliable information about a child's understanding of involved concepts, as well as affective information such as neatness, creativity, care taken, and so on. Always be sure the product is judged in accordance with the unit goals. The same child's electric project could show an excellent conceptual understanding and yet be messy and unappealing visually. It is not useful to give an overall rating somewhere in the middle when both concept and appearance are original goals. Rate for each goal separately.

Performance tests and *interviews* can be used to find out specific information about abilities, attitudes, and thinking. In this kind of evaluation, an individual child is asked to perform some particular task while you watch. Questions calling for verbal responses can be asked during the same test or separately, depending on the situation. The Piaget tasks described in Chapter 2 are examples of performance tests. If you have tried this kind of test/interview, you know that it is very powerful because you can follow up unclear responses with additional questions for more information. Unfortunately, individual interviews of this kind are time consuming and may not be practical to use routinely. They can be very helpful, however, when used selectively to get specific information from particular pupils for whom other evaluation methods have proved inadequate.

Be sure to record notes or a summary of the performance tests and interviews immediately. Everyone tends to have selective memory, especially for something as fluid as an interview. Consistent, unambiguous, readable records are important, not only in routine matters such as making out report cards but also in cases where a parent might have a question.

Paper-and-pencil tests are not always necessary. Generally, you can get the sort of information needed to assess learning in the various domains from the evaluation devices already described. The main advantage of these tests is that they gather specific information from every child in a relatively short time. The quality of the information gathered may be rather low, however, especially if the questions are unclear or misleading to pupils. It takes some experience and perceptiveness to children's misconceptions to write really good tests. When you are first starting out, a good rule is to use open-ended or full essay tests when you use paper-and-pencil tests at all. Objective tests that are both fair to the pupil and useful in picking out those who are not "getting it" are especially hard to write. When journals are used, formal written tests may not be needed at all.

STEPS IN DEVELOPING EVALUATION

With the Batteries and Bulbs unit in mind, consider the steps involved in developing some evaluation methods.

Step 1

Look at the list of goals, and jot down the types of evaluation that seem best suited for each goal.* Evaluation types are coded as follows: J = journal, WT = written test, BC = behavior checklist, PT = performance test, I = interview. Using the goals for the Batteries and Bulbs unit, here are some suggested evaluation types for each goal:

1. Cognitive content goals
   a. Know the elements of a simple circuit and their arrangement. (J, WT, PT, I)
   b. Diagram actual circuits using standard electrical symbols and construct actual circuits from provided diagrams. (J, PT)
   c. Know the effects of adding resistance to a circuit. (J, WT)
2. Cognitive process goals
   a. Predict and verify arrangements of elements that will cause a bulb to light. (BC, PT, I)
   b. Predict and verify the relationship of electromagnet strength to number of turns in the coil. (BC, PT, I)
   c. Infer pathways inside a mystery circuit board based on observed effects. (WT)
   d. Measure the brightness of a bulb with a simple meter. (J, PT)
3. Psychomotor goal
   a. Handle circuit elements and connectors with increasing skill. (BC)
4. Affective goals
   a. Show curiosity and persistence in working with materials and related problems. (BC, J)
   b. Behave responsibly toward use and care of materials. (BC, J)
5. Social goal
   a. Show cooperation and courtesy in group work. (BC, I)

Step 2

After assigning types to goals, regroup the goals according to evaluation type:

Journal: Goals 1a, 1b, 1c, 2d, 4a, 4b.

Written Test: Goals 1a, 1c, 2c.

Behavior Checklist: Goals 2a, 2b, 3a, 4a, 4b, 5a.

Performance Test: Goals 1a, 1b, 2a, 2b, 2d.

Interview: Goals 1a, 2a, 2b, 5a.

Step 3

Describe each evaluation method in general terms and how it will address each of its goals.

- Journal assignments will vary from one lesson to another in order to solicit responses useful in assessing the various goals.

---

* In this example, several evaluation types are indicated for some goals. In actual practice, you may choose to use only one evaluation for each goal.

- Written tests for Goals 1a, 1c, and 2c can consist of simple questions to which pupils respond by selecting from diagrams already present, by completing partial diagrams, or by drawing entire diagrams themselves.
- Behavior checklists are called for in assessing six different goals. Is it possible to put all behavior indicators for all of these goals on a single checklist? A judgment must be made. If too many behaviors are needed, two or more checklists should be made and used on alternate days. Remember to try to keep it simple.
- Is it possible to do the performance test and the interview for Goal 2a at the same time as the interview for Goal 5a? This should be fairly easy. Children are asked one at a time to construct a working circuit from materials, and then asked some questions about how group work is coming along.

STEP 4

Generate the specific questions, behavior lists, and so on, refining them for use. Consider a few specific examples of items for the various types of evaluation:

Journal

- Draw and label two diagrams of circuits that work and two diagrams of circuits that do not work. (Goal 1a)
- Tell how you measured the brightness of a bulb. Add a drawing if you like. (Goal 2d)
- Tell how you took care of your lab materials today. Why is this important? (Goal 4b)

Written Test

- Given some pictures showing simple circuits with (1) copper wire only, (2) a short length of Nichrome wire added, and (3) a long piece of Nichrome wire, answer the following written question: Would there be any differences in the brightness of the bulbs in these circuits? Write a short paragraph to tell what you know about these circuits. (Goal 1c)
- A mystery circuit board with four terminals gave these results when tested with a circuit tester: AB+, AC+, AD−, BC+, BD−, CD−. How many ways could the mystery circuit board be wired to give these results? Draw diagrams. (Goal 2c)

Behavior Checklist

- For Goal 3a, a checklist similar to those given for summarizing journals can be used. Make a checklist column for each behavior of interest. Figure 13.7 shows such a checklist.

Performance Test

- Jose, here are some materials to make a circuit. Would you please put them together to make the bulb light? (Goal 1a)
- What is each part called? (Goal 1a)

▼ FIGURE 13.7
Behavior checklist
for Goal 3a

	A	B	C	D	Comments
Susan					
Andy					
Jose					
Jared					
Kelly					

A: Uses clips efficiently.
B: Adjusts bulb in holder as needed.
C: Chooses to use holders when making complex circuits.
D: Is able to complete circuits without asking partner for help.

Interview

- For Goal 5a, the questions should be individualized to probe for further information after using other means of evaluation. You would have some initial information from using a behavior checklist. This is a case in which you may choose to use the interview only with those pupils who may be having difficulty working in their groups. The questions should be used flexibly, building on and probing pupil comments when possible.
- Do you enjoy working with your group? Why or why not? (Goal 5a)
- Have you done your part of the work? Tell me about it. (Goal 5a)
- What problems have you noticed? (Goal 5a)

STEP 5

After using your evaluation methods, decide whether the various items work as well as you would like. Then revise as needed and reuse if possible. If journals or behavior checklists do not work well, the opportunity to do them over may be lost when the unit ends. In such cases, devise a paper-and-pencil or performance test to salvage needed information.

STEP 6

Get ready for next time you will use the unit. After taking the time to develop a science unit, you probably will want to use it with more than one group of children. If possible, revise faulty evaluation methods as soon as you recognize a problem. If you cannot manage an immediate revision, at least make notes on what worked well and what needs rethinking and modification. If you are as specific as possible, your job will be easier when you come back to it. If results showed that a test was too hard, either fix the test or modify the instruction.

▼ *Mr. Newman*: Ms. Oldhand, I have a problem. Jennifer was absent the day we gave the written test for the electricity unit. I'm not sure what to do about her report card this time.

Ms. Oldhand: What about your other records for her work during that time? Do you have any behavior checklists or other records?

Mr. Newman: I was just learning to use the checklist, and I'm afraid I didn't always get a record for every pupil every science class. There are so many holes in Jennifer's record, I'm reluctant to base her grade on it.

Ms. Oldhand: What is your overall opinion of her science work for this unit?

Mr. Newman: She did pretty well, but I think there may be some areas that she never quite caught on to.

Ms. Oldhand: Why don't you give her a private performance test and interview? Make a list of the areas in the unit where you aren't sure of her understanding. Then turn those into questions or tasks to give her. Since you haven't done this before, you may want to tape record the interview so you can analyze your technique later.

Mr. Newman: Good idea. The tape will help me get my records straightened out, too.

▼ SUMMARY

The development of science units has many advantages over stand-alone lessons. The pupils can achieve depth in a topic at the same time the teacher can simplify concerns with materials and motivation. The selection of a topic for a unit should take into account the speed with which the changes involved take place. Topics involving slow changes, such as plant growth or decomposition of compost, require more careful scheduling than fast-change topics, such as pendulums or buoyancy.

Overall goals for a science unit should be identified for each of the various learning domains. The statement of goals will help greatly with the development of the rest of the unit, especially the evaluation, though it is not always necessary to have all the goals in place before working on other parts of the unit. Often, an important goal may be suggested by thinking about a particular activity. If so, do not hesitate to add it at that time. A certain working back and forth between parts is normal in any complex writing task.

After a sequence of activities for the unit has been determined, each activity should be tried out before finalizing the lesson plan. Later, you will need to try the activities again, with the actual materials to be used with pupils. These trials will not only deepen your own understanding of the science content but will also help you avoid problems with the materials during lessons.

Evaluation in elementary science is relatively easy to devise and use when it is coordinated with well-planned units. The goal statements will suggest various evaluation techniques which will fit logically. Some informal assessment methods such as journals and observation of pupils' working behavior can be made systematic by summarizing data in checklists. In this way, the teacher can ensure that each pupil has a record for each item on a regular basis. Systems of this sort also help teachers avoid unconscious bias and unexamined expectations that can cloud judgment.

Additional methods of evaluation described in the chapter are products, performance tests, paper-and-pencil tests, and interviews. Results of all methods used should be recorded systematically, regularly, unambiguously, and readably. Clear and meaningful records are important in planning instruction, in making grade reports, and in backing up your judgment in case of question.

▼ DISCUSSION QUESTIONS

1. React to this statement: "Science period should be for learning science. I don't see why I should be expected to teach children to get along with each other or to clean up after themselves at the same time."
2. Suppose the "worst" happens: The effect you wanted your pupils to discover did not happen because of problems with the materials. List several ways a teacher might react and then analyze the pros and cons of each.
3. When journals are used both for learning and for evaluation, is the learning function compromised? Should pupils be told their journal will be evaluated?
4. What do you think of when you hear the word *evaluation*? Make a list, bring it to class, and share in a general class discussion. Can you determine a general attitude from the lists? Do you think these same attitudes are held by elementary pupils? What effects on your teaching might unexamined attitudes have?

▼ ACTIVITIES FOR THE READER

1. Skim through one of the ESS teacher's guides or some other idea source identified by your instructor. Working in groups, identify seven or eight possible lessons for an instructional unit. Sequence the lessons in a logical order. Would any of the lesson objectives seem appropriate for direct instruction? For modified direct instruction?
2. Given below are some example goals for a unit on mealworms. Identify one or more types of evaluation that would work for each goal.

   1. *Cognitive Content Goals*
      a. Describe the characteristics of a mealworm.

b. Name and identify body parts of a mealworm.

c. Describe how mealworms walk.

d. Describe how mealworms act in the presence of barriers, light, heat, cold, or other specified stimuli.

e. Describe the stages of the mealworm's life cycle.

2. *Cognitive Process Goals*

a. Distinguish between observations and inferences.

b. Collect and organize experimental data into simple graphs.

c. Identify and investigate variables that affect the behavior of mealworms.

d. Construct and test hypotheses about the behavior of mealworms.

e. Identify inconsistencies in experiments and reports.

3. *Psychomotor Goals*

a. Effectively use a variety of tools and techniques to observe the mealworms.

b. Construct habitats to investigate mealworms.

4. *Affective Goals*

a. Show interest in the mealworm activities.

b. Develop sensitivity toward the proper care of living things.

c. Show responsibility in use and care of materials.

5. *Social Goals*

a. Show cooperation and courtesy in group work.

b. Demonstrate amicable but lively verbal interactive skills in class discussions.

3. Design some evaluation items for some of the mealworm unit goals. Try your hand at developing at least one evaluation item of each type described in this chapter.

▼ REFERENCES

Elementary Science Study (ESS). (1967). *Growing Seeds.* Nashua, NH: Delta.

Elementary Science Study (ESS). (1968). *Changes.* New York: McGraw-Hill.

Elementary Science Study (ESS). (1968). *The musical instrument recipe book.* Newton, MA: Education Development Center.

Elementary Science Study (ESS). (1970). *Butterflies.* New York: McGraw-Hill.

Elementary Science Study (ESS). (1971). *Earthworms.* Nashua, NH: Delta.

Elementary Science Study (ESS). (1971). *Starting from seeds.* New York: McGraw-Hill.

Elementary Science Study (ESS). (1971). *Tracks.* New York: McGraw-Hill.

Elementary Science Study (ESS). (1976). *Light and shadows.* New York, NY: McGraw-Hill.

Elementary Science Study (ESS). (1985). *Batteries and bulbs.* Nashua, NH: Delta.

Elementary Science Study (ESS). (1985). *Clay boats.* Nashua, NH: Delta.

Elementary Science Study (ESS). (1985). *Colored solutions.* Nashua, NH: Delta.

Elementary Science Study (ESS). (1985). *Eggs and tadpoles.* Nashua, NH: Delta.

Elementary Science Study (ESS). (1985). *Mapping.* Nashua, NH: Delta.

Elementary Science Study (ESS). (1985). *Microgardening, an introduction to the world of mold.* Nashua, NH: Delta.

Elementary Science Study (ESS). (1985). *Primary balancing.* Nashua, NH: Delta.

Elementary Science Study (ESS). (1985). *Structures.* Nashua, NH: Delta.

Elementary Science Study (ESS). (1986). *Behavior of mealworms.* Nashua, NH: Delta.

Elementary Science Study (ESS). (1986). *Kitchen physics.* Nashua, NH: Delta.

Elementary Science Study (ESS). (1986). *Mystery powders.* Nashua, NH: Delta.

Elementary Science Study (ESS). (1986). *Peas and particles.* Nashua, NH: Delta.

Elementary Science Study (ESS). (1986). *Sink or float.* Nashua, NH: Delta.

Science Topics for the Elementary School

▼
_____

The purpose of this book is to provide background and experiences that will help you build a repertoire of skills and strategies for teaching science to children. Science processes are emphasized because they are central to theory and practice in science but often neglected in high school and college science courses, where the emphasis is usually on "content." A working knowledge of science processes (sometimes called cognitive processes), combined with an understanding of the goals and uses of the teaching methods described in this book, will allow you to teach any topic in an appropriate way at any age level.

It is not the purpose of this book to teach science *per se* but to teach you how to teach it. Appendix A has been added to provide some ideas and examples of how the lesson plans and unit plans included in the book can be fitted into a science program that is organized by topics, as many programs and textbooks are.

In science there are a small number of very basic, very important ideas that underlie what sometimes seems to be an extremely complicated and confusing mass of concepts, theories, laws, hypotheses, and relationships. At one level, the ideas are complex, but every important idea in science can be understood at a simpler, less-complicated level. Take, for example, the topic of heredity. The details of DNA and RNA that govern heredity are certainly complicated and not understood without a great deal of study, but that is not the only level at which heredity can be understood. Even toddlers know that dogs do not produce kittens, and first graders in a multi-cultural society like that of the United States know that children resemble their parents in some basic physical characteristics. At a more complex level, there are experiments with fruit flies that sixth graders can carry out and understand—and so it goes with almost all important topics. This idea was expressed by Bruner in *The Process of Education:*

> The basic ideas that lie at the heart of all science and mathematics and the basic themes that give form to life and literature are as simple as they are powerful. To be in command of these basic ideas, to use them effectively, requires a continual deepening of one's understanding of them in progressively more complex ways. It is only when such basic ideas are put in formalized terms as equations or elaborated verbal concepts that they are out of reach of the young child if he has not first understood them intuitively and had a chance to try them out on his own. The early teaching of science, mathematics and social studies should be designed to teach these subjects with scrupulous intellectual honesty but with an emphasis on the intuitive grasp of ideas and upon the use of these basic ideas.*

When you understand how to use science processes and when to use the methods taught in this book, you will be able to apply your knowledge of the processes and methods to all the main topics of the curriculum. Regardless of the topic, direct instruction is useful for learning how to do something, guided discovery is useful for finding out about something, and independent investigations and projects are useful for planning and testing your own ideas.

Listed in this appendix are several topics taken from *Science for All Americans*, a book introduced in Chapter 1. Under each main topic are suggestions for subtopics that are developmentally appropriate in primary grades and in upper-elementary grades. References are included to lesson plans or unit plans that have been used in this book to illustrate teaching methods or science processes.

EARTH SCIENCE

THE SOLAR SYSTEM

The earth is part of a vast and ancient universe. Our sun is one star in a galaxy that contains billions of stars, and the universe contains billions of galaxies. The sun and the bodies orbiting it constitute our solar system. Knowledge of the solar system and the universe once came only from what could be directly observed, but now much knowledge comes though the use of tools such as the telescope, radio and X-ray applications, computers, satellites, and objects sent into deep space.

The earth is approximately spherical in shape and moves all the way around the sun once a year. The moon moves around the earth once in every 28 days. Day and night, summer and winter, the rising and falling of the tides, and winds and ocean currents are all consequences of these motions.

Some children will read about black holes, quasars, and various other phenomena in the universe, and they should have resources available to learn more about things of particular interest to them. But this will not be a main emphasis.

---

* J. Bruner, *The process of education* (New York: Vintage Books, 1960), pp. 12–13.

PRIMARY GRADES

The age and expanse of the solar system, much less the universe, are impossible for adults to fully comprehend; it is clearly not something that young children can understand. But there are many ways that children can become aware of the stars, the moon, the sun, and their relation to one another and to us. Some appropriate activities are:

- Reports of observations of stars and the moon.
- Outdoor activities about shadows.
- Observations about day and night; the cycle of the seasons.
- Questions and discussion about the moon similar to Example 2 in Chapter 2.

UPPER ELEMENTARY GRADES

Observations can now become more systematic and planned; data can be gathered and reported more formally. Relationships within the solar system and the place of our solar system in the universe are important understandings. Visits to a planetarium, if available, supplement the class activities and reading. Some appropriate activities are:

- Systematic personal observation and reporting of the changes in the movement and shape of the moon, as well as sunset and sunrise.
- Building or studying a model of our solar system. Some schools have small models. Pupils can construct and hang spheres representing the planets from the ceiling.
- Chapter 8, Predicting the Shortest Day lesson.
- Chapter 11, Moon Watching example.
- Chapter 12, Relativity unit.

THE EARTH

The earth is made mostly of rock, with three-fourths of its surface covered by water, and some of the rest covered by a thin layer of soil. Surrounding it all is another thin envelope of gases called the atmosphere. These conditions of water, soil, and atmosphere are, as far as is known, unique in our solar system and have allowed life to develop here. Minerals and rocks, fresh water, oceans, atmosphere, and energy from the sun are all resources of great importance.

The surface of the earth has been changed over time by the action of wind, running water, ocean waves, volcanic eruptions of melted rock that burst from inside the earth, earthquakes from shifts of rocks under the surface, and changes in climate. The earth's surface is still changing and will continue to change.

PRIMARY GRADES

Observations and experiences, followed by questions and discussion, help primary children begin to understand what the earth is made of, how it sustains us, and how we can sustain it. Some suggested ways to approach the topic are:

- Classifying rocks and minerals (adapted from Lesson 12.3 on classifying leaves). Let pupils develop their own schemes with guidance; the usual classification of rocks as igneous, sedimentary, or metamorphic is not useful at this age.
- Observation and discussion of forms of water (rain, snow, fog, dew, ice) as they occur.
- Use questions from Children's Ideas About the Earth in Chapter 1 as a basis for discussion.
- Chapter 11, Weather Chart example.

UPPER ELEMENTARY GRADES

Children are or can become interested in many aspects of the earth as the planet on which we live, including the interrelation of the physical environment and the ecosystem and the current threats to both. (Caution: Do not overemphasize the worst-case scenario of the effects of various forms of pollution to the extent that children become fearful.) Some ways to study the earth and the local environment are:

- What happens to water and/or snow that falls on the school grounds? Investigation of this question can involve observation, measurement, inference, communication of results, and other processes.
- Observation of effects of wind, water and other forces in nearby areas. A field trip where effects are more easily seen, followed by communication through photographs, drawings, written descriptions, and models may be possible.
- Attention to natural disasters or discoveries in the news with discussion of underlying causal configurations (tectonic plates) and forces.
- Chapter 1, Children's Ideas About the Earth. Use questions in this section as basis for discussion.
- Chapter 11, Weather Chart example. Upper-elementary pupils can carry this project further than primary children, including attention to the forces that shape our weather.
- Chapter 11, Square Meter of Earth example. This can emphasize soil, rocks, and physical features in place of or in combination with organisms found in the area studied.
- Chapter 12, Acid Rain unit.

PHYSICAL SCIENCE

STRUCTURE OF MATTER

Matter is what scientists call all the stuff that makes up the world and the universe. There are countless forms of matter that differ in shape, density, flexibility, texture, color, and hundreds of other ways. But, despite these differences, everything is composed of a relatively few kinds of basic materials, called elements. These are, in turn, made up of even smaller particles which will be studied in later years.

Although more than 100 elements exist, most of the materials most people are likely to encounter are made up of combinations of only a small number of them.

The elements that are the basic materials are combined in different ways, to form the great variety of materials that we know. When substances interact, their composition may change; this occurs in burning, corrosion, cooking, digestion, and other processes, resulting in the formation of new materials. These changes are generally not reversible; the original substances cannot be recovered by ordinary means. Some interactions do not produce new substances; this is the case when one substance dissolves in another one. In this case, the dissolved substance can usually be recovered.

Substances can exist in different states depending on temperature and pressure. Familiar examples are the changes of state of water that result from freezing, melting, boiling, evaporation, and condensation. These are reversible; that is, ice can be changed into liquid water and back again.

Primary Grades

Many appropriate activities are available. Simple experiments can be carried out. Mention of atoms, molecules and other particles should be avoided. Appropriate activities include:

- Understanding of properties of matter; observation and classification by property (length, color, size, shape, etc.) of many common objects.
- Freezing water; weighing before and after.
- Dissolving salt in water and recovering the salt through evaporation.
- Making indicators from plant materials to see different interactions that occur between indicator and other materials.
- Observing simple reactions (vinegar and soda; mild acid on rock, etc.).

Upper Elementary Grades

Children can continue observation and experiences, building on what has gone before and emphasizing physical and chemical interactions and changes. Avoid explanations based on behavior of atoms and molecules and provide opportunities for observations and experiences. Appropriate activities include:

- Making and labeling a collection of elements. This seems to be a passive activity, but it brings a bit of reality into a subject that is difficult to bring down to the elementary level.
- Growing crystals to show change in form from dissolved powder to crystalline structure.
- Observing simple titrations of safe-to-handle acids and bases using litmus or another indicator.
- Separating solutions through paper chromatography or other means.

ENERGY; FORCE AND MOTION

Energy appears in many forms, including heat, light, and sound, as well as gravitational and mechanical energy. Energy changes constantly from one form to another, but the total amount remains constant. Energy may be stored or expressed in motion. Changes in motion—speeding up, slowing down, changing direction —are due to the effects of forces. Two forces that are familiar are gravity and magnetism.

PRIMARY GRADES

This broad category includes many phenomena that children can experience and interact with, observing and describing the effect of their own actions. Appropriate activities include:

- Observing and describing objects in motion—balls, cars, trains.
- Working with magnets; trying out different materials; measuring how close a given magnet must be to attract a given object; attracting iron filings.
- Using a balance beam and other balancing activities.
- Experiencing sound and light; these are often included in primary science, but it is hard for children to make the connection between sound and light and energy.

UPPER ELEMENTARY GRADES

Appropriate activities include:

- Measuring speed of moving objects (no emphasis on accuracy here).
- Observing waves in water, a spring, or a rope.
- Working with electrical circuits.
- Experimenting with temperature and heat; mixing hot and cold water of known temperatures and masses (weights); measuring resulting temperature.
- Observing light phenomena—refraction in water, primary colors.
- Chapter 8, Inferring Hidden Circuits lesson.
- Chapter 8, Period of a Pendulum, and What is a Good Conductor? lessons.
- Chapter 10, Simple Machines lesson.
- Chapter 13, Beginning Circuits lesson.

LIFE SCIENCE

DIVERSITY

The two most general distinctions are between plants, which get their energy directly from sunlight, and animals, which get their energy indirectly from the same source by eating plants or other animals that have fed on plants. There are millions of different kinds of organisms, including many that are neither plants nor animals. Animals and plants have a great variety of parts and arrangements of parts. These are the basis for biologists' classification of animals and plants into classes that are useful for descriptive and other purposes but are not a part of nature, where the lines between classes are not always clear.

Primary Grades

Observation and study of animals and animal behavior and of plants and their responses are suitable classroom activities for children of all ages and abilities. In many ways these topics are closer to primary children's experience and interests than those related to physical science; science teaching should take advantage of this natural interest and use it to increase thinking and understanding through use of science processes. Appropriate activities include:

- Tending to animals in classroom. Focus attention on what animals need for a healthy life, how our needs are similar or different. Stress responsibility and co-operation.
- Observing animal anatomy and behavior (simple). Mealworms have been suggested, but similar methods can be used with other animals—earthworms, goldfish, hamsters. Set up stations with a different animal at each, and allow children to rotate, observe, report, and compare observations.
- Classifying animals.
- Growing plants. Bean seeds are popular but other plants can be grown, observed, measured, graphed and reported.
- Observing and measuring reaction of plants to growing in light versus dark, to amount of water, temperature, etc.
- Chapter 7, Introduction to Mealworms lesson and A Closer Look at Mealworms lesson.
- Chapter 10, Insects and "Bugs" lesson.
- Chapter 10, Flowering Plants lesson.
- Chapter 11, A Garden example.
- Chapter 12, Classifying Leaves lesson.

Upper Elementary Grades

Some of the same kinds of experiences and experiments can be continued with more careful observation and reporting. The microscope can be introduced and used to extend observations. Appropriate activities include:

- Observing (using microscope) and drawing organisms in pond water.
- Observing cells under microscope.
- Detailed and carefully controlled experimenting with plants.
- Continued attention to classroom animals and observation of animal behavior.
- Simple dissection (e.g., bovine eyes can be attempted by sixth grade).
- Chapter 8, Growth of Corn Plants.
- Chapter 10, Investigations of Trees unit and Small Creatures Found in Water example.
- Chapter 12, Change Over Time unit.

ECOSYSTEM

All living things are linked with others in a web of interdependent relationships called an ecosystem. The interactions of the multitude of living organisms is shaped by the nonliving environment of oceans, fresh water, earth, air, minerals, and the rays that come to us from beyond our planet. Ecosystems tend to reach equilibrium over thousands of years and remain in a relatively stable state unless great natural disasters overtake them.

PRIMARY GRADES

Since living things depend on the environment for food and shelter, they live in environments that provide what they need. Many animals live in groups for protection and other reasons. Appropriate activities include:

- Animal needs; observation and recall of what they know. (Where do squirrels live? What do they need?).
- Films and pictures. This is one area of the curriculum where films and videotapes can provide vicarious experiences that cannot otherwise be obtained. Discussion should always accompany any experiences, including the viewing of films.

UPPER ELEMENTARY GRADES

Observation can include more data collection, inference, and communication. Some of the activities listed under The Earth are related to this topic as well. The interrelations between the physical environment and the ecosystem can be emphasized. Appropriate activities include:

- A survey of local environmental threats and hazards with emphasis on reporting findings.
- Study of niches of plants and animals. Construction of models of animal homes; description of a plant able to live with certain environmental constraints.
- Study of ecosystem around the school.
- Study of changes in ecosystems wrought by past natural disasters.
- Chapter 11, A Garden example. Focus on ecosystem of the garden.
- Chapter 11, Square Meter of Earth example. Focus on interrelationships.
- Chapter 12, Acid Rain unit. Focus on changes to ecosystem.

SKILLS

The science processes emphasized in this book are thinking skills applied to problems of the kind scientists seek to solve. Skills that underlie these thinking skills or science processes include computational skills, manipulation and observation skills, communication skills, and computer skills. These skills are learned well enough to be useful only if they are applied to problems and are used over and over in different contexts. Throughout this book we have stressed the importance of pupils' keeping notebooks, writing about their work, making graphs, and doing simple computations related to their science activities.

PRIMARY GRADES

- Chapter 5, Getting Acquainted with the Equal-Arm Balance lesson.

- Chapter 8, Using the Trundle Wheel and Predicting Number of Beans in a Jar activities.
- Chapter 12, Describing and Identifying lesson.

Upper Elementary Grades

- Chapter 5, Lesson Plan 5.2. Communicating and Predicting with Line Graphs lesson.
- Chapter 6, graphing activities (see Using Process Activities with Children section).
- Chapter 13, The Secret Language lesson.

PIAGET TASKS

▼ _____

Piaget Tasks are problems for children to solve. Many of them are problems related to simple materials or apparatus. They are conducted on an individual basis and in private, usually with an interviewer or experimenter facing a child across a small table. It is important to have a relatively quiet place to give the tasks and to have time so that neither the child nor the interviewer feels rushed.

Start out by asking for the child's name, how old he or she is, and a few other questions such as the name of his or her teacher, whether the child has any brothers or sisters, and so on. Say that this is not a test, that it will not count for any kind of grade, and that you are doing it because you want to learn more about how children think so that you can become a good teacher. The point is to put the child at ease, to win the child's confidence, and to ease the natural nervousness everyone feels in a situation of this kind.

Do not prompt the child to make certain answers by smiling or nodding; however, you will not be able to probe the child's thinking unless the child feels comfortable with you. Try to encourage the child without giving cues. Piaget was said to have been very warm and sensitive; children liked him.

Have all of your materials ready ahead of time and practice what you are going to say and do. It's a good idea to practice with a friend or roommate if you can. This will help you get over your nervousness and the friend can give you feedback. Here are the steps you will need to take:

1. Read over the tasks until you know them almost by heart.
2. Copy the directions for the tasks on cards, one task per card.

3. Gather all the materials you will need.
4. Practice giving the tasks to a friend if possible; if not, practice them by yourself. (Now you are ready to give the tasks to children.)
5. Choose three children from your classroom or, if you are not teaching yet, persuade a friend or neighbor to allow you to give these non-threatening tasks to their children. (Actually, children usually enjoy these tasks.)
6. Interview each child individually and privately.
7. Have each child do a minimum of three tasks.
8. Include tasks that have a range of difficulty so that each child can do some but not all of the tasks.
9. Turn in a Record for each child. Your instructor may provide forms; if not, follow the style of the forms provided at the end of this appendix.

An important part of every Piagetian interview task is asking the child to explain the reason for a response, or give a *justification*. A simple "Why do you think so?" is usually sufficient, but occasionally you may wish to vary your wording. When a child gives a logical response, it is especially interesting to challenge the child a bit. Some examples are given here for a situation in which a child has said the liquid amount stays the same when poured into different containers:

- "Yesterday a boy told me that there was more orangeade when I poured it into the tall glass. Is there something you could say to convince him?"
- "But it looks like so much more in the tall glass! Are you sure?"
- "How do you know that? Is there something you could do to prove it?"

Note: We assume you will question both boys and girls. In order to prevent the constant use of he/she and her/his in referring to the child, we have alternated feminine and masculine pronouns among the tasks.

▼ TASK I: Conservation of Solid Amount

MATERIALS

- 2 equal-sized balls of modeling clay, about the size of a ping-pong ball

PROCEDURE

1. Let the child handle the balls of clay. Ask if the balls are the same size and, if not, how you can make them equal. Continue until the child is satisfied that the balls are equal.
2. Ask the child to flatten one ball out into a pancake shape and to leave the other ball unchanged.
3. Ask, "Does the pancake have the same amount, less or more clay than the ball? Can you tell why you think that they are the same (or that the pancake has more or that the pancake has less)?"
4. Now press the pancake back into a ball and ask the child to make a snake with one of the balls. Repeat the procedure and questions that you asked about the pancake.

▼ TASK II: Conservation of Liquid Amount

MATERIALS

- Colored water (orange and green)
- 2 glasses or beakers (100 ml)
- 1 tall thin glass
- 1 low wide glass or jar
- 2 smaller glasses or jars (25 ml)

PROCEDURE

1. Fill the two glasses about half full, one with orange water and the other with green water. Make sure that the child believes that the two glasses have the same amount of liquid.
2. Ask the child to pretend that she has the glass of orangeade and her friend has the glass of limeade. Pour the orange water into the tall thin glass and ask the child whether she has the same amount to drink as the friend. If the answer is no, ask the child whether she can say which child has more or less. Ask the child to explain why she answered as she did and record the answer.
3. Pour the water back into the original container. Ask the child to verify that the amounts are the same again. Now pour the orange water into the low, wide dish and repeat the questions and the request for justification. Record the answers.
4. Repeat the process, pouring the water into the two small containers this time. Ask the same questions and record the answers.

▼ TASK III: Conservation of Area

MATERIALS

- 2 sheets of green construction paper
- 20–30 identical 1-inch cubes or squares
- 2 small toy horses (or cows)

PROCEDURE

1. Show the child the pieces of paper and say that they are the same size. Show the cubes or squares and say that they, too, are all the same size. If the child questions this, or seems unsure, allow time for him to verify this.
2. Point to the pieces of paper and ask the child to pretend that these are fields of grass and that the horses are grazing in the fields. There is the same amount of grass for each of the horses to eat. Now the farmer builds a barn at one corner of one field and a barn of equal size in the middle of the other field. Ask the child whether the two horses still have the same amount to eat. Ask the child to explain the answer given. Record the answer.
3. Repeat as above, adding a barn beside the first one in the first field and a barn away from the first barn in the second field. Repeat the question. Record the answer.

▼ FIGURE B.1
Conservation of
area

4. Repeat as above, adding the third barn beside the first two barns in the first field and at a distance from the first two barns in the second field (see Figure B.1). Ask whether the horses now have the same amount to eat. Ask the child to explain his answer and record the answer. If the child thinks the amount of grass is different after a few cubes are placed, you can stop. If, however, he thinks the amount of grass is the same, continue adding cubes. Children who are transitional in their ability to conserve area will often change their minds when more "barns" are added.

5. If the children in your sample are not familiar with horses or cows and their eating habits, the task can be changed in one of the following ways:
   a. The two fields become a sheet of cookie dough and the barns are replaced by cookies that are cut out.
   b. The fields become lawns to be mowed and the barns become flower beds.

▼ TASK IV: Conservation of Number

MATERIALS
   - 1 sheet of paper
   - 6 black checkers
   - 8–10 red checkers

(Other small objects may be used. The traditional objects are tiny dolls and doll beds or tiny "eggs" and eggcups.)

PROCEDURE
1. Line up the 6 black checkers in a straight line. Ask the child to line up the same number of red checkers below the black checkers. (If the child cannot do this, discontinue this task.)
2. Do not move the black checkers, but stack the red checkers in a column.

3. Ask the following questions: "Are there now more red checkers than black checkers or the same number of red checkers as black checkers or more black checkers than red checkers?"
4. Ask the child to explain his answer. Record the answer.
5. Move the red checkers into a tight line (checkers touching) and move the black checkers farther apart. Repeat the questions as above. Ask for an explanation and record the answer.
6. If the child seems unsure, you can devise a third configuration and repeat the questions.

▼ TASK V: Conservation of Volume

MATERIALS
- 1 graduated cylinder or similar clear container that can be marked on the side
- 2 small objects of same size but different weights (e.g., a glass marble and a steel marble or a wood cube and a metal cube of equal sizes)
- water

PROCEDURE
1. Show the child that the two objects are the same size but weigh different amounts (or have different masses). Allow time for the child to verify this.
2. Fill the container about two-thirds full of water.
3. Ask the child, "What do you think will happen when I put this marble (the lighter-weight marble) into the water?" Accept the child's answer and say, "Well, let's see."
4. Drop the marble into the water (or lower it on a string) and *mark the water level*. Have the child confirm that the water level rose. Remove the marble carefully.
5. Say, "Now let's look at the other marble. It is the same size but heavier than the first one. What do you think will happen when I put this heavier marble in the water? Will the water level be higher, lower, or the same as when I put the first one in?"
6. Ask the child to explain her answer. Record the explanation. (You may show the child the result, but do not record the explanation after seeing the result.)

▼ TASK VI: Class Inclusion

MATERIALS
- 10 artificial daisies in a bunch
- 2–3 artificial red roses (or any combination of flowers of the same proportions)

PROCEDURE

1. Ask the child to name the flowers and make sure that he knows the term *flowers*. Ask, "Are the daisies flowers? Are the roses flowers?" When it is clear that the child understands the terms, proceed as follows.
2. Ask, "Are there more daisies or flowers here? How do you know?"
3. Ask, "More daisies than what? If I give you the daisies what will I have left? If I give you the flowers, what will I have left?"
4. Record the answers.

▼ TASK VII: Concept of Life

This is not really a task but a series of questions to determine the nature of the child's concept of life.

PROCEDURE

1. Ask the child whether various things are alive, following up each time with: "Why? Why do you think so?"
2. Ask, "Is the sun alive? A table? An automobile? A mountain? A lamp? A watch? A bell? A bird? The wind? A flower? The rain?"
3. Ask, "Is one of these more alive than another? The wind or the flower?" "The rain or the bell?" etc. "Why?"

RECORDING AND INTERPRETING INTERVIEWS

An Interview Record Form can be found toward the end of Appendix B. This form can be used to record the results of the task interviews for each child. Notice that the form appears first as it might be completed by a teacher (or some other interviewer). A blank form has been included so that you can copy it for use in doing these interviews.

The four columns of the Interview Record Form are:

TASK

You may wish to use a smaller selection of tasks in order to interview a larger number of children. If so, you can refer to the following list, which gives a rough indication of the acquisition age range for responding logically to the following tasks: Children younger than the stated range will almost all be unable to do the task; those older than the age range will almost all be able to do the task.

Task	*Age*
Conservation of number	5–7
Conservation of amount (liquid or solid)	6–8

Conservation of area	7–11
Class inclusion	7–9
Concept of life	5–10
Conservation of volume	9–12

RESPONSE

Two possible responses for each task are given. Circle the one that corresponds to the child's answer to your initial question.

JUSTIFICATION

In this space write what the child says when you ask for the reason for his or her response. It is important to summarize the child's actual words here. (See comment on justification earlier in this appendix.)

RESPONSE TYPE

Children's responses can be classified as logical or prelogical, and several subcategories can be made for each depending on the type of task. These response types are described in the next section, How to Classify Children's Responses.

An Interview Interpretation Form ends Appendix B. That form should also be completed for each child interviewed.

HOW TO CLASSIFY CHILDREN'S RESPONSES

CONSERVATION TASKS

The first four tasks included here are conservation tasks that distinguish between preoperational logic (nonlogic or prelogic) and concrete operational logic (logic applied to actions with objects). Task V, Conservation of Volume, requires more advanced thinking and is an indicator of the transition to formal operational thinking.

RESPONSE TYPES

Responses to the first four conservation tasks can be classified into Concrete Operational (ConO) or Preoperational (PreO) and into several categories within those classes:

Concrete Operational (Logical)

1. *Logical Necessity (LN).* Child explains that there is no logical alternative, such as "You didn't add anything or take anything away."
2. *Compensation (CP).* Child focuses on two dimensions or aspects and says that one cancels out the other, such as "This piece of clay is longer but skinnier so it's still the same amount."

3. *Reversibility (RV)*. The child understands that the transformation can be reversed, such as "If you poured the water back it would look the same as before."

Preoperational (Nonlogical or Prelogical)

1. *Object Centered (OC)*. Child focuses on the objects themselves rather than the transformations, such as "The horse can't move around here as well."
2. *Action Centered (AC)*. Child focuses on actions of the interviewer, such as "You changed it when you poured it."
3. *No Basis for Answer (NB)*. Cannot answer, gives silly response or totally irrelevant response.

CONSERVATION OF VOLUME

This task cannot be solved by reasoning at the concrete operational level and is useful in identifying those students who have advanced to a higher level of reasoning, the formal operational level. Responses can be classified into:

1. *Concrete Operational (CO)*. Pupil considers variables that might influence an outcome but chooses irrelevant variables or applies wrong algorithm.
2. *Formal Operational (FO)*. Pupil can separate variables and apply reasoning to overcome intuition or common sense.
3. *Transitional (TR)*. Pupil is unsure of answer or gives partially correct answer. Student seems to be struggling to decide what to say or changes mind.

CLASS INCLUSION

Task VI also distinguishes between logical and prelogical thinking. Responses can be classified into:

Logical

1. *Additive (AD)*. There are 10 daisies and 3 roses, so if you add the roses to the daisies you have more flowers.
2. *Part and Whole (PW)*. Child can think simultaneously of the whole and the part, such as "Because daisies are flowers and roses are flowers too."

Prelogical

1. *Focus on Quantities (QU)*. Child cannot focus on the part and the whole at the same time and focuses on the two parts, such as "There are more daisies than roses."
2. *No Basis (NB)*.

CONCEPT OF LIFE

This task explores the child's animism, that is, the tendency to consider all objects as endowed with consciousness and the ability to control their actions. Responses can be classified into:

1. *No Concept of life (NC)*. The child answers the questions with descriptions or free associations and uses the same criteria to attribute life or deny life.
2. *Life confused with Movement (Mo/Us)*. If it moves—or is useful—it must be alive. Thus, the moon, the wind, bicycles, and so on are alive, but a tree may not be.
3. *Autonomous movement makes something alive (AU)*. Anything that appears to move on its own accord is alive. Automobiles and bicycles are no longer thought to be alive, but the wind and the sun, which move without an agent, are alive.
4. *Only Animals and Plants are alive (An/Pl)*. Animals are thought to be more alive than plants but plants are recognized as alive, too.

Interview Record Form

Child's Name or Code __A. E.__   Grade _1_   Age _6_   Interviewer __K. Newly__ Date __Nov. 5__   Gender _F_

Comments about child (optional): __active, bright, top reading group.__

Task	Response (circle one)	Justification	Response Type
I. Conservation of Solid Amount	Same / **Different**	When you rolled it out, the snake was bigger.	AC
II. Conservation of Liquid Amount	Same / **Different**	The tall glass has more.	CO
III. Conservation of Area	Same / **Different**	One horse doesn't have as much grass. You can see it.	OC
IV. Conservation of Number	**Same** / Different	We still have the same amount. You just stacked yours up.	LN
V. Conservation of Volume	Same / **Different**	The water will go up higher because the heavy marble will push it harder.	CO
VI. Class Inclusion	**More daisies** / More flowers	Because there's more white and yellow.	QU
VII. Concept of Life Sun	**Yes** No	Because it gives light.	Mo/Us
Table	Yes **No**	It doesn't move, it can't eat.	AU
Automobile	**Yes** No	It moves itself.	Mo/Us
Mountain	**Yes** No	Because I know it.	NC
Lamp	Yes **No**	It's like a decoration. We make it. It doesn't make itself.	AnPl
Watch	Yes **No**	Because it runs.	NC
Bell	Yes **No**	It's made of iron, it doesn't speak.	An Pl
Bird	**Yes** No	It moves, it walks, it flies, it eats.	An Pl
Wind	**Yes** No	Because it pushes things.	MO
Flower	Yes No		
Rain	Yes **No**	It's water; it doesn't talk, it doesn't run, it doesn't move itself.	An/Pl

Interview Record Form

Interviewer _____ Date _____

Child's Name or Code _____ Grade _____ Age _____ Gender _____

Comments about child (optional):

Task	Response (circle one)	Justification	Response Type
I. Conservation of Solid Amount	Same Different		
II. Conservation of Liquid Amount	Same Different		
III. Conservation of Area	Same Different		
IV. Conservation of Number	Same Different		
V. Conservation of Volume	Same Different		
VI. Class Inclusion	More daisies More flowers		
VII. Concept of Life Sun	Yes No		
Table	Yes No		
Automobile	Yes No		
Mountain	Yes No		
Lamp	Yes No		
Watch	Yes No		
Bell	Yes No		
Bird	Yes No		
Wind	Yes No		
Flower	Yes No		
Rain	Yes No		

Interview Interpretation Form

Interviewer _____ Date _____

Child's Name or Code _____ Grade _____ Age _____ Gender _____

Your judgment about this child's stage of cognitive development.

___ Preoperational
___ Transitional to Concrete Operational
___ Concrete Operational
___ Transitional to Formal Operational

In the space below explain why you made the judgment above.

In this space, describe how your judgment about the stage of development would influence your teaching of this child.

TURN IN THIS AND THE RESPONSE SHEET FOR EACH CHILD.

INDEX

399